Corporate Social Responsibility Handbook

Third Edition

Corporate Social Responsibility Handbook

Making CSR and
Narrative Reporting
Work for Your Business

Third Edition

TONY HOSKINS

icsa.
Publishing

Published by ICSA Information & Training Ltd
16 Park Crescent
London W1B 1AH

First edition published 2005
Second edition published 2008
This edition published 2012

Typeset in Minion with Gill Sans by Hands Fotoset, Mapperley, Nottingham

Printed and bound in Great Britain by Hobbs the Printers Ltd, Totton, Hampshire

British Library Cataloguing in Publication Data
A catalogue record for this book is available from the British Library

ISBN 978-1-86072-481-7

Dedicated to all my family for putting up with me
with their continuing love and support

Contents

CONTENTS

Acknowledgements

My thanks and acknowledgements go to the following people and organisations:

- The Virtuous Circle team for its support, including giving me its permission to allow me to use the various CSR and reporting tools and analyses we have developed.
- My colleagues in The Virtuous Circle for their help in developing the approaches I have referred to, as well as their support with our projects and our clients whilst I have focused on writing the book.
- Our clients, whose experiences with CSR and Business Review reporting have taught me much about the issues of integrating these matters into the management cultures of large companies, as well as the strengths and weaknesses of the range of approaches that can be used to deal with them.
- My publisher, Fiona Tucker, for keeping me informed, motivated and focused on the deadline.
- My wife, Tricia, for her understanding and support in my writing this (in her words 'another edition!') book, that goes far beyond all my reasonable expectations.

In writing this book, I have taken the business manager as its audience. Certainly, there will be areas that could have benefited from more detail, if the reader's interest comes from the perspective of an NGO. However, my intention has been to help business understand more about the issues relating to narrative reporting and CSR and the range of possible actions they can take for their business.

Wherever possible, I have tried to provide business examples to demonstrate the point covered in the text. I have taken these examples from the corporate websites of the relevant companies. Any interpretation of these examples is down to me, and should not be considered to reflect any comments from the companies themselves.

Introduction

This book reflects the need for understanding of the non-financial aspects of business from the perspective of corporate social responsibility and corporate reporting in the UK (and across the EU) in the form of the enhanced directors' report.

It incorporates both an update of my ICSA book on corporate social responsibility,[1] published in 2005 (with its 2008 second edition), together with a review of the non-financial aspects of business review reporting, which are touched upon in my ICSA book on Corporate Reporting,[2] published in 2007.

Why the need for this book? Quite simply, it is because of the speed of change in terms of management thinking and management priorities.

In 2004, companies still considered CSR as an area that was 'nice to have', but was not necessarily related to business strategy. Having said that, notable business leaders of the time were making their voices heard on the subject. One was David Varney (then Chairman of O_2 subsequently Chairman of HM Revenue and Customs until 2006) whose comment represented one of the more committed:

> My belief is that responsible companies are more likely to prosper and thrive.

A similar quote came from Martin Hancock, then Chief Operating Officer in London for Westpac (and appointed Chair of the UN Environmental Programme Financial Initiative in 2005), who said:

> With globalisation, we have seen a shift in rights. Today, economic power lies very much with the private sector, rather than the public sector. And with those rights, there are certain responsibilities we must take on.[3]

It is fair to say that both those quotes came from individuals at the leading edge of CSR at the time. Perhaps as relevant was the quote from an individual who was at the more hard-nosed edge of commercial life – Ian Davis, then McKinsey's Managing Director:

> Business leaders should demonstrate more confidence on their moral position as creators of wealth, opportunity and rising living standards and should work proactively to build trust between their organisations and society at large.[4]

Today, it is not only the business visionaries who are committed to CSR. My observation is that companies are taking CSR more seriously. Their position is now based on a considered view of potential risks and opportunities relating to their action (or lack of action) in the areas of CSR.

This change in attitude has been helped by several factors. First, some of the legislation has begun to impact on how companies think. This is particularly true in the area of the environment, where legislation such as the EU's WEEE directive and the REACH directive, together with the UK's Carbon Reduction Commitment (which is essentially a carbon tax) have made companies change their corporate behaviour.

Secondly, the world is now much more aware of the dangers of climate change – helped, regrettably, by natural disasters such as Hurricane Katrina in the US and flooding both in the UK and in Europe. CSR was also very much helped in a business and economic rationale sense by the publication of the Stern Report. Scarcely a day goes by without an environmental subject being discussed on the national news – something that was very unusual in 2004.

Thirdly, in terms of business bottom-line pressure, requests about CSR performance have increasingly begun to form part of procurement tender documentation. Companies have begun to realise that CSR can have an influence on their ability to gain and retain contracts. This pressure has come from large quoted companies and also from the public sector procurement processes; it has affected all sizes and types of companies – not just the largest – or those quoted on the Stock Exchange. In addition, companies have begun to appreciate more strongly the importance of their being seen as a responsible company, particularly when recruiting new graduates – they have an expectation that their employer should perform responsibly and communicate their activities in a transparent manner.

Fourthly, corporate reporting legislation has changed and is beginning to have an impact. There has been ever-increasing pressure on companies to report on the non-financial aspects of their business. This was first introduced by the Companies Act 2006. In 2010, a new Code was introduced, and 2011 saw the Business Review consultation – so much change in such a short time!

The issue of narrative (or non financial) reporting forms a significant requirement for this book. Even with legislation in place, through my work, I have found companies uncertain of how and what they should be reporting upon in their Business Review. The challenge with the legislation is that it is not prescriptive in terms of the content – or, more importantly, the approach – to be adopted for the Business Review.

CSR and Business Review reporting are converging in terms of the nature of the activities and the measurements required. It is important to understand how each should be reported upon – and which elements of activity fall into each category.

This book takes CSR as being one of the bedrock constituents for narrative reporting – but not the only constituent. It represents a range of activities, policies and measures that *could* fit into the Business Review, without active CSR management a company's Business Review is likely to be a half-hearted attempt to reflect the requirements of the legislation. This is particularly the case for those listed companies, for whom an important aspect of the new enhanced Business Review is the requirement to comment on policies related to non-financial areas, and on their effectiveness.

However, in order to understand which elements of a company's CSR activity should be incorporated within its Business Review, the risks and opportunities represented by each CSR element need to be considered.

The good news for me in writing this book is that, unlike the first and second editions of the *CSR Handbook*, CSR is not a new topic for its readers. They see it as relevant to their job, but have varying levels of uncertainty about how it fits with their prime requirement – to contribute to the effectiveness of their company's corporate performance and its reporting.

The focus of this book

This book has been written to enable the directors of a business to answer five questions:

1. What is narrative reporting and how can it be communicated effectively?
2. How is CSR relevant to my business?
3. How can I make CSR work for my business?
4. What are the differences between CSR and Business Review reporting?
5. How can I ensure my Business Review reporting is at its most effective?

It is comprised of four sections:

1. Narrative reporting – what, why and how?
2. Why consider a CSR approach for your business?
3. How to implement CSR in your business.
4. What to do to make CSR work for your business.

Its objective is not only to inform the reader about CSR and its potential benefits, but also to consider how those benefits can be integrated into your business with the objective of influencing the bottom line – either directly or indirectly – and, for these companies with a wide investor base to determine how those actions can be communicated effectively to enhance shareholder value.It is written from the perspective of 'What are my business objectives, and how does CSR relate to my operation?' As such, it uses the focus of the Business Review 'to the extent necessary' as the basis for undertaking CSR activities and reflects that the business needs to determine what its approach should be in each CSR element, rather than adopting an 'everything but the kitchen sink' mentality.

The book has been designed for readers of all levels of familiarity with CSR and non-financial reporting; this enables each reader to select those sections where they feel they require more information or guidance.

Before dipping in and out of this book, it is worth pointing out that one of the challenges of this subject area is the great number of terms used by practitioners that have essentially the same meaning. Along with CSR are the terms Corporate Responsibility, Corporate Citizenship, and Sustainability. Amongst large companies Corporate Responsibility has become the more accepted term, but amongst smaller companies, the media, NGOs, and the EU, CSR is still the accepted term. For that reason, I have used CSR throughout this book. Similarly in the area of Business Review, as well as non financial information there are also narrative reporting and extra financial information. The latter is increasingly accepted amongst some forms of investors, but overall there seems to be greater recognition of the words 'narrative' and 'non financial', so these terms are used throughout the book. Both terms should be considered by the reader as having the same meaning as those above.

Sources

1 *The ICSA Corporate Responsibility Handbook – Making CSR work for business* – Tony Hoskins 2005.

2 *The ICSA Company Reporting Handbook* – Tony Hoskins 2007.

3 UNEP FI e-bulletin September 2004 – quote from Martin Hancock, as Westpac were declared sustainability leaders for the third year running.

4 *The Economist* 'The World in 2004 – Learning to Grow Again' by Ian Davis.

Narrative reporting – What, why and how?

Introduction to narrative reporting

What is narrative reporting?

'Narrative reporting' is a phrase that has come into much more common business parlance over the past decade. It can be interpreted in several ways, but the normal definition is that it is the term used to describe the textual information (both non-financial and financial commentaries) in company annual reports and accounts. It is important to emphasise the inclusion of the financial commentary (usually the section in the annual report that is produced by the finance director). However, it is also referred to as the 'front half of the book' and 'non-financial reporting' (although this may lead people to assume, incorrectly, that the financial review is separate). The relevance of this inclusion is that the financial commentary should be an integrated part of the narrative reporting, and not seen as a separate stand-alone element.

The UK Government's Department of Business Innovation and Skills (BIS), which has the governmental responsibility for company law, suggests that it comprises a number of elements, including:

- the directors' report, including the Business Review;
- the chairman's statement and the chief executive's review;
- the directors' remuneration report; and
- corporate governance disclosures.

However, for most observers, the focus is on the Business Review (including the finance review element), together with statements by both the chairman and the chief executive.

The information contained within the narrative report is intended to provide a broad and meaningful picture of the business, its market position, strategy, performance and future prospects. Both reports should complement each other, building a strong overall perspective of the company's business performance.

Is narrative reporting new?

Many practitioners may well assume that 'narrative reporting' is a new phenomenon. However, there has always been some form of a text commentary in the 'front half of the book'.

In this respect, company law stretches back to the South Sea Company, whose excesses led to the passage of the Bubble Act of 1720. However, the effects of the growth of the industrial revolution in the United Kingdom led to the avalanche of companies operating in the fields of canals and docks, railway, banks, and mining and quarrying. This growth resulted in a real need for public disclosure to their shareholders about the state of these businesses and led to the passing of the Joint Stock Companies Act of 1844, which required companies to provide for 'publicity' (or disclosure). The Limited Liability Act 1855 introduced 'general limited liability', with further requirements for disclosure.

This was then the last company law legislation in the nineteenth century, but since 1908, numerous committees have been formed to review company law, with Amending Act consolidations occurring roughly every 20 years. In these Amending Acts, the focus was UK-centric, reflecting events that had arisen with regard to UK corporations, together with the gradual modernisation of UK company law.

However, this changed when the UK became part of the European Union (EU) and there was the need to harmonise with EU company legislation and EU directives. The combination of piecemeal legislation since 1908 and compliance with European legislation meant that the overall effect resembled individual pieces of sticky tape trying to hold together a large parcel, or what some observers described as 'an Elastoplast approach to incremental legislation'. This haphazard and somewhat inconsistent approach was addressed with the company law reform consultation that started in 1998.

It was this reform process that ushered in what is now regarded as the modern day 'narrative reporting'.

The impact of the company law reform process

The objective behind the series of company law reform consultations was to modernise UK company law in a single act which addressed all the perceived issues. This was a new approach for the UK, and mirrored the actions of some of the old colonies. Countries such as Canada, Hong Kong, New Zealand, South Africa and Australia had traditionally taken UK legislation as their model, but, post-World War II, these countries had taken a more radical approach by undertaking major company law reviews to ensure their legislation was both up to date and suited to their own local circumstances.

The process started with the UK Government's 1998 consultation on company law reform. Its theme was 'Modern company law for a competitive economy'. In this respect there were many bodies involved in the review – over and above those that would be directly impacted. Representations to the consultations came from those that would be expected to respond, such as the CBI, the Institute of Directors and trade associations, together with other stakeholders, such as the TUC and individual trade unions, as well as non-governmental organisations (NGOs).

A key issue to be addressed by the process was that the reform should embrace the 'enlightened shareholder approach'. This was first stated in the report of the steering group for the reform. This represents 'an obligation on directors to achieve the success of the company for the benefit of the shareholders by taking account of all the relevant considerations for that purpose'.

This approach recognised that company managers (or more appropriately, boards of directors) should have regard, where appropriate, to the need to ensure productive relationships with a range of interested parties and have regard to the longer term. These interested parties are nowadays termed 'stakeholders', and include employees, local and central government, customers and suppliers, and communities.

The result of the series of consultations was the Companies Act 2006. This is perhaps the longest Act ever produced (comprising 44 Parts, 1,300 clauses, 16 Schedules, and 701 pages, excluding the table of contents), largely because of the complex issues it addressed. Even though the Act received Royal Assent in 2006, much of its intent had to be translated by subsequent secondary legislation; the effective dates of various parts of the Act stretched right through until 1 October 2008.

Given the focus of the consultations on the 'enlightened shareholder approach', it is hardly surprising that one of the key changes in the new Act was the introduction of a new director's duty (in all there are now seven such duties). It is worth pointing out at this stage that this duty applies to directors of all sizes and forms of UK incorporated companies.

This duty required a director to:

'Act in the way he considers, in good faith, would be most likely to promote the success of the company for the benefits of its members as a whole, and in so doing have regard (amongst other matters) to :

- The likely consequences of any decision in the long-term,
- The interests of the company's employees,
- The need to foster business relationships with suppliers, customers and others,
- The impact of the company's operations on the community and the environment, the desirability of the company maintaining a reputation for high standards of business conduct, and
- The need to act fairly between members of the company.'

Of these areas to be considered, the last point may be considered to reflect the content of older versions of company law. The others were new (although the duty often reflected a codification of other laws such as the range of employment and health and safety laws that were already in place). However, the wide scope of this director's duty became the basis for 'narrative reporting' in a company's annual report and accounts, especially since the duty provides an express statutory purpose for the Business Review (CA 2006, s 417(2)). This purpose is to assist members to assess how effectively the directors have performed their duty to promote the success of the company.

2

Narrative reporting legislative requirements

There are a variety of requirements relating to narrative reporting – some are legislative and some are guidance – both in terms of accounting standards and governance codes. There are new developments in the offing that may further change narrative reporting in the future.

The regulations

Before we can discuss how to implement narrative reporting there is a need to ensure the reader understands the range of regulations that have been in force.

There are three areas to be reviewed:

- the Business Review 2005;
- the operating and financial review; and
- the Business Review 2006.

The Business Review 2005 – the reporting requirements for all companies

This version of the Business Review was established under the Companies Act 1985 and was introduced via a statutory instrument in March 2005.[1] It was also known as an 'enhanced Directors' Report' (although this term has now fallen into disuse). This reflected the fact that the Business Review forms part of the front section of a company's annual report and accounts. The review is the responsibility of the company's board of directors, and they are accountable for its contents.

This version of the Business Review was introduced by the UK Government in order to ratify its obligations to the European Accounts Modernisation Directive[2] (EAMD). This was formulated in June 2000, when the Commission published its communication entitled 'EU Financial Reporting Strategy: The Way Forward'. It proposed that all listed companies prepare consolidated accounts in accordance with one single set of accounting standards – the International Accounting Standards. The deadline for achieving this was set for 2005. The impetus behind this communication was the EU Lisbon summit, which, amongst other matters, urged that 'steps be taken to enhance the comparability of financial statements prepared by Community companies whose securities are admitted to trading on a regulated market'.

The EAMD consolidated previous directives, as well as taking into account the concerns of the Lisbon summit. As a result, it was held to apply to *all* forms of companies. The deadline for its ratification by member states was 1 January 2005. All member states have ratified the EAMD with their own enacting legislation, although Italy and Greece were at one time taken to the European Court of Justice for their initial non-compliance with the directive. Any EU company (group holding companies as well as their subsidiaries) is required to produce a similar form of Business Review reporting. The exact format of the equivalent of the Business Review is defined by local country legislation and the approach may differ – the EAMD does not specify where the information will be held – it merely states 'in the annual report'. It was the UK Government that determined that within the UK it should be considered to be part of an enhanced directors' report.

The Business Review regulations require a company to produce a directors' report which includes the following information:

- the names of persons which held the position of director at any time during the financial year;
- the principal activities of the company;
- the amounts recommended as dividends;
- a Business Review; and
- with regard to Sch. 7 of the Companies Act 1985, disclosure of:
  - matters of general nature, such as changes in asset values, directors' shareholdings and other interests, and contributions for political and charitable purposes;
  - acquisition of its own shares (or a charge on them);
  - employment, training, and advancement of disabled persons;
  - involvement of employees in the affairs, policy and performance of the company; and
  - the policy and practice of the payment of amounts due to creditors.

Essentially, the Business Review was the new element in the requirement for the production of the directors' report. The required content and approach of the Business Review is as follows:

- it must contain a fair review of the business and a description of the principal risks and uncertainties facing the company;
- it must be a balanced and comprehensive analysis of the development and performance of the business during the financial year and the position of the company at the end of the financial year;
- it must (to the extent necessary to ensure understanding of the business) include an analysis using financial key performance indicators (KPIs) and, where appropriate, analysis using other KPIs, including information relating to environmental and employee matters; and
- it must (where appropriate) include references to, and additional explanations of, amounts included in the annual accounts.

It is relevant to note that the Business Review regulations are not prescriptive in terms of the detail of what information should appear in a Business Review.

These requirements apply to all UK companies – listed and unlisted, group companies and subsidiaries, UK owned and foreign owned – but there are different applications dependent upon the size of the company concerned.[3] The definition of the size of the company is one that is used consistently across the EU. A company will determine its size, if, at each level, it meets two out of three qualifying criteria (turnover, balance sheet total or employee numbers):

- A small company is one that has turnover not more than £5.6 million, a balance sheet total of not more than £2.8 million and not more than 50 employees.
- A medium company is one that has turnover not exceeding £22.8 million, a balance sheet total of not more than £11.4 million and not more than 250 employees.
- A large company is one whose turnover exceeds £22.8 million, whose balance sheet total exceeds £11.4 million and which has more than 250 employees.

It is relevant that the EU has a further definition for micro companies (those with less than ten employees) but these companies are incorporated under the small companies accounting regime. It should be noted that the definitions emanate from the EU[4] and the financial criteria are actually stated in Euros and are inflation linked. Hence these precise financial definitions may conceivably vary over time.

The difference in application of the requirements relate to the need for submission of a directors' report and the need to provide KPIs:

- small companies must produce a directors' report but do not have to file it with Companies' House if they choose to submit abbreviated accounts;
- medium companies must submit a directors' report but do not need to comply with the requirement to provide non-financial KPIs, if they choose not to do so.

These different applications do not apply if the company in question is a public company.

In addition, for those companies that are reporting as a group, their group report must produce a group directors' report covering the parent and those subsidiaries included in the consolidated accounts. However, there is no 'group exemption' and all UK subsidiaries have to produce their own Business Review (and for their EU subsidiaries, its equivalent in each member state).

Under the Business Review regulations, an enforcement regime was put in place. Companies that are deemed to be in breach of any aspect of the Business Review regulations are liable to:

- criminal penalties (for financial years beginning on or after 1 April 2005); and
- civil penalties (for financial years beginning on or after 1 April 2006).

The Financial Reporting Review Panel (FRRP), a sister body to the Accounting

Standards Board (ASB) and part of the Financial Reporting Council was given the legal authority under these regulations to review the directors' report from 1 April 2006. If deemed necessary, the FRRP has the power to go to court to force a company to review its report.

The Operating and Financial Review 2005

The Operating and Financial Review (OFR) is a more sophisticated form of the Business Review.

Some people may have the view that the OFR was a reporting methodology that emerged out of the Company Law reform process. However, it has an earlier origin. It was first introduced for listed companies by the Accounting Standards Board in 1993 and offered a framework for reporting by listed companies.[5] It was a non-mandatory approach, developed for shareholders and was intended to provide an analytical discussion of the company's results.

However, as a result of company law reform, a new OFR was developed by the ASB. In this case, there was a far greater consideration given to other stakeholders, such as employees and customers, as well as giving more non-financial information that was relevant to shareholders.

The intention was that the OFR should become a mandatory requirement for UK listed companies (and optional for other companies). In 2005, the government introduced combined legislation for a mandatory OFR for listed companies, together with the enabling legislation to introduce the Business Review. This legislation became effective for financial years starting on or after 1 April 2005, but this statutory requirement to produce an OFR for listed companies was removed by Gordon Brown, then Chancellor of the Exchequer, in the same year as it came into force.

The Business Review 2006 – the reporting impact for quoted companies

The 2006 Business Review legislation[6] consolidated the requirements under the Business Review 2005 with the inclusion of an enhanced set of requirements for quoted companies. In this area, it draws its pedigree from the operating and financial review. The Companies Act 2006 brought much of the OFR's requirements into law.

The revisions for the Business Review under the Companies Act 2006 for Business Reviews produced by quoted companies took effect for all financial years commencing on or after 1 October 2007. These revisions included additional or extended information in the following areas:

- the main trends and factors likely to affect the future developments, performance and position of the company's business;
- information concerning:
  - environmental matters (including the impact of the company's business on the environment)
  - the company's employees
  - social and community issues, including information about any policies

of the company in relation to those matters and the effectiveness of those policies and

- information on persons with whom the company has contractual or other arrangements which are essential to the business of the company.

If the company's Business Review does not contain information relating to the last two points, then it must clearly state which kinds of information are not contained in the Business Review.

The implications of this additional information requirement are as follows:

- The main trends and factors: This is much stronger wording than in the 2005 Business Review where the requirement was to give 'an indication of likely future developments'. As such, a quoted company's Business Review should include far more detailed explanation of current trends and future developments. It should be noted that as well as having cautionary statements, directors are provided with a 'safe harbour' protection against liability in the event that there are statements or omissions in (amongst other things) the directors' report, unless these statements were untrue or misleading.
- Information about environmental matters, employees, and social and community issues: This requirement continued with the 'to the extent necessary' ensuring that the board determines the amount of information that is necessary to understand the development and performance of the company's business. However, given the requirement to explain if any element has not been reported upon, most boards comment on all of these elements. The requirement for the provision of analysis using other key performance indicators, including information relating to environmental and employee matters remains separate. Most quoted companies provide information on the broader set of non-financial areas, and include some performance indicator data. A company may decide to include such indicators, but can emphasise that they are not deemed to be key to understanding the progress of the company's strategies. A more challenging requirement is the need to comment on the policies pertaining to these three areas, and to assess their effectiveness. This may be difficult for companies and they need to devise an appropriate way to determine their levels of effectiveness.
- Information about persons with contractual arrangements: This is in the manner of the operating and financial review requirement and could include major customers. The categories of customer will need to be identified, for example are they split between the public and private sectors, or are they national or international customers? It also includes suppliers of key components or services, for example, suppliers of call centre services to banks or outsourced distribution and logistics suppliers to retailers. A company would also be required to report on contractual activities such as its major joint ventures, including private finance initiatives (PFIs) which create public private partnerships (PPPs). There is no requirement to include KPIs for this area, although the board may decide to do this. It is important to note that the disclosure requirement regarding certain persons can be omitted if such disclosure

would 'be seriously prejudicial to that person and contrary to the public interest'. This distinction was included to prevent, say, animal rights activists targeting key suppliers to pharmaceutical laboratories. It is intended to provide some form of protection by not publicising details about those persons who have had a significant contractual arrangement with a company that was being targeted in this manner.

As noted in Chapter 1, the Companies Act 2006 introduced a new definition of directors' duties, driven by the concept of the need for directors to take account of 'enlightened shareholder value'. From the perspective of the Business Review, this new duty has considerable impact because of its wide scope of activities.

By introducing this new duty, an express statutory purpose is provided for the Business Review – namely to help members to assess how effectively the directors have performed their duty to promote the success of the company. This places more weight behind the enforcement regime of the FRRP.

From a board perspective, this new duty requires directors to consider to what extent they are aware that the managers of the company are running it in a manner that supports them in this duty. As such, this may be much more demanding for non-executive directors.

The Walker Review – the impact on private equity companies

In another form of semi-regulatory guidance, the Walker Review was a report on transparency and disclosure in private equity, published in 2007, on behalf of the British Venture Capital Association (BVCA). It was produced by a committee chaired by Sir David Walker (who also chaired the review of corporate governance amongst British banks). It recommended that all private equity portfolio companies should produce their Business Reviews as if they were a listed company. Part of the reasoning behind this guidance is that often such companies may be held by private equity companies for a relatively short time before they are floated back on to the listed market, and by maintaining listed status reporting standards, prospective investors have access to consistent corporate information.

If any private equity firm has a portfolio company which either has:

- more than 1,000 full-time employees in the UK, and generates more than 50% of its revenue in the UK;
- or which had an enterprise value at the time of purchase of £500 million;
- or where the market capitalisation together with the premium for acquisition of control was more than £300 million,

then these firms should ensure that those portfolio companies should produce an Annual Report and financial statement which is available on the company's website. This report should communicate who the private equity owners are, who the senior management team is, and include information about the company's employees, environmental and social issues *along the same lines* as would appear in the report of a public company. The Walker Review also said that private equity firms covered by these criteria should produce an annual review, again freely available on their website, setting out their values and providing information about governance, management, performance, etc.

This review requested venture capital firms to voluntarily give up a specific exemption under the Companies Act 2006 for all private companies. It also recommended putting in place a monitoring regime.[7]

Where these regulations impact

Given the variety of regulations described above, it may be helpful to summarise which companies are impacted by which regulation. These are as follows:

- *Listed companies* (London Stock Exchange) – enhanced requirements under Business Review 2006 (mandatory) and OFR (voluntary).
- *Quoted companies* (AIM and other markets) – the original requirements of the Business Review 2005 (mandatory) – consolidated in the Business Review 2006 – and OFR (voluntary).
- *Private and subsidiary companies* – the original requirements of the Business Review 2005 (mandatory) – consolidated in the Business Review 2006.
- *Venture capital portfolio companies (meeting specific criteria)* – Business Review 2006 (voluntary but effectively mandatory for BVCA members).

However, it is important to emphasise that, irrespective of the reporting, the new definition of directors' duties applies to all directors, regardless of the nature of the company.

The guidance

The Companies Act 2006 resulted in extra regulatory focus on the Business Review. Previously the descriptive elements of the annual report had not been subject to any form of regulation, although the governance aspects had been subject to the guidance of what was then the Combined Code. However, there are no standards on which company secretaries or boards of directors could base their annual report preparations. The Business Review legislation is not itself prescriptive – indeed, it is important to remind readers that having a *CR report within the Business Review* is not a requirement under the legislation!

The reporting statement

Whilst the OFR is a voluntary approach, it is the only form of non-financial reporting for which there is any form of guidance as to its content viz. the reporting statement.

The OFR was left as a voluntary form of non-financial reporting and the ASB modified its original Reporting Standard 1 to become a reporting statement,[8] that is guidelines for listed companies who are considering producing an OFR[9] on a voluntary basis. Its objective is to lay down guidance on best practice for completion of an OFR. The guidance is that this has to be a balanced and comprehensive analysis, as appropriate to the size and complexity of the business. The OFR should include a review of the following components:

- the development and performance of the business during the financial year;
- its position at the end of the financial year;
- the main trends and factors underlying its development, performance and position; and
- the main trends and factors likely to affect its future development, performance and position.

The purpose of the OFR is to assist members (i.e. shareholders) to assess the strategies adopted by the business and the potential for those strategies to succeed.

The reporting statement suggested that the OFR should disclose information relating to its subsidiary undertakings, including issues specific to business segments. This should include forward-looking views, but the reporting statement acknowledged that such statements may require a statement asking the shareholders to treat such element with caution (prior to the introduction of a 'safe harbour' provision under the Companies Act 2006).

In addition, the reporting statement suggests that the OFR should be used to provide an additional explanation of the information included within the financial statement. But the overwhelming intention of the reporting statement is that the OFR should be comprehensive and easy to understand, and that the emphasis is on the quality of the explanation of the business rather than the quantity of information provided. In addition, the reporting statement emphasises that the OFR should be balanced and neutral with an even-handed treatment of both the good and bad aspects of the business's development. In this respect, the intention is that the OFR should be comparable over time, although the length of time envisaged as the basis for reporting is not given in the reporting statement.

Within the reporting statement, the ASB has included a disclosure framework. The following are the main elements considered necessary to be included in this framework:

- A description of the business – featuring a description of the market, its competitive and regulatory environment, and its strategies and objectives.
- The development and performance of the business, both in the current financial year and for the future.
- The resources, principal risks and uncertainties and relationships that may affect the long-term value of the business.
- The financial position of the business, including its capital structure, treasury policies and objectives and its liquidity – both for the current financial year and the future.

As part of the above, the OFR is expected to include information about the business's involvement in:

- environmental matters;
- employee matters;
- social and community issues;
- individuals with whom the business has contractual (or other) arrangements that are essential to the business;
- receipts from and returns to the shareholders; and
- any other matters deemed relevant by the directors.

All of this information is to be reported '*to the extent necessary*', which again focuses on the directors' interpretation of what is necessary to help the shareholders understand the business's strategy and its development.

However if the directors comment on environmental, employees or social or community issues, then the OFR requires that they also comment on the policy for each area – and the extent to which these policies have been successfully implemented.

In addition, the OFR requires that KPIs should be included to allow shareholders to assess the business's progress against its stated objectives. These should cover both the financial and non-financial aspects of the business. Again the OFR uses the phrase '*to the extent necessary*' to ensure that it is the directors' interpretation and analysis of the business rather than that of a third party.

The business is expected to define any KPI used in the OFR (with an explanation of the method of calculation), describe its purpose and provide a quantification or commentary on future targets. Prior-year data for the KPI should be provided wherever possible (although, this may not be sufficient to allow a shareholder to understand the nature of the business).

The reporting statement gives a selection of 23 KPIs that may be considered for inclusion in an OFR, but makes the point that these are neither exhaustive, nor required, since it will be important to fit the choice of the KPIs to the nature of the industry in which the business operates.

Within the reporting statement, the KPIs have been chosen to relate to each area of the OFR, as can be seen below:

- **Nature, objectives and strategies of the business:**
  - return on capital employed;
  - incremental returns on investments;
  - economic profit; and
  - organic rates of growth and return.
- **Market positioning:**
  - market share.
- **Development, performance and position:**
  - average revenue per user;
  - number of subscribers;
  - sales per square foot;

- percentage of revenue from new products;
- numbers of product sold per customer;
- products in the development pipeline; and
- cost per unit produced.
- **Resources, principal risks and uncertainties and relationships:**
  - customer churn;
  - environmental spoilages;
  - CO_2 emissions;
  - waste;
  - employee morale;
  - employee health and safety;
  - monitoring of social risks in the supply chain;
  - noise infringements;
  - reserves;
  - market risk;
  - business continuity management;
  - economic capital; and
  - cash conversion rate.

When the reporting statement refers to the 'Principal risks and uncertainties', the emphasis is on the word 'principal'. The OFR does not have to include the business's entire risk register, but it should cover financial, commercial, operational and strategic risks – areas for which companies often had not provided full disclosure in the past. Previously, they had tended to focus on financial risks such as treasury, currency and interest rates, and had excluded areas such as risk to reputation.

The Accounting Standards Board (ASB) recommends that the reporting statement is a form of best practice for those quoted companies producing their Business Reviews under s 417 of the Companies Act 2006. However, the reporting statement has been criticised by some institutional investors as being overly prescriptive (especially since it recommends the OFR as the format that companies should follow).

The ABI

The Association of British Insurers (ABI) published its Responsible Investment Disclosure Guidelines in 2007.[10] These updated and replaced the Socially Responsible Investment (SRI) guidelines, launched by the ABI in 2001, and took account of the introduction of the Business Review under the Companies Act 2006.

The guidelines refer to the need for environmental, social and governance (ESG) matters to be commented upon in the Business Review. Previously these were described as social, environmental and ethical (SEE) matters and this change is important as it brings governance clearly into the discussion of non-financial matters.

The guidelines call on boards to report on their approach to managing environmental, social and governance risks within the Business Review and aim to help companies understand how to comply with the Business Review in ways that are useful to investors, without imposing additional requirements.

The guidelines also focus on providing forward-looking information, establishing a clear policy for risk management, publishing KPIs and a breakdown by business segment where appropriate, and describing how they actually handle environmental, social and governance risks of particular significance to the business.

The ABI went further and recommended verification of non-financial statements in the Business Review. It acknowledged that this verification could be undertaken either through internal resources or an external agency, stating that the verification procedure should achieve a reasonable level of credibility. This focus on verification was to overcome what had been quite 'glib statements' in early Business Reviews, such as 'Our people are our most important asset', without any further clarification of the statement.

The FRRP and Rio Tinto

The Financial Reporting Review Panel (FRRP) is part of the Financial Reporting Council (FRC), which is also responsible for the ASB. The FRRP's role is to review annual reports, and take action where it feels a report is less than adequate – typically by a private letter to the chair and company secretary. Appropriate action normally results, without any need to take a more rigorous approach.

The FRRP been responsible for reviewing the Business Reviews since 2006, but apparently has taken little public action in this area despite the fact that the statutory purpose for the Business Review, enshrined in s 417 of the Companies Act 2006, is one basis under which the panel should review companies' Business Reviews.

In its 2010 Annual Report (published in September 2010[11]), the FRRP stated that 'narrative reporting is claiming an increasing proportion of its attention'. It commented that it had questioned companies whose Corporate Social Responsibility (CSR) reports (i.e. the voluntary reports usually produced in web format or in hard copy) suggested environmental matters were material – but who had made no mention of these matters in their Annual Report and Accounts (ARA). This focus increased significantly in March 2011, when the FRRP issued a public notice via a press release about Rio Tinto's ARA,[12] following a complaint from a group of activist lawyers, ClientEarth, about inadequate non-financial disclosures, particularly related to the environmental impact on local communities of its mining operations. Rio Tinto's December 2010 ARA addressed these issues with a far fuller commentary than had been the case previously.

This move was significant because, for the first time, the FRRP was looking beyond just the statutory reports and comparison information included in voluntary, non-regulated reporting, with that included in statutory reports. Its intent was to focus attention on the need for adequate narrative reporting. The press release was circulated by the 'big four' accounting firms to all of their audit clients, advising them to step up their internal scrutiny of the adequacy of their narrative reporting.

Governance and accounting guidance

Whilst there are regulations that companies need to comply with in developing their narrative reports, there is also guidance which can be as influential, often because of its importance from the perspective of institutional investors or external auditors.

The UK Corporate Governance Code

In 2010, the Financial Reporting Council introduced the new UK Corporate Governance Code.[13] This took effect for financial years starting after 29 June 2010, and all UK-listed companies are now subject to its guidance. It replaced the Financial Reporting Council's Combined Code on Corporate Governance (commonly known as the Combined Code).

The new Code introduced two significant changes that relate to the new director's duty 'to promote the success of the company ... over the longer term':

> C.1.2 The directors should include in the annual report an explanation of the basis on which the company generates or preserves value over the longer term (the business model) and the strategy for delivering the objectives of the company. (Desirable that it is within the Business Review.)
> D.1.1 In designing schemes of performance-related remuneration for executive directors, the remuneration committee should follow the provisions in Schedule A to this Code ... all incentive schemes, including ... share option schemes, should be subject to challenging performance criteria reflecting the company's objectives, including non-financial performance metrics where appropriate.

Both relate to the quality of narrative reporting. They emphasise the need for a better description of the business model and the appropriate use of non-financial metrics. These are required both to evidence the performance of the company and as part of the criteria for executive remuneration. Over time, it is expected that both institutional investors and external auditors will be paying far more attention to the quality of narrative reporting in these two areas.

The management commentary

The International Accounting Standards Board (IASB), on which the ASB sits as the UK's representative, issued its Practice Statement for Management Commentary[14] in December 2010. The Management Commentary is a narrative report within Annual Report and Accounts (ARAs) and the Practice Statement is intended to enhance international consistency.

This Practice Statement represents a broad framework for the presentation of a Management Commentary. It is part of a series of IFRS financial statements which are non-binding unless countries specifically require them in their jurisdiction. A past example of this approach was the EAMD for which the EU took IASB guidance statements and made them mandatory for EU member states.

Whilst it is termed a 'management commentary', some countries may describe it as 'management's discussion and analysis' (known as MDA in USA), an 'operating and financial review' (UK), or a 'management's report'. These various forms of narrative reporting have not previously had any form of international guidance and it will be interesting to see how this form of international coordination develops.

UK Government bodies have a *mandatory* requirement to report their ARAs as a management commentary. This is based on the OFR, and these bodies use the ASB's reporting statement as the basis for their reporting. Some NHS trusts describe it as an OFR, rather than a management commentary.

Government-related developments

Narrative reporting is an area that is under constant review and development (to some extent regrettably, as any change needs time to bed down). At the time of writing, there are reviews taking place both by the UK Government and the EU, as well as an international voluntary programme to introduce integrated reporting. The regret stems from the view that too rapid a change may serve to create confusion and uncertainly amongst the practitioners responsible for producing annual reports. A more phased approach, ensuring greater comfort and confidence amongst practitioners in producing ARAs to current standards, such as the UK Corporate Governance Code, may be more beneficial.

EU developments

In early 2011, the EU launched a consultation on narrative reporting rules. This sought to improve disclosure on corporate social and environmental matters, including respect for human rights. The respondents were in general agreement that legal regimes on narrative reporting differ significantly across the EU member states. Half of them described the current regime applicable in their respective jurisdiction as poor or very poor. As a result, the EU set up a committee of experts to advise on improved reporting requirements, including whether or not to make such reporting mandatory, but with the addition of a 'comply or explain' rule. A lot of the discussion on this subject was incorporated in the EU's CSR strategy paper which was published in late 2011 (see Chapter 9).

UK Government developments

The UK coalition government's manifesto included a commitment to reinstate the OFR as mandatory reporting – which came out of the blue and surprised many observers. After initial consultation on this was completed, BIS issued a new consultation in September 2011 on further changes in annual reporting and the Business

Review, in conjunction with another, more publicised, consultation on executive remuneration. Details of the proposals in the annual report consultation are discussed below (in conjunction with FRC changes).

There is a very strong likelihood of mandatory Green House Gas reporting for UK-listed companies as required under the provisions of the Climate Change Act 2008. This may have the greatest repercussions for some companies (especially those with smaller market capitalisation). DEFRA consulted on how this should be applied, and it may be that the outcome of this consultation will be combined with the review by BIS of narrative reporting in the Business Review – although this may require joined up thinking by government departments!

Financial Reporting Council developments

In early September 2011, the FRC published two papers: 'Board and Risk – A Summary of Discussion with Companies, Investors and Advisers'; and 'Effective Company Stewardship – Next Steps'.[15] As with all FRC statements, the recommendations are in the form of guidance (the Turnbull Guidance is to be updated in the light of the risk recommendations), but the strength of the FRC statements is the impact they have upon practitioners and advisers. In reality, they are closer to directions than to guidance.

The proposed changes in annual reporting – BIS and FRC

Because the proposals from BIS and FRC (in 'Effective Company Stewardship') overlap, the nature of the proposed changes is described here as a summary in a combined format:

Narrative reporting

- **FRC**: Proposing that the audit committee would cover 'front and back' half of the annual report:
  - the FRC announced it would amend the UK Corporate Governance Code to enable the extension of the remit of an audit committee to include a consideration of the whole annual report, including the narrative report, with a view to determining whether it provides the information necessary for stakeholders to assess the performance and prospects of the company and that the annual report, viewed as a whole, is fair and balanced;
  - in addition to the increased scope of the audit committee, the FRC proposes that the reports by external auditors give greater transparency to the work carried out by auditors in relation to the annual report as a whole. This proposal implies that the external auditors will be expected to review the work by the audit committee with regard to the narrative report.
- **BIS**: Proposing a new reporting format for the annual report, effectively splitting it into two documents:

- a strategic report – comprising the business model, strategy, KPIs, significant risks, material environmental and social information and key executive remuneration information;
- an annual directors' statement – likely to be more detailed and possibly web-based. Content would include disclosures, corporate governance, remuneration report, and voluntary CSR information.

Risk reviews

- **FRC**: Proposing a more focused approach to risk reporting:
  - risks in narrative report to focus on strategic risks and major operational risks inherent in the business model and strategic implementation;
  - Turnbull Guidance to be updated accordingly;
  - changes in UK Corporate Governance Code to be considered to address this approach and ensure alignment.
- **BIS**: No additional comments.

Remuneration

- **FRC**: No comments made.
- **BIS**: Companies should consider (transparent) disclosure of key remuneration aspects in the strategic report, covering:
  - total director remuneration;
  - executive officer remuneration;
  - more appropriate measures/criteria of performance (with the use of the total shareholders' return (TSR) being criticised);
  - CEO pay to median pay ratio.

Other matters

- **FRC**:
  - the development of a new financial reporting laboratory to help practitioners with the quality of their narrative reporting;
  - developing the concept of, and model for, reporting standards for narrative reporting – this has echoes of its Reporting Standard 1 for the OFR, and one wonders how much support would be forthcoming; the likelihood is that standards will not be introduced.
- **BIS**:
  - proposing the introduction of a reporting statement (non-mandatory) – which will negate the FRC thoughts – and expects the existing reporting statement to be updated;
  - charitable donations disclosure to be dropped;
  - employee involvement disclosure to be dropped;
  - reporting on human rights matters is to be considered;
  - reporting on gender diversity – consider extending disclosure of women in the company as a whole, as well as on the board.

The Virtuous Circle's comments in its June 2011 research report (see Chapter 3) on business models, business strategy, related KPIs, risk reviews and remuneration criteria are addressed through the proposed changes in the BIS and FRC documents.

For those with preparation responsibilities for the ARA, the key implications of the BIS proposals and the FRC proposed changes that will need significant amounts of work are:

- the new audit committee remit – this may require more ARA preparation time;
- changes to remuneration policies – this will require delicate handling of executive directors' expectations, plus for some companies, considerable effort to determine median pay levels;
- for those companies not collating gender data, especially those multinationals without unified HR software systems, the broad gender diversity data disclosure will require a data collation system and its standards;
- the focus on defining business model will continue to be a challenge for many companies, which will include achieving a common understanding amongst directors and senior management.

It is also useful to consider the discussion in 'Boards and Risk', where the focus was on the risk management process and on the risks reported upon.

The former included emphasis on the board's overall responsibilities to determining the company's approach to risk, setting its culture, risk identification, oversight of risk management, and crisis management. It commented also on the board's need to agree its appetite or tolerance for key individual risks; to understand the company's exposure to risk and how this might change, both as a result of changes to strategy and the operating environment, and to take a view on these changes.

The latter commented on the need for boards to focus, especially on those risks capable of undermining the strategy or long-term viability of the company or damaging its reputation. As regards the latter, the paper acknowledged that reputational risk had grown in importance and required greater attention. It recognised that the increased 'velocity' of risk, with near-instantaneous global transmission of failure, required robust crisis management plans, including clear prior agreement on the respective roles of the chairman and chief executive in a crisis. The need to focus more on those risks capable of undermining the strategy or long-term viability of the company was deemed necessary because of the view that investors sought more meaningful reporting on risk (e.g. through an integrated discussion of the company's business model, strategy, key risks and mitigation).

The paper made suggestions for improving reporting which included:

- integrating commentary on risk throughout the report, rather than treating it as a standalone section;
- specifically, linking reporting on risk to discussion of strategy and the business model;
- explaining changes in the company's risk exposure over the previous 12 months, as a result of changes to the strategy or business environment, and indicating if it might change in the future; and
- disclosing how key risks were being mitigated.

The purpose of this paper was not an attempt to provide guidance, but rather to capture contributions from companies, investors and advisers to help other companies in thinking about their own approaches to risk. However, in *Effective Company Stewardship*, the FRC indicated it would update the Turnbull guidance to reflect the lessons from its work on risk, and will also consider whether changes should be made to the UK Corporate Governance Code as a result of that work and the Sharman Inquiry. This inquiry has been charged with the task of advising the FRC on lessons to be learned by companies and auditors addressing going concern and liquidity risks.

Voluntary developments

International Integrated Reporting Committee (IIRC)

The IIRC[16] was set up under the auspices of The Prince's Accounting for Sustainability Project. At the outset, it was viewed with some scepticism by observers. However, it has the backing and involvement of the Big 4 accounting firms and Professor Mervyn E King is deputy chairman (see King III below).

Integrated Reporting aims to demonstrate the link between a company's strategy, governance and financial performance and its social, environmental and economic context.

The intention is that an integrated report should be a single report which then becomes the company's primary report (instead of having an annual report with a Business Review, and a stand alone CSR document). Its focus is to communicate how a company creates and sustains value in the short, medium and longer term.

The work of the IIRC is still at an early stage. The schedule of the committee is that an international public consultation was held in late 2011. The consultation reviews the rationale for integrated reporting, offers initial proposals for the development of an international integrated reporting framework and outlines the next steps towards its creation and adoption. Assuming that there are positive responses it is planned that a pilot programme would operate with companies producing an integrated report in 2012. Over 50 companies have agreed to participate.

The question that needs to be asked is 'Will integrated reporting work?' In this respect, the next question is whether there is such a thing as 'an integrated stakeholder'. Experience has shown that the various stakeholders all have different information needs; this may inhibit the production of an integrated report.

King III

Having questioned whether integrated reporting will work, we now look to South Africa, where all Johannesburg listed companies must now submit an integrated report as their annual report.

Professor Mervyn E King (deputy chairman of the IIRC) is chair of South Africa's King Committee. This takes an integrated approach to corporate governance, based on enlightened shareholder value. It produced reports in 1994 and 2002 –

implemented as the King Code in South African company law – both of which had a significant influence on the UK's company law reform process.

King III,[17] which is the revised King Code and Report on Governance for South Africa, replaced the existing King II Code and Report on Corporate Governance. It was launched on 1 September 2009 and took effect in March 2010. It adopted an 'apply or explain' approach, thus enabling boards to apply a different practice with an accompanying explanation of practices adopted and reasons stated (compare this to the UK's 'comply or explain').

King III requires integrated reporting by listed companies, covering both a company's financial performance and its sustainability (disclosing positive and negative impacts of its operations on stakeholders).

This South African requirement is still in its initial year, and the continuing work of the IIRC will depend on the success or otherwise of King III. However, early review of reports published under King III suggest that they are very lengthy and this may be unacceptable in the longer term.

Sources

1 The Companies Act 1985 (Operating and Financial Review and Directors' Report etc.) Regulations 2005 (SI 2005/1011).

2 Directive 2003/51/EC of the European Parliament and of the Council of 18 June 2003.

3 Companies Act 2006 – ss. 382, 465 and 466.

4 The latest financial criteria can be found on the EU website: ec.europa.eu/enterprise/enterprise_policy/sme_definition/index_en.htm

5 ACCA – The operating and financial review – a catalyst for improved social and environmental disclosure – Research Report No. 89 – 2005.

6 Stated in s. 417 of the Companies Act 2006.

7 A review of the first year of progress of portfolio companies under the Walker Guidance can be found on the BVCA website: www.bvca.co.uk/search/features/DisclosureWalkerisWorkingandWhy

8 Reporting Statement: Operating and Financial Review – Accounting Standards Board January 2006.

9 It should be noted that whilst the OFR is intended for voluntary use by listed companies (and any others for which it may be an appropriate framework for reporting) it is a mandatory framework for some government bodies. In these cases, the OFR is described as a Management Commentary. Such bodies are those bodies that receive funding from government and include organisation such as NHS Trusts and the Post Office.

10 The press release announcing these guidelines can be found on the ABI website: www.abi.org.uk/Media/Releases/2007/02/ABI_publishes_Responsible_Investment_Disclosure_Guidelines.aspx

11 The FRRP's 2010 Annual Report can be found on its website: www.frc.org.uk/frrp/press/pub2349.html

12 The FRRP's statement in respect of the report and accounts of Rio Tinto Plc can be found on its website: www.frc.org.uk/frrp/press/pub2539.html

13 Details of the UK Corporate Governance Code and its application to listed companies can be found on the FRC's website: www.frc.org.uk/corporate/ukcgcode.cfm

14 Information about the Management Commentary can be found on the IFRS website: www.ifrs.org/News/Press+Releases/Management+Commentary+Practice+Statement.htm

15 The FRC press release, including links to the two papers can be found at: www.frc.org.uk/press/pub2632.html

16 Information about IIRC can be found on its website: www.theiirc.org/

17 Information on King III can be found on the South African Institute of Chartered Accountants website: www.saica.co.za/TechnicalInformation/LegalandGovernance/King/tabid/626/language/en-ZA/Default.aspx

3

Perspectives on the quality of business review reporting

How have companies met their Business Review reporting requirements?

In this section, two pieces of research undertaken by The Virtuous Circle into the quality of narrative reporting are reported upon. Whilst they are five years apart, their findings remain relevant today and, in fact, build upon each other.

The research[1] looked at the first Business Reviews to be produced in 2006 (this research was included by the Accounting Standards Board, in its own report[2] on the subject and was also presented at an ICSA conference on 5 October 2006).

This research looked at the first set of Business Reviews produced under the Business Review Regulations 2005. The objective was to understand how companies had coped with these regulations and to assess the quality of their corporate reporting. The listed companies researched included four FTSE350 companies, 12 FTSE100 companies and nine FTSE200 companies (representing about 65% of FTSE200 companies with a 31 March year end).

This research was commented upon in detail in the second edition of this book, but it is still relevant to review its conclusions and consider how far companies have come in their narrative reporting since then, given that then, as now, there is little or no laid down guidance for BR reporting.

Surprisingly, at that time, 48% of the companies studied had produced an OFR. This rose to over 50% of those companies that were part of the FTSE350 or FTSE100. Furthermore a few had both a BR and an OFR, which illustrated some confusion surrounding the subject. In 2011, whereas some may follow the OFR guidelines, few describe their report as an OFR.

The average length of a Business Review or OFR was 27 pages – but this ranged from 11 to 64 pages, with larger companies having longer reports. Length is not a good criterion to evaluate the quality of reporting. Most companies in 2011 are trying to reduce the length of their report, instead focusing on the quality of communication.

In that respect, bearing in mind the Business Review requirement to offer further explanation to the accounts, only about one-third of companies did so (around 50% of FTSE350 companies). Even today, there still seems to be a reluctance to make further explanatory references, with companies assuming that the notes to the accounts (not part of the Business Review) can fulfil that purpose.

In general and probably unsurprisingly, companies were generally good at giving 'a balanced and comprehensive review'. In many respects, this is what would have been produced in previous annual reports. However, the research identified the paucity of financial information at business unit or divisional levels. Where this was available, the information provided tended to be revenue and profit, but excluded capital employed or capital investment. This was still often the case in 2011. In addition, in 2006, there tended to be rather poor quality descriptions of the business environment faced at a business unit level, but this is one area where companies have improved the quality of their reporting.

For many companies, the more significant weaknesses lay in the 'fair review' – with a significantly lower level of attention being paid to the strategies and outlook for each business area. Where strategy was discussed, it tended to be at a group level rather than being segmented into the relevant business units. This remains the case in 2011, as will be demonstrated by the second piece of research.

Risks were reported upon by nearly all the companies studied – but they tended to be little more than a list. This was still the case in 2011. But whilst in 2006 very few companies reported upon their mitigation actions related to each risk area, this is an area that has improved since the first piece of research, with more statements about mitigating actions being employed.

Key performance indicators (KPIs) were an area which clearly caused problems. Too few companies appeared to be able to identify key measures which would demonstrate how the board was managing performance; this remained the case for non-financial metrics in 2011. In 2006, some companies failed to identify either financial or non-financial KPIs. This is not to say that there was no data, but there was nothing that could be described as an indicator of performance, with many of the indicators being an output, such as total sales revenue. Companies failed to identify which data represented the KPIs that they used to manage their business.

Surprisingly, very few non-financial KPIs related to key business areas such as customers or employees. This has changed since, but is still an aspect that can be improved upon. In addition, in terms of the quality of those KPIs that were reported, very few companies reported more than two years' data. Is this enough to help investors judge the quality of a company's performance? This is certainly an area that has changed since 2006, but most companies limit their reporting to around the previous three years.

Lastly, the impression gained was that the Business Review had been drawn from a series of silo functions – there was inadequate alignment between the descriptions of the business segments, the strategy and outlook, the risks and the KPIs used to manage the business. Regrettably, this is still very much the case in 2011.

The Virtuous Circle (TVC) published a further piece of narrative reporting research, published at the end of June 2011. Since the earlier research, TVC has interviewed institutional investors extensively on behalf of its clients. Institutional investors have said that they wanted the Business Review to 'tell the strategic story'. In other words, they want it to put the operational and strategic flesh on the bones provided by the financial data in the annual report and accounts.

In this latest research, the focus was on the extent to which companies were anticipating the guidance from the UK Corporate Governance Code (effective for financial years starting after 29 June 2010) by including its recommendations in their narrative reports and in their remuneration committee's report. In this context, the UK Corporate Governance Code encourages companies to take greater care in describing non-financial aspects of their operations in Annual Report and Accounts (ARA), including describing the business model and using relevant non-financial KPIs in executive remuneration policies. This research looks at how companies are following these guidelines.

The sample of companies was derived from those with December 2010 year ends. Based on client experience, it was expected that at least the larger market capitalisation companies would anticipate the outcome of the new Code in their planning for these year-end accounts.

Thirty-one companies were randomly selected as a sample of ARAs from the top 200 companies (in terms of market capitalisation) with December 2010 year ends (38% of the available population). The research was based on an evaluation framework, which considered:

- the quality of reporting of business models and business strategy and their links with the risk review;
- the use of non-financial metrics to explain the company's performance; and
- the use of appropriate non-financial metrics to determine remuneration practice.

The key findings of the research focused on two areas – the extent of commentary on business model, strategy and risks and the use of non-financial KPIs in executive remuneration policies.

The research found that only half of all companies analysed included a business model – but this was slightly higher for larger companies and business-to-business (B2B) companies. Also there was a great deal of variation in the quality of the business model statements.

More companies reported on strategy in their ARA, but few took the strategy statements into divisional reviews (as was found in the 2006 research). This represented a lack of consistency and suggested that strategic implementation was left to the head office, with little implementation at divisional level.

It was apparent that there was confusion between a business model and a business strategy. More importantly, those companies found to be stating a business model also were more effective in business strategy reporting.

In addition, the extent to which risks reported in an ARA relate to the business model and the strategic implementation was questionable in a majority of cases. Risk reviews were fairly 'predictable', with the normal focus on economic, financial and market risks, but less focus on operational or strategic risks. Again this was the case in 2006 research. This point was also commented upon in the FRC's paper 'Boards and Risk' (see Chapter 2), published in September 2011, shortly after this piece of research.

In terms of the provision of KPIs, almost every company reported what they described as 'KPIs'. However, where non-financial metrics (NFMs) are selected as

KPIs, there was often little linkage to the strategy/business model. Indeed, some of those selected appeared to be token issues, linked to legislation and the legislative burden on the board, rather than reflecting the ability to demonstrate the company's long-term performance success.

An example was where a health and safety performance indicator was chosen as a KPI. In such cases, it is difficult to understand how such an indicator can be an indicator of future performance and address the directors' duty to 'promote the success of the company …'. This issue may have been chosen as a KPI to alleviate directors' concerns over their potential liabilities regarding the Corporate Manslaughter Act.

NFMs were found to be more frequently identified as performance indicators in the CSR section of ARAs, with larger companies tending to be more expansive. The average number of NFMs selected as KPIs was 3.2 for FTSE100 companies and 1.8 for FTSE250 companies, whilst the average number of NFMs identified in the CSR section of the ARA was 4.0 and 3.3 respectively.

NFMs used as criteria within the remuneration committee's report was much more frequent for annual bonuses than for long-term incentives. Health and safety was a criterion in around 60% of cases, followed by employee and customer NFMs at around 30% (which in itself demonstrated how companies have begun to use a wider range of NFMs than in 2006). Several of those companies indicated that they would adopt NFMs as executive remuneration criteria in 2011.

Some concluding comments from the two pieces of research

The questions that should be asked by a company when preparing its Business Review are: To what extent does this help investors and shareholders to gain a more informed view of this company? and How well does the Business Review help to improve the reputation of the business and of the board's strategic thinking and implementation? The Business Review offers the opportunity for company executives to give a full and fair portrayal of the company's strategy and performance. Used properly, it has the potential to become a very significant tool in investor relations, ensuring that a true appreciation of shareholder value is achieved.

To do this effectively, however, the professionals producing the Business Review should see it as a planned piece of communication. As such, the comments about silo-based production (where individuals produce their sections of the repost independently of others) made in the 2006 research and amplified in the 2011 research, need to be addressed to enable the 'strategic story' to be told effectively.

It is clear, however, that, based on these two pieces of research, companies have improved the quality of their narrative reporting in their Business Reviews, but equally clearly, it is an ongoing process. Often there is a time lag before implementation, and new pieces of legislation are taken on board by companies only over time.

In addition, it is clear also that some assistance is needed to help companies describe business models and to select appropriate non-financial metrics for remuneration policies. From these business models, companies need to determine key business drivers, link NFM KPIs to them and avoid token KPIs. Alignment of NFMs to the business model and strategy needs to be reinforced and risk reviews in ARAs could be better structured to include comments on risks pertaining to both the business model and the business strategy.

Similarly, multiple-division companies should consider how to better convey that the overall business strategy leads to individual divisional initiatives.

Lastly, to reflect directors' duty to promote the success of the company, NFM criteria for incentive plans should be selected from longer term lead indicators, rather than choosing lag indicators that serve only to address the past or prior years' performances.

Investors' expectations of the Business Review

For the *ICSA Company Reporting Handbook*,[3] interviews were undertaken with regulators, company secretaries (representing companies with around £100 billion capitalisation) advisers, communicators and investors (representing funds under management of about £80 billion).

The latter were very forthcoming about how they viewed the Business Review. They ranged in investment style from the trader (for whom the numbers in the preliminary announcement was everything and who paid little attention to content of the annual report) to the activists (who used the annual report as the basis for having an intensive dialogue with company executives).

Their comments about the Business Review were very insightful and gave the opportunity to have extensive discussions with clients about how they should structure their own reviews.

Firstly, when commenting on the relevance of the OFR, there were comments that the ASB's reporting statement is overly prescriptive; they were hoping to see more of the company's personality and its culture when reading the Business Review.

Second, the investors' emphasis for the Business Review is that it should tell the company's strategic story. For them, the Business Review offers companies a platform to describe its strategy in more detail and relate it to risks in a more cohesive manner, with KPIs to demonstrate how well the strategy is currently performing and a forward outlook to demonstrate how well it will perform in the future.

Third, in terms of the choice of non-financial information to be included within the Business Review, the investors focused on the importance of business criticality. They commented that there is little benefit in disclosing non-financial information if it is not considered to be business critical to the success of the implementation of the strategy.

Fourth, when asked about risks and KPIs, investors commented that they wanted to see information that they were assured was relevant to the strategy and that represented quality information. They were not seeking an extensive range of information (on the basis that they did not believe that the board would be able to manage such in-depth information). An example was given of a company that published a total of around 40 risks – the comment of the investors was that if there really were 40 individual risk areas that were considered to be principal risks to the business, this suggested a business in decline – if not now, then certainly in the future!

Lastly, when asked about the forward-looking 'safe harbour' provision under the Companies Act 2006, they ventured that they were not looking for the equivalent of profit and loss forecasts. Instead, they were seeking medium-term views about the development of the strategy, including identifying any business or external develop-ments that may contribute to the success – or failure – of the strategy. Perhaps most telling was the comment of one investor that if there was no improvement on the part of companies in terms of providing forward-looking statements (given the 'safe har-bour' provision) then 'there may be some pressure from investors for the removal of the safe harbour provision … because it will not have done what it's there to do – encourage discussion about forward-looking prospects'.

In addition to this in-depth research into investors' attitudes and expectations of the 2006 Business Review, in January 2007, the Association of British Insurers (ABI) published its revisions to its Responsible Investment Guidelines. These are discussed in more detail in Chapter 2, but the important change is the reference to the inclusion of ESG (environmental, social and governance) matters in the Annual Report and accounts. For the first time, this brought issues of non-financial information clearly into the arena of corporate governance, including taking account of significant ESG risk matters in its regular risk assessment procedures.

In addition, the ASB has published its own guidance[4] on how its reporting state-ment on the OFR can be linked to the legislative requirements of the Companies Act 2006 Business Review (see Chapter 2). Their view (shared by TVC's own findings) is that the reporting statement offers good practice advice to listed companies prepar-ing their own Business Review. The benefit of this guidance is that it links the various regulatory requirements in their sections and identifies where to find the guidance in the relevant sections of the reporting statement.

Chapter 4 gives more detail about how a Business Review can be developed – the processes and the content.

Sources

1 'Preparedness for new corporate reporting requirements – A study of FTSE200 Business Reviews and a consideration of their readiness for the new Companies Act', The Virtuous Circle, November 2006.

2 A review of narrative reporting by UK listed companies in 2006 Accounting Standards Board – January 2007.

3 *The ICSA Company Reporting Handbook* – Tony Hoskins – ICSA Publishing – 2007.

4 Details of the ASB's guidance on linking its Reporting Statement to the 2006 Companies Act Business Review can be found on its website: www.apb.org.uk/asb/press/pub1480.html

4

Guidance on developing the Business Review

Different approaches for private and quoted companies

Private or subsidiary companies

In developing your company's Business Review, you are likely to have a different approach dependent upon whether the company is affected by the 2006 Business Review legislation. Almost all of the focus will be upon these quoted companies, but it is right first to address those companies that report as private or subsidiary companies.

Most accountancy practices provide advice on how to prepare a Business Review since they are required to provide their opinion on its consistency with the information provided in the annual accounts. One early example was PricewaterhouseCoopers' (PwC) templates for Business Reviews, which varied depending on the nature of the company reporting.

PwC's advice was very useful because of its provision of guidance for non-listed companies. It published a range of illustrative examples for such companies (for quoted companies, their advice at that time was to complete a voluntary OFR complying with the reporting statement).

For non-listed companies, PwC offered two forms of Business Review. 'The standard Business Review was for companies that have dispersed ownership – either privately owned or traded on exchanges such as the AIM – and covered the areas already discussed. The second is 'the simple Business Review'. This was for companies that are owner managed, as well as wholly owned subsidiaries.

PwC took the view that members of such companies will already have a good understanding of the development, performance and position of the company. Its conclusion was that 'little information, simply the minimum required to comply with the legislation, is necessary to present a clear picture to members in the Business Review'. The 'simple Business Review' was intended to contain only high-level disclosures in the directors' report. PwC's illustrative example limited the descriptions to the bare minimum and used the 'to the extent necessary' test to enable the directors to declare few, if any, KPIs.

The approach suggested by PwC is a realistic one, given the nature of the shareholders in such companies. However, care should be taken to avoid a minimalist approach, especially if the directors anticipate changing circumstances in the medium term. Such circumstances could include moving from privately owned to publicly quoted companies (most probably via AIM), as well as seeking significant additional capital through debt finance. In such circumstances, it may be preferable to move to a more complete form of Business Review, to enable the board or the company's owners to answer the questions of potential investors or lenders by having a track record of available information declared publicly via the annual report.

Quoted companies

In discussing guidance of how to prepare a Business Review for a quoted company, it is important to consider some wider aspects of corporate reporting. With the advent of the Companies Act 2006 came the opportunity for companies to provide their annual reports electronically. As a result, some bodies looked at the opportunities this change offered. One such body was the consortia known as the Report Leadership Initiative.

This initiative[1] was the output of a multi-stakeholder group that aimed to challenge the established thinking on corporate reporting. The stakeholders participating in the initiative at the outset were the Chartered Institute of Management Accountants (CIMA), PricewaterhouseCoopers, Radley Yeldar (the corporate communication design agency) and Tomkins plc. It was intended to be an ongoing activity, to which third parties could contribute via its website and was launched in November 2006.

The initiative took as its starting point the need to improve the annual report, on the basis that it should be more informative and accessible, by providing the information that investors want, without swamping them with unnecessary detail. Its objectives were to:

- help companies to report in ways that are more relevant and informative to their primary audience;
- encourage investors to push for the information they want; and
- prompt standards setters to consider how they might foster beneficial change.

It recognised that companies spend significant time aggregating and recalculating internal data to produce the regulatory information. This process was described as wasteful and ineffective. Instead a blueprint was developed for corporate reporting that aligns external reporting more closely with management reporting, acknowledges business complexities, is capable of being adapted to other media and offers relevance and accessibility to investors.

This blueprint covers aspects of corporate reporting:

- Effective communication
  - structure
  - messaging
  - navigation
- Modelling the future
  - value creation
  - forward-looking orientation

- – business environment
- – strategy
- – key performance indicators
- Rethinking the financials
  - – revenue and costs
  - – segmental disclosure
  - – pensions
  - – analysis of net debt.

The underlying intention of this blueprint is to provide greater contextual information, based on the conclusion from research that current reporting approaches are considered too backward looking and too compliance driven. It starts from the perspective of how to make the annual report more relevant by ensuring that more of the content tells investors what they want to know. It lines up with the outputs from another initiative – that of the Corporate Reporting Users Forum (CRUF) which has produced its guiding principles[2] on what analysts really want from accounts. This includes a cash flow statement that can be reconciled to the profit and loss statement, a P&L that differentiates between recurring and non-recurring activities, and a balance sheet that reflects the capital invested in the business, rather than its 'fair value'.

The strength of the Report Leadership initiative was that not only did it attempt to prescribe a course of action, but it also produced a draft company report – for an imaginary company, Generico – so that the audience for the initiative could touch and feel the concepts.

In February 2008, the Report Leadership team (by then without the participation of Tomkins plc) launched two more reporting publications – this time on remuneration reporting and online reporting.[3] The latter guidance for online reporting reflected the change in the Companies Act 2006 that permits companies to provide online reporting to shareholders as the default method instead of sending out hard copy versions of the annual report and accounts. This, of course, is subject to the board submitting a resolution to shareholders for this to be the case as a default. The Report Leadership publication focuses on how shareholders (or the wider stakeholder group) can navigate a company's reporting website. It emphasises the need for companies to create links between the various forms of reporting that are available online. In this context, companies should consider how they provide supporting evidence – non-financial information, covering areas such as customers, employees or environmental impacts – that will help stakeholders understand the interactions of activities that support the business strategy.

For the CSR professional, these reports provide many good signposts as to how CSR online reporting should be made available in the future. Just providing a PDF version of a report will not be enough. It will be necessary to consider providing Excel downloads of KPI data, as well as PDF downloads of documents such as policies. Provision of video and audio content is recommended as means of bringing the commentary to life. In addition it recommends making available analytical tools such as interactive charts and sensitivity analysis. If the CSR professional is to take on board the use of tools such as these, then CSR reporting will become more dynamic, and the dialogue with stakeholders will focus on the 'what if' rather than the 'what has' happened.

How to get consistency

As discussed earlier, experience shows that most Business Reviews appear to have been written in a silo approach, with different sections of the ARA being parcelled out to various divisions or departments. The result of this silo approach is that the ARA is often lacking a consistently persuasive communication.

To address this weakness, there are two options. The first (and most exhausting option for those concerned) is to ensure that the Business Review is written by no more than two people, to minimise variation of approach. This will often require a communication theme and message to be agreed beforehand.

As an example, Aggreko claims its 2010 report is written by its CEO and CFO. However, this can be a lot of work for those involved; the more senior the individuals are in the company, the less likely that they can devote sufficient time to produce a quality communication.

The second option is to gather the writing team together and plan the approach well in advance. Given that the Business Review is less dependent on year-end financial data, the writing process can start several months in advance. As an example, in one client interview held recently, National Grid stated they start their ARA process six months before the year end. This second approach is more effective, and can lead to a more in-depth communication.

Aspects that should be considered in the planning of the writing process include:

- How are the responsibilities split between the group and divisional team members?
- What is the overall message, and how should this be addressed in group and divisional sections of the ARA? In addition, a content style guide should be established at the outset to minimise subsequent style edits.
- What is the business model(s) and how should this be reinforced in the divisional reviews?
- What are the key strategies for the group as a whole?
- How are these strategies reinforced in divisional reviews, and are there any strategies that relate specifically to individual divisions?
- What are the key aspects to cover in each section of the ARA?
- What are KPIs and PIs (performance indicators) and how should they be reported at group and divisional levels?

As the Business Review forms a legal document, the need for compliance is high, so obtain a checklist from your legal advisers – or alternatively, contact solicitors, such as Addleshaw Goddard,[4] who produce a checklist that is regularly updated.

In planning the writing process, a key issue is the time available, and one individual should be allocated the task of project management and time planning.

When to start

As mentioned earlier, National Grid claims to start their narrative reporting process after the first half results are published. The Business Review should be 'a balanced and comprehensive analysis of the development and performance of the business during the financial year, and the position of the company at the end of the financial year'.

Given the need for time to develop a consistent communication approach, and that the focus is on the performance of the business during the financial year, then it is right to question why the preparation of the Business Review should be left until the year end.

In one client company, the investor relations director wanted to leave the preparation as late as possible to cover all events that occur in the year (this was overturned by a newly appointed CFO). The better approach is to start the planning and content development at the latest after the third quarter. If there is opposition to this from others that are responsible for the preparation of parts of the annual report, then ask them what activities will significantly change in narrative reporting terms in the last quarter? Even if there is a significant change, it is only likely to affect at most 20% of the content.

Bringing the preparation forward not only eases the burden on those responsible for the preparation but, more importantly, it ensures greater consistency of approach across all sections of the Business Review.

How to communicate the business model

An issue that many companies face is that of describing its business model. In this respect, it is important to avoid overlap between the business model and the business strategy. For its research, TVC defined the business model as:

- How a company makes and spends money *today*.
- How a company creates value for its shareholders.

It defined the business strategy as:

- How a company plans to make more money or change its business direction *for the future*.

Clearly, on most occasions, the business strategy serves to reinforce the current business model, but if the strategy is sufficiently radical, the result may be that the business model may change over time.

An example of such an occurrence occurred when Carphone Warehouse decided to set up its own phone company, Talk. This meant that its business model required a change to take account of the two business streams of retail and telecommunications. A similar change is occurring in the newspaper world as more companies look to generate profits through their online activities rather than through print media – the Guardian Media Group is a good example of these changes.

Effective shareholder communication requires there to be a simple and succinct description of its business model within its ARA. Components of the business model are derived from the company's key business drivers which would include aspects such as the company's current means of revenue generation, the key markets in which it operates (and why these markets were chosen), the company's main areas of competitive advantage, and its pricing and costing strategies. The latter would include aspects such as procurement policies if the raw materials are commodities, and hence may involve forward purchasing or hedging strategies.

It is important to emphasise that the financial review is part of narrative reporting – and as such the business model should include the financial management aspects relevant to that business. These may include capital management (equity and debt raising and dividend policies) and treasury and foreign exchange management. This was the intention with the introduction of the operating and financial review, although its lack of widespread take up has meant this message has been lost somewhat.

In this context, it is important that companies should take an integrated approach to their business model (i.e. integrating financial and non-financial – not the IIRC Integrated Report). Ideally, the business model should be featured at the front of the Business Review, so that it acts as a contextual platform for subsequent content. In addition, its presentation would benefit if it included a graphic presentation to aid the assimilation by the reader. However, whether or not this is appropriate will depend on the complexity of the business model.

It is important to recognise that it is acceptable to have more than one business model if the nature of its operations merit more than one model. As an example, Halfords is a relatively simple business and has one model, whereas Aggreko (providing mobile power generation) is more complex with two marketplaces – local, tending to be spot hire, and international, tending to be long-term power generation sources (e.g. providing power for hospitals in the developing world) and offers two models. Standard Life includes the business model in the CFO's statement (which was itself on p. 4 of the 2010 annual report), and discusses its capital management immediately after this business model statement, as well as discussing elsewhere both the business model and the company's strategy.

Demonstrating strategic alignment

Expectations of seasoned investors are that a Business Review should be like a stick of rock – the lettering reads the same, even if cut from different perspectives. To achieve this consistency, it is essential that there is a sound demonstration of strategic alignment.

As an example, Future Value is a consultancy used by many companies' investor relations teams to review the quality of their narrative reports. To do so, it assesses six factors: strategy and objectives; performance and KPIs; future factors and risk; sustainability; communication; and coherence. Each of these factors is assessed in its own right and also to the extent each consistently demonstrates alignment across all the sections in the Business Review.

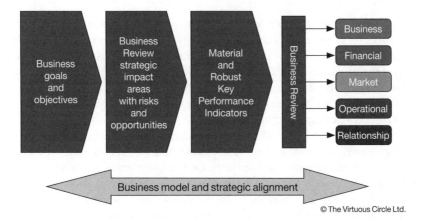

© The Virtuous Circle Ltd.

However, regardless of the guidance offered by authoritative bodies, developing a Business Review still represents a challenge for many companies. The key issue in the development of the Business Review is 'Who is responsible for its overall approach?' The graphic presentation above shows how the Business Review should be developed, demonstrating the need for alignment across all the sections.

It emphasises that the Business Review is as strong as its weakest link. If an investor sees one part of the Business Review that does not demonstrate strategic alignment, then for that investor, the rest of it is called into question.

The Business Review offers the board an opportunity to present the company's strategic thinking in a coherent manner and to demonstrate the quality of implementation of this thinking. As such, it is important that those contributing towards the Business Review should appreciate that their input is a part of the whole, not an individual item in its own right. The Business Review should demonstrate a flow of joined-up thinking, rather than a series of silo entities. In this respect, one question that requires answering at the outset is 'whose story is it?' In the past all annual reports had statements from both the chairman and the chief executive.

One of the areas to be addressed is the role of the chairman's letter. Some companies are incorporating both the chairman's letter and the chief executive's report within their Business Review, and some are combining both as one.

However, my recommendation is that the chairman's letter is separate from the Business Review, and addresses broad issues relating to shareholders, and makes references as necessary to areas that may be relevant to other stakeholders. The Business Review is then owned by the chief executive, representing, as it does, the performance and the strategy of the company. These are delegated by the board as the responsibility of the chief executive and the opening of the Business Review should include his report on performance against the strategy agreed by the board.

Business goals and objectives

The approach described in the route map above begins with the need to identify and define the business goals and objectives of the company. Ideally, these should be capable of being quantified, either directly (e.g. 'having the highest return on capital of any in our sector' (in which case the measure is easily determined by reference to the performance of others in the sector)), or indirectly, (e.g. 'being regarded as the leader of our sector' (in which case, some surrogate measures are required, such as market share percentages)). These statements will communicate the nature and scope of the company's business strategy.

It is worthwhile noting that identifying the business strategy is not as simple as it might sound – nor should it be!

Our experience of advising several companies on their development of their Business Reviews shows that many companies fail to communicate their strategy effectively in their annual report and accounts. One company made a great play of what it described as its strategy. However, our analysis showed that in fact, it was described as a 'strategy for growth' and represented its intentions relating to only about 10% of the current business. By omission, it failed to describe adequately what its strategy was for the other 90% of the business. For another company, the chairman's statement and that of the chief executive described what were in essence two separate strategies.

This lack of clarity was the issue commented upon by Paul Lee of Hermes, who, when interviewed for the *ICSA Company Reporting Handbook* said 'This may demonstrate something about the quality of strategic thinking at board level. Some cases suggest that the quality of thinking doesn't go on at board level, which is really quite concerning for the investor.'

It is worthwhile repeating the comment made in the latest research by TVC which highlighted that those companies that stated their business model in their Business Review were also better at communicating a succinct statement of their business strategy.

Business impact areas

Determining the objectives and underlying strategy should not be challenging, particularly once the business model has been communicated. However, there are examples such as those above where the strategy is more implicit than explicit and would require formalising for this purpose. Once this is done, the board must establish the key business impact areas and how they relate to the underlying strategy and its objectives. This requires a very precise description of the strategy and where it is expected to impact upon the company's performance. It will be important to ensure, therefore, that any superfluous material that may be regarded as diversionary from the main implementation aspects of the strategy is excluded.

What is required is a series of precise definitions of the key business drivers that will determine the success or otherwise of the strategy. These need to be set within the context of the business model. In reviewing annual reports and accounts on behalf of our clients, it is clear that there is insufficient clarity on this issue. This may be because companies do not wish to state their views on the business drivers or because they have not given sufficient time to their consideration. Either way, they are not being transparent to their investors, and particularly when it comes to providing the forward-looking statements that are required under the Act, this would be seen as a weakness from the perspective of investors. If they cannot see clearly how the business drivers will affect the implementation of the strategy, then how can investors take a longer term view of the potential success of the business?

In this respect, it is worthwhile reflecting on the new statement of the directors' duties which includes the need to consider 'the likely consequences of any decision in the long term'. The need to understand the impact of business drivers on the successful outcome of a strategy is even more important for non executive directors (with less time to understand the detailed operations of their company) than it is for the executive members of the board.

Risks and opportunities

Within the description of strategic impact areas it is important to spell out the underlying risks and opportunities that relate to the ongoing viability of the business (effectively the business model) together with those that relate to the business strategy in order to determine the extent to which the strategy will ultimately be considered to have been a success.

In this respect, it is clear from talking with major fund managers is that shareholders accept that running a business can be a risky activity – if this were not the case, they would be investing in gilt-edged securities rather than equities. However, what shareholders do expect is that the company will be endeavouring to manage all the relevant risks on their behalf.

In many respects, in the past, this aspect of the Business Review could be considered to overlap with what was regarded as part of the audit committee's report. However, whilst there remained a need for the audit committee to report on the process by which it governs the company's risk management process, there is also a need to put the identified risks in a strategic context within the Business Review. The combined nature of these activities are likely to be better addressed as a result of the proposals related to the FRC's 'Board and risks' and 'Effective stewardship – Next steps' published in September 2011 (see chapter 2).

There should be clear evidence that the company has identified the risks that may impact on the success of its strategy, should they arise. These risks can be described in the form of a list – which may be daunting to an investor.

To overcome this, it is important that alongside each risk, the company describes the controls it has in place to mitigate their effects, should they arise. This is critical if the confidence of the shareholders in the company's ability to manage its risks is not to be destroyed. Too many risks and too few mitigation controls will lead shareholders to take a more risk-averse attitude towards retaining their shareholding (or investing in more shares). A list of risks with no mitigation controls will lead to a series of questions on the minds of the shareholders about the ability of their company's management to be able to manage the inherent risks in the company's strategy.

Our experience of working with clients shows that, for many, their description of risks and opportunities are limited to financial or market risks – and little work has been undertaken to determine how non-financial aspects of a business can impact on its assessment of risks and opportunities.

For one company we worked with, the introduction of the Business Review caused the chief executive to look questioningly at his company's CSR programme along the lines of 'I get CSR – that's not in doubt – my question is what would happen to the business if we stopped doing some or all of it?' He was asking about the added value of CSR to his business strategy, and the prioritisation of the risks relating to its CSR programme.

Of course, not all CSR activities may pose a significant risk to the development of the business. However, the changes proposed by the FRC mean that there should be greater attention paid to CSR and operational risks to determine which are material to the business's performance, and should be reported upon.

The next step on the Business Review route map is the selection of material and robust KPIs. Such is the importance of this step – and the challenges that companies have found in their selection that it is treated as a separate chapter – see Chapter 5.

Communicating the strategic story

When interviewing investors for the *Company Reporting Handbook*, their concern was that the Business Review should 'tell the strategic story'. This is an area where we have offered considerable assistance to our clients. Too often, they find themselves to be highly internally focused and, as a result, find it very difficult to consider the extent to which they are effective in achieving this objective.

To help companies evaluate this important aspect of the Business Review reporting, we developed a benchmarking approach to enable them to assess the quality of their reporting against those that their board regarded as peers from an investors' perspective.

The following two charts[5] are the result of one piece of work we undertook. This was to help one company that was concerned with the quality of its reporting, but

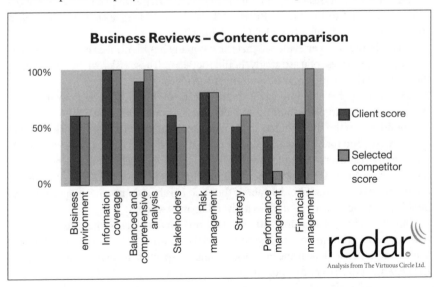

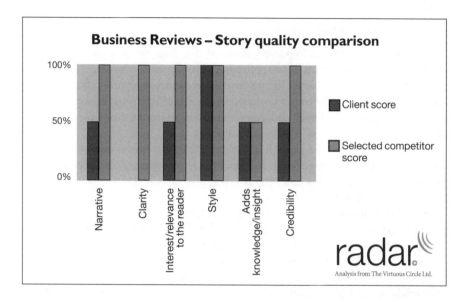

could not identify where its weakness lay. They did know, however, that their board regarded one company's reporting as being particularly effective and they asked us to benchmark their reporting against this other company.

We looked first at the content of the two Business Reviews, using the regulatory requirements as the basis for benchmarking. As can be seen from this first chart, there were areas where improvement could be made, but on the whole the content of the Business Review was not particularly deficient.

The areas for improvement could be seen much more clearly when consideration was given to the quality of the reporting, as can be seen from this second chart. This showed that one of the key issues was that of clarity of presentation, as well as the quality of the narrative and the levels of interest of relevance to the reader. Backed up by firm examples, we were able to advise the client that one of its key issues was that it had entered into a fundamentally new market leading to a new business stream. However, its reporting approach had continued along the lines of the previous report, where there had been only one business stream. As a result, its reporting was muddy and the reader could not clearly separate out the impact of each business stream on the company's business strategy.

For this client, we also looked at the investor relations presentations on its website. These had far greater levels of clarity than the information that was included in its Business Review. In our discussions with the client it became apparent that this was because these presentations were often written by one person for another person to deliver. As a result they were far more cohesive than the communication in the annual report, which suffered from a combination of silo-based writers.

As this example demonstrates, it is important not only to have the right content but also to have the right approach to compiling the Business Review.

How to handle divisional information

The International Financial Reporting Standard IFRS8 requires companies to report on their operating segments. It is important that companies ensure their divisional narrative reporting is in 100% alignment with the report on operating segments in the financial accounts and notes to the accounts. If not, then it is an aspect that is under closer scrutiny by FRRP, and may result in a letter from them to the company's chair.

But this focuses on the link on financial reporting. It is also important to decide what in the Business Review is group content (e.g. reporting on bribery avoidance procedures would be part of the group content, whereas market share statements are more likely to be divisional content).

In addition, if it is appropriate to state that there are differing business models for each division, then one option is to consider stating them within the divisional content, rather than featuring them at the beginning of the Business Review.

Similarly, whilst it is important to ensure that operating or divisional reviews are seen to clearly align to group strategy, some strategy implementation devolves to divisional responsibility. However, it is also important to comment upon, and convey, how the overall business strategy leads to divisional initiatives, and where divisional strategy is specific to that division.

Whilst there is often a section in a Business Review labelled key performance indicators, it is worthwhile considering including relevant non-financial performance indicators within divisional reports (as well as reporting them at group level). Examples of this approach could be to report on employee satisfaction or customer satisfaction indicators at divisional levels, as well as at group level. This would enable greater understanding of the performance of the business at divisional levels.

Similarly, if specific risks relate to a divisional context (e.g. where the company operates in two markets (such as Centrica with its upstream and downstream energy businesses)), then it is worth considering reporting upon these risks at a divisional as well as a group level. It is interesting that the FRC's 'Board and risk' suggested integrating commentary on risk throughout the report, rather than treating it as a stand alone section. No doubt this will emerge as good practice in the future, even if it may not be embraced in the proposed revised Turnbull Guidance.

Handling bad news

For every business, it is a truism that bad news happens – but the measure of good executives is how well they manage it!

Recent examples of poor management include News Corporation's handling of the hacking within News International; Eurostar's problems with snow entering their electric locomotives' engine compartments; and British Airways with the opening of T5. Each of these shows the importance of the executives managing bad news and demonstrating they are in control of the circumstances facing them.

Handling bad news in the annual report is just as important as the real-time disasters described above. What is important to recognise is that investment analysts are probably better informed than most executives believe, because they have a wide range of information sources and have easy access to competitor and market information.

So, if there has been bad news in the year, it is important that the annual report addresses it, including its causes, its impacts (both financial and non-financial), the company's response (how it handled it) and the company's mitigation to avoid such events happening again.

Examples of handling bad news include Rentokil Initial which published three profit warnings in a year as a result of the performance of its subsidiary City Link. The open and honest way it addressed the issues within City Link, and the actions it was taking as a result, won it the 2010 ICSA Hermes award for transparent discussion of the issues.

Similarly BP's 2009 ARA (prior to the Gulf of Mexico disaster) had a risk section where exploration risk merited one-third of a page. After this disaster, its 2010 report included six pages on the Gulf of Mexico – plus enhanced commentary in the risk section and elsewhere.

The key message for your annual report team is that if bad news happens, then it is important to be transparent about the causes and demonstrate that the company is in control of the circumstances, and is acting to reduce the impact on its performance.

Linking to analyst presentations

Investors gain information about companies from several sources; two of the main ones will be the annual report and analysts presentations. Yet sometimes these can tell differing stories.

One reason is that the analysts' presentations are often written by one person for delivery by another (often the CEO and/or the CFO). In contrast, the annual report has in the past been the result of a silo-based contribution to the overall document. The result can be that the analysts' presentation tells a better story, with more information than is provided in the annual report.

This may also be because, too often, directors (especially divisional ones) claim that information cannot be provided in the ARA because it is commercially confidential.

Yet our experience is that similar or relevant information can be easily obtained from sources such as publicly available market surveys (e.g. market assessments, competitors' annual reports and other analysts' presentations).

In developing the planning for the writing process, it is valuable to review the company's prior analyst presentation and to ensure that annual reports and analyst presentations tell the same story. Equally it is important to ensure that the willingness of the CEO to be open about non-financial performance in analysts' presentations is reflected in all aspects of the annual report.

Linking to CSR reporting

When considering the links between CSR reporting and the Business Review, it is very important to note that the Business Review legislation does not require an annual report to include a CSR section as such. However, it does require non-financial information to be linked to company performance.

The key criterion is 'to the extent necessary', by which is meant the extent of materiality as the criterion for reporting such matters in the annual report, although, for the Business Review, the board always has the 'comply or explain' option.

Increasingly, the preferred approach is to have *relevant* CSR information (based on business drivers) integrated into group and divisional reporting. In this respect, it would be expected that group reporting would include overall CSR KPIs and group-wide data (e.g. greenhouse gas emissions, breaches of the bribery code of conduct) whilst divisional reporting would cover specific CSR information (e.g. health and safety, customer satisfaction, employee retention) that is relevant to each division. This would avoid the need for a stand alone CSR section.

The stand alone section is often a default cop-out by the board, but it may cause CSR to be seen as a stand alone (and hence sometimes less than relevant). Certainly some institutional investors are critical of stand alone CSR sections in the annual report because they add size without necessarily adding relevance.

If the board adopts this format of integrating CSR into its group and divisional reporting, then the approach requires additional CSR reporting to meet compliance needs and to address relevant stakeholders' needs. This can either be in the form of a CSR report, or in the form of CSR web pages.

This would then allow the directors to adopt the 'comply or explain' approach. For example, for voluntary environmental reporting, the annual report may state 'The board judges its greenhouse gas emissions to be of low materiality for annual report reporting, but full details of our green house gas emissions can be found in our CSR report – www…'.

Business Reviews and CSR reporting – the differences

It is relevant to recognise the different aspects of Business Review and CSR reporting.

An important factor is business criticality – the focus of the Business Review is sharply on materiality and business criticality, whereas CSR reporting may cover these issues, but could also address matters that may be of low criticality, such as community activities.

Similarly, s. 417 of CA 2006 states the Business Review should *report on policies that underlie the non-financial matters* commented upon, and comment on the effectiveness of these policies (although few companies go this far in their Business Reviews). In contrast, CSR reports seldom go into depth on the governance of CSR activities, although this is an area that is developing quickly amongst major companies.

Similarly, risk is seldom reported upon in CSR reports, in contrast with the risk section in annual reports, although as discussed earlier, the quality of the latter can be very variable.

And lastly, the Business Review should incorporate a forward-looking statement – chairs and CEOs are getting better in terms of providing a quality statement for shareholders. CSR reporting tends to look back, with the exception of those companies that have rigorous CSR management systems, which include reporting upon activities and targets for the next financial year.

Convergence of CSR and non-financial reporting

By now, it should be clear to readers that CSR and non-financial reporting in companies' annual reports are converging, as is suggested in the Venn diagrams shown below.

However, this convergence does not mean that the two forms of reporting will become one and the same. There are different audiences for each set of information, and as a result, different needs that will need to be satisfied.

The paramount issue is the extent to which CSR activities are fundamental to the successful implementation of the company's business strategy. If they are not essential, then the directors of the company will not include them in their Business Review. Likely areas of omission will include community activities and the supply chain (particularly if the company involved is a people-based service organisation such as a support services company). However, exceptions can occur, dependent upon the company's *modus operandi*. One example would be where the company's activities are intertwined with those of the community in which it operates – examples may include retailers with large community footprints such as supermarkets, or steel manufacturers, where the community and the local plant are often one and the same, such is its importance.

The tendency for companies to date has been to avoid the question of business criticality by including a CSR section within the annual report. However, this is unlikely to continue as investors will begin to question its relevance if it is not seen to be adding value to the quality of the communication of the company's performance.

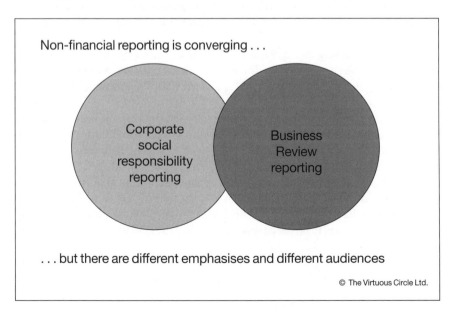

Non-financial reporting is converging . . .

Corporate social responsibility reporting

Business Review reporting

. . . but there are different emphases and different audiences

© The Virtuous Circle Ltd.

A more likely trend is for companies to integrate relevant CSR information into their description of the performance of each of their business divisions. As a result, this will make the CSR description much more relevant to the needs of each division.

The impact of the BIS proposed changes

It is almost 100% certain that the proposal will be implemented for there to be two parts to an annual report – the strategic report and the annual directors' statement.

In this respect, the information in the strategic report that relates to CSR matters will be heavily focused in those CSR elements that represent key business drivers. The remainder of information relating to the CSR elements could be part of the annual directors' statement. However, the latter is likely to be a particularly detailed (or even turgid) document, and if companies wish their CSR information to be available to external stakeholders, then this may not be the best place for it to be positioned.

Instead, the likelihood is that more information relating to CSR will be held on the companies' website. This will not negate the need for CSR reports, if companies feel it is appropriate for their stakeholders. However, these are likely to be web based. Those companies who provide their annual directors' statement electronically (as has been proposed as a method of communicating the detailed information to their share-holders) are likely to include links in their annual reports directly to the relevant sections of their CSR website or their web-based CSR reports.

Some concluding comments

The introduction of the Business Review (and the opportunity to commence on elec-tronic communications with shareholders) has caused many companies to consider in more depth what elements of non-financial activity are critical to the success of their business strategy.

As such, it is causing more critical questions from the board, including about the materiality of subjects such as CSR. These questions are undoubtedly right, since they are addressing the question of added value and the risk of not meeting stakeholders' expectations.

Once these questions have been answered satisfactorily, then the next issue is how best to communicate with all stakeholders, but most importantly, those that are criti-cal to the success of the business. The changes in electronic reporting of financial information will cause similar ripples in the reporting of non-financial information and could be like an unstoppable wave of a new thought process. CSR is an important element of non-financial information, but it is not the only element. The proposed introduction of the strategy report (under BIS proposals regarding annual reporting) will require companies to be selective about which of the CSR information is relevant to this report.

To ensure this process is totally effective, it is important to consider how best to understand the needs and expectations of stakeholders, and determine which are key to the business. A significant element in this process is the choice and reporting of key performance indicators.

Sources

1 More details about the initiative can be found on its website at: www.reportleadership.com

2 Details of CRUF's activities, including its guiding principles can be found on its website at: www.cruf.co.uk

3 Copies of the Report Leadership publication about online reporting can be found at: www.reportleadership.com/online_reporting/

4 Addleshaw Goddard have produced an annual checklist – information can be obtained on its website: www.addleshawgoddard.com

5 Reproduced with kind permission from The Virtuous Circle.

5

Which KPIs for the Business Review?

What does 'key' mean?

In looking at the wide variety of company's annual reports, it is apparent that KPIs can mean different things to different people. However, it is important to remember the context of the Business Review, in that *it is the board's report* on the company's performance.

A useful insight in this respect was the comment made by Simon Bicknell (Company Secretary of GSK when interviewed for the *ICSA Company Reporting Handbook*). He said that 'there are lots of PIs – the focus should be on disclosing those that are key!'

His view was that the selection of KPIs should reflect those that are a genuine management tool, and not simply a disclosure or PR exercise. For GSK, the board uses turnover, earnings per share and total shareholder return as its KPI management benchmarks. Recent annual reports have contained a section that showed these KPIs and related them to GSK's business model and strategy, with details of those performance indicators that were underlying the business drivers in each of its strategic areas. This enabled them to talk about performance indicators (PIs) such as product financials, research and development, staff motivation and providing medicines at not-for-profit prices to the developing world.

His reference point was to return to the statutory purpose of the Business Review and the duty to promote the success of the company. As a result, it is clear that the *key* PIs are those the board uses to review the company's performance on a regular basis (both financial and non financial). However, there may be a wider range of PIs that are used for the same purpose by the divisions (which may be incorporated within divisional reviews).

It is also relevant to consider what is meant by 'non-financial'. Many boards have interpreted this term to refer to CSR measures of activities. Yet, in fact, non-financial KPIs could include operational indicators (e.g. productivity), CSR indicators (e.g. relating to employees or environmental matters), and marketplace indicators (e.g. market share, average spend per customer or contractual pipelines). In this respect, it is important to emphasise that 'non-financial' does not necessarily mean 'CSR', and that 'key' relates to metrics used by the board regularly to evaluate the company's performance.

How to select KPIs

Recently, some company secretaries have commented on how valuable they have found it that the business model is well defined, so that business drivers and relevant PIs can be identified.

However, if the business model is still to be defined for a company, then it may be helpful to identify the range of PIs that are available, from which the KPIs can be selected. One approach used is the practical document-based approach for which a company secretary will review the various performance-related documents presented to the board (e.g. balanced score cards, performance dashboards, and annual planning documents) and, from these, identify the range of indicators provided. An alternative is the evidential approach. For this, one FTSE250 company secretary listed all the indicators mentioned by the board over the course of a year and made his recommendations on preferred selection on that basis.

However, whichever approach is adopted, there are some essential criteria that should determine the basis of the selection of KPIs from the range of PIs available. These criteria include:

- KPIs should be based on business success factors, and long-term performance indicators.
- Indicators should be leading rather than lagged (e.g. contract pipeline is a lead indicator, whereas customer revenue is a lag indicator).
- Indicators can be output based or input based (e.g. reportable accidents is an output indicator, whereas numbers of days training on health and safety is an input indicator) – in this case reportable accidents may be based on 'luck' rather than on management direction.
- Indicators could be based on qualitative measures (e.g. milestones towards achieving a strategic objective) but these may not be very satisfactory, or long lasting.
- Indicators should be capable of being presented in time trends – and with targets attached – which means they require an underlying management process.

The choice should be made carefully based on the materiality and deliverability of each KPI. Bear in mind that a good result in one year may not presage continuing good performance; the KPIs chosen need to be both material and robust.

Material and robust KPIs

The selection of material and robust KPIs is critical as a means of building shareholder confidence in the quality of their company's management. The choice of indicators needs to reflect the means by which the company's management is assessing the performance of the company in achieving its strategic objectives.

A poor selection of indicators could be interpreted as meaning that management is not clear about how it should be assessing the company's performance, provoking doubts about how well the strategy is, in fact, being managed. There should be clear

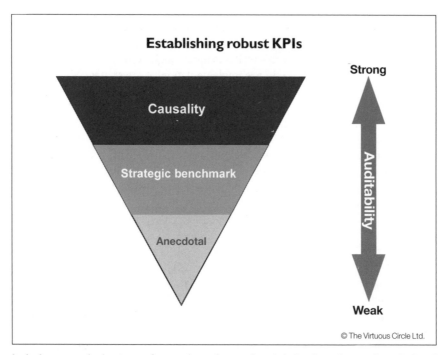

links between the business drivers (together with risks) that have been identified and the choice of performance indicators.

As an example, in the utilities sector, a common risk identified by management is the need to comply with the requirements of the regulators. This extends to their ability to manage expectations by performing well in the areas the regulators regard as being critical to fulfil the responsibilities towards utilities' customers. As a consequence, PIs that relate to these responsibilities should be included within the selection of KPIs.

In the water industry, one of the key areas of concern to utilities regulators is the amount of water leakage through the existing pipe network. Dealing with regulators about this problem is often quoted by water utility companies as one of their key risks. As a consequence, it is reasonable to expect that a KPI should measure leakage rate, since a poor leakage rate may result in potential fines; an increase in maintenance costs to address current pipe failures; and capital investment to correct more long-term issues. All these factors will affect the profit expectations of shareholders. Yet, in one of the companies we reviewed in the first set of research referred to in Chapter 4, one utility mentioned regulators as a risk, but not have a KPI that related to this.

In this respect, the board will need to review its selection of KPIs to ensure that they are both robust and material.

It is important that KPIs should be robust – that they can be regarded as being indicative of changes in the performance of a business area. Ideally, they should be seen as evidence of a high degree of causality. Take, as an example, 'numbers of customers'. If this was observed to be increasing, this might indicate increased turnover over the medium term.

However, it is often difficult to demonstrate causality because there may be other factors that will impact upon a business area. The more likely form of robust indicator is a 'strategic benchmark' – one that relates to the strategic activities and demonstrates the achievement of milestones in the implementation of the strategy. For example, this type of benchmark for a retail group would be 'the number of new store openings planned' and would be perceived as a better benchmark if it was supported by other indicators such as 'numbers achieved on time'.

An unacceptable robustness indicator would be one based on anecdotal or subjective data. For example, an unacceptable indicator for a company introducing a new product range would be the 'numbers of potential customers that expressed interest via a free phone or in an opinion survey' since this is unlikely to be replicated, and cannot be audited.

The key criterion in selecting the range of key performance indicators is the materiality of the indicators.

The graphic below shows how material indicators can be identified. The main question that needs to be asked is the extent to which the indicator selected relates to the company's business drivers, and as a result relates to the business model and strategic direction. This means that the board needs to think carefully how it manages its business, as was evidenced earlier in this chapter by the thoughtful comments of Simon Bicknell.

This approach shows how the board's KPIs can be effectively correlated with the PIs used by the various operations and departments within the company. Companies should consider presenting relatively few KPIs in the summary of their Business

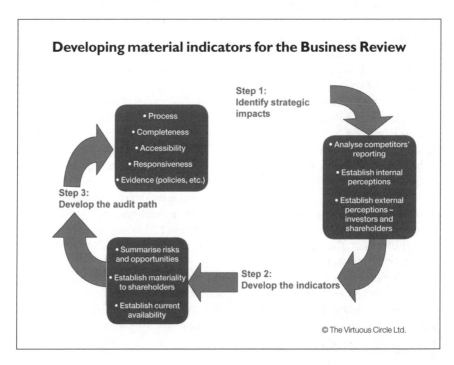

Developing material indicators for the Business Review

Step 1:
Identify strategic impacts

- Process
- Completeness
- Accessibility
- Responsiveness
- Evidence (policies, etc.)

Step 3:
Develop the audit path

- Analyse competitors' reporting
- Establish internal perceptions
- Establish external perceptions – investors and shareholders

- Summarise risks and opportunities
- Establish materiality to shareholders
- Establish current availability

Step 2:
Develop the indicators

© The Virtuous Circle Ltd.

Review, but add other PIs when describing the performance of their various subsidiaries and functional entities.

In this context, it is highly important that, in selecting one or more of non-financial KPIs as criteria for remuneration committee annual bonus or long-term incentive plans, they should be both material (i.e. truly reflective of long-term success) and robust, so that they will stand the test of time.

In terms of materiality, some companies use accident rates as one of the criteria for annual bonus plans. However, it is questionable whether health and safety is a business driver that determines the company's long-term success, important though this indicator is to the well being of the employees.

In this context, the KPI selected should be capable of demonstrating the executive's management skills in promoting the success of the business. It is essential that the KPI indicators are backed by adequate management processes, which ensure it is robust. With these in place, then the KPI is capable of long-term use as an indicator. Any KPI that is chosen has to stand the test of time and must be able to withstand changes in structure and market direction.

Assessing the business model and strategic impacts

In selecting material and robust KPIs, the first step in assessing strategic impacts includes the need to review and analyse competitors' reports to ensure that the indicators selected are in line with those actively used in the industry. Investment analysts are likely to compare and contrast the selection of indicators used by companies in the same sector.

Further there is a need to assess the internal perceptions of the business model and strategic impacts and the resulting range of possible performance indicators. If the PIs selected do not resonate with those who are measured by them, then they will fall into disuse. Alongside the internal review, it is prudent to ask investors and analysts about their perceptions and views of the relevant PIs.

Developing the indicators

The second step in developing the material indicators is an internal establishment of the risks and opportunities relating to the business model and the strategy, and an assessment of what would be regarded as the views of shareholders towards the materiality of these risks and opportunities. From this assessment, a range of possible PIs would be developed.

It is important at this stage to recognise the company may not have all the desirable indicators readily available (e.g. when considering indicators relating to non-financial areas, such as customers, suppliers, and employees). If these areas represent key business drivers, then it is advisable to include a statement within the annual report about including additional PIs in the future, as reporting systems develop.

Developing the audit path

The last step in developing material indicators is to ensure that the PIs are capable of being audited – at least by the internal audit team, particularly if some of these indicators are used as criteria for executive incentive schemes. The FRC proposals about the audit committee covering the full annual report means it is highly likely that external auditors will pay more attention to such data included in Business Reviews.

The audit needs to show how the performance indicator data are gathered and calculated. It should also show that the PIs are complete in describing the performance relating to any business driver or strategic impact area.

A good illustration of the need for completeness is the question of how to demonstrate improving customer relationships. Many companies use 'the number of customer complaints' as a measure of the quality of customer relationships. However, experience shows few customers are willing to complain, preferring instead to purchase elsewhere, or, in the case of subscription services, to cancel their subscriptions.

Performance indicators need to be easily accessible – to the extent that they can be produced for management review on a regular basis. Indicators presented only as part of the annual report cannot be regarded as 'key' by the shareholders. In a similar manner, 'key' indicators should be seen to be responsive to changes in strategic direction or performance variability.

Policies and effectiveness

It is important that companies have policies in place that ensure the indicators are being managed, rather than just reported upon; this ensures the indicators are robust operationally.

Under the 2006 Business Review requirements this has a more significant impact on listed companies. The directors should discuss the related policies in relation to every aspect of environmental, employee, social or community issues commented upon in the Business Review, and comment on their effectiveness.

This is a major challenge in a large company, especially one that operates internationally. Too often, cultural differences can mean that the existence of *common* policies will be few and far between. International companies often develop umbrella statements under which their subsidiaries develop the policies that are appropriate for their own business environment and the relevant legislation of their own country of operation.

However, behind this challenge lies an even greater one – establishing the extent to which the policies are regarded as being effective. The Virtuous Circle established a five-point scale for a client to evaluate the extent to which it had indicators backed by effective policies:

- no policy or evidence of best practice exists
- evidence of best practice exists
- policy exists
- policy exists and all are aware
- policy exists, all are aware and compliance is measured.

As can be seen, the existence of best practice is included in this scale. Best practice often depends on individuals driving activity because of their own conviction that the approach is correct. Inevitably, this best practice can deteriorate if the individuals concerned leave the company. However, assuming best practice does exist, it is normally a very simple task to move from best practice to develop a policy that regulates an existing method of operation. The real challenge in evaluating effectiveness of an individual policy is the extent to which managers and employees are aware of the policy, the extent to which they actively implement the policy and that its compliance is being measured.

Challenges in collating the data

Companies generally have very efficient financial information reporting systems, but non-financial reporting systems are some way behind them. This poses a challenge when producing KPIs that will be featured in the annual report – especially those that may be used as part of the remuneration committee's executive incentive schemes.

Furthermore, it is highly likely that, in the future, auditors will seek reassurance about the accuracy and completeness of data published in the annual report.

There are significant challenges in collating non-financial data and these challenges include whether:

- there are effective non-financial information systems in place;
- there is a consistent company-wide approach for measurement (e.g. for international companies, health and safety metrics can be difficult because of differing regulatory reporting measures, and most companies in this position have adopted their own company specific criteria for use in internal reporting);
- there are common units of measurement – the biggest international challenge in this respect is that of environmental measures, especially for utility bills, which can be in a variety of units;
- the data is verifiable/auditable – hence sufficiently rigorous to pass internal or external audit requirements;
- the period for the data collation has been adequately defined – and relates to the practicality of collating data.

Addressing these challenges in collating data

Some companies are using non-financial information software systems and the range of solutions includes linking to:

- existing internal financial systems (e.g. Cognos). The benefit of this approach is that data can link strongly to auditable data (e.g. energy costs). The disadvantage comes with KPIs such as customer satisfaction, where there are no financials associated with them;
- CSR systems (e.g. Credit 360). Here the benefit is that all non-financial measures can be accommodated within the one system, but the disadvantage is that it is not linked to financial data and hence may be more challenging for audit purposes; and
- scorecard dashboards (e.g. Matrix). In this case, the benefit is that the information is user friendly for management, and can cover a wide range of indicators. Again, the disadvantage is the lack of linkage to financial data for audit purposes.

However, the need to develop a consistent approach for measurement cannot be met through software solutions. As discussed above, one of the main challenges comes where regulatory reporting differs across countries (e.g. health and safety reporting which varies around the world). The answer is to develop a company-specific reporting measures that all operations report to (even though some may have to report using a different measurement basis than their own country's regulators) and then apply this measure in the non-financial software systems.

Delivering consistency means ensuring there is an effective procedure manual for each non-financial reporting area, with relevant customised training for each function reporting. This ensures a consistent approach at front-line level. To reinforce the effectiveness of these procedures, each operational MD should be required to sign off an internal control report on the effectiveness of reporting in that operation. This helps to ensure senior level buy-in.

Buy-in at all levels in individual operating units can be influenced heavily if some intra-company comparison is introduced (e.g. a performance league table by country). This ensures a competitive comparison culture, which should lead to more effective reporting. It also helps reporting anomalies to be addressed at an operational level.

The issue of having common units of measurement is greatest in the areas of the environment and health and safety. Health and safety, as discussed before, is the more easily addressed by having a common company system. Environmental data, especially energy, is more challenging.

Our experience is that units of gas measurements differ on a worldwide basis. In the USA, different suppliers invoice based on different units. An inexperienced administrator has to add up using two different invoices: the result? 'apples and pears'. Similar experiences arise with liquid fuels, and LPG bottles!

The first solution to this issue requires an effective procedures manual, backed up by an internal controls sign off by the senior manager for the operation. Ultimately, best practice would be to link data to financial data (e.g. via Cognos) to provide sanity checks (e.g. prices per unit volume).

The question of whether the data is verifiable or auditable can also be a challenge. The ABI in 2007 referred to environmental social and governance (ESG) matters and recommended verification of non-financial statements in Business Review:

> 'Independent external verification … would be regarded by shareholders as a highly significant advantage. Credible verification may also be achieved by other means, including internal audit. It would assist shareholders in their assessment of policies if the reason for choosing a particular method of verification were explained in the annual report.'

For this purpose the best solution is to have system-generated KPIs with internal controls reviewing specific data input processes (linked to internal control sign off), with a date-stamped audit trail incorporated into the system. An alternative is external verification, but this is likely to be costly and the best advice is only to do so where the reputation risks of incorrect reporting is high. In this context, the question to be asked is whether the company operates in a controversial or potentially regulated industry sector.

The question of what should be the period for non-financial data collation can be problematic because often non-financial data is not collated at the same time as financial data. Examples include utility invoices which may not be provided until after an ARA has to be sent for print, as well as customer or employee surveys, which often occur at certain points during the year which may not necessarily coincide with the financial year end.

The question is whether there is anything in the Companies Act that requires non-financial data to cover the same period as the financial data. It does give reference to the company's performance and states in s. 417 that:

> "Key performance indicators" mean factors by reference to which the development, performance or position of the company's business can be measured effectively.

The important words are 'measured effectively'. Where the provision of data falls outside the normal financial year reporting period, then the options are either to estimate calculations for the periods for which data is not available or to take a pragmatic approach, and use non-financial data with a different 12-month period to the year-end date (e.g. for a financial year end 31 December publish, say, a 12-month energy data for a calendar year to 30 September) with trends and targets based on the same approach.

A similar position arises for many companies that use employee satisfaction as a KPI. These employee satisfaction surveys are undertaken, at most, once a year. In the case of one client, the KPI quoted in a 31 December year end annual report is based on an employee survey that actually occurs in September each year. The benefit is that shareholders are provided with annual trend data of what is usually an important business driver for the company.

In either case, it is advisable to discuss the approach with the external auditors and it is essential to explain in the ARA that either the data is estimated or that is for a different 12-month period. It is also essential for the purposes of transparency to explain the reasons for adopting this approach (e.g. quarterly frequency of energy invoices, or the challenges of producing verified non-financial data in line with the financial year end).

In the next sections, the focus moves from narrative reporting in annual reports to the nature of CSR, and the processes required to manage it effectively.

PART

2

Why develop a CSR approach?

6

Background to CSR

So what does CSR comprise?

The thing that surprises most people when they begin to think about CSR is the extent to which it impacts on a wide range of business operations. To the newcomer or outsider, the view may be that CSR relates to charities or the environment. It does, but its reach is far wider than these two areas. CSR extends to issues including, but not limited to, employee practices, supply chain approaches, customer sales and marketing practices and human rights policies.

One of the challenges, in an area as innovative as CSR, is the difficulty of developing commonly accepted terminology and definitions. Each new observer seems to produce their own definition of what CSR comprises – and it's only when you go through all the relevant documentation that you appreciate that whilst the words may be different, the components are essentially the same.

For this book, I have resisted the urge to create new definitions, but have depended upon the components as defined by *Business in the Community*:

- *Community* – includes both community-linked activity and community investment.
- *Environment* – includes climate change and global warming, recycling, use of hazardous materials, water consumption and biodiversity.
- *Workplace* – covers prospective and current employees (both of a permanent and temporary nature and subcontractors).
- *Marketplace* – covers suppliers and clients or customers.

To which parts of the business does CSR relate?

As the reader will observe, the list above represents a wide range of business functions, and when corporate governance, risk management and investor relations are added to the melting pot, as is often the case for investor-related CSR surveys, it can be seen that CSR contains all the functions within a business.

In my experience, most companies are already doing some or all CSR elements. There is often no need to invest heavily in this area – it is much more important to ensure that all members of the company understand how their actions in these activities can impact.

One of the challenges for anyone trying to collate all the CSR activities within a company is that often those managers responsible for some of these activities may not see them as being part of CSR.

One example is that of health and safety – some managers may regard their task as being primarily legislation driven. Yet taken from an external perspective, this relates to how a company manages its impact on its internal stakeholders (its employees and subcontractors) and its external stakeholders (e.g. members of the community, as would be the case for a transport company aiming to improve its driver safety record).

The important thing for those responsible for gathering such information is to encourage their fellow managers to look at these activities from the stakeholder perspective, and recognise that these stakeholders want reassurance about the company's performance in these matters.

Indeed, because CSR encompasses many business disciplines, a business attempting to address the CSR agenda has the following issues: Where it should start? Where does the information lie? Where should a business position itself?

What is outside the scope of this book? One of the challenges for business is inherent within the term CSR – the implication of the word 'corporate' is that it is only relates to the private sector and only those company managers need to think about operating in a responsible manner towards their stakeholders. Yet there are enough examples within both the public and voluntary sectors in the UK to suggest that these areas also need the disciplines of a CSR-type agenda.

In fact, within the voluntary sector, the need to be seen as being a responsible operation (as well as supporting a good cause) has been recognised. It is becoming evident that new Charity Commission reporting regimes (in the form of the Summary Information Report[1]) place greater emphasis on the requirement to talk about charities' aims, activities and achievements. This recognises that as well as upholding a good cause, charities need to operate in a responsible and ethical manner towards their stakeholders.[2] These approaches came out of the Cabinet Office's paper *Private Action, Public Benefit*.[3] Added to this legislative pressure is the growing development that companies who donate to charities in major ways are now beginning to ask how these charities' own activities represent their CSR behaviour.

In this respect, of particular relevance is the new focus on public benefit. This was crystallised in the Charities Act 2006, which removed the previously held presumption that charities who relieve poverty, or advance education or religion are working for the public benefit. It is now up to the trustees of *all* charities to demonstrate that their charity's purposes are for the public benefit. This particularly affects the private education sector, which receives revenue in the form of school fees, but claims charitable status. As result this sector is looking at ways of demonstrating its public benefit, other than through the direct education benefit to its pupils (e.g. providing facilities to neighbouring local authority schools in the public sector, as well a providing senior teaching staff to act as mentors to teachers in neighbouring schools). Charities such as private schools will need to report on these matters within their SIRs.

Whilst apparently setting the agenda on CSR by raising the issues of corporate behaviour, many government departments themselves have been slow to address this area. Some seem to believe that as a public service, they are above such matters. However, some government departments have focused on the European Quality Model (EQM), whose components match up with much of the CSR agenda. The disadvantage of this model lies in the fact that one of the key advantages of CSR is public communication of CSR activities and performance in a transparent and honest manner – something that is not adequately addressed by the EQM, which tends to be an internally focused process.

However, there are exceptions. The Ministry of Justice (which replaced the Department for Constitutional Affairs) has gone out of its way to try to address some of these issues. Magistrates' courts (that come under its remit) now run a regular series of open days at weekends to help young people to understand more about the workings of the law and of the courts.

In a similar manner, HM Revenue and Customs (HMRC) includes a section on its own CSR on its website.[4] This includes its strategy for 2007–2012. Within the website, there are two CSR reports for 2007–08 and 2008–09. These tend to report in an anecdotal manner, with little or no trend data or targets (except for qualitative actions). There is a comparative section within the website – '2008/09 Progress Report against our Sustainable Development Action Plan for 2007/12' – but, as at the end of 2011, there were no subsequent reports of progress, which is a considerable disappointment. However, on the positive side, HMRC has appeared in the Business in the Community CR Index (being placed in the 'Gold' category for 2006, although it is no longer featured in later versions of this index).[5]

The Foreign and Commonwealth Office has also developed a CSR strategy.[6] This supports the DEFRA-led UK Sustainable Development Strategy.[7] The FCO approach is outward-looking, focusing on how it can help encourage responsible business practices. Its emphasis is on businesses in high-impact sectors that are operating overseas (such as the extractive industries). In March 2011, it published guidance for businesses dealing in the four 'conflict' minerals – Cassiterite, Coltan, Wolframite and Gold. In 2010, it celebrated the World Environment Day by declaring on its website that it has a corporate responsibility to reduce its carbon emissions.[8] However, in general, it pays relatively little attention to the internal aspects of its CSR approach.

Both the non-profit and public sectors are treated as being outside the scope of this book – not least because the development of CSR-related activity in these sectors lags far behind that of the private sector. Hopefully, this book may be used by them as a platform to decide how to develop the CSR approach that is relevant and appropriate to their sectors' needs.

The debate about CSR and its relevance

It is important for readers to understand some of the debate surrounding CSR in its early formative years. This debate has revolved around three arguments.

Relevance of CSR in modern capitalism

Regardless of the public commitments of leading business people towards CSR, there remain those for whom it is anathema. In this respect, they hanker back to an oft-quoted comment from Milton Friedman (dating back to 1970). The following statement is the inspiration for those that claim CSR is irrelevant to business and should not be part of the business planning process:

> There is one and only one social responsibility of business: to use its resources and engage in activities designed to increase its profits.

It should not be assumed that such a standpoint is the domain of reactionaries. In January 2005 *The Economist*[9] said that some CSR practices 'advance the interests of shareholders and the wider world'. However, its major criticism of CSR is that it is based on 'a faulty analysis of the capitalist system' and incorporates 'the dangers of muddle headed thinking'. This article provoked a lively debate in the magazine two weeks later, although, as will be seen later in this book, it has since modified its stance.

Whilst this type of argument is likely to continue to arise, the evidence of companies reporting on CSR matters, and the increasing requirement to report on relevant non-financial activities in a company's annual report suggests that this part of the CSR debate has become more academic than practical.

CSR as a public relations exercise

Consideration has to be given to the question of whether CSR can be regarded as 'spin'. This is often asked from the perspective of a non-governmental organisation (NGO). An issue some companies complain about is that NGOs are perceived to be one of the driving forces for CSR. In many respects, they have been very effective in drawing up the CSR agenda, and defining its component parts. Indeed, some seem to believe that CSR, and especially the reporting of CSR, should meet their specific requirements. But there is a need for both parties to accept they have their own separate agendas – and these may not be aligned in the same direction, or with the same priorities.

However, companies need to regard NGOs as being part of their stakeholder audience – and as such they have a right to comment on the quality and veracity of the information put before them. Companies need to be more rigorous in deciding the relative importance of their various NGO stakeholders and develop appropriate communications to meet their needs.

At the same time, the NGOs need to consider why companies are undertaking CSR – and how it benefits them. They need to better understand how CSR should form part of a business's policy and practice.

As will be described later, CSR relates to three forms of business management:

- Compliance
- Risk
- Reputation.

Given the last area, it is quite acceptable for companies to publicise their CSR performances to their stakeholders. But they can be justifiably accused of practising spin if this communication only refers to their successes or strengths without being equally transparent about those areas that are failures or weaknesses where the company should identify action programmes to rectify or improve these areas.

However, it is equally fair to say that the quality of company CSR reporting is the focus of more targeted criticism, particularly in the environmental arena, where the media are taking the approach of 'naming and shaming' companies on a comparative basis. One example is that of the *Guardian*'s report[10] on the 2007 Carbon Disclosure Project (CDP5). CDP5 published the names of those companies contributing to its analysis of corporate carbon emissions. The *Guardian* looked specifically at the FTSE100, and highlighted those companies that had reported to a lesser extent than others, and those that had not reported at all. All the information was already in the public domain, but the *Guardian* survey used this information as a very direct means of benchmarking the companies. It was not a criticism of companies using CSR for spin purposes, but a much more relevant comment on the quality of those companies' disclosure of relevant CSR information.

CSR terminology

The topic of extensive terminology was touched upon in the preface, but it is worth focusing on the argument over the term 'social'. CSR is often described as CR (Corporate Responsibility), particularly by the larger companies. The argument about CSR is the 'S' – Social – which some companies have suggested detracts from their business-related responsible activity by focusing on their social impacts (typically in the community area) whilst not giving due regard to the importance of ensuring that their company's operations are run ethically and responsibly. In that respect, they comment that their prime role is to ensure their business is sustainable, and if this relates to social activities, then all well and good, but if not, this should not be challenged because it is not part of their sustainable business strategy.

In my view, this remains an abstract argument, especially because it is generally the term used by the public, NGOs, smaller corporates and the media, as well as by governments, especially the EU. The key issue is not the choice of terminology; rather that the directors of a company make sure that companies act responsibly.

The next chapter discusses CSR and its relevance to your business.

Sources

1   More information about SIRs can be found on the Charity Commission's website: www.charity-commission.gov.uk/Charity_requirements_guidance/Accounting_and_reporting/Preparing_annual_returns/SIRs.aspx

2   A useful report – 'Narrative reporting by UK charities' – can be found at: www.cfdg.org.uk/~/media/Document%20library/02%20Reporting/04%20Impact%20Reporting%20incl%20narrative%20reporting/Narrative_Reporting_Executive_Summary_1001QUSH0001.ashx.

3   'Private Action, Public Benefit', Cabinet Office's Strategy Unit, September 2002.

4 See HMRC's website section on CSR: www.hmrc.gov.uk/about/corporate-responsibility/.

5 The full results of the BitC's CR Index for 2011 can be found via the FT's website: media.ft.com/cms/4b571b5a-a849-11e0-9f50-00144feabdc0.pdf

6 The FCO's CSR strategy is part of its overall approach towards sustainable development, which includes both intergovernmental activities and business support and encouragement. The latest details of this conflict minerals guidance can be found at: www.fco.gov.uk/en/news/latest-news/?view=News&id=574220082.

7 More details about the UK Sustainable Development Strategy (including the latest edition of 'Sustainable development indicators in your pocket' which gives an updated picture of the UK's environmental, social and economic wellbeing) can be found at: www.sustainable-development.gov.uk

8 Details of this carbon emissions statement can be found at: www.fco.gov.uk/en/news/latest-news/?view=News&id=22323610.

9 *The Economist* – 22 January 2005.

10 The Green List, *The Guardian*, 5 November 2007.

7

Why develop a CSR approach?

The forerunners of CSR

Those reading this book in the early part of the second decade of the twenty-first century will probably consider CSR to be a late twentieth, early twenty-first century phenomenon.

In their minds, they will consider that there have been a whole series of events in the 1980s and the 1990s that were catalysts to force companies to address the issues of their responsibility towards society and the environment. Events such as:

- the battle between the environmentalists (led by Greenpeace) over the proposed sinking by Shell of their Brentspar oil platform;
- the sinking of the *Exxon Valdez* and the consequent pollution of the Alaskan coast line;
- the fraudulent activity of the management of Enron leading to its collapse;
- the plundering of the Mirror Group's pension fund by its owner, Robert Maxwell;
- the collapse of WorldCom; and
- the issues surrounding TyCo International and its former Chief Executive, Dennis Kozlowski.

Equally, they will have been mindful of events that have occurred in the first few years of the twenty-first century, such as:

- the debate about the ethical product sourcing practices of companies such as Nike and Gap;
- the development of FairTrade products – initially sold in more ethically minded retailers such as the Co-op but now seen in shops across the retail spectrum;
- the publication of the Stern Review on the Economics of Climate Change and the release of Al Gore's film 'An Inconvenient Truth';
- The discussion about the ethical behaviour of the world's banking and finance system in the run up to the 2008 financial crisis;
- The environmental disaster resulting from the fire and explosion on BP's Deepwater Horizon rig in the Gulf of Mexico in April 2010.

Indeed, events such as these have been – and continue to be – catalysts in developing legislative and regulatory frameworks that relate to issues of CSR. However, whilst climate change is a modern phenomenon in terms of public debate, it is wrong to suggest that CSR did not exist before these events took place. It did exist, but people did not recognise it by this term.

Early examples of CSR

The first examples of company managers taking responsible attitudes to their businesses' dealings with society and the environment go back several hundred years. Philanthropic businessmen such as Robert Owen, Sir Titus Salt, the Cadbury family and later Lord Leverhulme were pioneers of a more socially responsible approach to doing business.

In the early 1800s, for instance, textile factory owner Robert Owen created a new type of community at the site of his four factories in New Lanark, because of his belief that a person's character is formed by the effects of his or her environment.

He built houses and schools and introduced reforms (e.g. refusing to employ children less than ten years of age). As importantly, he reduced the working day for all workers to 12 hours, ensured that young children attended his nursery and infant schools and that older children who worked in the factory attended his secondary school for part of the day.

Through his reforms, Owen was able to demonstrate that making a profit and adopting a more paternalistic approach were not mutually exclusive.

In the early 1850s, Sir Titus Salt provided similar accommodation for workers and their families surrounding his woollen mill in Yorkshire. The village he created comprised 22 streets, 850 houses, 45 alms houses and occupied an area of 25 acres.

Two decades later, the Cadbury family of Birmingham purchased what was then the Bournbrook estate, as the ideal location for their new factory. By the turn of the century the new factory employed some 2,500 workers. Far ahead of its time, the workers were provided with housing, education and training. Pension schemes for employees and medical facilities ensured a healthy and dedicated work force. The owner George Cadbury regarded the employees as part of his family and treated them well, with recognition for their services.

The reasons why these individuals took such responsible attitudes towards their employees were varied.

The Cadbury family were Quakers and no doubt their beliefs led them to take a more enlightened approach to their employees. Robert Owen and Lord Leverhulme were more business focused, reasoning that employees who had fewer burdens would be more productive. Some, such as Sir Titus Salt, reasoned that providing living accommodation in a more structured and organised environment would reduce the opportunities for his workforce to acquire alcohol – these were the days when the 'working classes' were prone to drinking cheap gin – and hence would limit their absenteeism and ensure they were more productive when they were in work.

Clearly, those businessmen taking responsible attitudes towards society and the environment had business objectives at heart even in those days. Yet it was social experiments such as these that had an impact upon the great social reformers of the day.

Robert Owen hoped that the way he treated children at his New Lanark community would encourage other factory owners to follow his example. In 1815 Robert Owen sent detailed proposals to Parliament about his ideas on factory reform.

The work of social reformers like Owen affected politicians such as Michael Sadler who introduced the concept of a minimum working time of ten hours for children under 18 introduced to Parliament in 1832. Their influence was long lasting, resulting in other social reform legislation, such as the Education Act of 1870, requiring compulsory education to be provided for children across the United Kingdom.

However, these social evangelists were still seen as unusual by the greater majority of the businessmen and managers of their age, even if their work was linked to business imperatives. In fact, in that same era, there were examples of businesses that were behaving in ways that would be seen as being totally irresponsible towards society and the environment.

One such example was referred to at the launch of a report, jointly written by The Virtuous Circle and The Work Foundation. Will Hutton, Chief Executive of The Work Foundation, asked a question along the lines of 'Which company has had its executives arrested for fraud, its operations criticised for unethical practices and has been accused of bribery and corruption of foreign officials'?

Many people in the audience suggested current examples. The answer, in fact, is the East India Company set up in 1600. Clearly, debacles like that of Enron are not new examples of mismanagement.

Indeed in the UK, these examples of enlightened businessmen have tended to wane, largely because the state took on much of their aspirations and converted them into reality through legislation for the benefit of the working population as a whole.

Why has CSR come on to the management agenda?

So why has CSR come to the forefront of public and business debate so strongly?

The latter years of the twentieth century saw some dramatic changes in world society and politics and there were further developments regarding climate change in the early twenty-first century. But there were several significant developments that made the ground more fertile for the development of CSR. There are seven reasons for these developments:

- wider shareholder franchise
- globalisation
- political initiatives
- corporate misgovernance
- changing world politics
- the internet
- public recognition of climate change.

der shareholder franchise

This relates to the extent to which the public at large has become a shareholder in modern European companies.

The general public has become enfranchised in terms of holding quoted equity as a result of the privatisation of nationalised industry in Britain in the 1980s when the likes of British Telecom (now BT) and British Gas (now Centrica) were sold by public offering. People who used these services when they were nationalised industries, were offered either free or discounted price shares.

The 1986 'tell Sid' campaign (developed to alert the British public to buy shares in British Gas) was one of the most significant in expanding the percentage of quoted companies shares held by the British public on a direct basis, rather than through pension funds and life assurance policies. This widening of the public franchise to equities was copied in most western companies, with extensive privatisation campaigns in Italy, France and Scandinavia.

The result of these privatisation campaigns was that the public became much more aware of corporate performance – and also of corporate transgressions, such as those already referred to, as well as the stories of 'Fat Cats'.

These were corporate executives who were considered as taking advantage of shareholders by paying themselves what were perceived as exceptional remuneration packages – even when the company's performance did not reflect such beneficial terms – resulting in the shareholders being disadvantaged relative to the perceived benefit of the executives. An earlier, but well-known example is that of Cedric Brown, who, as British Gas chief executive, saw his salary increase by 75 per cent in November 1994, prompting outrage from politicians, shareholders and unions. His performance and pay rise was ridiculed at an annual general meeting (AGM) when shareholders tried to bring in a pig to the AGM, inferring that the executives were like pigs at the trough. Such concerns about executive remuneration continue to the second decade of the twenty-first century, especially when compared to the average pay of the company's workforce. Fred Goodwin of RBS is one recent example where his perceived failure to manage the bank when he was chief executive led to both to the loss of his job and subsequently, the loss of his knighthood.

The result of public concerns such as these started to affect the consciences of pension fund managers. They began to recognise that, because of their influence due to the size of their investment, they had a role (on behalf of investors at large) to monitor the responsibility of the operations and the remuneration of the management of the companies in which they were investing.

Globalisation

Multinational companies were considered to be using their economic power without having due consideration for the national communities and environments in which they operated. This led to growing concerns of small groups of activists who were able to have considerable impact (out of kilter with the size of their groups) by demonstrating at Group 7 (now Group 8 (G8) and even Group 20 (G20)) summits of world leaders. What they perceived as being unacceptable was their perception of the lack of accountability of these companies, particularly bearing in mind that some of the world's major companies were creating more wealth than some of the world's developed economies.

One notable example in 2001 was that of JDS Uniphase – although little known to the general public, at the time, this was the world's largest supplier of fibre-optic components. This Ottawa-based firm declared its net loss to be $56.1 billion. At the time, this amount was the largest annual loss ever posted by a company in North American corporate history and represented more money than the entire annual national GDP of New Zealand at that time. This loss was eclipsed by the rather better known AOL Time Warner which posted losses of $98.7 billion in 2002. This remains one of the largest ever losses, only superseded by AIG's loss of $99.8 billion in 2008 – even the Fannie Mae debacle in 2009 resulted in a loss of 'only' $74.4 billion. In contrast the biggest ever earnings figure was that of Exxon Mobil, with its 2008 results of $45 billion profit.

Activists were concerned that the globalisation of companies was concentrating economic and, indirectly, social power in the hands of a few major business people, who were un-elected and were unrepresentative of the world's public. The public perception of large global companies (e.g. Nike and Gap) was that their prices benefited from the low wage levels in overseas countries; this was combined with a view that their sourcing depended on overseas suppliers operating unacceptable working conditions. Similar concerns were raised about the stringency of quality assurance amongst companies that outsourced their production to developing countries. One such example is Mattel, the world's leading toy company. In 2007, it suffered three product recalls in as many months. This was because of issues such as unacceptable quantities of lead in toys (manufactured in China) and small objects falling off toys (manufactured in Mexico) played with by small children – in one case leading to the hospitalisation of child who had swallowed an object. In the first instance, Mattel blamed the quality of workmanship of its Chinese suppliers. However, in a subsequent public apology to the Chinese, a senior Mattel Vice-President stated that: 'It is important for everyone to understand that the vast majority of these products that we recalled were the result of a flaw in Mattel's design, not through a manufacturing flaw in Chinese manufacturers.'

The support of production facilities in developing economies, without fully questioning the ways in which human rights, employment practices and environmental practices have been regulated, has caused some companies to gain opprobrium from some of the NGO representatives trying to address these issues. Whilst their attention focused on only a relatively few companies – the likes of Starbucks and Microsoft – the lesson was self-evident throughout the boardrooms of the western world. It was clear that public opinion could be marshalled by a few and the potential impact on a company as a result of such activity, not only in terms of short-term revenue and profit, but also in terms of long-term reputation, was something that needed to be given far greater consideration around the boardroom table.

The need for such consideration was reinforced by the fact that the companies targeted by the activists did change their policies to address the issues that the activists had focused upon. Starbucks has initiated ethical trading initiatives – and publicised them heavily in their outlets. Microsoft has developed a series of world-wide initiatives including support of Anytime, Anywhere Learning in the United Kingdom, with a simple goal – to help raise standards of achievement by providing teachers and students with one-to-one access to their own laptop computers running Microsoft Windows and Office in over 500 schools in the UK. In addition, Microsoft in the UK has been a significant contributor to the NSPCC's Full Stop campaign to stop child abuse.

Political initiatives

The World Summits held in Rio and Johannesburg, backed by the UN have resulted in the development of political initiatives such as:

- the eradication of poverty;
- changing consumption and production patterns;
- protecting and managing the natural resource base for economic and social development; and
- the development of environmental and global warming initiatives (e.g. the Kyoto Protocol of 1997).

Clearly not every country in the world is in favour of such initiatives – the USA has not endorsed the Kyoto Protocol – but every country has had to at least consider the outcomes of the initiatives.

In so doing, governments have had to realise that they could not deliver the required results of these initiatives on their own – they had to involve businesses in a manner they hadn't considered before. Previously, one of their views of business was as a source of tax revenue. Now they were asking business to take action, often without having legislation in place. Companies began to realise that politicians were beginning to see business people as being accountable for their actions.

What has become clear is that some of these initiatives would take time to become legislation. A good example is that of the Precautionary Principle,[1] enshrined in the 1992 Rio Declaration on Environment and Development. This is an ethical principle that states that if the consequences of an action, especially the development of science and technology, are unknown, but is judged by some scientists to have a high detrimental risk, then it is better not to undertake that action rather than risk the possible negative consequences.

As the reader might expect, there has been much debate on the use of precaution in science, but the European Commission finally adopted this Principle in 2000 and its REACH Directive[2] for the Research, Evaluation and Authorisation of Chemicals embodies this Principle. The REACH Directive has had a major impact, resulting in the exclusion of significant numbers of chemicals from business use, because they are considered to have potential long-term hazards. Similar changes occurred as a result of the Biocidal Products Directive, which addressed the issues of active substances contained in products such as pesticides and rodenticides. This was adopted by the EU in 1998, but in some areas of application, its remit is still to be fully enforced.

Corporate mis-governance

The widely publicised examples of corporate mis-governance, such as those already quoted, meant that the media (as well as those directly involved in financial matters) became more aware of issues of corporate governance and the effect that inappropriate actions could have upon society and the environment, as well as upon those individuals who were employees of the companies concerned.

Undoubtedly, the media has had a role in publicising such mis-governance. But, whilst some business people may decry the media in this respect, the more objective of the media (considered to be those such as the BBC's *Panorama* and investigative journalists on *The Times* and *Sunday Times*, often acting as whistle-blowers in their own right) have had a positive role in broadening the public's awareness of the way in which some businesses operate in an inappropriate manner. Certainly, without their actions, the issues of misappropriation of pension fund assets and corporate remuneration policies would have been left to the more lofty spires of the law journals and perhaps the inside pages of the *Financial Times*.

Changing world politics

World politics changed with the ending of the Cold War at the end of the 1980s and featured symbolic scenes like the pulling down of the Berlin Wall. This created the perception that capitalism had won over communism and, with it, a sense that capitalism was a good thing – especially from the US perspective. What this also did was to take away the spectre of the old Soviet Union (although the growth in economic strength of Russia has had some impact on this view). In some people's minds the threat of the Cold War was replaced by the spectre of corporate business as the new challenge to world society.

With these changes came the view that governments should aim to be less controlling of corporate behaviour, with fewer regulations and less bureaucracy. The result has been that over time, some people have questioned whether the pendulum has swung too far and have started to ask whether there should be more regulation of business and the manner in which it operates. In a sense, CSR is an attempt by business to become self-regulatory by becoming more transparent.

The internet and social media

The introduction of the internet (and over recent years, the development of social media) has created accessible information throughout the world. This had two areas of impact.

First, companies could place information about their activities on the internet – and outsiders could decide whether they liked or disliked what they saw.

Secondly, the internet could be used (by groups of activists as well as individuals) in a critical manner about companies' activities. Non-Governmental Organisations (NGOs) could comment on companies' activities, but so could current and ex-employees. Whilst beforehand disenchanted employees could only comment to their friends through the informal grapevine, now they could put it on the internet for all to see. The growth of social media has exacerbated this position and customers' opinions about company products or business approaches can be communicated virally in an extremely short time. Indeed, its use during the UK riots of August 2011 demonstrates how social media can develop a protest movement before the authorities are either aware of or are ready for it.

Shadow websites have existed for companies like Shell and Philips Electronics, where disenchanted employees can 'tell it like it is'. Whilst companies may try to ignore these sites, once information is published on the internet, it is in the public domain and journalists can use it without being concerned about libel actions.

Public recognition of climate change

Perhaps the biggest change of the first seven years of the twenty-first century has been that of public attitudes towards climate change. From a position where it was probably considered to be the reserve of environmentally conscious activists, who were not necessarily held in high regard by the general public, climate change has become an accepted (although still argued over) phenomenon for which public action is required.

Whilst the IPCC (Intergovernmental Panel on Climate Change)[3] – set up in 1998 by the UN and the World Meteorological Organisation – has had a significant impact on focusing government's minds on scientific issues of climate change, two other public activities have probably made more impact on the public.

The Stern Review report, released in September 2006,[4] was written by Baron (then Sir Nicholas) Stern, Head of the UK Government's Economic Service and Adviser to the Government on the economics of climate change and development (previously he had been Chief Economist and Senior Vice-President of the World Bank from 2000 to 2003 and Director of Policy and Research for the Commission for Africa). The strength of his report was that it brought into focus the economic impacts of climate change on government, business and society. As such, it meant that governments could no longer take the stance that this was a scientific matter – and one which was not relevant to the management of their countries and their economics.

The second was 'An Inconvenient Truth', an Oscar-winning documentary, presented by former US Vice President Al Gore Jr. It is one of the highest-grossing documentaries to date in the USA and Gore has donated all its proceeds to the Alliance for Climate Protection (of which he is both founder and chairman). The strength of this film is down significantly to Gore's own personal reputation – and the fact that he is American. As such, he has been effective in terms of helping to persuade both US and international public opinion about the dangerous consequences of climate change.

Both Al Gore Jr and the IPCC were awarded the Nobel Peace Prize in 2007 'for their efforts to build up and disseminate greater knowledge about man-made climate change and to lay the foundations for the measures that are needed to counteract such change'.

It is the confluence of scientific, economic and political contributions that has meant that climate change is now very high on the agendas of both government and business, although conflicting national interests have meant that progress has slowed after the perceived failure of the 2009 Copenhagen summit.

The developments described above have resulted in changes in investment attitudes and in developments in corporate governance. These changes are described below.

Changes in investment attitudes

There has been a growing recognition by members of the investment world that they do have a part to play in ensuring that the corporate world in which they are investing should behave responsibly, for the benefit of all including the investing public.

This started with the introduction of 'socially responsible investment' (SRI) as a vehicle for investors who wanted to invest their funds in ethically responsible companies. What was dismissed by some members of the investment community as a crank idea is now a significant percentage of all the *new* funds being invested in the US and the UK. In the US in 2002, a particularly bad year for stock market investment, SRI funds had a net inflow of $1.5 billion, compared to all other funds, which experienced net outflow of $10.5 billion. Since that time, SRI has continued to grow strongly. A recent study showed that in 2010, the SRI funds under management in Europe now represent €5 trillion – representing spectacular growth of nearly 90% since the data was collected two years previously, particularly in countries such as Spain and Austria.[5]

The emphasis on new funds is important, as the vast pool of funds invested on both sides of the Atlantic is in the form of long-term investment, supporting pension and life funds. Hence the ability to switch investments in these funds into other, SRI investment vehicles is difficult to achieve in the short and medium term, without significantly disrupting the market because of the immense value of the investments tied up in long-term funds.

This business growth has been reinforced by the Pension Fund Amendment Act of 1999 – a relatively small piece of government legislation, but one which has had a significant impact on fund manager attitudes. This required fund managers of pension funds to declare their SRI policy. When it was introduced, many independent observers felt it would have little or no impact, since it did not require a fund manager to have a proactive policy – indeed the fund managers could simply state they had no such policy. However, it changed attitudes – as was stated by the then Minister responsible for CSR, Douglas Alexander, in a Department of Trade and Industry conference, declaring that it had been a success, by being a 'soft touch on the tiller'.

This requirement for fund managers to declare their policy, as well as the development of a growing business opportunity, meant that some companies started to think about how they should approach their own responsibilities as the shareholders in quoted companies – regardless of whether or not they were seen as part of an SRI portfolio. As a consequence, some fund managers started to develop a proactive engagement strategy with the directors of the companies that are their main investments.

Typical of such fund managers is Hermes – the largest fund manager in the UK, with responsibility for major pension funds such as those of BT and the Post Office. It places great emphasis on exercising its ownership rights in those companies in which it invests as a means of delivering added value to its clients' investments in its 3,000 public company investments worldwide. It believes that good stewardship leads to superior corporate performance.

Hermes has taken this position further by recognising that such engagement strategies should be a two-way dialogue and it has published its own Responsible Code of Conduct to explain to the directors of the companies in which it invests what they should expect from Hermes as a responsible investor. Hermes has recently taken this further by developing a consortium approach for all investment fund managers that want positive engagement with the companies in which they invest – but who perhaps do not have the individual resources to do it as effectively as they would desire. This consortium is significant because it gives fund managers considerable voting power, if required, to persuade quoted companies to take a more positive responsible attitude towards society and the environment.

Out of actions like that of Hermes came the UK Stewardship Code,[6] established in 2010 by the Financial Reporting Council (FRC). Its objective was to enhance the quality of engagement between institutional investors and companies to help improve long-term returns to shareholders and the efficient exercise of governance responsibilities. Engagement included dialogue on strategy, performance and risk management. The Code is addressed to firms who manage assets such as pension funds, insurance companies, investment trusts and other collective investment vehicles. All UK-authorised asset managers were required to produce a statement of commitment to the Stewardship Code or to explain why it is not appropriate to their business model. By the end of 2011, nearly 150 asset managers and over 40 asset owners had signed up to the Code.

Whilst this is specifically a UK example, it has been emulated worldwide. This demonstrates that fund managers have moved from a position of offering their investors the option to buy into funds that consist of socially responsible companies, to a position of recognising that they should be active rather than passive investors, with a responsibility to work with the managers of those companies in which they invest to help them develop socially responsible strategies, in the interests of stakeholders and long-term prosperity.

One example of international collaboration between asset owners and asset managers that demonstrated the more enlightened way some investors have been considering issues regarding, amongst other factors, socially responsible practices was that of the Enhanced Analytics Initiative.[7] This was aimed at encouraging better investment research, in particular research that takes account of the impact of extra-financial issues on long-term investment. At the end of 2007, its members had total assets under management of €1.8 trillion. It incentivised research providers (stock analysts) to compile better and more detailed analysis of extra financial issues (including aspects such as a company's environmental impact) as part of their mainstream research. It was concluded as a self-standing initiative in December 2008 after four years when a more global partnership was formed with the UN Principles for Responsible Investment (UNPRI).[8]

These principles were formulated in 2006, as a result of dialogue between the UN

Environmental Programme Finance Initiative, the UN Global Compact and major institutional investors. They reflect the belief of activist institutional investors that environmental, social and corporate governance (ESG) issues can affect the performance of investment portfolios and also recognise that by developing and applying these principles they may be better able to align their investment actions with the broader objectives of society. By the end of 2011 over 900 investment institutions had become signatories, with approximately US$ 30 trillion of assets under management.

Changes in corporate governance

Coincidental with the emergence of CSR onto the management agenda was an understanding by the professions that regulate business behaviour – the accountants and the solicitors – that they needed to consider the means by which they could influence business behaviour and the manner in which business operates. Their activities in influencing the actions of corporates are likely to be in advance of the legislative action taken by governments, but can often be the result of even limited regulation – especially in the UK where, as previously mentioned, governments (and particularly the previous Labour government) have had a policy of developing a soft touch on the tiller to avoiding claims that it was imposing additional regulatory burdens on business.

There have been series of governance procedures in the UK by various professional bodies that have had a significant impact on the ways in which British business has approached corporate governance. These developments have run parallel with the development of CSR, so that in many respects, corporate governance and CSR now go hand in hand. An investment term illustrating this point, which is becoming commonly accepted, is that of ESG – environmental, social and governance – which is the successor term to SEE (social, environmental and ethical).

Developments in governance procedures

Developments in governance procedures include:

- *The Cadbury Report* or, to give it its full title, 'The Report of the Committee on the Financial Aspects of Corporate Governance'. This was published in 1992 and was described as a landmark in thinking on corporate governance. It included the development of a Code of Best Practice, which focused on the presentation of the accounts of a company (to ensure they were not misleading or suffered from 'window dressing') as well as the development of a board of independent-minded directors, acting in the best interests of the shareholders of the company. UK-listed companies came under increasing pressure from the investment world to comply with this Code.
- *The Myners Report.* Published in 1995, this focused on the relationship between companies and their institutional investors. In particular, it urged institutional investors to reassess their role as shareholders and to consider their

responsibilities for ensuring good corporate governance and the success of the companies in which they invested. In many respects, this report helped focus the minds of such investors on issues outside the direct area of financial performance and to include consideration of issues that may ultimately affect corporate reputation and hence share values.

- *The Greenbury Report.* Published in 1995, this focused on better governance of directors' remuneration. This was at a time when the UK media was commenting on 'fat cat' directors and the report issued a Code of Best Practice for establishing remuneration committees.

- *The Hampel Committee.* This was set up to review the recommendations of both the Cadbury and Greenbury committees. It covered a range of governance issues, such as the composition of the board, the role of directors, the role of shareholders and the communication between shareholders and the company. It suggested that in addition to the prevention of abuses, there should be equal focus on the positive contribution that good corporate governance could make. It recommended that the findings of all three bodies should be combined into one single code of governance, published in 1998 as The Combined Code, which would apply to all UK-listed companies.

- *The Turnbull Report.* Published in 1999, this was the result of a working party of accountants from the Institute of Chartered Accountants in England and Wales. This report gave added emphasis to the responsibilities of directors to take account of inherent risk and to look forward in respect of performance impacts.

- *The Higgs Report of 2003.* This was commissioned by the DTI and focused on the role of independent non-executive directors (NEDs) on the boards of companies.

- *The Smith Report of 2003.* This was established by the FRC and focused on the role of the audit committee of the board.

- The responsibility for the Combined Code was transferred to the FRC in 2003 and a revised Combined Code was published in that year. This revision of the 1998 Code incorporated many of the recommendations from the Turnbull Report, the Higgs Report and the Smith Report. As well as consolidating the earlier reports, it recommended regular review of the Combined Code.

- The latest review culminated in the publication in June 2010 of the UK Corporate Governance Code (referred to in detail in chapter 2) which placed added emphasis on the reporting of relevant non-financial information and KPIs within a company's annual report.

- *The Association of British Insurers (ABI) Disclosure Guidelines on Social Responsibility.* This was published in 2001and determined the levels of reporting on CSR in annual accounts that the main institutional investors expected to see. The ABI updated its Guidelines in the light of the changes in reporting requirements for UK-listed and registered companies, resulting from the Companies Act 2006. The new version is titled 'The ABI's Responsible Investment Disclosure Guidelines'.[9] These guidelines emphasise the importance of a board taking account of environmental, social and governance (ESG) risks. It went further when commenting on ESG disclosures in corporate reporting, by suggesting that an independent external verification of ESG statements in reports offers a significant advantage to the investor.

The scope of corporate governance

The issues of corporate governance have included risk management, financial reporting and auditing, directors' remuneration and ethical concerns (especially where these knock on to affecting the company's corporate reputation). At the outset, the focus was upon safeguarding the rights of the shareholder, but increasingly the concerns of other stakeholders have been taken into account.

For example, the OECD, in its introduction to its principles of corporate governance, states that from a company's perspective, corporate governance is about:

> Maximising value subject to meeting the corporation's financial and other legal and contractual obligations. This inclusive definition stresses the need for boards of directors to balance the interests of shareholders with those of other stakeholders – employees, customers, suppliers, investors, communities – in order to achieve long-term sustained value.

Shareholder versus stakeholders

The benefit of this approach towards corporate governance is that it recognises the broad objective of maximising shareholder value, whilst acting fairly in the interests of other stakeholders with an interest in the company's affairs. However, there are more stringent interpretations of corporate governance, which suggest that it is concerned with achieving a balance between economic and social goals and between individual and communal goals. In South Africa, the King Reports, published in 1993 and 2002, advocated an inclusive approach, taking the view that a company has a wide range of stakeholders whose views should be considered and that a participative corporate governance system was required, applied with integrity. The third King Report (King III) took this approach a stage further with the introduction of integrated reporting (see chapter 2).

These interpretations struggled when put into the context of a UK company law system that gives certain rights to shareholders. The Company Law Committee of the Law Society, in its response to the UK Company Law Review Steering Group in 1998 stated that it did not accept the pluralist approach.

In its view there is already scope to apply enlightened shareholder concepts and most boards do take into account the interests of stakeholders in the decisions they take. As a consequence, the corporate governance approach that is generally accepted is that of maximising shareholder values whilst acting responsibly in the interests of other stakeholders. This was embodied in the concept of 'enlightened shareholders' value' that was the basis for the approach developed in the Companies Act 2006.

These stakeholder-based developments encouraged companies to actively consider their responsible approach towards society and the environment, including the wide range of stakeholders – customers, supplies, employees, the community and government. At the outset it was only the largest companies that were active in this respect, often because it was perceived as a 'nice to have' rather than a process embedded within business. However, since the turn of the millennium, this has changed to embrace all sizes of quoted companies, as well as some of the larger unquoted companies in the UK, such as the John Lewis Partnership, as well as subsidiaries of foreign companies, such as Vauxhall Motors and publicly owned bodies such as BNFL and the BBC.

Large and small enterprises

It is argued that CSR should embrace small and medium-sized enterprises (SMEs) – defined in the UK as a company with less than 500 employees. However, whilst activity in this direction has been pursued by the government, this area of SMEs has not been so strongly developed in the UK, partly because providing the relevant information to demonstrate a company's responsible approach towards its society and environment can be perceived to be costly, especially if that company is not already recording such information for its management purposes. Many owner-managers are already participating in responsible approaches, although they may not describe them as being part of CSR. Equally, it is accepted that the nature of CSR in an SME can be significantly different to CSR in a large company.

Indeed, the argument is that SMEs are often undertaking their own forms of CSR and that the focus for CSR should be on the larger companies, where the levels of impact on society and the environment are more substantial. Yet, it is the larger companies, through their supply chain CSR activity, that are beginning to encourage SME suppliers to become more CSR active. The challenge is to ensure that the practices suitable in larger companies can be modified to be appropriate for the SMEs.

Sources

1 The Precautionary Principle is referred to at: ec.europa.eu/legislation_summaries/consumers/consumer_safety/l32042_en.htm.

2 The Reach Directive took effect on 1 June 2007. See: ec.europa.eu/environment/chemicals/reach/reach_intro.htm.

3 More information on IPCC can be found at: www.ipcc.ch.

4 A summary of the Stern Review and the report itself can be found at: www.direct.gov.uk/en/Nl1/Newsroom/DG_064854.

5 The study was undertaken by the European Social Investment Forum, (Eurosif) and was published in October 2010. See www.eurosif.org/publications/sri_studies.

6 Details of the Code are on the FRC website: www.frc.org.uk/corporate/investorgovernance.cfm.

7 More information about the Enhanced Analytics Initiative can be found on the website of USS, one of the initiating partners. See: www.uss.co.uk/UssInvestments/Responsibleinvestment/RIResources/ArchivedMaterials/Pages/EnhancedAnalyticsInitiative.aspx.

8 More details about UNPRI can be found at: www.unpri.org.

9 A press release detailing the position of the ABI on these guidelines can be found at: www.abi.org.uk/Media/Releases/2007/02/ABI_publishes_Responsible_Investment_Disclosure_Guidelines.aspx.

Indices, analysts and researchers

'Nice to have' or 'need to have'

Whilst there is much greater acceptance of CSR amongst business leaders, there are still questions about the extent to which companies are legally obliged to undertake CSR activities. This leads to some confusion and to the question 'Is it just a nice to have?', almost in the same way that people used to ask about marketing and training.

The answer is not as simple as people in business would like. Whilst there is a requirement for some forms of non-financial reporting through legislation such as the European Accounts Modernisation Directive and the UK's Business Review, much of the 'regulatory driving forces' for CSR have come from the investment side and the quasi-regulators (those who have been influential in focusing the minds of governments and major businesses), as well as from business-based influencers such as Business in the Community.

These bodies have been developing reporting and policy standards that have been perceived by business as being necessary requirements for them in their approach towards and the reporting of CSR. It is likely that any regulatory forms of CSR that may be introduced will first have been developed by investors and non-governmental bodies in the form of these reports and standards.

Stock market and other indices

Consequently, the standards developed by the investment side and the 'quasi regulators' are the precursor of our review of the legal requirements in chapter 9.

The Business in the Community Corporate Responsibility Index (BitC CR Index)

The BitC CR Index, although not stock-market based, is important because of the level of influence it has had on UK perceptions of CSR.

The BitC was established in 1982, following a government conference on inner city unrest, following the riots in Toxteth and Brixton. It was a business-based charity, but with the significant advantage of having had the Prince of Wales as its President since 1985. BitC is one of the Prince's charities, and his influence can be significant in its choice of topics and the direction it takes. It now has over 850 company members, and claims that nearly 11,000 companies are involved in its campaigns globally.

It established the CR Index in 2002 as a means of challenging companies to manage, monitor and benchmark their responsible business activities. The index is compiled based on companies' submissions to an annual questionnaire. These submissions are reviewed and challenged by BitC's own staff, which then scores the submission on a common basis. In the early days, the scores were published based on percentages, but these were changed as it was realised that the leading companies were plateauing at the highest percentage levels. This approach was not considered to be sufficiently inspiring to encourage companies to continue their participation, so instead companies were grouped into four categories – platinum, gold, silver and bronze – based on their scores. The BitC has always published the results of its index, in conjunction with a media sponsor – *The Times* and the *Sunday Times* are past sponsors; in 2011, the *Financial Times* was the media sponsor. This approach has given additional credibility to the index.

The overall format has been unchanged since 2002, comprising sections on companies' responsible business approach to corporate strategy, integration, management, and disclosure, together with their activities in four impact areas – community, environment, workplace and market place. Whilst the overall format has remained reasonably constant, the weighting of the questions has changed over the years and in the impact areas, additional topics have been added from time to time. These additions reflect the political influences, as well as the Prince of Wales' perceptions of current issues. For example, topics such as employees' commuter travel and immigration polices have been inserted into the question topics – matters that do not often occur generally in other indices.

Whilst the CR Index has been very influential in driving broad business opinion towards positive action on CSR, its approach is very UK oriented (e.g. its position on diversity fails to take into account the difficulties faced by multinational companies in capturing diversity data from worldwide operations). It also allows some organisations – either UK subsidiaries of overseas companies (e.g. Toyota UK in 2011), or the UK arm of professional practices (e.g. Deloittes and Accenture, both in 2011) – to report solely on their UK operations, whilst listed companies are expected to report on their worldwide operations. It is much easier to do well in the index if a company reports solely on its UK operations.

On being asked by clients which index to enter – a stock market index, or the BitC, or both – my answer is to ask what is the purpose of their submission? If it is to build credibility within UK influencers, including government, then BitC should be high on the list. However, if the focus is to build a worldwide reputation, especially with investors, then my preference would be for one of the stock market indices.

The stock market indices

These indices have been set up to deliver the means of addressing the needs of those investors that wish to invest in 'responsible companies'. As a result, the indices develop criteria and questions that define 'what is a responsible company' – at least in the eyes of the investment community.

The two main indices are the DJSI (Dow Jones Sustainability Index) and the FTSE4Good set of indices, both of which aim to provide coverage of all the major stock markets in the world. The DJSI is a more selective index, whilst the FTSE4Good has significantly wider coverage in terms of the numbers of companies included in the index, in the numbers of countries covered by these companies, and by the numbers of independent stock markets setting up their own version of the FTSE4Good index (such as the Johannesburg Stock Market in South Africa). In addition, Bloomberg, the financial data giant, set up its own survey to provide ESG information on major companies.

The Dow Jones Sustainability Index (DJSI)

The DJSI[1] was set up in 1998 as a result of collaboration between Dow Jones (the publishing company that publishes the *Wall Street Journal*, together with all the US-based Dow Jones stock market indices) and SAM Group[2] (Sustainable Asset Management), a Zurich-based company that specialises in investment management and research linked to issues of sustainability. There was a further collaboration between Dow Jones and STOXX – a joint venture between SWX (Swiss Exchange) and Deutsche Boerse (the German stock exchange).

The DJSI is in fact a series of indices. It started with DJSI World (1999) and DJSI STOXX (2001) – now called DJSI Europe – and has been extended to cover DJSI North America and US (a subset of North America) which were both launched in 2005. As result, the DJSI family currently comprises global, European, Eurozone, North American and US benchmarks.

Unusually in terms of ethical investment indices or surveys, DJSI does not exclude the investment areas often regarded as the pariah areas by the purist ethical investor (i.e. alcohol, tobacco, gambling, and armaments). However, it does publish separate indices, in which these areas are excluded, if a fund manager wishes to focus on the 'pure ethical investment areas' – this is often the case for those fund managers using the index to manage investments on behalf of churches, universities and charities.

In terms of impact, as at September 2011, 60 licensees in 16 countries were using the DJSI data as the basis for their fund management purposes. These licenses had total funds of $8 billion under management, based on the DJSI.

The DJSI indices are based on an objective assessment rating system that leads to the subsequent selecting of companies. This selection is a distinctive element in the DJSI approach, leading to the DJSI World Index consisting of just under 350 companies, representing the top 10% of the leading sustainability companies in 60 industry groups (weighted by the free market capitalisation). The target for selection is that no more than 10% of the companies in each eligible DJSI industry group are selected from a universe covering the biggest 2,500 companies in the parent Dow Jones Global Indices (which covers 30 countries in all).

Of the 342 companies that are constituent members of the DJSI list, the highest percentage in terms of market capitalisation is represented by USA-based corporates (28%) followed by UK-based corporates (17%), as can be seen in Table 8.1 on the following page.

Table 8.1: Components of the DJSI List as of 31 October 2011

Country of origin	Percentage of market capitalisation
France	7
Germany	7
United Kingdom	17
Switzerland	9
Spain	4
Other European countries	8
Australia	6
Japan	4
South Korea	2
Other Asia Pacific	2
USA	28
Canada	3
Brazil	2
South Africa	1
Total constituents	100

What is of interest since the index started in 2004 is the growth in the numbers of companies listed that are based in the newly developing world, especially the BRICs. Companies from Brazil, China and India, together with Taiwan and South Africa now represent over 4% of the index value. This reflects the increasing interest in CSR issues and awareness by companies in these countries, although at this stage there are no companies listed in the fourth of the BRIC countries – Russia. These companies may instead seek a London listing as their primary listing.

Overall, European companies represent 52% of the DJSI World Index's market capitalisation and North and South America companies represent 33%. In contrast, for the DJ Global Index (from which the DJSI is derived), the Americas represent nearly 51% of the market capitalisation. This is indicative of the way in which European companies tend to lead the way on CSR. But it is also indicative of the way in which US companies (other than those that are multinational in reach) see CSR in a different light – often focusing on the philanthropic aspects, and downplaying the environmental matters (led by the US government's stance on issues such as greenhouse gas emissions).

The strength of the DJSI lies in the fact that it is updated on an annual basis, based on objective assessments. For the 2011 list of participants in DJSI World, the final list deleted 23 companies from the previous year's list and added 41 new companies.

The DJSI requires companies to apply to be included for the first time in the index. All participating companies (whether new or existing) are required to undertake a regular assessment. This assessment occurs once a year, with the results being published every September.

In my opinion, the DJSI approach is the most rigorous of the stock market indices, involving a range of questions that are scored as part of the assessment. These scores are then weighted to give an overall score for the company. These questions cover a wide range of areas, representing economic, environmental and social dimensions. The three dimensions each contribute towards the overall company score, covering the following aspects, which have been taken from one sector reviewed for one client by The Virtuous Circle in 2011. The percentages in brackets represent the weighting of the score in the assessment:

- *Economic dimension* (29%)
    - codes of conduct/compliance/corruption and bribery 6
    - corporate governance 6
    - risk and crisis management 6
    - customer relationship management 11
- *Environment dimension* (25%)
    - environmental performance (eco-efficiency) 11
    - environmental reporting 3
    - environmental policy/management system 11
- *Social dimension* (46%)
    - corporate citizenship/philanthropy 3
    - labour practice indicators 5
    - human capital development 6
    - social reporting 3
    - talent attraction and retention 6
    - standards for suppliers 11
    - occupational health and safety 12

These elements will be modified slightly for each sector with several industry-specific questions within each dimension. This ensures that the DJSI has a sector-customised approach that is not found in other indices, addressing CSR issues that relate individual industry sectors. As an example, based on experience of a company categorised as being in the hotels and restaurants sector, the DJSI questionnaire included a series of questions that related only to its sector. In this instance there were questions relating to:

- gambling, alcohol and tobacco
- brand management
- healthy living and food safety
- genetically modified organisms
- sustainable tourism, sustainable agriculture and fisheries
- advanced environmental management systems
- local impact of business operations and global sourcing.

Perhaps for the reader unfamiliar with CSR, the breadth and depth of this list will give an understanding for the first time of the unusual scope of the CSR agenda. In no other business discipline with which I am familiar is there so much coverage of the entire activity of a business operation. It is this scope that often makes the subject of CSR difficult to grasp by the functional management, and equally why the role of the CSR co-ordinator requires individuals with an unusual depth of experience of business matters if they are to ensure that the business can answer requests for information in the most effective and comprehensive manner.

It is also important to reflect that the DJSI is very active in modifying the elements of the individual dimensions to cover changes in importance on aspects of sustainability. Question topics have been dropped from the various dimensions as their application has become more of the norm for companies. In addition, the relative weightings for question topics have changed over time, which also means that the relative positioning of each dimension can change. The 2011 index was the first year in my experience where weightings have remained unchanged.

The results of the annual DJSI assessment is an overall ranking of companies based on their assessed scores, together with a ranking within the sectors, which is the most appropriate for outside observers, since league tables that go across sectors can be highly misleading. What is particularly relevant here is that the sectors used are the same as used within the main Dow Jones indices, so for companies quoted on the London Stock Exchange and being assessed also for the DJSI, there will be a degree of 'apples and pears' in terms of comparing their performance. However, the sector approach gives a much more relevant comparison between those DJSI companies in the same sector.

Only a limited number of companies are permitted to join the index. This does not prohibit other companies from the same sector being assessed for entry, but only if their total score is high enough will it result in their being in the top 10% and becoming constituents of the index.

This works both for the individual index, and as a result for the combined World Index, the latter being the composition of the 'highest achievers' in their industry sectors from around the world. The current 'super sector' leaders for DJSI World (as at September 2011) are shown in Table 8.2 opposite.

These 'super sector leaders' are under constant pressure to retain their place. In the 2007 edition of this book, the retail leader was Marks and Spencer – it has been replaced by Lotte Shopping Co Ltd, a South Korean retailer. In 2007, the real estate leader was Land Securities – it has been replaced by Stockland, an Australian property group.

The companies that become part of the index receive the right to include the DJSI logo on their literature (of more value for literature related to investor relations and corporate reputation, such as the corporate website, than for the general public) and also receive a comparison against the best and average scores of all companies in their sector across the following DJSI areas:

- total score
- economic dimension
- environmental dimension
- social dimension.

Table 8.2: 'Super sector' leaders for DJSI World

Market sector	2011 DJSI world leader
Automobiles and parts	BMW AG
Banks	Westpac Banking Corp.
Basic resources	Xstrata PLC
Chemicals	Koninklijke DSM N.V.
Construction and materials	Hyundai Engineering & Construction Co. Ltd.
Financial services	Itausa-Investimentos Itau S/A
Food and beverage	PepsiCo Inc
Healthcare	Roche Holding AG
Industrial goods and services	PostNL N.V.
Insurance	Swiss Re Limited
Media	Pearson PLC
Oil and gas	Repsol YPF S.A.
Personal and household goods	Koninklijke Philips Electronics N.V.
Real estate	Stockland
Retail	Lotte Shopping Co. Ltd
Technology	Samsung Electronics Co. Ltd.
Telecommunications	KT Corp
Travel and leisure	Air France-KLM
Utilities	Enagas S.A.

Being part of the DJSI is more than just an accolade for those companies that are its constituents. It benefits them in developing investor reputation, as the DJSI is used as the basis for fund management. However, its selectivity (probably based on the effort in assessing the companies making submissions) may not encourage other smaller companies to follow the CSR route.

The FTSE4Good Index

Like the DJSI, the FTSE4Good[3] index is assessed by an independent assessment research company – EIRIS (otherwise known as the Ethical Investment Research and Information Service) that is a long-established provider of investment analysis. The index was set up in July 2001 by FTSE (the global index company that is independent, despite having *Financial Times* (FT) in its name). It is unusual in that it was conceived originally with the support of UNICEF and this link continues today, in so far as UNICEF receives all the profits from licensing the FTSE4Good index. This position had drawn criticism, as UNICEF has an *ex officio* representative on the committee that reviews the standards set for the index. Also, FTSE4Good established a Breast Milk Substitutes (BMS) Committee, as part of its support for the aims of UNICEF. Some observers have been critical of this link, suggesting it is an ambiguous position to have a powerful Non-Governmental Organisation (NGO) like UNICEF having an influence in the standards setting.

Until 2011, companies such as Heinz, Danone, Nestlé and Abbott Laboratories (which produce breast milk substitutes) had never been members of FTSE4Good. However this changed when FTSE introduced new Breast Milk Substitutes criteria for the FTSE4Good Index in September 2010. FTSE Chief Executive, Mark Makepeace, explained the reason for the change, stating: 'In the infant food sector we were not able to engage the companies as they were all being excluded from the index.' In March 2011, Nestlé was the first manufacturer to join the index having met the full range of criteria.

Like DJSI it has extended its portfolio of indices, and covers over 20 markets, with a potential of over 2,000 companies. The following are the indices included in the FTSE4Good index series:

- FTSE4Good Europe
- FTSE4Good UK
- FTSE4Good US
- FTSE4Good Global
- FTSE4Good Japan.

In addition, there are four tradable indices (covering the UK, Europe and Global markets) to provide asset managers with a cheap and efficient basis for investment products. Also, there is a FTSE4 Good Environmental Leaders Europe 40 Index which focuses specifically on European companies within the FTSE4Good universe that demonstrates leading environmental practices.

The criteria for possible inclusion is that the companies concerned are either in the FTSE All Share Index or in the FTSE All-World Developed Index – the latter covers both large and medium capitalisation companies across the world, whilst the former is UK focused and includes small capitalisation companies.

However, FTSE4Good has developed a different approach towards the selection criteria for its constituents in the index, compared with that of the DJSI. Whilst there is a questionnaire, similar to that of the DJSI, this is not scored – EIRIS, the survey company, uses the data to develop an analysis summary for use by its clients. The data collected as part of the survey questionnaire serves to establish whether or not the company has passed the FTSE4Good criteria.

Initially these criteria were based on the nature of the company's activity (rather than their methods of operation). Hence all companies were considered eligible for inclusion within FTSE4Good, unless they fell into one of the following categories:

- tobacco producers
- manufacture of whole weapon systems
- manufacture of nuclear weapons (in whole or in part)
- owners or operators of nuclear power stations.

These excluded categories remain in place, with the exception of nuclear power generation. The latter's inclusion is a recognition that many utility companies now use a wide range of energy sources, including nuclear power, to generate electricity. A good example was that of Powergen, a UK utility company that is now part of E.ON. This was excluded from FTSE4Good when it acquired a US utility company which had a small element of nuclear power generation.

In 2002, FTSE4Good introduced additional criteria that were intended to challenge companies to improve their CSR commitment, focused on three areas of environmental sustainability, human rights and relations with stakeholders. More recent additions include climate change and bribery. The areas that the index covers now are:

- environmental management
- climate change mitigation and adaptation
- countering bribery
- upholding human and labour rights
- supply chain labour standards.

In terms of human rights, FTSE4Good's focus has been on two areas – companies in what they described as the global resource sector (oil, gas and mining) and companies with significant presence in countries of major human rights concern (for which FTSE4Good developed an agreed list).

For the environmental criteria, FTSE4Good categorised companies as falling into high, medium or low environmental impact areas. Those in the highest environmental impact companies were required to have rigorous environmental management systems. All companies were required to have an environmental policy. The categorisation is open to question, since included in the low-impact area are sectors such as telecommunications (which would include mobile telephone companies, whose communication masts are thought by some to represent environmental and health risks), whilst the high impact area includes sectors such as fast food chains and agriculture (as well as agricultural pest control).

The area of promoting positive relationships with stakeholders is less well defined, being based on a best practice framework, including areas such as having:

- a code of ethics
- an equal opportunity policy
- a health and safety management system
- training and development systems, and
- employee relations programmes including union recognition or consultative agreements.

In addition, the company was expected to make charitable donations in excess of £50,000.

These latest criteria of countering bribery and climate change focus on a company's approach and cover areas such as policy and governance, management and strategy, disclosure and performance. There are differing levels of criteria requirements for each of these, depending on the level of operational impact of the company.

In addition, the index has introduced a set of criteria for those companies involved in uranium mining.

As can be seen from this description of the criteria, their focus has been on encouraging companies to address what FTSE4Good has seen as key CSR issues. The extent to which FTSE4Good is responsible for achieving this desired effect may be open to question – since undoubtedly there are other pressures on companies to address these issues – but FTSE4Good does claim to have been successful.

This is largely because of the Responsible Investment Unit at FTSE, which is responsible for engaging with companies and developing an ongoing dialogue. The FTSE4Good Tenth Anniversary Report[4] claimed that as a result of this dialogue, 60% of the 1,000 sets of engagement that FTSE has had with companies has resulted in improvements in disclosure and improvement in practices.

The review of the membership of the indices is an ongoing process, and its September 2011 semi-annual review indicated that there were 20 new entrants, and 15 deletions (because the companies concerned had been deleted from the FTSE All World Developed Index). It is worth considering these deletions. In 2011, both 3M and Pfizer were excluded on the grounds that they 'no longer meet FTSE4Good Criteria'. Previous years have seen the exclusions of both Honda and Toyota for not meeting the human rights criteria; JC Penney was excluded for not meeting the environmental and supply chain criteria; and Agilent Technology was deleted for failing to meet the criteria for human rights and countering bribery. How far these companies concur with their reasons for deletion is not commented upon.

However, the strength of FTSE4Good has been in drawing attention to CSR issues such as these, in this respect, it can argue that it has been successful. In particular, its early approach to the selection criteria meant that it has gained a wider number of quoted companies as part of its index constituents than the DJSI approach. The subsequent improvement in the selection criteria has meant that these companies have had to address those CSR issues raised by FTSE4Good. The fact that it has been willing to name the companies who have both improved their approach towards the new criteria, and those who have failed to meet the criteria, can be considered to have given it greater influence.

FTSE4Good cannot be accused of standing still: in 2011 it introduced the FTSE4Good ESG Ratings. These are designed to offer an objective means of integrating ESG considerations into investment and stewardship approaches.

The extent to which it can claim to have been a useful management tool for investment fund managers who are seeking to focus on those companies that show better CSR performance in the sectors in which they operate, is left open to question. This is because of its use of the criteria-based approach, unlike the DJSI, which attempts to rank these companies based on objective measurement. However, the ESG Ratings service may go some way to offsetting this position, since included within it are various analytical tools for use by investment fund managers.

The Bloomberg ESG survey

Bloomberg describes itself as the leader in global business and financial information as well as financial software, offering similar services to the financial markets as those of Reuters. It makes up one-third of the global financial data market, and has over 300,000 subscribers to its Bloomberg terminal service.

In 2009, it launched its Environmental, Social and Governance (ESG) service, integrating ESG data into its core product offering. As a result, institutional investors are given ESG data alongside traditional financial data.

It was initially derived from publicly available data. However, due to what it considered to be unacceptable inconsistencies, Bloomberg created its own sustainability survey, using Global Reporting Initiative data; it then sent this partially completed survey to CSR professionals and asked them to complete the data on the behalf of their companies. This data collation commenced in 2008 (before the data was made publicly available). Bloomberg comments that the extent of gap filling remains a work in progress, and to encourage improvements in this area, it scores companies on their ESG disclosure. With the maximum being 100, Bloomberg has stated that only eight companies have scored above 70, with the maximum being 83. Nevertheless, Bloomberg is committed to extending its ESG offering, and believes that the standards of disclosure will improve, especially as the US Securities and Exchange Commission (SEC) extends its regulatory remit to this area.

Bloomberg's approach is unlike that of DJSI or FTSE4Good, which produce a selected list of companies from which fund managers can develop their portfolio. Instead, it aims to deliver comparable ESG data to analysts, leaving to them to decide how to use it. Over a 60-day period in 2010, Bloomberg found that ESG data sets were viewed 11.5 million times by over 1,000 global users.

The investment fund managers' approach

Whilst the DJSI and the FTSE4Good are both examples of indices created by stock market 'authorities', it would be wrong to assume that all the other players in the stock markets have been compliant users of these surveys as their ethical investment bible.

Indeed the area of social responsibility investment (SRI), as it has become known, is a burgeoning part of the stock market.

The Social Investment Forum Foundation is the USA's equivalent to Europe's SIF. Its 2010 report[5] 'Socially Responsible Investing Trends in the United States' stated that despite the recent economic downturn, SRI in the United States was growing at a faster pace than the total universe of investment assets under professional management. Since 2005, SRI assets have increased more than 34%, while the broader universe of professionally managed assets has increased by only 3%. From the start of 2007 to the end of 2009, when broad market indices such as the S&P 500 declined and the broader universe of professionally managed assets increased by less than 1%, assets involved in sustainable and socially responsible investing increased more than 13% (from $2.71 trillion to $3.07 trillion). Over 12% of assets under professional management in the United States are involved in some strategy of socially responsible and sustainable investing. This is perceived to be due to net inflows into existing SRI products; the development of new SRI products; and the adoption of SRI strategies by managers and institutions not previously involved in the field.

Whilst at one time it was felt that the SRI market would remain a niche area, this is clearly not the case today. In addition, as evidenced by Bloomberg providing ESG data sets, it is clear that ESG considerations have become a significant aspect of mainstream investment decision making.

As was commented upon within chapter 7, the evidence of the Eurosif survey shows that this growth is not only in the USA. This survey showed that in 2010, the European SRI market was estimated to be €5 trillion – up 15 fold since 2003.

Within the area of SRI, there are a number of companies that have developed their own approaches towards evaluating a company's CSR performance, including investment fund managers, such as Henderson (previously part of AMP, but since 2007 a listed asset management house) and Morley (now part of Aviva).

The Aviva approach

The Aviva approach[6] was originally a rigorous analysis to enable it to develop its own categorisation of companies. Its security selection starts with a broad universe of companies, which are screened with its own sustainability matrix and valuation tool to isolate the most attractive ideas. This sustainability matrix is based on what it regards as two key elements:

- product (or business) sustainability
- management quality (including vision and strategy)

In terms of business sustainability, this focus is on the extent to which the business products and services provide a 'sustainability solution' – in other words, help overcome some of the key hurdles to sustainable development.

This approach is based on scoring over a five-point scale (ranging from the business being 'most sustainable' to 'least sustainable') and assesses the extent to which a business helps society and/or the environment. Sustainability is measured against Aviva's four key themes of climate change, quality of life, sustainable consumption and risk and governance management. The company then practises ongoing engagement with companies, to gain more information about them, their operations and approaches to corporate governance and corporate social responsibility issues, including offering Aviva's views on best practice.

The Henderson approach

The Henderson approach[7] is slightly different. Henderson is smaller than Aviva (having £74 billion funds in management compared with Aviva's £402 billion in mid-2011).

Its philosophy focuses on the sustainable development of its investments, and uses a three-strand approach, covering the sustainability, responsibility and ethics of companies in which it invests.

In terms of sustainability, Henderson has developed an SRI investment policy that focuses on 'companies that contribute to, benefit from and best adapt to the environmentally sustainable and socially responsible global economy'. They describe these companies as being part of the 'industries of the future'. In their opinion, these industries cover ten main themes (not necessarily industry sector-based). These include:

- cleaner energy – companies that develop sources of energy that combat the effects of climate change through developing more renewable energy;
- efficiency – companies that provide products and processes that reduce energy consumption;
- environmental services – companies providing goods and services that improve the quality of the environment and reduce pollution and waste;
- health – companies offering products or services that enable longer and healthier lives;
- knowledge – companies supplying education or training services to enhance quality of life and opportunities in the workplace for students and those in employment;
- quality of life – companies that promote sustainable lifestyles across all age groups;
- safety – companies providing goods or services that minimise the risk of safety incidents – at work, home or for the public at large;
- social property and finance – companies providing property for social benefit and regeneration and companies providing better and wider access to financial services;
- sustainable transport – companies providing cleaner forms of transport technologies; and
- water management – companies managing water conservation and minimising pollution.

It is probably important to note that Henderson actively reviews these categories – and its list has expanded from seven to ten categories since 2003, with social property and finance being included and others such as sustainable transport and water management being classified as separate categories – and hence with tighter remits. In assessing the universe of companies available, it uses five categories:

- industries of the future
- gatekeepers/enablers
- sensitive
- controversial
- extreme.

Before a company can be included within the 'industries of the future' portfolios, Henderson assesses its CSR approach. It does so by assessing the company's approach in terms of its corporate standards – its environmental management, its workplace practices and its interactions with society. In addition, reference is made to the company's involvement in recognised standards, such as the Global Reporting Initiative (GRI) and the UN Global Compact.

It then categorises each company on the basis of its responsible approach in terms of five grades:

- leaders
- integrating
- developing
- reacting
- resisting.

Its approach generally is to invest in companies that it regards as leaders, but it will also include companies that are in lower-risk sectors where it believes their management has made a commitment to progress.

In terms of its ethics component of its philosophy, each of its funds have exclusion sectors and the sectors that it may consider avoiding include:

- alcohol production
- animal testing
- arms
- automotive
- carbon intensive industries and fossil fuels
- extractives (e.g. mining)
- fur
- gambling
- genetic engineering
- meat and dairy production
- nuclear
- ozone layer depletion
- pesticides
- pornography
- road building
- tobacco
- unsustainable forestry.

This avoidance is based on the recognition that some of its clients will apply their own ethical values in their selection of their investment portfolios. Whilst the Henderson approach includes active engagement in those companies in which it has invested, this avoidance strategy is known as negative screening.

In late 2011, Henderson announced it was modifying the rigorous approach described above. In its place, it has stated that responsible investment is the approach it uses to cover its work on environmental, social and corporate governance (ESG) issues in the companies in which it invests on clients' behalf, across all funds. This suggests that Henderson has moved away from specific SRI funds to including ESG as criteria for all its investments.

There are a number of means by which pension fund managers address the issues of socially responsible investment. The alternatives include:

- negative screening of investments – excluding businesses which do not meet defined social responsibility standards, such as tobacco, gambling, armaments, etc;
- positive screening – actively selecting business that are at the forefront of social responsibility;
- active engagement – working with businesses in which investments are held to develop practices to meet defined social responsibility criteria on behalf of its investor clients.

Over the past five years or so active engagement has emerged amongst other fund managers as a favoured SRI approach, but it can represent a time-consuming activity on the part of fund managers. This active screening has been taken further by Hermes,[8] which has developed its set of principles describing 'what shareholders should expect of their companies, and what companies should expect of their investors'. In all there are 12 principles, covering communication, financial, strategic and social ethical and environmental issues. The latter contributes two of the principles:

- *Principle 9* – Companies should manage effectively relationships with employees, suppliers and customers and with others who have a legitimate interest in the company's activities. Companies should behave ethically and have regard for the environment and society as a whole.
- *Principle 10* – Companies should manage effectively environmental and social factors that affect their business and society at large with a view to enhancing their long-term sustainability.

These principles are the basis for Hermes policy of active shareholder engagement funds – 'Focus Funds' – although much of the focus is on under-performing companies.

The investment researchers' approach

Within the investment community, there are also the parties that can be best described as investment researchers – organisations that exist to provide independent advice to investment fund managers.

EIRIS

EIRIS[9] is a not-for-profit organisation that was established in 1983, as a charity, with the help of a group of churches and other charities which all had investments and strong convictions of what they thought was right and wrong. They needed a research organisation to help them put their principles into practice when making investment decisions. Its Board and Council members reflect that early approach, with members coming from bodies such as the Methodist Church, as well as more recent activist bodies such as the Carbon Disclosure Project.

It researches 3,000 companies from the UK, Continental Europe, North America and Asia-Pacific covering all the companies on the FTSE All World Developed Index, covering over 100 different environmental, social and governance issues.

Its quality of research is best indicated by the nature of its clients, which as well as the NGOs and religious bodies, include major names in the financial world, such as Aegon Asset Management, Aviva Investors, Blackrock, Insight Investment, Legal and General Investment Management and Rothschild and Standard Life Investments. It is also a signatory of the UN Principles of Responsible Investment (UNPRI). It does not investigate companies' financial status but instead looks at their ethical approach and conduct, covering three research areas – governance, the environment and social issues. It does not provide financial advice, but provides information to enable investment managers to make their own decisions in these areas.

EIRIS uses a questionnaire as the basis for its research. These are sent to the companies it researches. The level of detail stretches to nearly 90 areas relating to governance and social issues and about 20 areas relating to the environmental area. It should be noted, however, that not all of the environmental areas are required to be answered by all companies – EIRIS provides a guide to which areas of environmental impact are considered relevant to specific industry sectors. The EIRIS questionnaires are used as the basis for assessment of a company's eligibility for inclusion in the FTSE4Good Index – there are no separate questionnaires for that purpose.

PIRC

Another investment research organisation is PIRC (Pensions Investment Research Consultants Ltd.). PIRC[10] is an independent provider of research and advisory services, covering corporate governance, proxy voting and socially responsible investment to pension fund managers and fund managers. At one time in the early years of this decade, it was the source for comparative data used by *The Times* in a regular article about individual companies.

PIRC sees itself as the pioneer and champion of good corporate governance within the UK. As such it offers a high level of public advocacy, resulting in a high public profile, positioning itself as advocates of transparent markets, accountable corporations and responsible investment. It was the first organisation to monitor companies' corporate governance and the first to publish shareholder voting guidelines. It has been highly visible in corporate controversies such as that of British Gas over executive pay in 1995 and environmental issues such as that of Shell in 1997. More recently in late 2011, it was very vocal on the subject of placing greater constraints on executive remuneration and put forward a shareholder motion at the BSkyB AGM that James Murdoch should resign as CEO after he became engulfed in the phone-hacking inquiry. PIRC prides itself on its independence, encouraging its analysts to develop a critical stance about the companies to be researched and analysed.

As you might expect, this approach is not without its critics, particularly amongst the companies researched. The research sources used include archives of the press and other media articles about the companies in question, details of any fines or outstanding legal action, as well as the companies' published information. PIRC does send its analysis and recommendations to companies in a draft form for comment. However, some companies have been concerned about the extent to which this information used is up to date, as well as the extent to which the analysis (and hence the recommendation) is accurate.

PIRC adopts an approach that suggests it is their wholly independent analysis, based on in-depth research. As a consequence, companies often feel they have little opportunity to challenge the analysis and recommendations. It describes itself as maintaining a reputation for investigative analysis unmatched in the UK and has 'an unrivalled reputation as independent and professional experts on UK corporate governance'. Some of the companies that have been the subject of PIRC assessments may argue with this claim.

Risk Metrics Group

A similar investment research company is the Risk Metrics Group, which acquired Innovest Strategic Value Advisors.[11] Risk Metrics was itself acquired by MSCI in 2010. As a result MSCI offers a range of ESG-based indices for use by investment fund managers. These cover best in class, values based (socially responsible and religious) and environmental, as well as customised ESG indices. MSCI claims to be the only major index provider with a separate in-house ESG research business unit. This provides in-depth ESG analysis and ratings covering five areas: the environment, community and society, employees and its supply chain and customers and governance. A company's ESG score is mapped to a nine-point letter scale, with ratings from AAA (highest) to C (lowest). ESG ratings also determine peer group rankings for MSCI ESG best-in-class index methodology.

So which indices and surveys matter?

When a company director faces the deluge of paper that these indices and surveys represent, they may be forgiven for responding to all of them without questioning their relevance or their importance. However, it is necessary to think beyond each survey, and ask what is each trying to achieve?

Several years ago, a client asked for an analysis of four surveys it had received. This compared the topic questions covered by each organisation with the resulting comparison:

Table 8.3: Surveys and indicies – They aren't all the same!

	BitC	EIRIS	PIRC	DJSI
Corporate governance	0	7	8	10
Investor relations	0	1	0	3
Corporate strategy	6	1	2	6
Integration	9	6	1	2
Community	8	2	1	4
Environment	7	4	10	3
Marketplace	8	5	1	9
Workplace	7	9	0	6
Performance and impact	10	9	0	8

This shows the importance given by each surveying organisation. As can be seen, the Business in the Community CR index had no coverage on issues of corporate governance or investor relations – not surprising as it is not intended to be used as the basis for investment decisions. In contrast, the DJSI is particularly strong in this area. In the case of PIRC, the emphasis on the environment in the case of our client in question outweighed its apparent interest in matters concerning the workplace – a surprising omission given the importance of workforce to the ongoing performance of the company in question.

None of these surveys and indices is wrong – but they are all different – and if any chief executive starts questioning the company's finance director about apparent poor performance in a particular survey, then the best course of action is to review what questions were asked – and how relevant they are to the company's industry sector. For those of you who do complete several of these surveys, then replicating the exercise we undertook for our client is a useful task that can help you to compare the results from each survey you have completed.

What is equally important is to recognise that the surveys themselves will change over time. The constituents of the DJSI have often changed as has the weighting given to each constituent. Equally, some surveys, such as the BitC's CR Index, will try to reflect current issues in their surveys. So for example, in its 2007 questionnaire, it included for the first time an optional question about migrant workers. This was because it was seen as a subject of concern to both the UK Government and the EU Commission. In itself, the inclusion of this question means that the BitC CR Index has become more UK- or European-centric than DJSI. In 2007, it reduced the weighting for the verification of CSR reports on the basis that many companies were now having such verification undertaken.

What such changes mean for company executives involved with these surveys is that the results from consecutive years can change without the company itself having made any significant change in its own CSR approach. Consequently, there is a need for such executives to manage the expectations of their CEO as to how they are likely to perform on a year-on-year basis – their CSR performance may remain the same, but this is no assurance that the surveys results will be the same.

The importance of completing the surveys that suit you

Our advice to our clients – and the advice to the readers of this book – is to decide which indices and surveys are important to you. If you want to develop a strong CSR image in the UK with influential stakeholders, then the BitC CR Index would be a very useful survey to focus upon. In contrast, if you are keen to develop a high-profile image amongst international SRI analysts and investors, then the DJSI should be the survey that is given the most attention.

This need to prioritise goes beyond focusing on chosen indices and surveys, and extends to developing an information provision strategy for the various stakeholders. This includes focusing on specific indices, but also involves a more positive approach to information requests. Too often, we have seen all such requests being treated with the same level of importance by company executives. This extends to researching some information for specific survey requests. A better approach is to refer all other requests for information and completion of questionnaires (outside of the selected indices) to the information provided on the website (or in hard copy elsewhere) – more of that in Chapter 17 on stakeholder engagement and communications.

Sources

1 Full information about the DJSI (including the list of companies that are members) can be found on its website: www.sustainability-indexes.com.

2 Information about SAM can be found on its website: www.sam-group.com.

3 Information about FTSE4Good can be found the FTSE website: www.ftse.com/Indices/FTSE4Good_Index_Series/index.jsp.

4 See www.ftse.com/Indices/FTSE4Good_Index_Series/Downloads/FTSE4Good_10_Year_Report.pdf.

5 The press release associated with this report can be found on the USA SIF website: ussif.org/news/releases/pressrelease.cfm?id=168.

6 A more in-depth review of Aviva's investment approach can be found on its website: www.avivainvestors.co.uk/asset_classes/equities/sustainable_and_responsible_investment/SRI_Process/index.htm

7 Information about Henderson's approach towards sustainable and responsible investment can be found on the SRI part of its website: www.3.henderson.com/sites/henderson/sri/philosophy.aspx.

8 Details of the Hermes Principles can be found in its responsible investment section on its website: www.hermes.co.uk/corporate_governance/corporate_governance_introduction.htm.

9 For more information about EIRIS, see: www.eiris.org.

10 For more information about PIRC, see: www.pirc.co.uk.

11 For more information about MSCI, see: www.msci.com/products/indices/thematic/esg/.

9

CSR – the legal and the quasi-regulatory background

Observers of the developments in CSR have often asked 'What is the legal background to it?' In many respects, this question can be interpreted as – is CSR a 'must do'? As ever, the answer is not that simple, since it implies that CSR is a new discipline – and hence new legislation is expected to relate to it which would be the driving force for its introduction by a company. For CSR, however, the driving forces come from a wide range of legal and quasi-legal sources.

In trying to answer this question, we will look at three areas:

- legislation that exists relating to the individual components of CSR;
- legislation that exists, or is proposed, that relates to the reporting of CSR; and
- the quasi-regulatory areas that have influence (but are not mandatory) on companies to operate within their guidelines.

An overview for each area is provided below. More detail of the legislation that relates to the individual CSR components is given in subsequent chapters

Legislation relating to CSR components

CSR can be described as relating to five main elements:

- corporate governance;
- the community;
- the environment;
- the workplace; and
- the marketplace – customers and suppliers.

Corporate governance

Most readers, particularly those involved in the legal or financial issues facing a company, are expected to be familiar with the detail of the current business law pertaining to the United Kingdom. Consequently, this chapter will give an overview of the general issues of the laws that relate to CSR, rather than providing chapter and verse, although more details are given in the chapters focusing on individual CSR elements.

For corporate governance, the key elements to be considered by listed companies are described in what is now known as the UK Corporate Governance Code (previously the Combined Code). It is being constantly updated by the Financial Reporting Council (FRC) – the body responsible for the Code. Prior to the introduction of the UK Corporate Governance Code in 2010, the last revisions were recommended in 2007, and the FRC has already indicated it intends to revise the new code in the light of its paper 'Effective Company Stewardship – Next Steps' (see chapter 2). The code incorporates corporate reporting, risk management and executive remuneration as well as board structures and practices.

As has been seen in chapter 2, corporate governance is now considered to take account of CSR-related elements – what the ABI calls ESG (environmental, social and governance) issues relating to non-financial information included within annual reports and accounts – as well as the use of non-financial key performance indicators (KPIs) as the criteria for executive remuneration incentive programmes.

Corporate governance also relates to CSR in the context of business practices, particularly in the UK, where the Bribery Act 2010 heightened the need for companies to have anti-bribery and corruption procedures in place by introducing a new corporate crime of 'failure to prevent' bribery.

This means that companies unable to demonstrate that they have implemented 'adequate procedures' to prevent corrupt practices within their ranks or by third parties on their behalf could be exposed to unlimited fines as well as other collateral consequences, such as debarment from government business. The Act makes it clear that it is immaterial whether a bribe is paid by a company itself or by a third party acting on its behalf (i.e. agents, etc). The company, not the third party, is ultimately accountable.

To comply with this Act, companies should ensure they have the following in place:

- a code of conduct with detailed policies and procedures;
- an effective anti-bribery/corruption policy;
- clear clauses in agency and other agreements to make it clear that bribery is not acceptable when working on behalf of the company;
- procedures to rapidly report (and enable staff/others to report) any bribery or potential bribery issues;
- investigative procedures (including internal audit) and means of resolution for (potential) bribery issues;
- training and communication processes in place for staff and agents;
- regular monitoring/audit processes to effectively be able to measure and demonstrate that 'adequate procedures' are in place and that there is a clear understanding that bribery in any form is unacceptable.

The community

In terms of the community, there is little legislation – if any – that guides a company regarding how it should relate to its local or national community, other than that which defines how it should operate in matters to do with noise or effluent pollution.

The environment

This is an area that is already well regulated and the following are but a few of the regulatory requirements with which a company has to comply. This list has been selected to relate to the key questions that would be asked of a company in terms of its CSR performance:

- pollution standards;
- use of hazardous chemicals;
- disposal of waste materials (including packaging);
- duty of care;
- standards of road transport safety; and
- green house gas emissions (both from the perspective of air quality, and for those companies affected by carbon trading and reporting, from the perspective of reduction in carbon dioxide emissions or their equivalent).

The workplace

In the workplace there is also a high degree of regulation, often driven by the EU's Social Chapter,[1] to which the UK Government is now driving compliance – somewhat belatedly compared with the approach adopted in other EU countries. The social chapter was developed as part of the Maastricht Treaty in 1992. The UK Government initially negotiated an opt-out, but the Labour government, elected in 1997, signed up to the Social Chapter in the Amsterdam Treaty of 1997 (which came into force in 1999). The social policy element of the chapter covers four main areas regarding workers:

- workers' health and safety;
- workers' communication;
- workers' rights; and
- working conditions.

Some of these were already in place in the legislation of the United Kingdom. A good example is the workers' health and safety legislation now dealt with under the umbrella of the Health and Safety Commission, based on the Health and Safety at Work Act of 1974. The work of this Commission has been instrumental in major advances in reducing injuries and ill-health including established occupational diseases. Throughout that time, consultation with industry, unions, local government and other stakeholders has been a core principle of the way the Commission works. But in addition, for certain occupations there has also been specific legislation. An example is that of transport drivers, for whom the Road Transport Directive[2] (based on the Working Time Directive, derived from the Social Chapter) defines the numbers of hours that a transport driver can drive in a working day, as well as the number and length of breaks they are required to take.

The workers' communications legislation has been driven by the EU directives – especially the Information and Consultation Directive that gives employees (in businesses of over 50 employees) the right to be informed about the business' economic situation, informed and consulted about employment prospects and informed and consulted about substantial changes in work organisation. This directive came into force in March 2005, on a phased basis.

Workers' rights have been defined by a number of different sets of UK legislation. Probably those longest standing have been those relating to discrimination, based on gender, race, and now disability. The first piece of legislation enacted in the UK was that relating to equal opportunities, starting with the Equal Pay Act of 1970, followed by the Sex Discrimination Act of 1975. These were followed by the Race Relations Act of 1976, and most recently by the Disability Discrimination Act (DDA) – first introduced in 1995, although with its implementation is being phased-in three parts. Part 3 of the DDA (including extending the Act to small enterprises and treating cancer as a disability) finally became law in October 2004, and brought UK legislation into line with the European Union Equal Rights Directive so far as it relates to disability discrimination. This focus on non-discrimination continues as the UK Government has brought all legislative areas under the auspices of the Equality and Human Rights Commission; this has been reinforced by the passing of the Equality Act 2010.[3]

This consolidated previous Acts, and instigated further reporting requirements. These are being phased in. The majority of the requirements affect the bodies in the public sector, with the following key actions and dates of implementation:

- employee profile: January 2012 (Schools April 2012) (and annual update);
- equality objectives: April 2012;
- age goods and services: April 2012;
- gender pay gap reporting: 250+ employees April 2013; and
- political parties – diversity data: April 2013.

Whilst these relate to public bodies, it is highly possible that organisations that supply goods or services to the public sector will be affected. The likelihood is that a public body's requests for quotation will require similar statements and information from those organisations seeking to supply to that public body.

Having said that, it is important to be mindful of the BIS consultation that is seeking listed companies to report upon gender-based information relating to their workforce (see chapter 2).

Other legislation affecting the workplace includes the Working Time Regulations of 1998 that laid down the maximum number of hours that a worker could work in a week, as well as the Trade Union Acts that determined the right of the workforce to freedom of association. There have been many of these since 1871, the most recent being the Trade Union Reform and Employment Rights Act of 1993 and the Employment Rights Act of 1999 that assists unions in claiming recognition.

The marketplace

This area is less well defined – at least as far as the supply chain is concerned. In the case of supply, there is little legislation that can be deemed to be focused on issues that relate to CSR. Even the issue of prompt payment (which is relevant to small suppliers) is seen as an item of government agenda, rather than a legislative right, with the UK Government being supportive of the *Better Payment Practice Guide*.

However, often health and safety legislation relating to customers can impact on the supply chain – as is the case with products such as toys. The issues that Mattel faced regarding its recall of toys in 2007 called into question the quality of its outsourced manufacturing in places such as China. Whilst this was found subsequently to be due to design faults within the initial specifications, the EU Commission called toy companies together to discuss their use of outsourced supply chains. As a result, the EU deliberated whether to introduce additional legislation about the quality of toy manufacture;[4] it issued a new Toy Safety Directive in 2009.

Customers (as distinct from clients, who are typically companies in their own right) are better protected by legislation that has elements of CSR within it. Such legislation includes:

- the rights of the customer with respect to misleading advertising and marketing (overseen by the Office for Fair Trading through such legislation as the Control of Misleading Advertisements Regulations of 1988);
- responsibility for product safety (enacted as the General Product Safety Regulations of 1994 and the EC Product Liability Directive);
- product labelling (covered by a variety of legislation, dependent on the nature of the product – for example, the UK Register of Food Standards for Organic Food Production, enacted in 2001); and
- the right to return inferior goods bought over the internet or by mail order (enacted as the Consumer Protection (Distance Selling) Regulations 2000).

As can be seen from the list above, for a company based in, and wholly operating in, the UK (or for that matter the EU) the components of CSR are already well regulated. In this respect, performing better than average in CSR means exceeding the minimum legislative requirements already laid down.

However, the challenge becomes greater for those companies operating outside the UK and the EU, and the more they are involved with developing countries, as distinct from developed countries, the greater is the challenge.

The issues in these instances revolve around the extent to which the companies in question use their corporate power to influence their *modus operandi* in these countries – using their home country standards as the basis for their operational approaches as distinct from the legislative framework in the developing countries (which will generally tend to be less demanding of companies than is the case in the developed world).

In both these circumstances – those companies who operate solely within the UK, and those who operate particularly within the developing world – the challenges of CSR relate to the extent to which they are willing to use their corporate ethos to demonstrate responsible approaches to the manner in which they do business – *over and above* what may be expected by reason of the legislative environment in the countries in which they operate.

Legislation relating to CSR reporting

It is in this area that much of the discussion about CSR and legislation generally focuses. The debate is to what extent companies should be required to tell their stakeholders about the ways in which they operate and the extent to which these operations are acting responsibly.

One of the challenges for the drafters of any legislation that prescribes how a company should operate is the difficulty of describing activity that often may be considered to be intangible – or at the very least subject to several different interpretations. Nevertheless, this difficulty has not deterred government legislators from attempting to develop legislative frameworks for such activities.

French legislation

The French government enacted the New Economic Regulations law in May 2001,[5] compelling companies to report about the social and environmental impacts of their activity. The law applied to the annual reports of 2002 that were first published in 2003.

The law required companies to include the following information in their company reports:

The workplace:

- total workforce;
- working hours, for full- and part-time employees;
- earnings and welfare costs;
- absenteeism and its grounds;
- recruitment, with distinction between fixed-term contracts and permanent contracts;
- analysis of possible difficulties with recruitment;
- lay-offs and their grounds;
- overtime;
- labour from outside the company;
- plans for staff cuts;
- protection of employment;
- efforts of redeployment, reemployment and attendant measures;
- assessment of collective agreements;
- health and safety;
- training; and
- gender profiles and the employment and the integration of disabled workers.

The company must demonstrate how it ensures that its subcontractors and its subsidiaries respect the measures stipulated by the fundamental conventions of the International Labour Organisation.

The environment:

The company's annual report is required to include the following environmental information:

- consumption of water resources, raw materials, energy;
- measures taken to improve energy efficiency including use of renewable energy sources;
- emissions – air, water and soil;
- pollution – noise and olfactory pollution;
- waste;
- biodiversity – measures taken to reduce damage to biological equilibrium, natural ecosystems, protected animal and plant species;
- the company's course of action for certification of environmental issues;
- conformity to legal procedures and regulations relating to environment;
- incurred environmental expenditure;
- environmental management, training and information of the employees;
- provisions and guaranties allocated to environmental risks; and
- fines and compensations relating to environmental issues.

In addition to these detailed analyses, the company's report must show also how the company takes into account the territorial impact of its activities as far as employment and regional development are concerned (wherever its operations are based).

Also, it is required to describe its relationships (both for the French parent and any foreign subsidiaries) with education institutions, associations for the protection of the environment, consumer's associations and populations living locally to the company's operations.

Ground breaking as this law was (not only for French companies, but also for countries within the EU) the issue is whether it has had an impact on the operations of those companies to which it applies. The manager of one of our clients had recently moved from a French company and her view was that companies conformed to the law, but had not necessarily taken it into their culture and embedded it within their operating processes.

In some respects, having the legislation define what should be reported leads to a 'dumbing down' of individual companies' approaches.

Certainly, Arese (now known as Vigeo[6]), a French corporate responsibility rating agency, commented that the law failed in defining specific indicators, did not require any auditing of the required information and had no sanctions for failure to comply with the reporting requirements.

Other EU countries

Certainly the French legislation is the widest-ranging CSR-related legislation of all EU countries. Others have some, if not a wide, form of CSR reporting-related legislation. Denmark, Norway and Sweden all have legislation requiring companies to report on their environmental impacts. Others have legislation relating to pension funds and their position on social and environmental matters in their investment decisions (e.g. Germany, Italy, Belgium and Sweden). Belgian companies (and subsidiaries of foreign corporations based there) have, since 1996, been obliged to report on their social performance over a three-year period. Others have voluntary guidelines (e.g. Austria). However, the most influential government initiative has been that of the Netherlands, whose government issued an annual benchmark which ranks companies on the quality of their CSR reports. Clearly not all government initiatives that result in positive change need to be legislative driven.

Legislative activity in the European Union

In many respects, the French law was seen as pre-empting anticipated EU legislation in the area of CSR. However, this was less forthcoming than expected.

The process commenced in July 2001 when the EU published its Green Paper 'Promoting a European framework for corporate social responsibility'.[7] This was one of the outcomes of the Lisbon Summit of 2000. This summit set the strategic goals for Europe and, for the first time, the European Council made statements about CSR, seeking contributions from businesses in meeting those strategic goals.

The Green Paper was followed in 2002 by the EC Commission's 'Communication on corporate social responsibility'. The outcome of these deliberations emphasised the need for business to operate responsibly, but surprisingly to many observers (especially the NGOs), avoided the regulatory path, stressing the need for voluntary action on the part of companies.

As a result, the EU set up its Multi-stakeholder Forum on CSR. This took contributions from nearly 50 representatives, covering business, consumer groups, and NGOs. Its objectives were to:

- direct EC efforts to put the business case for CSR to large and small companies;
- consider how best to achieve convergence among codes of business conduct;
- strengthen research on CSR;
- attempt to use the European Social Fund to promote CSR in management training; and
- agree guidelines for voluntary social labelling schemes.

It concluded its deliberations in June 2004 after what it described as its '20 months intense learning and dialogue'. Its analysis continued to focus on reporting in the mode of voluntary rather than regulatory. Its recommendations covered three aspects:

- raising awareness and improving knowledge on CSR – which included the recommendation that public authorities should include CSR within their procurement tendering approaches;
- developing the competencies and capacity is to help mainstreaming CSR; and
- ensuring an enabling environment for CSR.

The EU Council had to respond to the findings of the Multi-stakeholder Forum. It is apparent that some other stakeholders – NGOs and union representatives – believed that regulation would be forthcoming in the future, and indeed, felt that the forum failed in its aim to lay the groundwork of a European framework for CSR.

However, others, typically companies, felt that the forum had been successful. This was in helping all those involved to gain a common understanding of corporate social responsibility and its complexities. But in addition, it was felt that, within the three aspects described above, the forum made nine recommendations on the way forward at a European level. In particular, they felt its progress on two recommendations – the need for transparency, and the role of public authorities in encouraging corporate social responsibility – was beyond what might have been expected at the outset.

Given the political complexities of an expanded EU, it was difficult to anticipate what might be the outcomes of the Multi-stakeholder Forum. However, the appointment of new Commissioners in late 2004 meant that the EU took a political swing away from the strategic goals of the Lisbon summit.

However, there were milestones scheduled that related to the EU's deliberations. These were in many respects more of a series of low key actions, rather the announcement of the anticipated EU-based legislation. First, the Dutch, as President of the EU, placed CSR on its agenda for the November 2004 presidency conference. However, this did not add anything of substance. Secondly, the new European Commission produced its 'Communication on CSR' in March 2006 – a year later than had been expected. Grandly entitled 'Implementing the partnership for growth and jobs: Making Europe a pole of excellence on corporate social responsibility', the communication took a voluntary stance – 'because CSR is fundamentally about voluntary business behaviour, an approach involving additional obligations and administrative requirements for business risks being counter-productive and would be contrary to the principles of better regulation. Acknowledging that enterprises are the primary actors in CSR, the Commission has decided that it can best achieve its objectives by working more closely with European business'. This move was of concern to both NGOs and trade unions, who thought that CSR legislation was a way they could achieve their aims.

The third milestone that was planned for 2006 was a 'state of the union' EU stakeholder meeting on CSR. This proved to be another false dawn and the position of the Commission currently (and for some time to come) is that the voluntary stance is one that it continues to advocate as the only way forward.

However, CSR remains on the agenda for the EU and in 2011 it published its communication on its renewed CSR strategy. CSR at EU level will remain voluntary, but the Commission believes that, given the current economic crises, by renewing efforts to promote CSR now, it will assist the creation of conditions favourable to sustainable growth, responsible business behaviour and durable employment generation in the medium and long term.

The communication indicated the Commission will seek to introduce measures to encourage governments and corporations to adopt more extensive CSR programmes. These measures divide into those that are in the control of the Commission which intends to:

- create in 2013 multi-stakeholder CSR platforms in a number of relevant industrial sectors, for enterprises, their workers and other stakeholders to make public commitments on the CSR issues relevant to each sector and jointly monitor progress;
- launch, from 2012 onwards, a European award scheme for CSR partnerships between enterprises and other stakeholders;
- address the issue of misleading marketing related to the environmental impacts of products (so-called 'green-washing') in the context of the report on the application of the Unfair Commercial Practices Directive, foreseen for 2012, and considers the need for possible specific measures on this issue;
- initiate an open debate with citizens, enterprises and other stakeholders on the role and potential of business in the twenty-first century, with the aim of encouraging common understanding and expectations, and carry out periodic surveys of citizen trust in business and attitudes towards CSR;
- launch a process in 2012 with enterprises and other stakeholders to develop a code of good practice for self- and co-regulation exercises, which should improve the effectiveness of the CSR process;
- facilitate the better integration of social and environmental considerations into public procurement as part of the 2011 review of the Public Procurement Directives, without introducing additional administrative burdens for contracting authorities or enterprises, and without undermining the principle of awarding contracts to the most economically advantageous tender;
- consider a requirement on all investment funds and financial institutions to inform all their clients (citizens, enterprises, public authorities etc.) about any ethical or responsible investment criteria they apply or any standards and codes to which they adhere;
- provide further financial support for education and training projects on CSR under the EU Lifelong Learning and Youth in Action Programmes, and launch an action in 2012 to raise the awareness of education professionals and enterprises on the importance of cooperation on CSR;
- create with Member States in 2012 a peer review mechanism for national CSR policies;
- monitor the commitments made by European enterprises with more than 1,000 employees to take account of internationally recognised CSR principles and guidelines, and take account of the ISO Standard 26000 Guidance on Social Responsibility in its own operations;
- work with enterprises and stakeholders in 2012 to develop human rights guidance for a limited number of relevant industrial sectors, as well as guidance for small and medium-sized enterprises, based on the UN Guiding Principles;
- publish by the end of 2012 a report on EU priorities in the implementation of the UN Guiding Principles, and thereafter to issue periodic progress reports; and
- identify ways to promote responsible business conduct in its future policy initiatives towards more inclusive and sustainable recovery and growth in third countries, and those that require actions by governments of member states for which the Commission:

- invites member states to develop or update by mid-2012 their own plans or national lists of priority actions to promote CSR in support of the Europe 2020 strategy, with reference to internationally recognised CSR principles and guidelines and in cooperation with enterprises and other stakeholders, taking account of the issues raised in this communication;
- invites all large European enterprises to make a commitment by 2014 to take account of at least one of the following sets of principles and guidelines when developing their approach to CSR: the UN Global Compact, the OECD Guidelines for Multinational Enterprises, or the ISO Standard 26000: Guidance on Social Responsibility;
- invites all European-based multinational enterprises to make a commitment by 2014 to respect the ILO Tri-partite Declaration of Principles Concerning Multinational Enterprises and Social Policy;
- expects all European enterprises to meet the corporate responsibility to respect human rights, as defined in the UN Guiding Principles; and
- invites EU member states to develop by the end of 2012 national plans for the implementation of the UN Guiding Principles.

Whilst some of the 'intends to' are of an awareness and persuasive nature, some are more powerful because they involve responsibilities that the EU can directly impact upon. The two that are of significance are:

- the issue of misleading marketing related to the environmental impacts of products – which, given a Directive is to be introduced, could have an impact on the nature of marketing approaches towards 'eco friendly' products and services;
- facilitate the better integration of social and environmental considerations into public procurement as part of the 2011 review of the Public Procurement Directives – since this Directive will impact the procurement approaches by all states this is likely to have a significant impact for all corporations dealing with supplies to the public sector.

In addition, there are actions that indicate the Commission may attempt to engage public opinion in the debate about levels of trust in corporations. It may:

- initiate an open debate with citizens, enterprises and other stakeholders on the role and potential of business in the twenty-first century – which could lead into a public debate about trust in business and would play into the hands of those states that are concerned about corporate governance, as is the case with Germany, which is seeking to eliminate the comply or explain principle, and move purely to a 'comply' principle;
- consider a requirement on all investment funds and financial institutions to inform all their clients about any ethical or responsible investment criteria – whilst this is already in place in the UK with the Pension Funds Amendment Act, a possible interpretation of the Commission's statement is a further tightening, and moving from a 'light touch' to a compliance approach.

But developments along the lines described above relate to the Commission's priorities and its own authority. Much will depend on the outcomes of European politics and economic fortunes when, or if, the Eurozone financial crisis is finally resolved.

But whilst the EU has moved from legislation to voluntary actions, other countries – notably in the developing world – have moved the other way. Both Indonesia and the Philippines passed legislation in 2007 requiring companies to implement CSR programmes. The Indonesian action is possibly the first instance of CSR being mandated by law. Much of the focus relates to the activities of the extractive industries and is intended to ensure that indigenous people are given fair reward and community benefit for the industrial activities taking place in their midst.

UK legislative developments

The EU's approach of encouraging individual member states to decide upon their own appropriate legislative action brings us to UK legislation: the Operating and Financial Review (OFR) and the Business Review.

The Pension Fund Amendment Act

Before we discuss the Operating and Financial Review (OFR), let us first address an earlier example of government legislation, whose tone has set the scene for the OFR in terms of a 'soft touch on the tiller'. This was the amendment to the Occupational Pension Schemes (Investment) Regulations 1996 that took effect from July 2000. This required trustees of pension funds to include in their Statement of Investment Principles the following two statements:

- 'The extent (if at all), to which social, environmental or ethical considerations are taken into account in the selection, retention and realisation of investments.'
- 'The policy (if any), directing the exercise of the rights (include voting rights), attaching to investments.'

At the time this amendment was issued, there were concerns that it had few or no teeth. Indeed, if pension fund trustees were so minded, their response to these two statements could be in the negative. The Minister involved, Stephen Timms, indicated that he was more interested in achieving increased transparency, rather than securing direction of investment by the back door.

Since this amendment, the view has changed; most observers now believe that the amendment has caused pension fund trust trustees to take far greater cognisance of the CSR issues relating to the companies in which they have invested. This was, indeed, an example of the government successfully taking 'a soft touch on the tiller' to achieve attitudinal changes without heavy regulatory burdens.

This 'soft touch' approach was supposed to have been emulated in the government's approach towards the OFR and the Business Review, with the latter being non-prescriptive.

The Business Review reporting legislation

The UK's Business Review reporting legislation (described in detail in chapter 2, including a description of the OFR) has impacted on the requirement for companies to address CSR elements within their annual report and accounts. These elements, referred to as non-financial matters, are included 'to the extent necessary' as deemed by the directors. This phrase means that the directors could determine which non-financial aspects are pertinent to the success of their business strategy. This does not mean that all CSR aspects need to be referred to in the Annual Report or that an annual report requires a CSR report to be included.

The requirement initially was fairly light and required all companies to include information relating to environmental matters and employee matters. In the Companies Act 2006, this was enhanced for listed companies to 'include information about:

- environmental matters, including the impact of the company's business on the environment, with appropriate KPIs;
- the company's employees (with appropriate KPIs);
- social and community issues;
- any policies of the company in relation to those matters and the effectiveness of those policies; and
- information about the person with whom the company has contractual or other arrangements which are essential to the business of the company'.

The impact of the non-financial corporate reporting has been to raise the profile of CSR, to the extent that nowadays there are few, if any, listed companies that do not report on CSR items within their annual reports. Indeed there are many that provide a considerable amount of CSR detail within them. This impact has been reinforced by actions taken by the likes of the Association of British Insurers advising companies of the expectations of their members (representing significant investors in British industry and commerce) as regards reporting on ESG matters.

It can be seen that the legislative background is somewhat lagging behind the pressures that are building for companies to demonstrate CSR from the investment and benchmarking indices. Legislation and investment are not the only pressures that companies are facing. When considering CSR, there are also the quasi-regulatory pressures.

The quasi-regulatory background

So far we have looked at legislation driven from national governments, such as the UK and France, as well as legislative attempts from the EU. Just like the UK's legislative framework is driven by EU directives (it is estimated that at least 80% of UK current legislative activity is based on EU legislation) so too is national (and EU) legislation driven by international activities, which are often UN-led.

First, we will review international laws that both impact governments, and also affect companies that operate internationally. These laws (or treaties) act to form guidelines under which companies should operate, particularly in the developing world. Subsequently, we will review the activities being undertaken by the UN, particularly those instigated by Kofi Annan, when he was Secretary General. Perhaps unlike previous Secretary Generals, he has recognised that, as well as the UN's role as a peacekeeper, it also has a role to promote the economic and health development of the emerging countries. In recognising this role, he came to understand that the power of the multinationals can be turned to good, provided they are given an infrastructure and rules within which to play their part.

The ILO

Firstly, looking at the laws and treaties, it is remarkable how many of them have their foundations in the First or Second World Wars. The International Labour Organisation (ILO) is the oldest institution. It was set up in 1919 as a result of the Treaty of Versailles, which brought the League of Nations into being. It became the first specialised agency of the United Nations in 1946.

Its role is to formulate international labour standards, which take the form of conventions and recommendations[8]. Its work is wide-ranging in the area of employment and it is unique in having a tripartite structure in which employers' and workers' representatives have an equal voice with governments in shaping policies and programmes. The key ILO conventions represent eight areas that have become the basis of many other international laws:

- The 'forced labour' convention (established in 1930);
- The 'freedom of association and protection of the right to organise' convention (1948);
- The 'right to organise and collective bargaining' convention (1949);
- The 'equal remuneration' convention (1951);
- The 'abolition of forced labour' convention (1957);
- The 'discrimination (employment occupation)' convention (1958);
- The 'minimum wage' convention (1973);
- The 'worst forms of child labour' convention (1999).

Whilst business representatives form part of the ILO, multinational businesses are actually not signatories of the ILO. Only countries can sign up to the ILO conventions and be bound by them. Once countries have ratified the conventions, any company operating within those countries, or under the law of those countries, has to comply. As you will see when we look at the workplace components of CSR, much of the measurements and policies required of companies relate back to these ILO conventions.

The UN's UDHR

The next institution (or treaty) to be established was the United Nations Universal Declaration of Human Rights (UNHDR) constituted by the United Nations in 1948. Remarkably, the content of this declaration has changed little since that time. It now represents a total of 30 articles,[9] including those conventions established by the ILO, but also covering aspects such as personal privacy, freedom to marry and found a family and the right to be presumed innocent until proven guilty.

The issue of human rights is often considered by companies to be of relevance only if they are operating in the developing world. However, the EU has developed human rights as one of its legislative platforms, with a result that all EU countries are required to have human rights legislation. This requires governments to consider issues relating to individual human rights, but also requires companies to think about how their actions impinge upon individual human rights. A good example is that one of the earliest instances of litigation against a company in the UK was initiated by the local community living around Heathrow, who contended that their human rights were being affected as a result of the noise pollution created by night flights landing at Heathrow. Rightly or wrongly, human rights is now becoming an argument that has some potency when an individual wishes to complain against the operations or actions of corporations.

The OECD

Similarly becoming a significant force, particularly on multinational corporations, are the Organisation for Economic Cooperation and Development's (OECD) Guidelines for Multinational Enterprises – or more correctly – 'The declaration on international investment and multinational enterprises'.[10] The OECD was set up in 1960 and its original members reflected those nations from the developed world. Its membership has since expanded, but, in essence, this 'developed world' characteristic still remains.

This characteristic has some value since the Guidelines have been written from the perspective of how companies located in the developed world should act in their dealings with, and their operations in, the developing world.

The Guidelines (updated in 2011) are intended to reflect good practice in terms of business relations and avoidance of exploitation. The general policies cover 11 areas that an enterprise should take into account in the countries in which they operate and include:

- contributing to economic, social and environmental progress, aiming to achieve sustainable development;
- respecting human rights;
- encouraging local capacity building;
- encouraging human capital formation;
- refraining from seeking or accepting exemptions from statutory frameworks related to human rights, environmental, social or financial issues;
- supporting and upholding good corporate governance;
- fostering confidence and mutual trust between Enterprises and societies in which they operate;
- promoting employee awareness of and compliance with company policies;
- refraining from action against employees who make bona fide whistleblowing reports;

- encouraging business partners to follow the guidelines; and
- abstaining from improper political involvement.

Whilst these 11 areas form the basis for legislation in the developed countries, the Guidelines take the form of principles to which multinational corporations are expected to adhere in their operations in the developing world. Again, many of the measures, used in indices and surveys assessing performance in terms of CSR, relate back to these 11 areas.

The UN Global Compact

A similar approach to gaining influence amongst corporate leaders has been developed by United Nations in the form of its UN Global Compact. This was introduced at the World Economic Forum, in Davos in January 1999, when the then UN Secretary General, Kofi Annan, challenged world business leaders to 'embrace and enact' the Global Compact.[11]

This challenge covered both business leaders' corporate practices, and also their support of appropriate public policies. Initially it covered nine principles, covering human rights, employment practices, and environmental practices:

- supporting and respecting the protection of international human rights;
- ensuring their own corporations are not implicit in human rights abuses;
- upholding the right of freedom of association and recognition of the right for collective bargaining;
- eliminating forced and compulsory labour;
- abolishing child labour;
- eliminating discrimination in employment and occupation;
- supporting precautionary approaches to environmental challenges;
- undertaking initiatives to promote greater environmental responsibility; and
- encouraging the development and diffusion of environmentally friendly technologies.

The UN has been effective in bringing companies on board with this Global Compact. First, it has encouraged all its suppliers to the UN to participate in the Global Compact – a good example of governmental organisations leading by example in the purchasing field. Secondly, the UN has been successfully lobbying to bring on board major corporate leaders and encourage those that are already participating in the Global Compact to bring on board their peers.

In addition, the UN has used the power of the internet. Not only are companies expected to make clear statement of their support for the Global Compact, informing their stakeholders and introducing it into their staff training and development programmes, but they are also expected, once a year, to produce a concrete example of progress made or lessons learned in implementing the principles for posting on the UN's Global Compact website.

In the Global Compact Summit of 2004, the feeling was that it had become more than a top-down directive, to such an extent that as a result of an extensive consultation, the overwhelming majority of participants wanted to strengthen the Compact. A tenth principle has been added:

- Businesses should work against corruption in all its forms, including extortion and bribery.

In addition, various groups have created their own initiatives (e.g. cotton in Africa) aiming to establish Africa and cotton as a quality label for cotton produced in the developing world.

The UN Global Compact has gained momentum each year since its launch in 2000; by December 2007, it had grown to over 3,600 businesses in 100 countries around the world. In 2011, over 8,000 businesses had signed up to the Compact around the world (around 5,000 of which are classified as active). The number of EU businesses has risen from 600 in 2006 to nearly 2,000. Nevertheless, the US participation remains low – with only 208 businesses participating listed as active, of which about 50 are classified as publicly traded companies.

The Global Compact structure has continued to evolve and following a comprehensive review of the Global Compact's governance during 2004–05, a new governance framework was adopted in August 2005. Based on its voluntary nature, the governance framework is designed to be non-bureaucratic and to foster greater involvement in and ownership of the initiative by participants and other stakeholders. Governance functions are shared by six entities, including local networks.

However, although it has become an important driver for CSR, with over 40% of companies surveyed by McKinsey[12] saying that it has had a positive effect on their organisation, if the participants' geographic distribution does not reflect the real corporate universe, it may not be considered as wholly legitimate.

There remains the feeling that the UN Global Compact is only relevant to those companies that have large international footprints (and hence face business risks of an international nature) which is probably the reason why in the US (which has a very large internal market) so few companies have signed up.

The Global Sullivan Principles

The UN Global Compact owes much to the groundbreaking work undertaken by the Rev. Sullivan, an American Baptist Preacher who helped developed minority owned businesses and non-profit ventures for inner-city residents in Philadelphia. He was also a member of the Board of Directors of the General Motors Corp from 1970–90. In 1977, he developed the Sullivan Principles (now known as Global Sullivan Principles of Social Responsibility).[13] These were targeted at companies for their endorsement; the eight main principles are fairly common with that of the Global Compact, the ILO conventions, and the UN declaration of human rights. The Sullivan Principles are a common feature of US business commitment and the companies and organisations endorsing them tend to be either US-owned, or have a strong presence in the USA, where the status of the UN is perhaps not as high as in Europe or the developing world.

The Earth Summits

The UN is using its political clout to ensure that governments and corporations are aware of CSR issues, particularly as regards sustainability. It first held the UN Conference on Human Environment (now known as the 'Earth Summits') in 1970 in Stockholm. The Rio Summit in 1992 ended with the Rio Declaration on environment and development and included legally binding conventions on Climate Change and Biological Diversity, as well as the endorsing of the Precautionary Principle. The talks relating to the UN climate convention led to the development of the Kyoto Protocol, established in 1997 (which committed countries to reductions in emissions, but which the US has never ratified).

The last Earth Summit, which was held in 2002 in Johannesburg,[14] focused on other issues of sustainable development, with the introduction of Millennium Development Goals – the availability of drinking water and sanitation, access to modern energy services, improving health (and reducing infant mortality), improving global agricultural productivity, reducing the rate of biodiversity losses, along with the introduction of ecosystem management and providing global, economic and financial rules systems and markets that support sustainable development.

Since 2002, there have been no further Earth Summits – although the Millennium Development Goals remain under international government review. However, the focus has now shifted to climate change, and the successor to the Earth Summit is the Climate Change Summit, held in Bali in 2007. Its purpose was to agree the successor to the Kyoto Protocol. Its outcome was an agreement to spend the subsequent two years discussing with all parties – especially the USA – how to go about developing its successor. The Copenhagen summit in 2009 was intended to produce a consensus that delivered the replacement for Kyoto. Regrettably, the different national agendas (especially those of the USA and China) meant that this was not to be. The Durban summit, held in late 2011, was supposed to end the impasse with a legally binding framework and agreement on emissions reductions – the outcome (now known as the Durban platform) is discussed in more detail in chapter 13.

The WBCSD

The Earth Summits are not merely government jaunts. As one would expect, given the agenda of these summits, the NGOs are regular participants. However, corporate representatives are also present and a consistent presence has been the World Business Council for Sustainable Development (WBCSD).[15] This Council came together as a provider of business input for the Rio Summit, and the team of CEOs' from about 50 companies started the Council. Now, the WBCSD is a CEO-led, global association of some 200 companies dealing exclusively with business and sustainable development. These companies are drawn from nearly 40 countries with, significantly, nearly 50 companies coming from the USA. As well as participation in the Earth Summits, the WBSCD partners with the OECD, the UN Development Programme and the UN Environmental Program. The Council's aims include being the leading business advocates on issues connected with sustainable development, participating in policy development, demonstrating best practice and sharing these practices and contributing to a sustainable future for developing nations. It focuses on four key areas:

- energy and climate;
- development;
- the business role; and
- ecosystems.

In 2010, the WBCSD published its *Vision 2050* report calling for a new agenda for business. The report features a set of agreed 'must haves', which represent vital developments that WBCSD hopes organisations will consider putting in place within the next decade, to help ensure that a steady course towards global sustainability is set. They include:

- incorporating the costs of externalities – starting with carbon, ecosystem services and water – into the structure of the marketplace;
- doubling agricultural output without increasing the amount of land or water used;
- halting deforestation and increasing yields from planted forests;
- halving carbon emissions worldwide (based on 2005 levels) by 2050 through a shift to low-carbon energy systems;
- improved demand-side energy efficiency, and providing universal access to low-carbon mobility.

Reporting Standards – SA 8000, AA1000, the UN GRI and ISO 26000

There are several different sets of Reporting Standards. The first in the field were the SA8000 and the AA1000.

The SA8000 is the standard set by Social Accountability International (previously known as the Council on Economic Priorities Accreditation Agency). Its focus has been on auditing and certifying labour practices in companies and their suppliers. As such it is a more limited approach, one that has been used more by companies in the USA than in Europe, partly because of its lack of focus on issues such as the environment. However, it is often used as a benchmark by those companies seeking suppliers in the developing world and enables these companies to select those suppliers certified to SA8000, without themselves needing to undertake supplier assessment visits regarding these issues.

The AA1000 Assurance Standard (AA1000 AS)[16] has been developed by the Institute for Social Accountability (also known as Accountability). The AA1000 AS is a process standard for assessing the quality of an organisation's social, economic and environmental reporting, and related management systems. It particularly emphasises stakeholder engagement. The standard is based on an overarching principle of 'inclusivity', described as the accountability commitment (interpreted as the right of stakeholders' interests to be heard, and for companies to respond to these interests) which underpins three principles of reporting:

- materiality;
- completeness; and
- responsiveness.

The Institute is based in the UK, and this, together with its broader CSR approach, has meant it is a standard more favoured by European business.

However, of growing significance is the UN Global Reporting Initiative[17] (GRI). The GRI is a set of guidelines for companies to use in the development of their CSR reports.

This was established in 1997 as a joint initiative between CERES (The Coalition for Environmentally Responsible Economies, a US NGO) and the United Nations Environment Programme. Since its launch it has developed several versions of its guidelines, building on the experience of the companies' using them.

In 2002 it produced its second version of the Sustainability Reporting Guidelines and, based on this version, it has moved into developing guidelines for specific industry sectors, after comments that some of its indicators were too focused on manufacturing. In addition, it developed Technical Protocols, detailing the definitions and calculations for the various indicators in its Guidelines.

In 2006, it produced its third version of the Guidelines (the G3 Guidelines) which are now at version 3.1. The G4 guidelines are scheduled for 2013 and are currently being piloted. Echoing the AA100AS, the G3 Guidelines have four reporting principles to determine the context of the report – materiality, stakeholder inclusiveness, sustainability and completeness. They continue with principles to determine the quality of the report – balance, comparability, accuracy, timeliness, clarity and reliability. Sector supplements for specific industries have been produced: Financial Services (published October 2008), Electric Utilities (published April 2009), Mining and Metals (published March 2010), Food processing (published May 2010), and NGO (Published May 2010).

The G3 Guidelines do not attempt to advise on the nature or method of reporting, but focus instead on the information contained within the reports. As such, one of its main features is that every report that uses the G3 Guidelines should have a section that cross-refers between the various GRI indicators and the sections of the company's report where they would be found (and also requires the company to state if the indicators are not reported on). To meet differing levels of reporting quality, there are three levels in the system, entitled C, B, and A. The reporting criteria at each level reflect a measure of the extent of application or coverage of the GRI Reporting Framework. A 'plus' (+) is available at each level if external assurance was utilised for the report.

The G3 Guidelines are designed to ensure that reports using them will be transparent, inclusive and auditable. There are three areas of standard disclosures: strategy and profile, management approach and performance indicators. For the latter, the G3 version is both shorter and much tighter, indicating the benefit of the extensive consultation that occurred.

The guidelines structure performance indicators according to a hierarchy of category, aspect and indicator. The hierarchy is structured as follows: the figures in brackets represent the numbers of indicators for each section:

- *Direct economic impacts (9)* – covering economic performance (value generated, risks relating to climate change, coverage of benefit plan obligations, financial assistance from government), market presence (minimum wage compliance, local supply sourcing, hiring of local management), and indirect economic impacts such as infrastructure investments
- *Environmental (30)* – covering materials, energy, water, biodiversity, emissions, effluents and waste, suppliers, products and services, compliance, and transport.
- *Social:*
  - *Labour practices and decent work (14)* – covering employment, labour and management relations, occupational health and safety, training and education, and diversity and opportunity;
  - *Human rights (9)* – covering investment and procurement practices, non-discrimination, freedom of association and collective bargaining, child labour, forced and compulsory labour, security practices and indigenous rights;
  - *Society (8)* – community, corruption, public policy, anti-competitive behaviour and compliance; and
  - *Product responsibility (9)* – covering customer health and safety, products and service labelling, marketing communications, customer privacy and compliance.

In total, as at March 2011, GRI claims that around 1,800 companies have submitted reports that have been compiled according to GRI Principles. This is more than are covered in the DJSI, but less than are present in the FTSE4Good Index. These are mainly large international companies – SME's represent around 200 of the reports, of which around 60% were from Europe. With the introduction of the NGO sector supplement, there is an increase in their reporting to GRI standards, with around 50 compiling their reports to GRI. Of the total, Europe accounts for about 45% of these reports, whilst the US presence amongst GRI reports remains low with about 10% of all companies compiling GRI reports. Forty seven percent of all reports were externally assured.

However, the importance of the GRI lies not so much in its corporate coverage (many of those that may like to consider doing so are put off by the GRI's complexity of information) but rather in the fact that it is becoming seen to be an international standard for reporting. Hence it is being used as a reference point for legislators and regulators in their development of CSR-related legislation (as well as that corporate governance legislation that refers to CSR elements). In addition in 2006, GRI and the Global Compact announced they had formed a strategic alliance in which they will undertake advocacy and other partnership efforts to encourage companies and CSR organisations to support the synergistic platforms of the Global Compact and the GRI.

ISO 26000 Guidance on Social Responsibility

It is particularly interesting that the EU's CSR strategy, produced in 2011, invited all large EU companies to commit to take account of one of the following sets of guidelines – the UN Global Compact, the OECD Guidelines or the ISO 26000 Guidance on Social Responsibility.[18] Of these, ISO 26000 is the most recent.

ISO 26000 is an international standard giving guidance on CSR. It is intended for use by a wide range of organisations of all types, both public and private and in a wide range of countries both developed and developing. It aims to assist companies to operate in a socially responsible manner. It offers guidance, not requirements and, as such, is not a certification standard. It hopes to integrate international expertise on social responsibility in terms of the issues needed to be addressed and best practice in implementing CSR.

It is dubious how useful ISO 26000 will be to organisations that have already started their CSR journey, but clearly it could be of use in the developing world. Governments could use it as a benchmark for assessing companies' CSR positions.

Conclusion

This chapter has discussed both the legal and the quasi-regulatory background to CSR. I hope that what has become apparent to you is that the legal CSR initiatives are less important than the wide range of quasi-regulatory developments.

Initiatives by the UN are having significant impact with major corporate leaders especially those of multinational corporates. What is becoming the norm is that the precedents set by the likes of the UN Global Compact are being adopted by major corporations, who are then communicating their expectations and their standards to their peers in other industrial sectors, to their competitors in their own sector and to their suppliers.

Whilst it is unlikely that there will be some form of regulatory action by the EU sometime in the future, the pressure from the quasi-regulatory players means that a level playing field has been established in terms of what is expected of companies.

Sources

1 A useful guide to the EU Social Chapter and the UK's opt out was produced as a research paper for the House of Commons Library and can be found at: www.parliament.uk/briefing-papers/RP97-102.pdf.

2 Details of RoSPA's response to the consultation on rules regulating drivers' hours can be found at: www.rospa.com/roadsafety/consultations/info/domestic_drivers_hours.pdf.

3 For the latest update on the introduction of the Equality Act (and to check on latest implementation dates) access the EHRC website section at: www.equalityhumanrights.com/legal-and-policy/equality-act/.

4 To access the report on these deliberations see: ec.europa.eu/consumers/citizen/my_safety/docs/safety_measures_toy_supply_chain.pdf.

5 Information about the French Law can be found through the ORSE website: www.orse.org/gb/home/report_regulation.html

6 Information about Vigeo's work can be found at: www.vigeo.com/csr-rating-agency/.

7 Reference COM (2001) 366 Final.

8 For more detailed information about the ILO and its work, see: www.ilo.org/global/about-the-ilo/lang--en/index.htm.

9 The text of the UDHR can be found at: www.un.org/Overview/rights.html.

10 The text for the OECD Guidelines is available at: www.oecd.org.

11 Further information about the Global Compact can be found at: www.unglobalcompact.org/.

12 'The UN's role in CSR', Blair, Bugg-Levine, and Rippin: *The McKinsey Quarterly*, 17 November 2004.

13 Full details of the Global Sullivan Principles, including those organisations endorsing them can be found on the Global Sullivan Principles website: globalsullivanprinciples.org/principles.htm.

14 For information about the Johannesburg Summit, see: www.earthsummit2002.org/.

15 Information about WBCSD can be found at: www.wbcsd.ch.

16 Copies of the AA100 AS can be downloaded from the Accountability website: www.accountability.org/standards/aa1000as/index.html.

17 Further information on the GRI, including details of its Guidelines and Protocols as well as the list of companies compiling their reports according to GRI Principles, can be accessed via its website: www.globalreporting.org.

18 More details about ISO 26000 can be found at: www.iso.org/iso/social_responsibility.

PART

3

How to implement CSR in your business

The scope of CSR

This chapter reviews the scope of CSR, discusses the rationale behind it and addresses how to implement a CSR strategy by means of a simple route map. This has been developed to help companies to understand how to implement it. It also examines the differences in company approaches towards CSR, differences by size, and sector and the company's country of incorporation. Also addressed is the question of a business case for CSR.

The rationale behind CSR

Let's start by asking what is the rationale for a company to develop a CSR strategy? The challenge for companies is that they get lots of people – particularly from organisations such as trade unions and NGOs – telling them what they should do, usually on the basis that it is good for them to do so.

But corporate decision making does not work on the basis of what is good to do – it requires analysis and a rational explanation, especially if it is something that will need to be communicated and explained to shareholders.

The Chief Executive of one of our clients, a FTSE100 company, had a conversation with our direct contact (the Head of CSR) along the lines of: 'I get CSR, and why it is good for us to do it – you don't need to explain that to me. What I need to know is what the issues are if I don't do some or all of CSR?' This question is faced by every chief executive. All of them have a range of potential activities and, in selecting their chosen activities, need to develop a rationale-based set of priorities.

The answer lies in the extent to which CSR-related activities represent potential risks or opportunities to the delivery of the company's overall business strategy. The support we provided to the head of CSR was to take each of the CSR activities currently undertaken by his company, and place them into a risk management framework. This enabled us to identify those CSR activities where potential risk and associated probability meant that they should have priority as part of CSR support for the business strategy.

In that respect, the rationale for CSR should be based on the potential impact of corporate actions related to the range of stakeholders and the possible business risk or opportunity associated with each.

Developing and implementing the CSR strategy

Let's start by identifying how a company should start to develop its CSR strategy. When I started in CSR consultancy, the biggest challenge was to find a simple way to show our clients what areas they should be addressing; and how they should be developing their CSR strategy. When we met one of our clients in 2001, his desk was covered with fund manager surveys, as well as a PIRC evaluation. His request to us was simple: 'Tell me what I need to do to answer all these surveys.'

A simple enough question, but not so easy to answer! To help him we developed the CSR Route Map, an easy-to-read graphical presentation, which, in our experience, has helped many companies to consider both where they're at and where they have to go in developing their CSR approach. The Route Map is shown below:

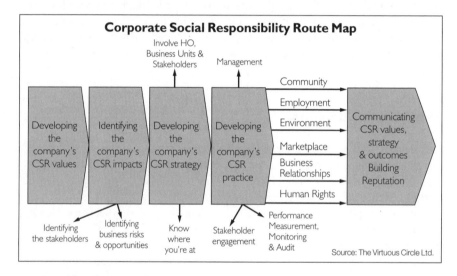

Let's take each of those block arrows and discuss briefly what each of them means. We will go into more detail about each activity as we move through the various chapters, where you will see the Route Map used as a consistent reference point.

Developing the company's CSR values

This should be the first step in considering how to develop a CSR strategy. It seems logical that the company should determine its CSR values before embarking upon a strategy. However, we have seen companies where logic does not play a strong part in developing the CSR strategy. The result is often a CSR strategy that does not relate to the company's culture and that cannot be embedded into the organisation, because the CSR values have not been established in advance.

It is important at this time to emphasise that the CSR values may be different from the corporate values. The latter are often defined as part of the *vision, mission*, and *values* that many companies now have in place. However, when you look at the values that are being described, there are often internally based values (e.g. how staff will talk to each other, the importance of teams, and importance of achieving profit, etc).

These are all perfectly acceptable – indeed, there is nothing wrong with them. However, they may not be the same as CSR values, where the focus is upon the company's relationship with stakeholders – how they're treated, how they're valued, and the manner of communication to the stakeholders. Hence, when following this Route Map, the first step is to consider the company stakeholders and to decide the company's CSR values.

Identifying the company's impact

This requires the CSR team to stand back, take an external perspective and have an objective discussion about the company's impacts. This discussion revolves around the need to consider in-depth the question: 'Who are the company's stakeholders?', with the implicit question 'Who are the key stakeholders and what are their priorities?' Once these questions are answered (do not assume that this is easy), the real question becomes apparent: What are the risks and opportunities to the business, relating to each of the key stakeholders? This comes back to the earlier discussion about the rationale for CSR. The real challenges are in considering how well you understand the views and attitudes of your stakeholders – too many companies assume they do and then are surprised when some of these stakeholders protest about one of the company's activities. There is a need to fully engage your stakeholders. The process of developing a programme of stakeholder engagement can be very challenging (see chapter 17 for an in-depth discussion).

Deciding the company's CSR strategy

Strategy development should not be new to the readers of this book. However, the CSR strategy poses challenges that I suspect few managers will have faced. One of the primary issues is the relative lack of information – generally, CSR has not been the subject of regular management reporting systems and, as a consequence, there will be significant amounts of information that are not available and will require a detailed 'data mining operation'. Frequently I need to describe the challenge of this 'mining operation' to our clients. When we go into a company to do a CSR review or audit, we are looking for 'gold nuggets' that can demonstrate the company's surprising CSR qualities. It is like turning over a stone, and finding a gold nugget underneath – except that the staff member doesn't recognise it. The reason they don't is because they become complacent about it. To quote a phrase I use often:

They don't see it as exceptional, because they don't see it as the exception.

The other aspect that represents a challenge in developing a CSR strategy is that of reconciling different attitudes towards CSR between the head office and the business units. We have often found that the attitude of head office towards CSR will be dramatically different to those of the business units.

Not only are these attitudes different, but often the business units will not make a full and frank declaration of their activities. The reasons for this are varied, but they are usually along the lines that the business units are concerned that their CSR activities are not consistent with corporate strategy and that this will result in criticism from (at the very least) the local managers if this is discovered. Alternatively, the business units 'hide their CSR activities' by allocating them to misleading account codes. So if the local business unit wants, for example, to provide a football kit to the local school's girls football team, then the cost of that kit is likely to be allocated to an account code such as sales promotion. Lastly, there is a need to involve the stakeholders, but if there is a lack of understanding about who the stakeholders are and who the priority stakeholders are, then it is a safe bet that they have not been involved in discussions about potential CSR strategic developments.

Developing a CSR practice

This is moving from the strategy to the implementation phase, and covers each of the key elements of CSR – community, workplace, environment, the marketplace and human rights. We will go into each of these in more detail later, but at this stage it is important to emphasise that each of them will require a management and governance system to ensure effective implementation. There should be an involvement with the stakeholders and, following on from the previous comments, there needs to be a performance measurement system with targets in place and an audit of the performance achieved to ensure it is realistic.

Communicating CSR values, strategies, and outcomes

This is an area that is often overlooked by companies, largely because of their failure to appreciate the value that CSR can provide in helping to build the reputation of a company. In the course of our work, we became aware of one finance institution that was very active in providing support for employee volunteering – to the tune of a seven-figure sum. This continued for some years until financial pressures caused the analysts to question the value of the activity. The issue is not whether the activity itself was right or wrong, but rather that the activity (and the business case) was not communicated to the stakeholders at large; as a result there was no perception of the resulting value added. The value of undertaking CSR strategy development and then implementing the practice is only realised if there is an effective communications programme supporting it which explains the nature of the activity and how it benefits the company.

Even using a Route Map, such as the one above, we still get asked 'What are the most important aspects'?

To me, there are three key elements to this Route Map. The first two are probably obvious – they are the block arrows at each end of the map. If you are not clear about the values, then you cannot decide the direction; if you have not communicated the direction in the actions, you've wasted the investment.

But the third key element is probably less obvious – it is 'know where you're at'. I cannot emphasise enough the need to fully understand the range of activities (usually at the front-line level) before you proceed to develop the strategy.

A strong CSR strategy will usually be built from within the company using the cultural norms that are already in place to make the company an effective organisation. If you try to build the strategy without first recognising the activities that are already in place, then the task of gaining commitment will be greater and the task of making CSR part of business practice will be almost impossible.

I will deal with the detail of each of the individual components of CSR in subsequent chapters. What is important is how different companies have different approaches towards CSR.

The difference in company approaches to CSR

Company attitudes towards CSR – by size

This section looks at how different sizes of companies have different approaches towards CSR. It is important to treat each size of company separately and we will start with the smallest companies first.

The small business

Much recent government focus in UK (and also in the EU) has been upon how it can introduce CSR to SMEs (small and medium-sized enterprises). Yet for many small businesses, there may already be a culture akin to CSR. Many of them are owner-managed. For these organisations, there is often a framework of employee support (sometimes encompassing family support in difficult circumstances). The smaller the organisation, the closer the ties between employees and it is almost impossible to develop an approach which would result in them being exploited. You, as the reader, may challenge that, giving examples of sweat shops and gang masters and you would be right to cite such instances. Yet in reality these tend to be the extreme examples of what are more often positive approaches adopted by small businesses towards their employees

Similarly in small businesses, there are already examples of the owner-manager providing personal and company support to the community – these activities are not put under the banner of 'corporate social responsibility'. The owner managers are often regular contributors to the community through associations such as the Lions Club and the local Rotary Association.

The same is true for the environment – the family nature of small businesses means that, generally speaking, they are more environmentally friendly. There will be discussions about recycling, whether it involves paper or ink cartridges (in a small office), or recycling waste material (in a small workshop).

The area where CSR is less evident for small business is in the marketplace – dealing with customers and suppliers. In many respects, this comes down to the economic power of the business. Unless it is in a particularly niche market, then a small business will be unable to monopolise its position with its customer base, or even its supplier base. The CSR issues of treating customers fairly and building relationships with suppliers are likely to be less relevant for a small business that, by implication, is not likely to be strong in either of these relationships.

The medium-sized business

The medium-sized business is where the CSR challenges become greatest. Here, the administrative structures are lean compared with those of the large businesses, primarily because of economies of scale. Often their main customers are larger organisations, so not only do they have to have CSR policies in place, but also they need to ensure they are practised, and their results measured.

The government – then in the form of the DTI (now the Department for Business, Innovation and Skills – BIS) has been concerned about this and has instituted approaches towards SMEs which have helped them to develop approaches for CSR which are in line with their own capability and capacity. However, it remains fair to say that the biggest focus on CSR is amongst the larger companies.

Larger companies

It should be easier for the large businesses to cope, but even here, their approaches vary. These variations tend to be because of the need of the organisation to demonstrate its responsible approach. Quoted companies on AIM, or FTSE500, as well as privately owned companies, can often state that CSR is not a burning issue for them and as a consequence, they have decided not to invest in collating the necessary information or supporting the appropriate CSR activities.

It's a bit like saying marketing or advertising is not important, or doesn't work – the answer is to ensure that the nature of the activity is appropriate to the nature of the company concerned. Similarly, the challenge is to make CSR relevant to the needs of the company. One of the most important contributions that we can make to our clients is to reassure them that they do not need to do everything that they read about CSR. What is important is to decide what is right for their business.

In summary, it is fair to say that the reporting of CSR has, in the main, been a large quoted company initiative, but this does not mean that CSR activities lie solely in this sector. On the contrary, there is evidence of CSR across all the sectors. What is important is for SME companies to collate all the evidence available about these activities to enable them to respond to supply chain requests for CSR information that will increasingly come from their larger clients.

Sector attitudes towards CSR

Reinforcing the need to 'do what is right for their business', companies need to appreciate that different sectors will have different approaches towards CSR. Most importantly, external stakeholders will have different expectation levels for different sectors.

As an example, a local community group will expect more from a local supermarket in terms of its support for the community than it will an office-based business.

Similarly, the local expectations of a chemical business in terms of meeting environmental challenges will be greater than the expectations of a local supermarket.

To help our businesses understand how they should position themselves, we developed The Virtuous Circle's (TVC's) Radar approach. This is designed to help companies understand how they compare with their competitors, as well as the companies they aspire to emulate. This approach relies totally on information which is available on company websites. The reason for this is that if you are an external stakeholder, the website will, or is likely to be, the most complete set of information available regarding a company's CSR performance – even if the company itself is actually performing at higher levels than it makes available to the public. For the external stakeholder, 'perception is reality'.

In the Radar approach we use a scale, using ten different attributes relating to the CSR position:

- vision, values and CSR management;
- signatories and accords;
- community activities;
- environmental activities;
- marketplace activities;
- CSR communications;
- CSR innovations and initiatives;
- stakeholder engagement; and
- the extent of the CSR verification.

Each attribute is scored out of ten, giving a maximum of 100. The results of this evaluation gives us the *Radar Thermometer* providing an overall positioning of the company in question, versus its targeted competitors and peers as shown below:

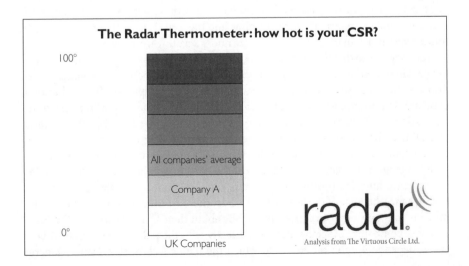

135

From the same evaluation, we are also able to produce an in-depth insight of its performance for each of the ten attributes – the Radar CSR Content Map – as can be seen below:

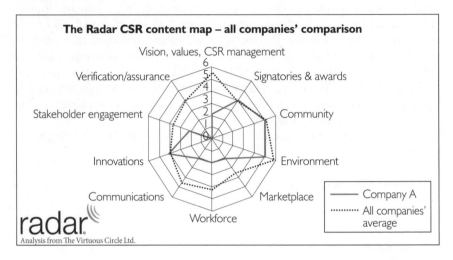

The Radar CSR content map – all companies' comparison

— Company A
·········· All companies' average

radar.
Analysis from The Virtuous Circle Ltd.

The two charts above are based on an evaluation carried out for a client. This involved a comparison of 22 companies followed by a presentation made to the board. The objective was to help directors decide the extent to which they were comfortable (or not) in being behind their peers and competitors. It also highlighted the areas in which they were strong and those in which they needed to improve their CSR performance.

High performers

In total, we have now compared over 500 companies – over 75% of them are UK quoted. Of these, the highest performers have been those within the telecom, food and drug retailers, pharmaceutical, mining, and tobacco sectors. These industry sectors are very much in the public eye and are under scrutiny from the NGOs.

You may notice that the oil and gas sector did not feature amongst the highest performers in our studies. Our studies for this sector included both oil and gas exploration companies as well as oil and gas support services companies. The exploration companies rank among the highest overall performers, but the support services companies do not feature as highly. This is largely because they do not perceive themselves as dealing with the end user; they see themselves as providing a service to the exploration companies and do not consider that they are in public eye to the same extent.

It is being in the public eye that drives the comparison between sectors. So, for example, we find that business-to-business support services will have a lower CSR performance, because of the fact that their customers are other businesses; hence, the pressure for communication from the public about their CSR activity is lower. Even for those companies in sectors that deal directly with the public, there can be differences, dependent upon the extent to which the public feels at risk. Hence, general retailers perform at a lower level than food and drug retailers because the public expectation of them is somewhat lower.

This differentiation continues into the various CSR components. So, for example, in the environmental component, food and drug retailers, together with mining, are the highest performers, largely because of public expectation that they should have the relevant policies, measures and initiatives in place to reduce their environmental impact. Contrast this with, for example, insurance companies and support services companies, whose environmental impact is lower, hence their environmental activities are also lower.

The issue of businesses providing services or products to other businesses is key in terms of affecting their CSR performance rating. In our studies, the examples of food producers and processors and the manufacturers of personal and household products (some of whom only provide private-label products so have no more than five or so direct customers) aligned with that of the support services industry, where all its customers or clients are other businesses. The fact that these companies are not in the public eye will affect the extent to which they feel the need to publish their CSR performance. However, it will not limit the extent of their CSR activity, because the businesses themselves will be under procurement pressures from their customers or clients to provide information on operational aspects such as environmental performance. They often provide this information on a confidential basis to their customers, rather than publishing it in the public domain.

Companies' published CSR performance varies by sector, depending on the extent to which they are in the public eye (and hence subject to pressure or lobbying), as well as the extent to which their direct customers impose their own CSR-related evaluation through their procurement procedures.

Country attitudes to CSR

Just as different industrial sectors will have different performance standards for CSR, so too do different countries. Our Radar approach covered a selection of European, US and rest of the world companies and the Radar Thermometer overleaf demonstrates how strongly CSR has affected UK companies in contrast to those in the USA and the rest of the world (evidenced by the extensive presence of UK companies in the DJSI).

There are several reasons for this differing level of CSR performance.

European companies

Our experience of working with companies with operations in countries such as Germany and Holland is that the different social security systems place different expectations on companies compared with similar ones in the UK. So, for example, when I asked Dutch or German subsidiary operations about their links with charities, I experienced blank looks. When probed, their response was that the taxes they paid to their government were meant to provide support for disadvantaged groups and, as a result, companies were not expected to give donations or create programmes for charities, as these areas were adequately covered by social security programmes.

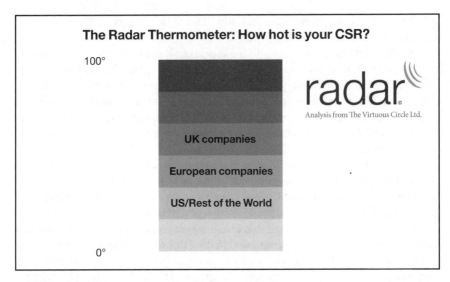

Similarly, legislation in some European countries, particularly the Nordic countries and Germany, means that environmental initiatives are the norm (for example, recycling waste material in these countries results in a far higher percentage achievement than in the UK). Consequently, they are expected to perform at a high standard in the environment area and as a result, find less benefit in communicating what is already the accepted standard. The same is true for the workplace. In the past, European governments have tended to be more socialist. This means that they have also accepted the EU's Social Chapter more readily than the UK so they have greater levels of legislation in areas such as flexible working, discrimination, etc., resulting in a greater number of employment practices.

US companies

In terms of US companies, the differences are much more cultural than political. CSR in the UK and in Europe has, at its heart, pressure on companies from governments and NGOs to perform more responsibly. This is not the same in the US, where entrepreneurialism (and sometimes a 'gung ho' attitude) is considered to be both acceptable and admired. As a consequence, CSR is not perceived in the same light in the US. Here, they interpret CSR rather differently.

For US corporations, CSR relates more to corporate citizenship and communities than it does in the rest of the world. As an example, when the US Chamber of Commerce announced its 2011 Corporate Citizenship awards, the award categories were: Best US Business Neighbour, Best International Ambassador, Best Corporate Stewardship and Best Partnership.

The US culture in is driven by governance issues. When George W. Bush spoke about corporate responsibility in March 2002, he launched his 'Ten Point Plan to Improve Corporate Responsibility and Protect America's Shareholders' based on his three core principles of information accuracy and accessibility, management accountability and auditor independence. However, he was referring to corporate governance, linking it to the Enron and WorldCom financial scandals. His speech was strongly linked to the introduction of the Sarbanes Oxley Act (also known as SOX), which addresses corporate governance and, in particular, conflicts of interest in the boardroom.

As a result, US companies focus more on corporate governance than on CSR in the sense of the European definition. This is reinforced by the US Federal Government's approach to the world's environment, being one of only a few countries that did not ratify the Kyoto protocol, largely because of the knock-on effect it would have on motorists in the US, where the average fuel consumption for cars was still only 22.6 miles per gallon in 2008 (but a massive improvement from the 14.3 miles per gallon of 1960).[1] This was considerably less than in Europe and the UK. Consequently, from a corporate position, being seen to be strong on environment for a US company does not have the advantage that exists in the UK and Europe. The same reticence is seen towards the US Government ratifying the Precautionary Principle, although in this case, the reason is different – it appears that there is a concern that ratifying it might lead to litigation claims from activists.

Similarly, the US attitude towards community is different from the UK and Europe. Not only is the language different – 'donations' are seen as being patronising, whilst 'philanthropy' is considered highly worthy – but also the involvement of corporations in the community is significantly lower. This is due to the strength of church organisations in the US, as much community activity is driven at local level, often through individual activity as part of church-based giving activity. The popularity of individual giving in the US also affects the amount of corporate giving and is related to the personal tax regime in the US, where such giving has tax benefits.

In a presentation given by Business for Social Responsibility at the European Conference on CSR,[2] these differences in attitudes were put into sharp focus. The point was made that there is no US government source of inspiration for business to embrace CSR, although, equally, US-based corporations are under increased pressure from civil society (including SRI organisations) to answer questions on voluntary codes, business conduct guidelines, expanded reporting guidelines and social or sustainability performance indexes. One of the most important points made was that public attitudes toward business is different in the US than in Europe as a whole – this next chart overleaf illustrates that US citizens are more positively inclined towards corporate bodies.

But even this US public attitude appears to be changing. In mid-2007, an article appeared in *The Huffington Post* (or HuffPo), the online news US website described as the US's most popular 'analysis and opinion website'.

The article was written by Jim Talent, Republican Senator for Missouri until 2006, who played an active role in Governor Mitt Romney's nomination campaign for the 2008 Republican Presidential candidate and who currently serves as a member of Romney's 2012 Economic Policy Team. Entitled 'Beyond the Bottom Line: Redefining Corporate Social Responsibility', one of his conclusions was that whilst 'business success is still about making money … it can't only be about that' – hardly world shattering, you might suggest.

He referred to a survey conducted by Fleishmann-Hillard and the National

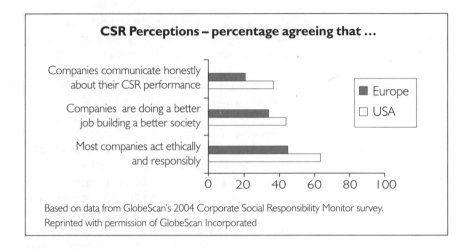

CSR Perceptions – percentage agreeing that …

Based on data from GlobeScan's 2004 Corporate Social Responsibility Monitor survey.
Reprinted with permission of GlobeScan Incorporated

Consumers League.[3] This found that a majority of Americans believe the most important thing a company can do to be viewed as socially responsible is to 'treat their employees well'. It also found Americans who evaluate a company's CSR commitment modify their views depending on whether they are considering their own position as employees, investors, customers, or voters.

Remarkably, the survey found Americans are united in their view of corporate performance and, regardless of political affiliation, the overwhelming majority believe:

- corporate priorities are out of alignment with Americans' priorities;
- US corporations *do not* act responsibly; and
- government should intervene.

Probably few of these findings (or even Senator Talent's views) will be particularly surprising if read from a UK perspective, but the article and the survey represented new ground in the USA. As relevant was the range of online responses that Talent's article provoked, which ranged from supportive to outright abuse (often accusing Talent of relinquishing his Republican heritage).

Perhaps the message from both Talent and his accusers is that CSR is seen through the eyes of the culture in which it is being practised.

Today, more than ever, in evaluating CSR programmes, account must be taken of both the culture and the politics of regions in which the company is located.

The business case for CSR

Given the variations in approaches to CSR caused by differences in size, sector, or corporate nationality, the question that the reader may be posing is: What is the business case for CSR?

Compliance, risk and reputation

Firstly it's important to recognise that CSR is not about reporting – it's about doing! As I have already declared, from a corporate perspective, the rationale for CSR lies in terms of assessing risk and opportunity. In that respect, CSR is about the management of three critical areas:

- compliance
- risk
- reputation (which some people also link into risk).

Compliance is legislative driven and covers aspects such as occupational health and safety, employment practice, environmental performance and customer safeguards. Put bluntly, if a company considering CSR does not have compliance well in hand, there is little point in taking any steps regarding CSR.

Risk management is extending significantly into the corporate domain, driven by corporate law developments and following the requirements of codes such as the UK Corporate Governance Code. In CSR circles, probably the biggest aspect of risk management is in the area of the environment, followed by employment practices. In the UK, the risk is of employment tribunals, but for those companies operating in the USA, the development of class actions is a far more worrying and costly reason. The key issue in determining risk is understanding how stakeholders can impact on your business strategy; this is likely to be different for different business sectors.

The area which is least developed is that of reputation management. It is difficult to explain why this is the case, but my intuition suggests there are four reasons:

- The responsibility for the development of the corporate brand is often unclear – the marketing department tends to focus on products, rather than the brand of the company itself.
- The average length of tenure of the UK CEO is of the order of four years – and as a consequence, his or her management and development of the corporate brand is unlikely to be high on the priority list for action.
- Similarly, where the marketing department might have the inclination to consider corporate brands, their focus is, generally speaking, short term; this is not helped by a similarly short average length of tenure for the marketing director.
- Lastly, the extent of the corporate brand covers many different departments, and being able to manage and develop the corporate brand requires a coordinated approach, the skills and resources for which the company may need to acquire.

Perhaps at this stage it is worthwhile outlining the relevance of CSR to the wide range of corporate brands. The chart on the following page contains the individual components of the corporate brands and demonstrates that CSR can influence the preference of the various stakeholders towards these brands.

Given this interpretation of corporate brands and reputation management, what is the business case for CSR?

Source: The Virtuous Circle Ltd.

Achieving high performance – CSR at the heart of business

There are many studies focused on customer attitudes towards products and ethics. A report[4] that TVC wrote with The Work Foundation reviewed a range of different research studies relating to CSR and its components, with a view to identifying the key elements that supported the business case for CSR.

One study in the report demonstrated that consumers' perceptions of a company's ethical business practices and ethical products and services had a significant impact on their spending. It showed that 52% of consumers have boycotted a product or service for ethical reasons and, most importantly, two-thirds of them reported that they never returned to the product once it had been associated with an unethical practice.

The purpose of the report was to look at a wider range of business drivers, especially those that demonstrated that where CSR is embedded at the heart of business, it can have an impact on business performance.

We highlighted four areas from previous research studies that supported how CSR affected business performance:

- CSR – enhancing the 'employer brand'
- CSR – delivering performance through committed employees
- CSR – and customer preferences
- CSR – and strategic business fit.

Enhancing the 'employer brand'

The research above highlighted that about 20% of employees were positively attracted to employers with a socially responsible image. Of particular importance were the age bands of the employees who are likely to take into account CSR performance in determining their attitudes towards their current (or prospective) employer. Unsurprisingly, perhaps, older employees (45+) were one of those age brackets –

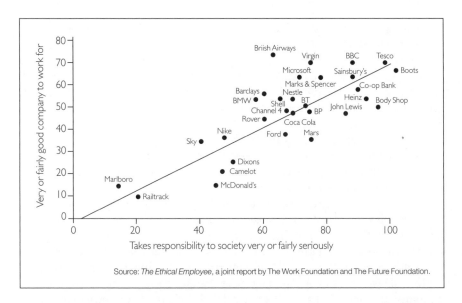

Source: *The Ethical Employee*, a joint report by The Work Foundation and The Future Foundation.

probably because of the need to be sure that their pensions were safeguarded. The other age bracket that was influenced is that of the younger generation (18–24). In this instance, given the well-publicised 'Talent War', their attitude towards an employer's image is significant in terms of determining a company's ability to gain the right skills for future business growth.

It was also evident from the research that those companies who match their values with those of employees improve the retention of employees. Overall, this research showed that committed employees made a great contribution towards the organisation. If an employer's promises at the time of recruitment are seen as being kept by the employer, then this will influence the employee's decision to remain with that employer.

Conducted in 2001 amongst over 1,000 economically active adults, the research also highlighted employees' attitudes towards 30 leading British companies. As the graph above shows, there is a strong positive correlation between companies seen to take their responsibilities towards society seriously and those seen as a good employer to work for.

Given the cost of recruiting the necessary skills required in business, it is clear that developing a positive perception of a company's CSR approach will both improve the quality of talent available to the company and also contribute to reducing the cost of recruiting it.

The findings above demonstrate a positive business case for using CSR as a means of improving the recruitment and retention of employees.

Delivering performance through committed employees

Another aspect of this report investigates the extent to which CSR could be effective in developing the relationship between employee attitudes and the performance of their companies – also known also as 'the service-profit chain' which establishes relationships between profitability, customer loyalty, and employee satisfaction, loyalty, and productivity.

The study was undertaken in 1999 and demonstrated a positive correlation between employee commitment, customer satisfaction and revenue. Its approach was based on a similar study conducted at Sears in the USA, which showed that the service climate created by committed employees was a central driver of business success.

In the research referred to in The Work Foundation report, the study was based in the UK, focusing on one of the UK's largest retailers, using a selection of almost 100 of its stores, with a database collected over two years, containing the attitudes of over 65,000 employees as well as 25,000 customers.

The study used structural equation modelling techniques, allowing the relationship between a complex set of variables to be mapped, and, as a result, demonstrated a strong correlation between the perceived quality of line management, corporate culture, employee commitment, customer retention and sales volume. The model below illustrates the strength and direction of the relationships found by the study.

This shows the most important relationships between employee attitudes, customer attitudes and changes in sales. All of the relationships shown in the model are statistically significant, and a positive relationship means the items move in the same direction, whilst a negative relationship occurs where one item increases as the other decreases.

Also it shows that perceptions of line management are strongly related to perceived company culture, which in turn is strongly linked to employee commitment. This is a very important part of the chain as it is directly positively related to a change in sales and also indirectly influences sales through its effect on customer satisfaction with service. The direct effect of employee commitment is slightly greater than its effect on customer service satisfaction.

This 'People to Profits' study emphasises the importance of measuring commitment, rather than just satisfaction. An important conclusion is that positive employee

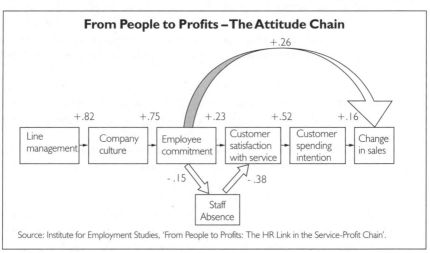

From People to Profits – The Attitude Chain

Source: Institute for Employment Studies, 'From People to Profits: The HR Link in the Service-Profit Chain'.

commitment, based on pride in the company and identity with its values, is an important factor in delivering high-value customer relationships and, as a result, revenue improvement.

This research demonstrates that one business case for CSR is the way in which it can play a significant role in terms of developing employee commitment and can ultimately improve customer revenue.

CSR and customer preferences

Whilst the previous study showed the importance of developing a positive image through CSR for the employees of a company, another study that was featured in the report demonstrated the relevance of CSR in driving customer satisfaction and profit.

This study was undertaken by British Telecom. It analysed the variables that might have an impact on customer satisfaction. BT's conclusion was that specific CSR activities represented more than 25% of the image and reputation component and that if BT was to lose its positive reputation for its CSR activities, its customer satisfaction levels would drop by up to 10%.

BT wanted to take this further and undertook two further studies to relate customer satisfaction to the bottom line. It identified that the highest levels of satisfaction correlated to the highest levels of customer loyalty (which it related to its 8 million most valuable customers, delivering some £560 million in earnings before interest and tax). It also looked at how dissatisfaction with customer service would hit profits and indicated that its research showed that a single call centre adviser with poor customer service skills would reduce profits by up to £300,000.

The three studies confirmed to BT the importance of its CSR activities in developing employee satisfaction and commitment as a means of supporting the driving of revenue, and ultimately the bottom line.

CSR and the strategic business fit

The final category of research looked at the impact on CSR when it becomes embedded within the overall business policy and practice. This was based on two studies. The first research, based on interviews with over 1,000 UK CEOs, showed that there is a strong correlation between Total Factor Productivity (the UK performance measure preferred by many economists) and four overlapping areas:

- customers and markets
- shareholders and governments
- stakeholders
- HR practices creativity and innovation.

What was clear was that no one area on its own influenced performance – they are all interdependent – and these four areas relate closely to the broad definition of CSR.

A second survey took this further, and drew two important conclusions:

- *Profit growth* – firms in the manufacturing, business services and service sectors that reported CSR to be a primary or strong business focus were twice as likely to experience profit growth, as those that reported CSR to be a minor or negligible focus.

- *Market share growth* – firms in the business services and services sectors that reported CSR to be a primary or strong business focus were twice as likely to increase market share as those that reported CSR to be a minor or negligible focus.

These two research studies showed that if CSR is embedded in an organisation, it contributes to both profit and market share growth.

The correlation between ESG actions and financial performance

Environment and financial performance

A study[5] produced by the Environment Agency and Innovest sought to answer the question of whether there is a link between corporate environmental governance (covering values, policy, oversight, processes and performance) and financial performance.

The study undertook an assessment of 15 case studies of companies, as well as a literature review of 70 separate studies, including those by academia. The individual company case studies were analysed in depth to establish evidence of correlation. The findings were significant – in over 85% of the studies assessed, a positive correlation was found between environmental governance and/or events and financial performance. The findings showed that in the case studies, changes in financial performance stemming from environmental governance measures can be demonstrated and quantified, although the study did accept that the extent to which these changes are entirely due to environmental governance issues is not always clear. It also identified that where companies had set up appropriate environmental accounting and reporting procedures, these benefits could be more accurately measured.

ESG and share performance

In 2009, for an environmental book,[6] I interviewed Michelle Clayman, Managing Partner and Chief Investment Officer of New Amsterdam Partners (NAP), an asset management firm with about 30 employees, specialising in offering a blend of quantitative and fundamental investment research. NAP had $2.7 billion of assets under management at the end of 2008, with funds focusing on ESG amounting to $679 million (about 25% of their total assets).

NAP's Director of Quantitative Research was exploring the time horizons affecting environmental and governance practices of companies. The findings indicated that better governance practices are reflected in share out-performance in the nearer term, whereas better environmental practices result in stock out-performance in the long term. NAP's quantitative team completed a study in mid-2008 showing that companies with neutral or positive ESG scores outperform companies with negative scores.

The NAP study looked at share price performance results over a three to five year time frame. A more recent Harvard Business School working paper, 'The Impact of a Corporate Culture of Sustainability on Corporate Behavior and Performance',[7] looked at share price performance over the far longer time frame of 20 years.

It found that corporations that voluntarily adopted environmental and social policies many years ago – termed as *high sustainability* companies – exhibit fundamentally different characteristics from those that adopted almost none of these policies – termed as *low sustainability* companies. In particular, the research found that the boards of these companies are more likely to be responsible for sustainability and top executive incentives are more likely to be a function of sustainability metrics. Moreover, they are more likely to have organised procedures for stakeholder engagement, to be more long-term oriented and to exhibit better measurement and disclosure of non-financial information.

Finally and perhaps most importantly from the perspective of using this research persuasively within companies, the research provided evidence that High Sustainability companies significantly outperform their counterparts over the long term, both in terms of stock market and accounting performance.

Is there a business case for CSR?

As the reader will probably now appreciate, the challenge of CSR is that it cuts across all aspects of the business. The research studies quoted above demonstrated that CSR can impact upon business performance, but is almost impossible to state unequivocally that CSR has a unilateral impact upon business revenue or bottom line profit over the short term. It's like the old quote that 50% of advertising works, but you never know which 50%!

However, there is clear research-based evidence that CSR can impact both financial performance and share price performance. The challenge of these research studies is that (with the exception of more medium-term employee commitment studies) their results tend to be long-term. Regrettably, not many chief executives are interested in the performance of their company in the years after their departure! Nevertheless, these studies are powerful and can be used effectively in stimulating internal debate.

What is important is to recognise that CSR does have an impact upon business performance – along with other important business activities. The studies indicate that ignoring CSR can be a perilous action for any board to take and understanding the risks implied in this action is an important task for the director or manager responsible for CSR.

What is more relevant is not to ask 'Does CSR work?' but instead to ask 'How can I make CSR work better for my company?' 'How can I decide what elements of CSR are critical to the business objectives of my company?' Much of the remainder of the book is devoted to this question.

Sources

1   US fuel consumption information is available for the US Bureau of Transportation Statistics at: www.bts.gov/publications/national_transportation_statistics/2010/index.html.

2   'Are Americans From Mars? CSR in North America'. Presentation given at the European Conference on CSR in Maastricht on 8 November 2004 by Kate Fish, Managing Director, Europe, Business for Social Responsibility.

3   The survey is referred to in Fleishmann-Hillard's Sustainability Blog at: sustainability.fleishmanhillard.com/tag/national-consumer-league/.

4   'Achieving high performance: CSR at the heart of business' Stephen Bevan, Nick Isles, Peter Emery and Tony Hoskins (2004) The Virtuous Circle and The Work Foundation.

5   'Corporate Environmental Governance – A study into the influence of Environmental Governance and Financial Performance', White and Kiernan, on behalf of the Environment Agency and Innovest. The full report can be accessed at: www.publications.environment-agency.gov.uk/PDF/GEHO0904BKFE-E-E.pdf.

6   The case study based on the interview was published in *Environmental Alpha: Institutional Investors and Climate Change*, Angelo Calvello (ed.), John Wiley & Sons, 2009. The research was subsequently published in the *Finance Professionals Post*, the journal of New York Society of Security Analysts. Available at: www.post.nyssa.org/nyssa-news/2010/07/the-impact-of-esg-on-stock-returns-and-profitability.html.

7   The HBS working paper, written and researched by Robert G. Eccles, Ioannis Ioannou and George Serafeim can be found on the HBS website at: www.hbs.edu/research/pdf/12-035.pdf.

A management culture

One of the major criticisms of CSR is that it is 'all management spin'. Sometimes, this can be true and, where this is the case, it may be because the company concerned has adopted a tick box attitude towards the individual CSR components and has communicated only the most favourable aspects of its CSR performance.

To correct this criticism, the management of the company needs to embed CSR as part of its management culture. It is easy enough to say, but challenging to implement. But it can be done, as was demonstrated in the research undertaken by Harvard Business School, referred to at the end of the previous chapter, entitled 'The Impact of a Corporate Culture of Sustainability' – it's the culture that counts!

Making CSR part of the normal business process

CSR must become part of the normal business process, by which I mean CSR is considered by the company's management and staff in all aspects of the business as part of:

- its business decision making;
- its performance measurement system;
- its employee and management incentive programmes; and
- its business planning process.

Some companies question the need for this development of a management culture based on CSR and revert to questioning the business case. As can be seen from Chapter 10, identifying the business case is difficult – but not impossible – and often requires more detailed thinking (and sometimes over a longer time horizon) than may normally be the case in a company's business planning process.

In only a few of the companies in which I have worked has the business planning been long term, such as can be seen from the nature of the following businesses:

- in a life assurance company that related to the maturity of the life and pension funds, the planning process was roughly 20 years' duration;
- in a manufacturing company, business planning was medium term (three to five years);

- in a business-to-business services company the view of the president of the company was that anything over one year was too difficult to plan; and
- and in a consultancy business, you are as good as next week's billings

Clearly, the shorter the time horizon, the more difficult it is to plan for CSR activities that develop business benefits – CSR has a long-term effect on the management culture and this effect cannot be easily demonstrated in a one-year planning horizon.

To integrate CSR into the management culture requires a clearly signposted strategy and for this purpose, I will revert to the route map already discussed in the previous chapter and focus on a more detailed view of its components.

The vision and values

The vision and values are at the core of CSR. How can you define the responsible approach for a company, unless you first define the values by which the company would wish its approach to be judged? Yet, what does the term 'values' mean in CSR?

In my experience, many companies spend a lot of time and effort in creating their 'mission, vision and values', but these are usually developed solely from a commercial and internal viewpoint. There will often be talk about the need to develop adequate returns for shareholders, being innovative in product development and utilising the resources appropriately – a few companies will go on to talk about meeting the needs of customers and developing their employees. Seldom will there be any discussion of understanding customer and employee feedback, the needs of the community in which they operate, the business impact on the environment, or the human rights of individuals (especially relevant, where the company is operating in developing countries).

The company's commercial values are, in fact, the starting point for considering the CSR values. But to achieve an appropriate set of CSR values that reflects an under-standing of relationships with stakeholders (and subsequently to prioritise their

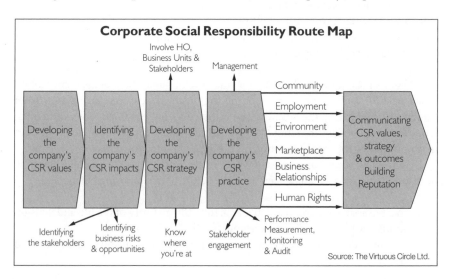

stakeholders, given the nature of the company concerned), the managers responsible need to stand back and take an objective external view. They need to identify the stakeholders in the various markets where they operate and to review how the company impacts upon the stakeholders. Only then can the company decide what its CSR values are.

In determining what values the company should have for its CSR, a useful starting point is some of the international standards already referred to in chapter 9.

So for example, a company should consider how its values, relating to its employees, line up with the ILO conventions. Similarly, in terms of companies that operate internationally, the OECD guidelines provide a useful checklist. For companies that operate both nationally and internationally, the UN Global Compact provide a useful set of standards against which to benchmark their values. If a company is purchasing commodities, the Ethical Trading Initiative Basic Code will offer a useful set of guidelines for how it should handle its purchases from developing countries.

The benefit of having a code of ethics

The beginning for this evaluation of the company's values is the company's own code of ethics. These may also be termed as a code of conduct and whilst the two terms are used interchangeably, in reality, they are different.

A code of conduct is a set of rules outlining the responsibilities of or proper practices for an individual, party or organisation. In the case of a corporation, the code of conduct usually defines the conduct expected by employees on behalf of the company. A code of ethics is adopted to assist those in the company, called upon to make decisions on behalf of the company, to understand the difference the company's attitudes towards what are 'right' and 'wrong' decisions. The code of ethics will usually involve training with scenarios to help employees apply their understanding of the company's ethical position to their decision making.

Many companies embed their code of ethics within their code of conduct so that employees have only one document to consider. Company practice now requires employees to acknowledge receipt and understanding of the code of conduct as part of their induction programmes. As a result, the code of conduct can form the backbone for a company's compliance system and can be used in employee disciplinary procedures.

Such codes are now found in most major companies – research undertaken in 2003 by the Institute of Business Ethics (IBE) showed that over 90 companies in the FTSE 100 had such a code. The exact number varies dependent upon the number of investment trusts in the FTSE100 (they would not normally be expected to have a code) and the number of foreign companies in the FTSE100, but the position in 2012 remains around the same level. The foreign companies tend to be mining companies and have chosen to list in the UK because of capital management reasons. At the outset of their listing, they tend to have less governance systems than their more longstanding FTSE100 partners.

But the presence of the code of ethics declines with the size of the company. In a similar piece of research, the IBE showed that only 163 of the FTSE 350 stated that they had a code in place.

'Do business ethics pay?' The IBE[1] has undertaken several research studies to establish the extent of a positive correlation between the presence of a code of ethics and financial performance measures. In 2003, it took a sample from the FTSE350 for which full and comparable company data were available over the years 1997–2001.

It used four measures of corporate financial performance – market value added, economic value added, price earnings ratio and return on capital employed. Its research demonstrated that for three of these four measures, it was found that those companies in the sample with a code of ethics had outperformed a similar size group, who said they did not have a code. Similarly, those companies with a code of ethics generated significantly more economic value added and market value added in the years in question than those without a code of ethics.

Importantly, companies with a code of ethics showed less price/earnings ratio volatility over a four-year period than those without a code, suggesting that these companies may be a more secure investment over the longer term.

The IBE referred to other research, which indicated that a stable price/earnings ratio attracted capital at below average cost and inferred that having a code of ethics may be considered to be a significant indicator of consistent management.

The IBE commented that the Return on Capital Employee showed a different pattern of results. In the first two years, there is no discernible difference found in this indicator between those with did not have a code. However, in the last two years covered by the study (from 1999 to 2001), the average return of those with codes showed an increase of about 50%, whilst those without a code fell over the same time. Backing up this result was the fact that the research showed that that those companies with codes of ethics had produced profits to turnover ratios 18% higher than those without such codes over the four years in all.

The IBE's general conclusion was that there is strong evidence to indicate that companies with a code of ethics have performed better (in financial terms) than those without a code. This conclusion is in line with the findings of studies referred to in the previous chapter, which indicate that corporate governance has a positive correlation to share price.

In 2007, the IBE revisited this question with a new[2] research study, which looked at the relationship between the provision of business ethics training and corporate financial performance. Their standpoint is that because most companies in the FTSE100 have some form of ethics code, this in itself does not indicate that the company is more ethical. Instead they hypothesised that a commitment to embedding ethical values into business practice through a training programme should differentiate companies and should enable them to enjoy a stronger financial performance as a result. The research took 50 companies in the FTSE350 and split them between those that disclosed a code of ethics (labelled *corporate revealed ethics*) and those that both disclosed their code and provided training programmes to reinforce these codes with their employees (labelled *corporate applied ethics*).

The research took four financial performance measures – return on capital employed, return on assets, total return and market value added – and adjusted them for size, risk and price to book value. The analysis showed that over the long term (here, the study covered 2001–05) there was a significantly greater positive relationship between those companies in the applied ethics group and their financial performance than those in the revealed ethics group.

The conclusions from both these studies indicate that having a code of ethics will deliver better financial performance for a company but that living your ethical values – through using training programmes to embed them in staff behaviour – will have an even greater impact.

Developing a code of ethics

Given this relatively strong indicator that a code of ethics will have a beneficial impact upon the company's performance, how does a company develop such a code?

There are several steps to this development. Most importantly, the management of the company should not assume that having a written code of ethics means that demonstrates it is operating ethically. It has also to show that the code of ethics is operational throughout the company.

To achieve this objective requires a four-stage approach:

- developing the code of ethics;
- developing the compliance system;
- communicating the code, together with the compliance system; and
- developing a culture of trust, to ensure that employees are comfortable in declaring what they may perceive to be a breach of the code.

The IBE has developed a set of guidelines for the best practice for the development of any code of business ethics.[3] This highlighted that development of codes usually take one of two forms. There can be the 'stakeholder approach,' which reviews and sets out the company's approach to its stakeholders, including:

- employees
- shareholders and investors
- suppliers or business partners
- customers and clients
- the local and national community (including governments) and the environment.

The alternative approach is 'issues based' and consists of policy statements that cover the company's key areas of concern.

Both approaches can be correct and it depends very much upon the management's focus as to which is chosen. For either, is essential that employees are able to use the code as a means of offering them guidance on their behaviour with regard to stakeholders, particularly where potential conflicts of interest may exist.

The code should be a living document. If once written it is locked away in a filing cabinet, then its value is questionable. In that respect, the code should be reviewed regularly – as a minimum, every three years – and updated, if appropriate, to reflect any new issues that the company's business approach is facing.

In developing the code, it is essential that there is a board level champion who not only has a conviction to develop it, but also has the support from the board to ensure it is implemented. Subsequently it is essential that a draft code be reviewed with a representative group of managers, as part of its internal development (and to ensure that the commitment of the board and the champion is ongoing).

Identifying areas of consistency and conflicts in a code

In one of the codes of ethics that we helped to develop for a client, we used IBE's Illustrative Code of Business Ethics as the benchmark for internal development. We fragmented this illustrative code into sections that related to our client company's various functional departments. The sections were sent to these departments in the form of a consultation with a simple question:

'For all its clauses, do you have the view that:

- policies are in place that match the clauses;
- practices are in place that would meet the needs of the clauses; or
- that there are clauses that create conflict with existing business practice?'

The outcome of this consultation gave us a very rapid assessment on the extent to which the company had policies in place, the extent to which practices could be con-verted into policies without any real burden being placed on the company and the extent to which imposing a code would cause difficulties in continuing the existing business practices.

In the case of our client, a multinational company, operating in a decentralised manner, it became apparent that there were a few policies that were group wide, but there was much practice on a country-by-country basis that would enable a code to be easily implemented.

It also highlighted very specific concerns that a code would create conflict of inter-est. This enabled us to develop a code which could be reviewed with the main board in a very focused way. As a result of this analysis, the clients' management was well prepared for the valuable debates about potential conflicts of interest. This resulted in a satisfactory resolution of the need to introduce specific areas of group policy.

Phasing the development of a code

Such a resolution may not necessarily be an immediate fix. Indeed, in some com-panies, the conflict of interest areas may be ingrained in the business culture. In such cases, the code of ethics should include aspirational terms, indicating that the company intends to move towards a position that ensures that such conflicts of interest disappear over time.

However a company should not assume that it can include aspirational statements in its code of ethics forever and a day. Regular reviews of the code should include moving from aspirational to factual statements.

Bribery and facilitation

An area which will typically cause challenges for a company is that of bribery and corruption. Until the passing of the Bribery Act 2010, for most companies operating solely within the United Kingdom, this was unlikely to be an issue, although it could be the case for a company involved in overseas trade or operations. Of course, not all countries are subject to corrupt practices, but for some these practices are endemic, particularly with government officials. Transparency International publishes an annual Corruption Perception Index, providing an indication of perceived levels of public sector corruption in 183 countries and territories. It defines corruption as the abuse of entrusted power for private gain. For its 2011 Index,[4] the top ten countries perceived as having high levels of corruption were Venezuela, Haiti, Iraq, Sudan, Turkmenistan, Uzbekistan, Afghanistan, Myanmar, North Korea and Somalia. This Index addresses public sector corruption, but where this is high, the pervading culture will affect both the public and the private sector.

However, under the Bribery Act (discussed in more detail in Chapter 9), UK-based companies need to be able to demonstrate that they have implemented 'adequate procedures' to prevent corrupt practices within their ranks or by third parties acting on their behalf; if not, they may be liable under the new corporate crime of 'failure to prevent' bribery. As such, all UK companies need to take their anti-bribery procedures extremely seriously, regardless of where they trade.

Most countries regard bribery as being illegal and have stringent legislation to counter it. Bribery involves the payment to an individual, normally actively concerned in the transaction, to ensure that your company gains a competitive advantage over any others that may be involved in competing for that transaction. As such, bribery is generally easier to investigate and identify.

However, facilitation payments are where issues generally arise. Facilitation payments are best described as payments made to enable an activity to occur. Often they are paid to local government officials, but sometimes to third parties, such as 'rebels' who may be the *de facto* government of the region in question.

These activities are normally those that occur in the general course of business. They may include business activities such as enabling shipments of goods to leave ports, ensuring that genuine shipments are delivered to the customers without being unduly delayed, or enabling a genuine application for building permission to be made in the normal planning process.

Issues with facilitation payments

There are two challenges with such payments. The first of these is that, in developing countries, salaries paid to local government officials are often below the levels necessary to maintain the standard of living in the country concerned. As a result, what we know as facilitation payments may be accepted methods of doing business in that country. They are often seen by the government concerned as part of those local government officials' own salary. The challenge is, therefore, whether it is acceptable to impose some Western standards of ethics on a culture which does not comply with these standards.

The approach advocated by companies that face such a dilemma is a pragmatic one. Whilst not condoning the practice, they accept that it is a way of life and agree to make such payments, but only if they receive an invoice or receipt from the individual in question.

By so doing, the view is that both the employee agreeing to such payments and the individuals receiving them are made aware of the company's disapproval of the practice, with a view that, ultimately, the open approach to such practices will lead to their demise.

The other challenge is more difficult. In the UK, facilitation payments are illegal and the terms of the Anti-Terrorism Crime and Security Act of 2001 mean that the directors of UK-based firms participating in such activity are liable to prosecution (this has been reinforced by the Bribery Act). However, the US has no such legislation and, as a result, facilitation payments are perfectly legal. The result is an imbalance in business practices, which is unlikely to change in the near future. This imposes a possible additional cost to UK companies operating in the developing world, over and above the costs of their international competitors.

US versus UK codes

There is a further example that demonstrates the different attitudes towards codes of ethics between the US and the UK. In the UK, there is, currently, no legal requirement for a company to have a code of ethics. However, for UK-listed companies, the UK Corporate Governance Code requires disclosure of corporate governance arrangements, including risk management and internal control. The 2005 Turnbull guidance on internal control, which underlies it, refers to the presence of a code of conduct. Nevertheless, this is merely for guidance, so having a code of ethics is voluntary in the UK. This is not the case in the US, where the Sarbanes-Oxley Act of 2002 (SOX) requires US SEC-registered companies to have a code of business conduct.

When you look at the codes of business conduct developed by US companies it is very clear that they do not have the same wide scope as the codes of ethics suggested by the likes of the IBE. Instead, they tend to focus on declaring any conflict of interest and ensuring that the directors are aware that they are responsible for maintaining good business practice in the company.

Indeed, whilst employees are referred to in such codes, in the main, the intended audience appears to be the directors and officers of the company concerned. As a result, there is little reference to external stakeholders in the manner described in the IBE Illustrative Code. The SOX Act was the US Government's reaction to financial fiascos such as Enron and WorldCom, hence the US approach to codes of ethics is far more about corporate governance than it is about CSR and stakeholders.

Developing the ethics compliance system

The compliance system should be seen as an integral part of the code of ethics – not just because that is good business practice, but also because legislation requires an element of it to be in place. This involves the requirements to have confidential helplines for 'whistleblowers'.

Whistle blowing

In the UK, the idea that 'whistle blowers' should be 'protected' came first with the Public Information Disclosure Act of 1998. The UK regulatory requirements of the Combined Code C.3.4/Smith Guidance 4.8, introduced in July 2003, required companies to provide a confidential helpline for employees with concerns about their operating approach. This has been restated in section C.3.2 of the UK Corporate Governance Code under the broader title of the company's 'internal control and risk management systems'. On a similar line, the SOX Act requires US-listed companies to keep a register of 'whistle blowers' complaints and the results of any subsequent investigation.

In terms of the business practice involved in the compliance system, then the tendency of UK companies appears to involve the audit committee of the board as the recipient of performance information regarding compliance (or otherwise) of the code of ethics. Sometimes, the board will give another committee – the ethics committee – specific responsibility for this area. In either instance, this generally means that the company secretary (and/or the general legal counsel) will be the corporate officer responsible for the code of ethics.

Beneath this level, the handling of 'whistle blowing' needs to be well-defined. First of all employees need to understand the definition of 'whistle blowing'. There is likely to be some confusion with personal grievances – for which many companies have well-established grievance procedures as part of their HR policies. It needs to be made clear that 'whistle blowing' relates to any matters that an individual has observed – but with which they are not directly involved in themselves or affected by them – which could be construed as being a breach of the company's code of ethics.

Once this definition has been communicated, the procedure should show how the breach should be handled and who should receive it. As regards the latter, most companies encourage their employees to report a breach through the line if the employee feels comfortable with that process. However, it has been reported that as many as 54% of employees[5] who were aware of malpractice did not report it, because such *confidential* help lines were not available.

Dealing with whistle blowing

A company must consider two options in terms of receiving confidential information from an employee. One option is to make an internal manager, or a management team, responsible for receiving these calls. The alternative option is to use an external service provider. The factors involved in choosing between these two options include the following:

- cost of providing 24-hour cover;
- ability to cover all languages (not just for overseas operations, but also for UK staff for whom English is not their mother tongue);
- confidentiality; and

- objectivity –with no conflict of interest.

I have seen clients who have selected an external service provider (which may not be overly expensive on a cost-per-employee basis) as well as clients who have selected the internal route. Provided the option selected is seen to be confidential and objective by the employees of the company, then either would suit. What would be wrong, however, would be to choose the internal route to ensure that any whistle blowing is kept within the company; this would suggest a lack of transparency and would risk criticism of an unethical approach. The choice of system also should have regard to the company's own operating circumstances. In one workshop of international managers that we ran for a FTSE100 company, the Australian that ran the company's China operations complained about the internal whistle blowing system. He said that for his local employees the system was failing because of the failure to recognise the time differences between China and the head office in Solihull and, perhaps more importantly, because no-one in Solihull spoke Mandarin!

Once a complaint has been received, it is important that it is registered by the manager concerned. For those companies using an external service provider, it is worthwhile considering how the external service provider links with the internal manager responsible for considering the reported breach. Generally speaking, the external service provider will submit a report of the breach (which could be either on an anonymous or an open, but confidential, basis) to nominated managers, who receive a faxed report of the breach only after a confidential and secure procedure (e.g. declaring their security PIN number to the external service provider).

The quality of the approach should be consistent between the internal and external approaches, particularly from the point of view of establishing an audit trail. This is also the case when it comes to the investigation of the breach. This needs to be reviewed independently within the company (ideally by a company's internal audit department, if it exists) to ensure that the investigation was undertaken in a confidential and objective manner, totally consistent with the intent expressed in the code of ethics.

Communicating the code and the compliance system

Communicating the code requires more than merely handing out a copy to all the employees. Instead, the communication process should combine communication and training programmes.

The training programmes should include:

- a presentation made to employees, describing and explaining the contents of the code and the process for compliance;
- documentation for employees, providing Frequently Asked Questions;
- documentation for use in role play, providing scenarios related to the ethical issues that the company may face;
- documentation to allow an employee to write to the company's ethical champion about any areas that they believe are not covered satisfactorily by the code; and

- documentation to be placed on the employee's personnel file to indicate receipt of their copy of the code and that they had received the appropriate training.

It is worth remembering that the communication process should be available as an ongoing process, not just as part of the induction of any new employee. It should also be available to employees throughout the duration of their employment with a company, as a form of reference, should they have any questions about the code or its implementation.

In some companies, the code is available in hard copy and communication devices such as posters on employee notice boards or in credit card style formats are used. Others ensure that the code, together with all associated documentation, is available on the company's intranet. Probably the best route is a combination of both.

Developing a culture of trust

The real challenge is to ensure that the employees believe the company will uphold the code and that any declaration of a possible breach is handled in a responsible and objective manner.

The company should publish regular reports on the performance of the confidential helpline and should communicate the results of investigations to the employees as appropriate. In practice, companies would not necessarily want to publicly disclose (including its employees) the results of investigations in every case.

For the code to be seen to be effective internally, the employees must come to regard it as being transparent, honest and fair. If this can be achieved satisfactorily, then communicating its effectiveness externally will be relatively easy. Where a company uses regular internal employee satisfaction surveys these should include questions about employees' perceptions of the code, as well as its workings. Similarly, there should be some formal consultation with representatives of employees about a regular review of the code, so they can see that their views have been taken on board.

In addition to the internal communication, the shareholders should be informed about the effectiveness of the code, starting with information in the annual report about the launch of the code and continuing with regular performance information in subsequent reports.

Only by being open about the effectiveness of the code can a company develop an internal culture of trust and an external acceptance of the company's responsible approach on ethical matters. In time, this will lead to positive cultural changes in terms of how the employees demonstrate commitment towards the company as a whole and as a result, will demonstrate improvements in company performance.

One last word about the importance of having a culture of trust. We have been involved in the development and implementation of codes of ethics for around five companies. We have also helped one major charity to develop its own code of ethics. In many respects, this latter experience demonstrated forcefully to us that having the culture of trust internally is an essential precursor to having an effective code. In the case of charities, there are three internal stakeholder groups that need to be involved in the development of the code: the senior management team, the employees (as would be the case in a company) and the trustees of the charity. It was the last group that demonstrated the need for the culture of trust. Trustees are usually involved in the charity because of an emotional attachment to its cause, whereas the senior management team and the staff will have a more rational business or employment-focused reason for their association. Our challenge was to enable all the groups to come to a common conclusion about the contents of the code of ethics, but developing a unified approach across groups that were coming from different perspectives meant that initially, the trust was not there. Developing the code took nearly two years, but by the end of the process there was a greater unity of understanding and direction.

Understanding your stakeholders

So far, we have focused upon the company's values and the code of ethics that the company uses to 'regulate' its methods of operation. However, to ensure this ethical approach takes account of all aspects of the business operations, it is necessary to understand your stakeholders and their attitudes towards your business, its operational approach and the risks and opportunities related to it (a more detailed review of stakeholder engagement and communications is contained in Chapter 17).

In our experience of working with companies, understanding your stakeholders' attitudes is of considerable importance, largely because the company's approach towards its stakeholders is likely to have been in the past reactive (often in a crisis mode), rather than proactively attempting to understand the views and attitudes of stakeholders.

The approach we have adopted involves three stages:

- identifying the range of stakeholders;
- stakeholder issues: identification and ranking; and
- stakeholder mapping against the issues.

The key task is to prioritise the issues that those stakeholders regard as important so that a meaningful communication can take place about the range of risks and opportunities that exist.

To undertake this communication will require a judgement to be formed with the management of the company as to the importance of the different stakeholder categories with regard to the issues considered to be important and, within each category, the relevance of the stakeholders.

In one example, a wind farm (then the biggest in the UK) was scheduled to be built on the Romney Marshes. As well as having a significant impact on the amount of renewable energy produced in the UK, this area is a significant habitat for wildlife, particularly migrant birds. nPower, the power generator company planning to build this wind farm, needed to prioritise between the NGOs representing wildlife on the Romney Marshes (such as Natural England in its earlier guise as English Nature and the Royal Society for the Protection of Birds) and those NGOs advocating renewable energy resource throughout the UK. The wind farm has been built, but not without significant delays.

The scheme finally got the go ahead in October 2006, after the High Court in London had rejected a legal challenge in order to protect local birdlife, particularly Bewick Swans. The Judge who heard the case ruled that the planning inspector who handled the public inquiry into the 'green' energy proposal had taken a 'precaution-ary approach' in respect of the alleged threat to birdlife.

Companies would be extremely challenged to satisfy the wide range of the NGO objectives that may relate to their business. Instead they need to evaluate the importance of the different categories of NGOs to determine their response to those objections that they may face.

Undertaking this prioritisation is not a one-off activity, but one that should be repeated regularly, to ensure account is taken of changes in attitudes, not only for the company, but also within the stakeholders.

Our experience has shown that stakeholders are willing to participate in this type of issue prioritisation, although we have had NGOs stating that they do not wish to support a commercial company. Thankfully, these were very much in the minority, but these reactions serve to demonstrate the range of different agendas between those of the NGOs and those of the corporates.

Similarly, if the company is multinational, then it is essential that this external approach should reflect its scope. There will be a width of cultural and political differ-ences, needing different approaches dependent upon the different cultural norms that exist in different parts of the world.

This external review generally throws up a wide range of attitudes, from the internal perspective of the managers of the company to those offered by the external stakeholders. The internal perspective inevitably focuses on those issues seen as important by the company, whereas the external perspective can highlight issues not even considered relevant within the company. The resolution of the two sets of opinion is the basis for the development of strategy.

Developing the CSR strategy

In developing your business's CSR strategy, several key aspects must be considered. However, because these aspects tend to overlap, there is a need to ensure that the evaluation process for each of them links to the evaluation of the other aspects in an iterative manner.

There are five key areas to be considered:

- understanding the range of stakeholders (and their relative priority) and iden-tifying their key issues in terms of both risks and opportunities;
- auditing the range of activities that already exist within the business;
- deciding where you want to position the business in terms of its CSR approach compared to those of its competitors and peers;

- involving management and employees, both at the centre and in the operational business units, to determine the focused range of activities to which the company should be committed; and
- developing a CSR management system so that CSR becomes integrated within the business rather than being an add-on, or standing to one side.

Addressing the needs of the stakeholders

We have already addressed the issues about understanding stakeholders and determining the key issues with which they are concerned. In developing its CSR strategy, a company needs to take a business objective-based approach relating to these issues when considering the extent to which action can be taken to reduce or eliminate these risks and to optimise the opportunities that may be presented.

From an external stakeholders' perspective, it is easy to take the views of stakeholders and key issues and assume that they will be acted upon. However, from a company's perspective, it may simply not be possible to go anywhere near satisfying the concerns of the stakeholders. A good example in this respect is that of BAT. As long as it is legal to manufacture and sell tobacco products, there will be companies meeting the needs of consumers that want to buy such products. For BAT to enter into a stakeholder engagement process, inferring that they could or would stop their prime business activity would have been unethical. Instead, they took a very transparent approach and stated that their business was the manufacture and selling of cigarettes. The way in which the company should operate responsibly would involve considering how they should produce the tobacco (particularly relevant in developing countries) and how they should sell and market such products (in this instance, with a special regard to the young and easily influenced customers).

As a result, the company needs to undertake a form of a cost–benefit analysis against each of the risks and opportunities they have identified, which should include the timescales required to undertake each of the activities to address these risks and opportunities. In addition, the functional department responsible for each area of risk or opportunity should identify the probability of each occurring, so as to determine the likely value of their impact.

This cost–benefit analysis will enable any manager responsible for the development of the CSR strategy to prioritise the range of initiatives against the likely cost impact of their occurring.

The biggest challenge in undertaking this analysis is that of evaluating reputation risk. The functional management is generally well placed to be able to identify the financial risks that may arise, but may be less able to consider the impact that such risks would have upon the corporate reputation. This aspect needs to be addressed in the last stage of the cost–benefit analysis and should include a discussion including all the functional departments, as well as those involved in the reputation area – departments such as corporate affairs and investor relations. Inevitably, such an evaluation will be subjective, but provided the cost–benefit analysis has been undertaken by the functional departments in advance, then the risk of this subjectivity is lessened.

Knowing where you are at – auditing CSR activities

I said at the outset that aspects can overlap to a great extent and a good example of this is the need to 'know where you are at'.

In evaluating risks and opportunities, a functional viewpoint (usually head office) can be unnecessarily pessimistic, unless there is good knowledge of the range of activities that exist at the operational business unit level. In my own experience of talking with both head office and relevant business unit staff, the head office knowledge is less detailed than might be expected (e.g. because local operations disguise certain activities by using different budget headings for, say, donations to local community groups).

In a meeting involving a company working in a highly technical field, its central management had a tendency to view involvement in community work as being irrelevant to its business. However, in my discussions with the management of the local business unit, it became apparent that a great deal of community activity did occur; this was widely publicised in the business's regional magazine circulated to all the staff. This was seen as being important in terms of developing a good employer image for potential recruits.

Similarly, in a discussion with a support services company, it became apparent that a lot of environmental initiatives were being directed through the supply management. As such, the client's environmental management often had only limited knowledge of the activity or of the impact of such initiatives.

With another client, with a head office in the UK, but whose main operations were in Eastern Europe, the key dilemma was how to get information from operational management who were unused to discussing CSR – and who still had a thought process linked to the old 'command and control' management style of the previous communist era. To help them get their minds around identifying CSR activities, we asked them about activities they were particularly proud of and would want to talk about with external parties – either in their locality or with bodies such as their own central government.

Two approaches – the use of structured questionnaires with site visits and data collection surveys – can be adopted to understand where a company stands in terms of its CSR activities. The first approach is highly relevant where a company has made little or no inroads into determining their level of CSR activity – especially where this activity is generally undertaken in a totally autonomous manner to the other parts of the business. This approach is particularly suitable for large companies, operating in the form of stand alone business sites. Clearly, these units have to provide detailed information on their health and safety and environmental activity for regulatory purposes, but the other aspects of the CSR range of components tend to be managed at a local level, with little or no reporting to the centre.

Structured questionnaires

To overcome a lack of central reporting, a structured questionnaire can be used when visiting different sites. Designed to identify the range of activities occurring at each site and to produce data from each site as evidence in the form of relevant statistics, this type of questionnaire can also be used to elicit case studies to inform stakeholders about the quality of the activity.

Site visits

Information from the site visits can be used to develop an internal CSR report covering only those specific sites visited. This can show internal management how information will be communicated to the general public, once it has had been collated. It also shows the relevant site managers the benefits of providing information, which previously had not been requested.

One of the key issues that faces companies developing a CSR report for the first time is the amount of information that is required for the report, which is usually not part of the regular reporting system. This can represent a significant additional burden and the benefits of providing such information need to be sold in to management at the outset.

Data collection surveys

The second approach, one that I have developed for client companies, builds upon the first and is a data collection survey that can be used either as a stand alone PC version, with completed Excel spreadsheets being e-mailed to a central point of collation, or as a central questionnaire hosted on the company's intranet, with the respondents' data being collated into a central database.

This approach is particularly relevant for companies with multiple locations and is particularly helpful in the central management of information requests from the various relevant investment or CSR surveys. However it is a much more sophisticated approach than the first. In developing a CSR strategy, the more basic approach is often better in providing a simplistic overview from which to base the analysis necessary to develop the CSR strategy. The latter approach is relevant once the strategy has been developed and implemented. There are now a variety of software solutions for companies that want to collate their CSR information in this way – but the challenge is always that of GIGO (garbage in and garbage out); for these software solutions to work effectively, CSR must be fully embedded within the company.

Deciding your CSR positioning

We have already described how we used the Radar approach as part of the CSR positioning. To develop CSR strategy there is a need to go into more detail about the extent of the activities and positioning of the competitors. The company needs to decide if it wants to be seen as cutting edge or middle of the road in its market sector and needs to consider what it must do to maintain or to achieve its chosen position.

In reviewing the competitors' CSR activity, the following areas need to be considered:

- the extent to which the competitor companies are involved in CSR, in terms of policies and management systems;
- their level of performance in each of the CSR components;

- the focus areas of each competitor – in other words, those areas that they are trying to claim as being their own, where they can demonstrate leadership; and
- the areas of risk that are apparently relevant to each competitor.

For one of our clients, a support services company, we undertook a threefold approach in developing the CSR positioning, in each approach, drilling down more deeply into the available published and researched information. This involved:

- the Radar evaluation, reviewing competitors and their clients and the companies that the board aspired to be positioned against;
- a more detailed update of the above, specifically targeted at competitors; and
- a much more in-depth investigation, looking at the one competitor that was deemed to be considered to be the most advanced in CSR.

The investigation included reviewing the competitor's corporate and national websites (covering all of its country operations) and undertaking an in-depth search of its CSR-related coverage. It also included undertaking a personal contact exercise (in the form of mystery shopping of the competitor's field operations) to establish the extent to which the policies could be perceived as being implemented in practice – to assess the extent to which they 'walk the talk'.

At this last stage, we were able to map out our client's positioning against that of its key competitor in terms of CSR. As a result, we were able to identify those areas where investment and activity was necessary to achieve cutting-edge status. Equally, we were able to identify those areas where our client was ahead of its competitor, and areas where stakeholders drew an unfavourable comparison between the competitor and our client. This gave our client a competitive advantage. It could then consider whether it was of commercial value to build on those areas to the detriment of its competitor.

Again, as stated at the start of this section, an evaluation of competitive CSR positioning needs to be undertaken as part of an integrated approach with the other three areas, especially that of stakeholder prioritisation. It is sometimes easy for a company's management to become annoyed at a seemingly effective activity on the part of the competitor. Instead, it first needs to ask about the intended stakeholder audience and then to assess whether or not they would see the competitors' activity as being valuable and effective in CSR terms.

Involving management and employees

Clearly management should be involved in the development of CSR strategy, but it is less often accepted that employees should play a part. The reason why their involvement is important relates to 'knowing where you are at'. Often employees have already been carrying out the activities that are now to be consolidated into a CSR strategy. Dialogue is important to ensure that employees feel that their individual efforts have not been hijacked, but have been built up through consultation with them.

The EU introduced its Information and Consultation Directive to ensure that employees are regularly informed and consulted about major changes in the nature of the company's strategy (implemented in the UK via the Information and Consultation of Employees Regulations 2004). However this is probably too formal an approach for the development of a CSR strategy. Instead a low-key series of working groups based either at a functional level or at a business unit level would suffice. This will only be successful if there is adequate publicity about the nature of the activity, so that the employees can see both that their representatives are being consulted and that the results of this consultation have been communicated to them. As a consequence, whilst only a very small percentage of employees may be involved in the development of the CSR strategy, the vast majority will feel that the company values their opinions. This ensures they are committed to the outcomes.

Employee surveys

Where companies undertake employee satisfaction surveys, this mechanism should be used as a means of understanding more about employee attitudes towards CSR-related activities. If the timing of the development of CSR strategy can incorporate a proposed employee satisfaction survey then this should include specific questions about attitudes towards CSR. These answers could then be used to help formulate the CSR strategy. However, often it is difficult to time the employment satisfaction survey to line up with events such as the development of the CSR strategy. One alternative is to have a specific CSR employee survey. If this is not feasible, then once the CSR strategy has been developed, the results of the strategy should be included in subsequent employee satisfaction surveys. This will enable benchmark tracking to be developed to ensure the strategy is in line with the attitudes of employees.

Local involvement

There is a particularly strong need to involve local managers where the company is based in a variety of locations, especially if these locations are in different countries. Our experience of multinational CSR means that the development of the strategy has to take account of a range of different cultures.

Ultimately, the best route in such multinational circumstances is to develop an 'umbrella' approach under which the company sets out its aims and the objectives of the policies and practices that it expects every country operation to implement. It then allows the individual operations to decide how best to achieve this implementation in relation to their local cultures.

Integrating CSR into the business

As part of strategy development, it is important to plan a management system in advance so that CSR becomes embedded within the business. CSR should not be a separate activity undertaken by the centre, but rather a part of the normal business process and practice for all business units.

Several elements should be considered to ensure that CSR is integrated into business.

- The inclusion of a range of CSR performance indicators (PIs) that are reviewed on a regular basis at main board level. These do not need to be as extensive as those KPIs that may be communicated to the company's stakeholders, but they should relate to the way in which CSR can impact on business performance. As such, it will be relevant both to the main board and to the management groups that have ownership for these PIs.
- CSR-related elements should be included in the performance incentive pay structure, so that management and employees recognise the importance of CSR to the business (and to their own position). These incentives should relate to the CSR PIs discussed above. Clearly these should also be discussed as part of performance appraisal of management and staff.
- CSR should be included in the business planning and review process, so that any business planning decision takes account of the impact upon the various CSR elements. These impacts need to be taken into account both at the time of the annual planning cycle and also in the regular (monthly or quarterly) reviews of performance by the relevant business unit.

These three elements can be best described as 'winning the hearts and minds of management and staff'. However, to make sure CSR is truly embedded within the company there is another element: leadership and governance.

It is essential that the main board and particularly the CEO should be seen to be leading on CSR. There should be a governance system to support this leadership. It should not be left to local business operation units to develop tactical rather than strategic responses. As a consequence, it is important that the CEO becomes an advocate on the key CSR elements relevant to the nature and focus of the business. This advocacy needs to be communicated effectively throughout the company. This will ensure not only that the employees are aware of the company's commitment towards CSR, but also by demonstrating advocacy, will encourage management staff to consider ways to develop initiatives that can contribute to the company's CSR positioning and business performance. It will also show that the CEO believes in the integrity of the CSR process.

Monitoring and audit

In ensuring this integrity, the monitoring and audit of the CSR measurements and activities is a key consideration that must be addressed at the outset of developing a CSR strategy. The reason is that of transparency. If a company seeks to develop its CSR approach to meet the needs of its stakeholders, then it – and they – must be assured that what is being reported is both relevant and realistic.

Some elements of CSR already have some form of monitoring and audit built in. These include the environment (for those companies that have ISO 14000 certification), the marketplace (for those companies that have ISO 9000 certification for supplier and customer quality management) and the occupational health and safety area (for those companies that have the OSHAS 18001 certification).

However, not all companies have followed these certification paths and for them and for those that only have some of them, there is a need to ensure that the information provided as part of the CSR process is accurate.

For this purpose, most companies that have developed their CSR programmes have given this task to their internal audit department. When members of this department undertake their reviews as part of their normal audit role covering financial and governance issues, they also include CSR activity and measurement.

Internal and external verification

The question that many companies are considering is whether this internal audit process is sufficient. From an NGO perspective, the relevance of having an external audit of such activity is considered to be very high. This relates to the amount of trust that NGOs have in corporates and their accusations of the 'greenwash' of companies' CSR reports that they felt were high on corporate spin and low on social and environmental relevance.

However, from a corporate perspective, the value of such external audit and verification has been questioned. One leading FTSE350 CSR director holds the view that more effort is spent on explaining the nature and risks and opportunities of the business to the external verifiers than is ever gained in value by improvements gained from their insight into the process.

As a consequence, some corporates avoid any form of external verification. Others limit it to low-scale reviews of what is in their CSR report. A study in 2002 by KPMG showed that in 2002, only 29% of the top 250 global companies had had their CSR verified (or assured as it is often described nowadays). Since then report verification has increased, as is indicated by the GRI[6] which showed that 47% of reports submitted to GRI were externally assured in 2010 (although only 16% of those North American companies that submitted their reports under GRI were externally assured).

However, verification is becoming more important as the impact of the new Business Review comes into play. As will be seen later, the Association of British Insurers (ABI) has recommended that all ESG (environmental, social and governance) statements included within the Business Review should be verified – either through a rigorous internal process, or preferably by some form of external verification.

The possibility is that over time the company's auditors will acquire the role of the verifier of the CSR data included within the Business Review, as was alluded to in a report by the ICAEW,[7] whose President said:

I personally think that the profession should take the lead on sustainability because it is in the public interest.

However, such an approach is unlikely to satisfy the NGOs, because of its reliance on process, rather than enquiring of the stakeholders the extent to which they are satisfied with the company's performance and the materiality of its reporting.

Accountability's AA1000 Assurance Standard[8] was developed to offer an assurance standard that companies could use with a high level of credibility in terms of the transparency, quality and relevance of their CSR information. The standard is specifically compatible with the UN Global Reporting Initiative, ensuring its use around the world. Its key principles include:

- materiality;
- completeness;
- responsiveness;
- accessibility; and
- evidence.

The standard is certainly thorough, although the investment required for a company to use it as its verification method may be a stumbling block to its being taken up on an extensive basis.

Regardless of what method is used, there is a need to demonstrate to an external stakeholder that the CSR process and measurements have been monitored and that they have been audited to ensure accuracy and relevance. The likelihood is that this is an area that will grow in importance and more companies will come to accept some form of verification of the CSR statements made in published reports.

CSR and sustainability – a developing approach

Sustainability is a concept which is defined as being mankind's impact, through development, on the environment. The WBSCD description is that sustainable development is 'development which meets the needs of the present without compromising the ability of future generations to meet their own needs'.

It starts from the premise that current environmental and resource issues, like climate change, are the result of unmanaged and hence unsustainable, consumption of natural resources. It takes its task to be how to meet the needs of a world population that is expected to rise from 7 billion currently to 9 billion by 2050.

In many respects, the issues addressed by sustainability are no different to those addressed by CSR – it could be described as a new form of terminology. However, there is interest in business as to how such longer term sustainability issues can be taken into account in management decision making. One route is that promoted by the Prince of Wales with his Accounting for Sustainability project.[9] The project has focused on developing systems to help business to take into account and report the wider social and environmental costs of their actions. It has received support from accounting practices such as PwC and KPMG in order to develop methodology to measure these costs. It has been closely associated with the International Integrated Reporting Committee (described in Chapter 2). There are several large companies (including Marks and Spencer with its Plan A) that are beginning to develop sustainability decision-making models as part of their longer term planning, which will ensure sustainability becomes part of their management culture.

Conclusion

This chapter set out to describe CSR as being a means of developing a management culture. We have highlighted the importance of CSR values and especially the development of the code of ethics and its compliance system. In addition, we have described how the CSR strategy can be developed, with the objective of embedding it within the culture.

However, the fundamental success factor of CSR is that it is seen to be a living management process. The strategy needs to be set and reviewed regularly. But the key activity is ensuring it is implemented across all business units and across all CSR components. The delivery of CSR practice is a critical activity. If any of the components are weak, they detract from the effectiveness of the other components. It is to the issues of developing effective practices for each of the individual CSR components that we now turn in the following chapters.

Sources

1 Webley and More *Does Business Ethics Pay? Ethics and financial performance* (2003) The Institute of Business Ethics.

2 K. Ugoji, N. Dando, L. Moir *Does Business Ethics Pay? – Revisited* (2007) IBE.

3 S. Webley *Developing a Code of Business Ethics – A guide to best practice including the IBE Illustrative Code of Business Ethics* (2003) The Institute of Business Ethics.

4 The detailed results of Transparency International's 2011 Index can be found at: cpi.transparency.org/cpi2011/results/

5 'Strategies to Combat Fraud'. A presentation made by David Crook, chairman of Expolink, a provider of external confidential helplines, in an IIR seminar in September 2004.

6 For more information about GRI reporting trends, see *GRI Sustainability Reporting Statistics*: *Publication 2010* at: www.globalreporting.org/resourcelibrary/GRI-Reporting-Stats-2010.pdf.

7 'Sustainability: the role of the accountants' can be viewed at: www.icaew.co.uk/bettermarkets.

8 Details of the AA1000 Assurance Standard can be found at: www.accountability.org.uk.

9 Details of this project, including access to the toolkits provided can be found at: www.accountingforsustainability.org.uk.

12

CSR – The community

Perceptions of CSR

The 'community' is what those less knowledgeable outsiders often perceive CSR to be all about. The reason is the use of the word 'social'. For many company observers, this equates to providing donations to charity and community acts of goodwill, which is why some corporate practitioners prefer to call it CR (corporate responsibility).

But the attitude goes both ways – in our stakeholder research, we found environmental NGOs, who are convinced that there is too much focus on 'community' activities in the information provided by companies.

The background to this perception is based on the way companies have historically managed those areas that are now perceived to relate to the community element of CSR. Within the human resources department there was usually an individual with a title that referred to either 'community relations' or 'community affairs' and who was responsible for activities such as charitable donations, as well as liaison with community groups.

Usually the budget involved was a relatively small amount and the extent to which there was any strategic consideration was limited – indeed, the view was that these donations were a whim of the chairman or the chief executive, often as a result of some personal involvement, as distinct from determining what was best from a corporate perspective.

This perception of the community is different in North America to that in the UK. In North America the amount of corporate giving to charities is limited, largely because the idea of 'donation' is considered patronising and the concept of 'philanthropy' is considered more acceptable. This view relates especially to individual giving, sometimes via personal or family foundations. Corporate philanthropy tends to involve employee activity and is usually focused on a few themes relative to the company.

The case is similar in Europe, but for different reasons. In Europe, the level of social security tends to be higher than in the UK and companies perceive that the higher rate rates of tax they pay are, as a consequence, linked to the provision of such social benefits to the disadvantaged. As a result, they do not feel the need to contribute to education or to those who are disadvantaged in the same manner as companies might do in the UK.

For this purpose, we are focusing on the community activities of a UK company, from the perspective of how it can help meet business objectives. This will cover the following aspects:

- community affairs, including the benefits of such giving, the Giving List and corporate foundations;
- cause-related marketing;
- community investment;
- employee volunteering and community activity;
- overseas activities involving activities such as sponsorship as well as community investment;
- developing corporate reputation through community-related CSR activity; and
- measurement of community activities.

Community affairs

Let's start by defining community affairs for the purposes of this section:

> Community affairs represent involvement by companies by giving donations to charities and community groups, for them then to decide how they should spend these donations.

The company has no responsibility or authority in terms of how the money should be spent by those who receive these donations, regardless of how they originally advocated it should be spent. As such, the responsibility for ensuring that the donations are spent in the manner originally intended by the company is down to the managers or the trustees of the charity concerned.

This form of giving has evolved over the past decade to include three forms of donations:

- gifts in kind – also known as value in kind;
- cash; and
- management time.

The differences between the three forms of giving will affect the way in which charities or community groups can benefit from the donations.

Gifts in kind

Clearly gifts in kind are a highly focused method for a company giving to a community-based group.

As an example, if a company wants to donate some of its assets, such as computer equipment, then the community group concerned will only benefit if they have the need for such equipment. Making it a relevant form of gift in kind to the charity concerned is key (e.g. providing paint and building materials to a charity that is involved in refurbishing houses for use by the homeless).

Similarly, the provision of medicinal drugs to communities can be a highly targeted activity designed to alleviate specific community issues. Such donations need not only be focused on the developing countries (as in the case of AIDS-related medicine for African countries), but also can include the donation of drugs to the poor in the developing world who do not have any medical insurance to pay for them (e.g. Astra Zeneca and Glaxo Smith Kline both gave drug donations to patient assistance programmes in the USA).

Whilst the value of such gifts in kind are generally recorded on the basis of their wholesale price, the community benefits in terms of the much higher retail value, which improves the public's perception of the company.

Staff time as a gift in kind

The provision of management and staff time is a form of gift in kind and can be highly motivating to the individual employees concerned, provided the community group finds the resource of benefit to them. Traditionally, such staff time focused on providing charities with legal and accountancy skills – skills that are usually expensive for a charity to resource. As a consequence, such time typically came from the higher echelons of the management of the company concerned.

Now, however, there is a growing tendency for companies to provide staff as part of a personal development programme – for instance, the provision of junior staff as mentors, either in education, or in supporting young disadvantaged people. In these instances, the use of junior staff can be appropriate because they can relate to the younger generation target audience.

To maximise the benefit for the company concerned, the skills developed through such activity must align to the company's requirement for those job-related skills to be developed in the staff concerned.

The ideal win-win for a company providing management or staff time as a donation to a charity is that the charity benefits from the skills it needs, the company benefits from developing a new set of skills in its employees and the individuals concerned can see an improvement in their career prospects as a result of developing those skills.

Generally speaking, management or staff time is donated free of charge. Ironically, these donations are not always valued as much as they should be, *because* they are seen as being free. Certainly when we have worked for charities, our early experience of pro bono (or free) work was that unless it was conducted for a senior executive, it tended to be valued (and acted upon) less than if we charged for the work.

As a result some companies have started to provide skilled support to charities by charging for the provision of their staff time at 'not for profit rates'. A good example of such a programme is that offered by Accenture – the Accenture Development Partnerships.[1]

Accenture's programme

Accenture has always been very zealous in deriving statistical data from all its management activities. In terms of recruitment of new staff, it discovered a correlation between the high career performance of the individual and the desire to 'give something back'. Their Development Partnerships programme was established recognising that, even in a high flying technology-based management consultancy, many of their staff, particularly their newly qualified or graduate employees, have socially related needs and aspirations.

Accenture has developed this programme to enable these individuals to work for not for profit organisations, usually in the developing world, offering high quality consulting expertise to bodies that would not normally be able to afford such skills at full consultancy rates. As such, Accenture involvement does not imply a donation, since the individual's services are charged to the organisation concerned, but on an 'at cost/cost neutral' basis rather than on a 'with profit' basis. The employees that take part on these programmes also volunteer to take a temporary salary reduction. The additional benefit the receiving organisation gains is the back up experience that Accenture provides to its staff working on such projects – experience that is provided as part of the package.

The programme has been remarkably successful. In considering setting up the programme, they canvassed the views of their UK employees in the first instance, 70% of whom indicated they would be willing to consider participating in such a placement programme. This is quite a significant response, considering the average placement was six months, with the employee taking a reduced salary and living in conditions that would be below what they were used to. The key finding was that a disproportionate number of Accenture's best performers were interested in this kind of work; this very much underpins Accenture's business case based on retention and recruitment.

Cash donations

The final option is cash donations. These can be specified to be used for certain activities. Such donations are defined as 'restricted income' by the charities involved.

However, from a charity perspective this may be less attractive. They try to avoid 'restrictive income', since they are unable to switch from using it for one activity to using it for another, even if the latter is a more needy cause. The issue of 'restrictive income' is particularly challenging for charities that receive high levels of legacy income. One of our charity clients received a legacy for a sizeable sum, with the restriction that it was to be spent providing support to the charity's causes in the Isle of Man – a location where they had no base and where the cost of setting up such a base would have been more than the size of the legacy itself. This restriction effectively made it a worthless donation. As a result, charities would normally prefer cash donations with no restrictions, but most corporate donations (often agreed via the company's Charity Committee) are for specific activities, when usually the corporate donation is part of a larger amount of funding, obtained via personal donations, trusts funding or lottery grants.

The benefit of giving

The benefits gained from making charitable donations can often be intangible. At most they will represent developing relationships in the form of a body of support for the company amongst those individuals or organisations seen as being influential within the community.

The nature of the benefits can be seen in many forms. They:

- align the interests of the organisation alongside those of the local government bodies for the community concerned;
- gain allies within the community amongst groups that could be seen as being influential in the event of the company facing problems; and
- simply allow the company to be seen as a citizen within the community.

However, to gain these benefits, the nature of the giving is important. Sponsorship, such as a floral decoration on a roundabout, is unlikely to generate the same sense of goodwill towards a company compared with a gift to the local school (e.g. additional resources for the library, sports kit, or supporting the extension to the science block).

Similarly, the nature of the process will determine the extent of goodwill. Much charitable giving is channelled through a company's charitable donations committee (often with a maximum authority in the order of £5,000) and the process becomes administrative in nature, rather than acting as the basis for relationship building with the community organisation involved. Most charities or community groups would prefer a more involved approach from the company rather than an administrative approach for a charitable donation.

The Giving List

The change to include the three different forms of giving has led to an increase in the value of corporate giving – helped also by the recognition that companies need to be better able to collate all their community involvement activity and report on a more complete basis than previously.

This need to report was driven by the production of 'The Giving List' by the *Guardian* newspaper.[2] Until 2006, this list collated all the giving for charitable purposes for the UK's leading quoted companies. Initially, the information about their giving came from the companies' annual report and accounts, which required that cash donations to charities (and to political parties) were stated (although the BIS consultation referred to in Chapter 2 does suggest that the requirement to disclose this information may be at an end). The *Guardian* stopped publishing The Giving List in 2006, but more detailed information about corporate giving is available from the Directory of Social Change.[3]

However, the change to reporting on the three forms of donations came as the companies pointed out that this form of measure did not reflect the true levels of community involvement on their part.

The Giving List was assembled by Business in the Community. At best it was a useful indicator of the intentions of the companies featured in the list, but the quality of the information was inconsistent, driven as it was by company submissions which may not have been fully audited or comprehensive. Indeed, on some occasions, companies have not made a submission, but have had information included in the list based on published data. Inevitably, this will be less than complete.

The challenge was that the List developed as a league table comparing corporate donations as a percentage of pre-tax profits. Some of the company's submissions were based only on UK data – not such a problem when companies such as BSkyB are involved, but a fairly large omission when companies such as Shell International's performance was based on its UK data compared with worldwide pre-tax profits.

Equally, the year-on-year comparison is made more difficult by companies improving the quality of their data – a good example of which was Shire Pharmaceuticals, whose performance in 2003 improved by 92% as a result of the inclusion of the donations of flu vaccines to Argentina and Colombia, as well as anti-cancer drugs to a US NGO, Americare. The comment of the company's Head of Corporate Communications indicates that the level of gifts in kind was roughly the same year on year, but that the quality of information had improved, based on reporting to the Giving List!

Our own analysis of the Giving List for one of our clients bore out the relevance of this comment. This research showed that those companies that were scoring highly were doing so by undertaking activities (involving measurement of gifts in kind, staff time or management costs) which greatly improved the percentage of pre-tax profits that they contributed to community activities. In fact, for those companies contributing 0.5% or less, not one of them had included any form of gift in kind giving within their measurements. Yet from my own experience of reviewing companies' community activities, such gift in kind giving does exist – but it is often not part of the company recording system.

Nevertheless, the List was widely used – often by charities to identify targets for future corporate donation campaigns, as well as by corporates who looked at their position in the league table as a means of comparison with their peers and competitors.

Of the companies featured in the List, a total of 0.8% of pre-tax profits was given to charities, voluntary organisations and community projects in 2002/2003, representing a total of £818 million. But by 2006, little appeared to have changed – FTSE100 companies gave about the same in percentage terms (0.79%) but the total amount invested in community responsibilities had increased to £986m due to an increase in corporate profitability.

The objective of the List was to encourage more companies to achieve the Percent Club – later called the Business in the Community's Percent Standard (i.e. those companies that give more than 1% of their pre-tax profits to community activities). Launched in 1986, this was used as benchmark for corporate community investment in the UK. Every kind of business was measured against a minimum investment into the community of 1% of UK or global pre-tax profits. Over 122 companies in the UK were achieving this standard in 2003. But even with these companies donating a total of £854 million in 2002, the impact of corporate giving on the income of the voluntary sector was still small, standing at 4.9% of the total cash income of the voluntary sector in 2002. Corporate giving still represents a significant development area of potential fundraising for charities.

However, by 2007, Business in the Community had responded to companies becoming more sophisticated in their range of community activities. Its members (all corporate) challenged Business in the Community to develop a new standard to recognise their more holistic approach to corporate community investment. As a result, Business in the Community developed the CommunityMark[4] and 2006 was the final year that the Percent Standard existed as a stand alone activity. The CommunityMark utilises a survey approach that focuses on the evaluation of key community projects by companies and assesses the difference that made to the community and the business and identification of commitments for the next three years. It is a more comprehensive approach than the Percent Club, which tended to focus on giving rather than a company's relationship with its communities.

Corporate foundations

More companies are considering the use of corporate foundations for community giving. These are foundations formed by companies for the sole purpose of channelling their donations for charitable purposes.

This is distinct from foundations founded by individuals endowed with the wealth they accrued through their corporate endeavours. These include the Leverhulme Foundation, based on the wealth created by the Lever family, or the Wellcome Trust, created by Sir Henry Wellcome, who endowed the Trust with the entire share capital of The Wellcome Foundation Ltd (now part of GSK).

Corporate foundations can either be funded by initial endowment or annual endowments (or a combination of both). These corporate foundations are totally independent of the companies that formed them – and the trustees are equally independent of the company, except in so far as the foundation's articles of association allow them to take into account the company's interests in their charitable decision making.

One of the first companies to form such a foundation was Lloyds TSB. The Lloyds TSB Foundation was set up as a result of the merger agreement between Lloyds Bank and TSB (at that time a mutually owned organisation). This agreement was intended to reflect the loss of the mutuality in a way whereby the new business could still demonstrate the community activity upheld as important by the old TSB. As a consequence the foundation was set up with an annual sum paid into it equivalent to 1% of the new company's pre-tax profits. The result is that this foundation became one of Britain's larger charitable bodies in terms of both endowed capital and new income. Lloyds TSB changed its position regarding the foundation after it acquired HBOS and became the Lloyds Banking Group. The very much enlarged group would result in significant additional income for the foundation and the agreement changed from a percentage of profits to fixed income amounts agreed on a regular basis.

Why are more companies considering following a similar path? The reason is to channel their giving (often so as to reinforce the corporate discipline within the employee base) as well as to reduce the number of unsolicited requests for funding. The 'benefit' of such foundations is that their charitable articles mean that they are directed to certain specific community activity areas – so, for example, the foundation established by Shell has its focus 'finding sustainable solutions to social and environmental problems linked to energy production and consumption' – rather than being open to all forms of requests for charity and community funding. It is noteworthy that the Lloyds TSB Foundation was an exception to this – the Foundation is independent of the Lloyds TSB CSR management direction.

However, there is no UK tax advantage or disadvantage to the company of funding such a foundation although, once endowed, the foundation may benefit from favourable tax treatment of its investment income. Not every major company has gone down the foundation route – BT for one has decided against putting its significant CSR community budget into a foundation.

So why would a company set up a foundation (at considerable legal expense)? Currently there are just over 100 registered corporate foundations, 50% of which have been set up since 1990. Business in the Community conducted some research on the reasons why these had been established – and the most often quoted was 'to provide a governance structure and arm's length independence of giving from the business' – or to quote the foundation secretary for the Morgan Stanley Foundation:

> It sends good messages internally and externally that we are committed to supporting the community because the money is ring fenced. Once it comes into the Foundation, the company can't get it out.

Others have found that corporate foundations can have other advantages. They can be more attractive as a partner to charities than the parent company itself. This can be because the charities see the foundation as being a charity like themselves and hence 'speaking the same language'. Also, corporate foundations can raise funds through co-sponsoring that a company itself may never be able to realise.

Yet, others do not favour corporate foundations as vehicles for their community involvement. Their reasons vary, but the three main ones are:

- Once you endow the foundation, decisions about its activities are down to the trustees, whose role is guided by the articles of association, rather than the endowing company's business objectives.
- The reputation benefit to the company can be more difficult to secure, because the community sees it as coming from the foundation, as distinct from the company that provided the funds.
- Setting up a foundation can separate community affairs from the rest of the company's CSR agenda and as such can reduce the company's integrated approach towards CSR. This can cause difficulties, since at times it can be of benefit to link, for example, environmental and community activities.

Certainly companies like BT and also Barclays (who gave 1.14% of its pre-tax profits to community activities in the 2006 Giving List) have clearly weighed up the pros and cons of setting up their foundation. Barclays' then Director of Consumer and Community Affairs Martin Mosley said that:

> You get more ownership and flexibility channelling investment through community affairs.

The foundation can offer benefits of focus but there is a risk of a company washing its hands of the community activity by setting up an independent body to tackle it. If a company is serious about its community impact then it should not be delegating this responsibility to trustees who may not always have the company's business objectives as their first priority.

Cause-related marketing

Cause-related Marketing (CRM) is a more commercial form of community involvement. Business in the Community[5] defines it as:

> A commercial activity by which businesses and charities or causes form a partnership with each other to market and package products or services for mutual benefit.

The phrase 'form a partnership' is slightly misleading, as there are two forms of CRM – one where a company promotes a charity's cause and the other where a company defines a cause it wishes to support and then contributes directly to the recipients of such a cause, instead of via an intermediary, such as a charity.

A good example of the former was Ford UK's 'Drive Towards a Cure'. Whenever individual members of the public test drove various vehicles, Ford made a payment to the Breakthrough Breast Cancer charity.

In contrast, an example of the latter is Tesco's Computers for Schools, probably one of the longest running CRM campaigns, which generated vouchers, based on an individual's spend in store; these were then collected by the recipient and given to the school of their choice (which can be their children's school, or as is often the case, their grandchildren's or nephews' or nieces' school). The school then exchanged them for computer hardware and software. Once schools had become better equipped in IT, Tesco modified this scheme in 2008 and repositioned it as Tesco for Schools and Clubs, and changed the 'offer' to cover a variety of useful pieces of equipment for schools and amateur clubs. In effect, Tesco created its own cause, whereas Ford partnered with an existing one.

Choosing the right approach to CRM

The choice of approach depends on several factors:

- Can the company afford to select and support its own cause? Tesco has provided logistical and distribution support as well as funding the equipment.
- Does the company have the status to create its own cause or would it benefit in reputation by developing a partnership with its chosen cause? Ford's choice of Breakthrough Breast Cancer helped it to strengthen its position with the women's car purchasers market.
- Can the company find a partner whose brand attributes match those of the company – and hence establishes the rationale for the partnership – giving the company potential for greater reputation improvement?

The last point is highly significant. Having helped charities develop their corporate fundraising programmes, I am constantly amazed at how many proposals are sent out by charities that are effectively a standardised approach, with only the company name being changed. The development of a partnership has to be based on a common aim and a consistency of brand attributes.

Both the charity and the company involved need to satisfy themselves about the latter before considering proceeding with such a CRM programme. A good example of this was evidenced when Cadbury set up its 'Get Active' campaign to promote healthier lifestyle through encouraging young people to become more active in school sports, in conjunction with the Youth Sports Trust charity. The criticism that it received was unprecedented and based around the fact that the process involved exchanging chocolate wrappers for school sports equipment.

As The Food Commission (publishers of *Food* magazine) wrote:

If British school children purchase all of the 160 million tokens that Cadbury's plans to issue, they would have to purchase nearly two million kilograms of fat.

Their analysis took this further by highlighting that if a ten-year-old was to earn enough vouchers to gain a basketball, then that same child would need to play 90 hours to burn off the calories gained through eating the chocolate. Added to which they highlighted that the value of the equipment purchased was (not surprisingly) considerably more than the cost of the chocolate consumed – for a cricket set worth £150, about £1,150 of chocolate would need to be purchased, equivalent to about 15% of the value of the goods purchased. This last equation is misleading since it fails to take account of the various levels of cost and profit involved in the distribution chain, which are built into the final retail price but it is often quoted by NGOs.

This criticism did not revolve around the nature of the food and its impact upon young people's health. There was no direct criticism of the chocolate eaten by the young people.

In contrast, Walker's Crisps had CRM campaigns targeted at providing books for school children, but their cause was that of providing more books in school.

The difference lies in the degree of the affinity between the cause and the company (or the brand in the event of a consumer product CRM) as perceived by the stakeholders. A similar free books for schools scheme is now being run by Nestlé cereals, which is probably a healthier scheme than potato crisps and hence more acceptable to schools' stakeholders!

Essentials of successful CRM

This highlights two of the key tenets of a successful CRM campaign – the need for transparency in the relationship between a company and its chosen cause and the need for the cause to be seen to be gaining in value as result of the partnership. Both of these can depend on the nature of the CRM programme, which can be:

- A money-related donation – such as a donation per customer survey completed;
- a redemption-related donation – such as vouchers provided to an individual and redeemed by the ultimate recipient; or
- an awareness and business relationship-related activity.

This last context is often one that can be overlooked, usually because CRM is considered to be appropriate only for consumer-related products. Yet, in one of my previous roles as Marketing Director of Manpower plc in the UK, I undertook several CRM programmes based on a business-to-business market, which had the development of business relationships as its main objective.

One example was when we undertook a CRM programme with Capital Radio (now Capital FM) which runs the Help a London Child appeal at Christmas time. Their challenge was that they received a lot of toys from London's stores, but only after the end of Christmas – too late to meet the expectations of the children receiving them. Manpower's business challenge was how to stimulate discussion in January with its HR clients about their temporary workers – a particularly low time for business-to-business discussions in this market.

To match both these needs, we developed the simple approach of advising our clients (typically HR directors) that we would be delivering a Christmas tree, some plastic sacks and sufficient posters to cover their office needs at the beginning of December. The posters encouraged the client's staff to collect toys and put them into the sacks – which we promised to collect in the week before Christmas. The result was that we collected about £100,000 of toys for the Help a London Child appeal on each of the three years we ran the campaign – and London's deserving kids received them on Christmas Day as Capital had intended. So one side of the equation was satisfied. On the other side of the equation, our branch staff were able to go in to their clients in early January to say 'thank you' for their support. This provided a 'no pressure' opportunity to recommence business discussions well in advance of the normal business season and it gave us a commercial advantage over our competitors.

Having identified the various forms of CRM, there are three questions to be asked:

- How successful is it for corporates?
- What are the key factors to ensure this success?
- Is CRM part of CSR?

How successful is CRM for corporates?

Perhaps the easiest way to answer this is to look at the experience of Tesco, which started its Computers for Schools programme in 1992, initially as a sales promotion programme. When it ended in 2008, it was probably one of the longest running CRM programmes – certainly in the UK, but effectively it continued in its new format 'Tesco for Schools and Clubs', reflecting that the school focused approach is now coming up to its twentieth year.

As the largest private employer in the UK, Tesco believes it has a role to play to contribute to workforce educational skills. Over 80% of primary and secondary schools in the UK were active participants, receiving computers and equipment such as digital cameras, digital movie creators, microscopes and interactive encyclopaedias. Since 1992, Tesco has given away equipment worth nearly £200 million. In 2010, UK schools and clubs (clubs were an extension beyond the formal education sector) collected computers and items of school equipment worth £9.3 million through Tesco's CRM initiative.

Whilst the Tesco management will admit they cannot see a direct statistical link in terms of relating sales revenue to their investment in this programme, they are also very much aware that each time their programme runs, there is a very noticeable rise in sales revenue for the period of the programme. What is of particular interest is that Tesco has used this initiative as a platform to introduce other school-based initiatives (perhaps now more topical than was the case in 1992), such as Sport for Schools and Clubs and the FA Tesco Skills Programme aimed at improving football skills for children aged 5–11.

Whilst not every CRM programme has this level of success, the Brand Benefit research undertaken in 2003 for Business in the Community does demonstrate good reasons for a company to consider a CRM programme as part of its community involvement:

- 83% of consumers had participated in at least one CRM programme (compared with 68% in 2000);
- 70% of consumers involved in CRM programmes reported a positive impact on their behaviour or perceptions of the brand concerned;
- 48% of them changed their behaviour as a result of the CRM programme, switching brands, increasing usage, or sampling new products.

What are the key factors for success?

There are four key factors to ensure the success of a CRM programme. The first involves ensuring there is sufficient expenditure on communication and relates to how effectively the programme is to be communicated to the target audience. The estimate of the levels of communication expenditure for a successful sponsorship programme is that the company that acquires a sponsorship should spend two to three times the amount of the sponsorship to ensure the target audience is fully aware of the sponsorship link.

The same is true for CRM, although the multiplier will be slightly different given the presence of a partner in the form of a charity that may bring their own communication to the party. It is wrong to believe that just because a company is supporting a good cause its target audience will hear about it, or understand it. There is a need to have adequate communication to get the message across to the intended audience.

The second involves the affinity of the brands involved. The target audience's perception of a programme will be stronger if they believe that there is a sound reason for the two bodies to work together. Tesco has been able to build a strong community brand, based upon its support of the educational programmes (as will be seen with another Tesco case study, featured in the next section).

The third involves visibility and transparency – the target audience should be able to see and understand that there is a fair balance of the benefits to each party. Without an equitable balance (but particularly if the balance is weighted in favour of the company partner), the target audience will not be inclined to support the programme, however much they wish to support the charity or the cause.

The fourth is about longevity. Two of the most successful CRM campaigns have been long running – Tesco's is in its second decade, whilst Walker's Crisps ended its Free Books for School CRM in 2003, after five years and 6.6 million books. Longevity of a CRM Programme is a double-edged sword. The target audience becomes much more familiar with it the longer that the programme runs – and hence the return on investment improves. However, a long-running programme can become too familiar to the target audience and as a result its impact is lessened. Equally in an area as socially deserving as education, there is a further issue that the longer the programme runs, the more the schools come to depend upon it – and for a company to terminate it, a discussion is required about the extent to which such a decision would be likely to be a public uproar. In my judgement, aiming to run a CRM programme for about five years is probably about the right length, while the 19 years of the Tesco programme may be considered by some to be too long to continue deriving commercial benefits.

Is CRM part of CSR?

Alternatively, is CRM just another form of marketing? Well the answer is yes and no. As long as CRM drives increased community involvement, it is part of CSR and should fit into the CSR strategy – indeed if it did not fit into the strategy, it should be axed. But it is a marketing vehicle to drive revenue and profit and this should not be forgotten. The issue is that of tempering the marketer's natural exuberance with the CSR requirement that community programmes should be transparent and drive real community benefit – which will always result in an intense discussion between the marketer and the CSR manager!

Community investment

Community investment[6] is different from community affairs in so far as the company sets a community strategy that means it directly involves itself in some manner in the delivery of the community activities, rather than purely making donations for the charity or community group to decide how to use it. Invariably it involves a larger investment on the part of the company than would normally be expected for a community affairs programme. Business in the Community's Community Mark is a benchmark for excellence in community investment but only 41 companies had achieved this by the end of 2011.

The nature of such activities will vary, but because of the expenditure involved, for a company to consider community investment, it needs to regard itself as already having a high presence and a high impact with communities and consumers. The following are some examples that indicate how companies are using community investment:

Targeting local communities

- *Tata (ex Corus) in Port Talbot, South Wales* is a large steel-making site, located in a town where the dominant employer is the steel works. Its presence not only physically dominates the town, but its noise and dust is part of everyday life. Our work with Corus highlighted a particular example of community investment, which involved cash, management time and using company influence effectively for the benefit of the cause.

  In the UK every user of packaging and producer of waste material has to pay a landfill tax for disposal of waste. However, if a company donated up to 6.8% of their landfill tax liability to environmental projects it can receive in return 90% tax credit. These are provided on a 'use it or lose it' basis. Corus had such tax credits available to it.

  It was approached by parents of children with special educational needs who were seeking support for the development of a centre for such children. Their previous efforts to gain funding of £250,000 had proved unsuccessful. Corus identified that it could use its credits to support projects that provide or maintain public amenities and that a Special Needs Activity Centre would fall into this category.

  Only when Corus supported the parents' proposal with management resources and an allocation of £180,000 from its tax credits could an approach for matching funding be opened up to the UK Lottery for capital and revenue funding, enabling the centre to open its doors in 2001 to children with such needs from the local community. When I visited the centre, the company was still active in supporting its management and the company's employees had been active in subsequent funding of the activities in the centre, which, being a prominent part of the local community, was a strong example of the company's commitment to the community.

- *Compass Group* is well known as the largest food service provider in the world.

Prior to divestments in 2006 it operated in the public domain with UK brand names such as Upper Crust, Moto motorway service stations and Café Ritazza. However, its businesses extend to communities in the developing world as a result of the support services it provides to oil exploration companies and other extractive industry sites.

The workers it employs are typically from the local communities rather than the more highly qualified personnel that are the oil exploration workers. As a result of its involvement with the local employees, it has recognised the importance of being involved with local communities in a more positive manner.

It has developed its own policy for working with the organisations representing indigenous people and has been active in developing the skills and resources available to these communities. Good examples of its proactive approach exist in its operations in places such as Angola and Alaska, where Compass is working with such organisations to:
- develop the community's employable skills (including setting targets for the percentage of managers being local nationals over a four year period)
- help local agriculture to become more efficient in meeting the standards of multinational consumers, benefiting both the local Compass operation (which would use the local sources to supplement its existing supply chain) and also enabling these agricultural producers to gain access to a wider geographic market place.
- *Boots* developed a series of initiatives with NHS Trusts local to its Nottingham headquarters. An award winning example is its development of the transformation of a room in a Nottingham hospital into a beauty room for cancer patients, providing a unique massage service for in-patients and creating a health spa for NHS staff with Boots' cosmetic products provided as part of the on-going service.

Developing educational initiatives

- *BT's* example of community investment involved their funding of a Communication Skills Road show. This involved BT working with over 1,400 schools across the UK in 2004–2006 to improve the communication skills of children aged between nine and 12 with visiting teams of actor facilitators.

The event consisted of a 30-minute drama performance, followed by around one hour's worth of classroom-based communication activities relating to effective speaking and listening skills. The 30-minute drama tells the story of a new girl at school who is bullied for being different. The bullying aspect is used as an example of how poor communication can lead to undesirable situations and explores the themes of citizenship, bullying, communication and personal responsibility.

BT's support to help young people communicate more effectively continues and in 2011 it was the lead sponsor of *'Hello', the National Year of Communication*[7] to help more young people develop their communication skills.

- *McDonald's* community programme[8] with The Scottish Football Association, Community Partners has been a collaboration between two organisations to encourage active lifestyles and promote learning skills to benefit local school-children through a community football coaching programme.

  The programme involves over 16,000 primary school children and is designed so that annually 200 primary school teachers and 100 community volunteers are trained, where applicable , to achieve Level 2 coaching status. This provides a personal development opportunity for them as well as pro-viding a continuum to the programme, enabling children in future years to benefit. It also provides a sustainable work programme for previously part-time coaches. Since its inception in August 2002, over 500 schools have been involved in the programme. The first four-year programme produced 1,270 new volunteer grassroots community football coaches. The current programme (which runs until 2014) will see McDonald's helping the Scottish FA to attract 13,000 new volunteers and 10,000 new coaches before 2014, as well as supporting 600 clubs and 52,000 players.

Skills development and regeneration

- *Tesco* has been active in bringing together public services, employers and com-munity groups to deliver economic and environmental change in deprived areas. Their first regeneration partnership[9] was in the Seacroft area of Leeds, which was once one of the largest council estates in Europe. The partnership with the local council, the Employment Service, a Family Learning Centre and a group of employers led by Tesco involved training residents for up to a year – with the benefit of guaranteed jobs at the end of that period.

  Since then, Tesco has developed further regeneration partnerships amount-ing to a total of 35 stores and around 4,000 jobs for long-term unemployed people by 2011. All of them have involved new Tesco stores being opened and each of them involved the environmental development of what were previously derelict sites.

- *Marks and Spencer's* Marks & Start programme[10] targets individuals who are facing real barriers to getting a job, because of issues such as homelessness, dis-ability, single parents wishing to return to work or youth unemployed. The scheme involves work experience placement in a Marks and Spencer store or office, the allocation of a Marks and Spencer employee as a mentor (buddies or coaches) to each participant and the provision of travelling expenses, lunch, uniforms and a reference if requested. Employees act as mentors to the partici-pants. In 2010, 840 people took part in the programme, supported by a coach and M&S buddy. Approximately 40% of those involved in the programme go on to gain full time employment.

Venture philanthropy

Clearly, all of the above schemes are significant in their impact on the community groups at which they are targeted and represent significant levels of investment (not only in money, but more importantly in management time and resources) for the companies concerned. As a consequence, it may be thought that community investment is only for the larger companies.

However, developing in the UK is the concept of venture philanthropy, where individuals or companies take a shareholding in new ventures developed to meet social needs. This approach is emulating the development of venture philanthropy in the USA – largely on the back of Silicon Valley millionaires who wanted to put their funds to some good use and where they wanted to share their management expertise with the socially focused venture. However, such approaches can be highly vexatious, especially if the ownership is more like a corporate shareholdings rather than a social enterprise. Social enterprises don't really have 'equity' to sell and comments from the Co-op's finance director suggest that a 30% holding is about as far as a single investor can go before the enterprise loses its status as a mutual undertaking or social enterprise.

This approach has been reinforced in the UK with the introduction of the Community Investment Tax Relief (CITR) scheme in 2002. This is a tax incentive for individuals and companies to invest in under-invested communities through accredited intermediary organisations – Community Development Finance Institutions (CDFI's[11]) – that, in turn, invest in enterprises that operate within or for disadvantaged communities. The scheme applies to investments in accredited CDFI's made on or after 17 April 2002.

The tax incentive is a tax relief worth up to 25% of the value of the investment in the CDFI and is spread over five years, starting with the year in which the investment is made. To obtain maximum tax relief under the scheme investors must hold the investment for at least five years.

To keep its accreditation, the CDFI must (amongst other conditions) invest most of the money raised under the CITR scheme across a range of small and medium-sized enterprises that would otherwise struggle to obtain finance.

In this respect, if a company were to invest in a CDFI, it is doubtful whether it could use this method of community investment as a means of either directing the investment to certain groups that it sees as being needful, or gain community based reputation through the investment in such groups. Although if the CDFI brand were strong enough, then engagement with the CDFI would mean that a company could relate to the totality of its impact.

However, this scheme, linked to the concept of venture philanthropy, enables smaller companies than those quoted in the above examples, to participate in community investment schemes that are more appropriate to the size of the company involved. However, as has been outlined before, they should do so only if, when considering their business objectives, they believe having a strong presence in the target community would have a positive benefit to the company concerned.

For the year ended March 2010, CDFIs had lent £200 million (up 77% on the prior year), comprising 19,000 individual loans. Total loans disbursed since the inception of CDFIs amounts to £678 million. Its association, the CDFA, now has 66 members lending in the UK, operating across 175 branches across the UK.

The idea of venture philanthropy, combined with social enterprises, is likely to continue to create interest as the recent CSR strategy published by the EU includes a Social Business Initiative action plan. This includes a European regulatory framework for social investment funds.

Employee volunteering and community activity

Employee volunteering is a regular part of the British corporate community affairs activity, unlike on the continent, where volunteering occurs at a personal rather than a corporate level.

The reason for this British phenomenon is that companies see it as a way of gaining commitment from employees by supporting them – often on a matched giving basis if the volunteering involves fundraising for a charity.

There can be a lot of goodwill generated by these activities, but companies may not be making the most of the money and resources they are providing to support employee volunteering. The challenge is that employee volunteering involves a personal commitment on the part of the employee and there may be reluctance on the part of an individual to share any limelight gained by themselves with their employer.

Instead, companies operating employee volunteering need to ensure they are seen to provide an umbrella under which employees are capable of 'doing their own thing', but where the employees recognise the part played by the company – and do not object to the company gaining reputation as a result.

A good example was identified by a member of our team in some research undertaken on a call centre run by British Gas in South Wales. It had wanted to develop employee volunteering in this centre and had canvassed the opinions of the staff about the types of cause they should be supporting. From the results of this exercise, they chose one cause that the company supported with matched giving and publicity (based around the fact that it was British Gas employees that were doing the volunteering, rather than a group of individuals that happened to work for British Gas).

The company was concerned that only a small percentage (less than 5%) of the staff had actually volunteered and they wanted to know whether the scheme was a success or not. The research showed that because it had canvassed beforehand and had communicated after the event, there was a 'halo effect' amongst the other 95% of the employees, which generated significant goodwill about the project and towards the company.

Since then, it has developed its employee volunteering by linking activity-based employee volunteering (e.g. acting as mentors to the disadvantaged) to their employee development appraisal system. This has included identifying the skills gained in the volunteering activity and mapping them against the skills required in their work for the job they are doing and for future possible jobs. In this manner, they reinforced the importance that the company places on employee volunteering and it enables the company to make the employee feel that the company is genuinely sharing with them the effort and investment in the various programmes.

Overseas community activities

It is relevant to consider overseas community activities, because there is a risk that all community activities are considered through a western developed economy perspective. Part of our work has included working for clients such as mining companies. Typically these will operate within the developing world – Africa or Southern America, as well as within the old Soviet republics. For these countries the concept of community activity can be markedly different from that in Europe or North America.

Often their community activities include programmes such as sponsorship of sports clubs. In the UK, these would be frowned upon as being marketing rather than community programmes. Yet for these companies, the very nature of their operations means that the location of their extraction sites are often in underdeveloped areas and their presence is often highly intermingled with that of the community – in fact, to all intents and purposes they are the community.

Their role reflects what the case in the UK was in the early days of the industrial revolution and they will act in a manner similar to that of Salt, Rowntree and Leverhulme. As a result, they will not only sponsor (and perhaps nearly 100% fund) sports clubs, but will also invest in hospitals, religious and educational facilities. They will also support the communities that are peripheral to their own operational site, providing them with business guidance and educational support.

For them, doing so represents part of the cost of their licence to operate. These activities are not the same as the charity of the year programmes of some totally UK-based companies, but in many respects, they are not dissimilar to cause-related marketing. As such, they are right to describe these activities as part of their community activities.

There are also examples from the developing world, where governments have established legislation requiring companies investing in these countries to participate in local community investment. This is the case in Indonesia and Philippines, where legislation was targeted at foreign extraction companies. It was designed to ensure that these companies reinvested into those communities on whose lands they were locating their extraction operations. Essentially, this approach adds greater clarification on the cost of obtaining a 'licence to operate' for those industries.

Developing corporate reputation through community-related activity

The last example of employee volunteering shows how a well thought out approach can ensure that both the company and the employee can gain personal and corporate reputation through a well coordinated corporate approach towards employee volunteering.

Some companies allow the community element of their CSR programme to 'just happen' without aiming to deliver improvements in corporate reputation as a result. To identify the opportunities offered in developing corporate reputation we developed our 'Grid for a Rewarding Business', shown below, that identifies the need to have both a CSR stakeholder focus and also a brand reputation focus for all the activities.

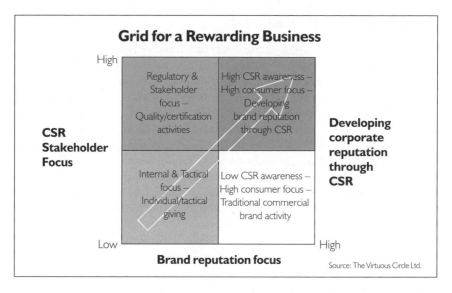

The bottom left quadrant represents those activities that are typically tactical, whilst the bottom right quadrant represents the typical marketing activity and involves activities such as corporate sponsorship and advertising programmes. The top left quadrant represents those activities that are typically compliance related, such as having the range of social, ethical and environmental policies. It is the top right quadrant that should be the target, where the activities combine both a stakeholder and a brand reputation focus.

The grid below illustrates how the community-related activities for a company can be plotted out on the grid – the example shown is that of a company which asked us to identify how it could improve its community activities in terms of reputation building.

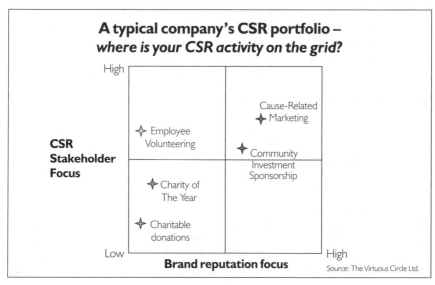

The challenge for each company is to revisit their community-related activities with an open mind and ask whether they are really delivering a satisfactory return on investment for all the effort that is being expended. As an example, what is the benefit to the company of having a charity of the year? Most companies have gone down this path at some stage with the result that few if any of them are receiving any significant competitive advantage from their having one. This potential disadvantage is compounded by the fact that by having an annual charity, their ability to deliver a consistent themed message is diluted every year they change the charity.

A good example of one company that focused its community activity is BT, who previously had a multitude of charitable support projects. After reviewing their community activity, they focused on one charity, Childline (established by the NSPCC), because research amongst their community stakeholders had identified child-related activities as the most appropriate type of charity they thought BT should relate to. Their view was also that the company should be seen to be having a significant impact in their actions – indicating a requirement to have a critical mass of activity.

BT decided that the only way it could deliver the visible impact that it was seeking was by concentrating its efforts on one charity and then to have a long-term plan of development with that charity. It commenced its support in 1986. It has since extended its financial support to Childline by bringing together a wide range of activities, including working with its supply chain to identify suitable joint programmes. BT people also dedicate their time as ChildLine volunteer counsellors. Since 2002, BT has raised over £7.5million for ChildLine.

The Head of NSPCC Corporate Partnerships attributes ChildLine's continued success to BT:

> I am in no doubt that part of this success is down to the longstanding relationship between ChildLine and BT. Indeed, it's impossible to talk about the work of ChildLine without mentioning BT.

Measuring community activities

In developing a CSR strategy, a key element is the setting of quantifiable measures and targets through which the extent to which a company is developing its community programme in the right direction can be seen.

In setting these measures, there needs to be both measures of inputs and measures of outputs.

For inputs, the range of measures is reasonably clear and includes aspects such as:

- value of donations in the form of cash, management time and gifts in kind;
- value of management time and resources used in delivering other community based activities (other than straight donations); and
- numbers of employee days spent on company supported volunteering.

However, the outputs can be far more complex and the question is whether the company can actually demonstrate that its community-related work has delivered the results that were expected. The community outputs need to be created in a series of Performance Indicators (PIs) that relate to the purpose of each type of activity or project, rather than as a series of financial data as may be the case with the inputs PIs.

So, for example, looking at the Marks & Start project, outputs could be of the nature of 'How many of the participants in the project were still in paid work a year after completing their work experience and mentoring?' or 'How did the skills of the participants improve over the period of their work experience placement?'

Similarly for the Tata (ex Corus) Special Needs Activity Centre, the output measurement would revolve around the ability to give the children a better quality of educational care, with questions such as 'How many of the children that attended the Centre were able to develop themselves over a period of a year from commencing attending the Centre?'

As can be seen, there is little likelihood of being able to have an identical set of indicators for all companies, because they depend on the nature of the project. But the indicators used should enable the company concerned to demonstrate that their community involvement has produced demonstrable results that have met the objectives set at the outset.

As well as these project related outputs, measures are required that demonstrate the benefits for the company concerned. These involve understanding how the image and reputation of the company has changed as a result of its embarking on community related initiatives. This requires the company to establish the opinions and attitudes of the various stakeholders and review them in the light of the various community activities that have been undertaken.

Where a company undertakes a regular employee survey, this should include questions about the extent to which the employees are aware of the activities undertaken, understand the part their fellow employees have played in them and are supportive of the nature of activities that are being undertaken.

Similarly, there should be regular surveys of community-based stakeholders – either in the form of opinion research surveys, or through some form of panel or focus group of stakeholders that is convened to take on board their opinions as representatives of the wider range of community stakeholders.

Conclusion

The community element of the CSR strategy is one of the areas where traditionally it has been difficult to relate a business case to the activities. Hopefully, the aspects covered in this chapter and the examples given will demonstrate to the reader that the community activities can be related to a series of business objectives. But to do so may require more careful thinking on the part of the management about how to deliver these objectives. Regardless of whether companies operate only in the UK or have an international presence, companies need to ensure their approach to the community is integrated into their CSR business process, rather than it being a 'stand alone'.

Sources

1 Information on Accenture's Development Partnerships can be obtained via the corporate citizenship section at: www.accenture.com.

2 Information about the *Guardian*'s 'Giving List' for the FTSE100 for 2006 can be found as a pdf at: image.guardian.co.uk/sys-files/Society/documents/2006/11/08/ftse100.pdf.

3 Details of the *Guide to UK Company Giving 2011/2012* can be found on the DSC's website at: www.dsc.org.uk/Publications/Fundraisingsources/@2727.

4 More information about the CommunityMark can be found on BitC's website at: www.bitc.org.uk/community/communitymark/index.html.

5 Business in the Community has long been an advocate of CRM and its website has a report on the brand benefits of it: www.bitc.org.uk/resources/publications/brand_benefits.html.

6 For information about community investment, Business in the Community offers guidance on its website at: www.bitc.org.uk/community/community_investment/.

7 Details of BT's sponsorship for 'Hello' and other community communications programmes can be found in its online Sustainability Report. See www.btplc.com/Responsiblebusiness/Ourstory/Sustainabilityreport/section/index.aspx?sectionid=dc06b50a-96ec-4d5e-9f5a-3fbddd5b373d.

8 Information on McDonald's Scottish community football coaching programme, can be obtained via the Scottish FA website: www.scottishfa.co.uk/scottish_football.cfm?page=197.

9 Information about Tesco's regeneration programmes can be obtained via its website: www.tescoplc.com/corporate-responsibility/our-community-promises/actively-supporting-local-communities/.

10 Information on the Marks and Start programme can be obtained from its 2011 Annual Report: http://annualreport.marksandspencer.com/downloads/PDFs/annual-report/OperatingReviewOurPeople.pdf.

11 More information about CDFIs can be found on the CDFA website at: www.cdfa.org.uk.

CSR – The environment

What is the environment?

'The environment' is a term that can be used as a catch-all phrase under which all manner of different activities can occur – a little bit like 'the economy' can be all things to all men – especially since former President Bill Clinton used the phrase 'It's the economy, stupid'.

For most readers, it is probably fair to assume a generally low technical knowledge regarding the environment (although it is doubtful if anyone has not now heard of climate change and carbon dioxide emissions – even if they don't fully know what the latter means). As a consequence, the purpose of this chapter is to ensure that you are adequately informed about the various issues surrounding the environment as it is understood from a CSR perspective.

So what are the areas involved in the environment? If you take a CSR survey as a benchmark, the general issues that are covered include:

- the extent to which there are environmental policies, environmental management systems and environmental certification in place;
- the extent to which the company has signed up to environmental standards or international accords;
- measurement of specific environmental areas such as global warming and emissions, energy usage, resource usage and recycling and waste, including the impact of international measurement standards such as the greenhouse gas protocol, the carbon disclosure project (CDP) and the carbon reduction commitment (CRC) in the UK;
- availability of plans for specific environmental areas such as biodiversity conservation (if appropriate), reduction in the use of ozone depleting substances, developing local environmental heritage and implementing employee environmental programmes; and
- development of screening of suppliers for environmental programmes.

For those readers who come from the industrial sectors where environmental programmes are commonplace, the list above will not be surprising, but for those readers working for companies who do not consider that they have a significant environmental impact – such as office-based industries involved in business support services – this list may be daunting or thought to be unnecessary. However, our experience suggests that this need not be the case and I will give an example later of how assessing these impacts may be achieved in a simple manner.

The important challenge is that companies need to understand how their operations impact upon the environment in which they operate and develop initiatives to minimise them. These initiatives can be as simple as having paper recycling schemes, using video conferencing to reduce travel costs and hence reducing greenhouse emissions or vehicle speed inhibitors to reduce energy use.

This chapter will address each of these areas separately so that the reader can appreciate what each means and how it may relate to the reader's company, in the context of:

- environmental legislation, regulation and protocols; and
- environmental policies, environmental management systems and environmental certification.

At the end of the chapter, I will discuss environmental performance measurement and the range of environmental initiatives that have been developed so that readers can appreciate what may be feasibly used in their business.

Environmental legislation, regulation and protocols

The environment is heavily bound by legislation – probably as much as in the workplace. The legislation that exists in this area is a combination of long standing and new actions as well as being more quantitatively based than in other areas.

The legislation is based on three levels:

- world (UN) protocols and conventions, which are binding on the states that sign them;
- European regulations, which commit member states' governments and businesses within each state to follow specific environmental measures; and
- national legislation, for specific purposes.

Even though the world protocols do not relate to businesses you should not assume that you can ignore them – those companies that look at their supply chain in the context of CSR are asking questions, such as 'Does your company proactively review and comply with international conventions or protocols concerning the environment?'

In an area as wide as the environment, the numbers of different pieces of legislation can be extensive. Highlighted below are the major aspects that all companies need to consider.

UN protocols

In this area, there are three main conventions or protocols, plus the output from the last Earth Summit (which are not yet in the form of Conventions).

The UN Conventions on Biological Diversity[1]

Biological diversity – or biodiversity – is the term given to the variety of life on Earth and the natural patterns it forms.

Scientists believe that there are actually about 13 million species of plants, animals and micro organisms, of which about 1.75 million species have been identified – and scientists are identifying more every year. But biodiversity also includes genetic differences within each species – for example, between varieties of crops and breeds of livestock. Biodiversity covers the variety of ecosystems such as those that occur in deserts, forests, wetlands, mountains, lakes, rivers and agricultural landscapes.

At the 1992 Earth Summit in Rio de Janeiro, world leaders agreed on a comprehensive strategy for 'sustainable development' – with one of the key agreements adopted being the Convention on Biological Diversity. This pact among the vast majority of the world's governments set out a commitment to maintain the world's ecological systems or underpinnings.

There are 193 parties to this Convention, with states such as Iraq and Somalia becoming parties as late as 2009. However, there are some notable exceptions, such as the Vatican State and Andorra, which have never signed or ratified the Convention and the United States, which signed in 1993, but subsequently failed to ratify and has never become a party to the Convention. This turnaround was seen by some as a victory for the owners of private property rights and the natural resources providers in the USA. Nevertheless, the US has produced some thorough implementation of Recovery Programs for species conservation.

Business managers may regard biodiversity as being 'airy-fairy' in how it affects business. But, clearly, there is an impact on all those companies involved in the extractive industry sector and there is also an impact on those companies involved in activities such as tourism. In the UK, the major impact is on property companies, or on those companies that own their own offices. Current legislation requires that each new property build should have a biodiversity plan attached to it, the impact of which may be small or large, dependent upon the location of the new property.

In addition, there was a supplementary agreement to the Convention in 2000 known as the Cartagena Protocol on Biosafety. This protocol focuses on the potential risk resulting from modern biotechnology. In particular, it focuses on genetically modified organisms (GMO) and is based upon the Precautionary Principle referred to in chapter 9.

In April 2002, the parties to the convention committed themselves to achieve, by 2010, a significant reduction of the current rate of biodiversity loss at the global, regional and national level as a contribution to poverty alleviation and to the benefit of all life on Earth.

This was subsequently endorsed by the World Summit on Sustainable Development and the United Nations General Assembly and was incorporated as a new target under the Millennium Development Goals – known as the 2010 Biodiversity Target.

In 2010, the convention promulgated the Nagoya Protocol on Access to Genetic Resources and the Fair and Equitable Sharing of Benefits Arising from their Utilization to the Convention on Biological Diversity. This is an international agreement which aims to share the benefits arising from the utilisation of genetic resources in a fair and equitable way, including by appropriate access to genetic resources and by appropriate transfer of relevant technologies, with the aim of contributing to the conservation of biological diversity and the sustainable use of its components. This protocol is open for signing by the parties until February 2012. Also at Nagoya, the parties to the convention recommended to the UN that it should declare the period from 2011 to 2020 as the UN Decade on Biodiversity, which it did in late 2010.

Why is biodiversity important for business to consider? Perhaps the best answer is that given by former UN Deputy Secretary-General Louise Fréchette who said that the unprecedented loss of biodiversity has reduced the amount of food available to the world's 900 million rural poor and should receive widespread attention:

> Given the growing interdependence among countries and expanding trade in agricultural goods and services, maintaining biodiversity for food security is as much a global priority as a local one. Many freshwater fish species, which can provide crucial dietary diversity to the poorest households, have become extinct and many of the world's most important fisheries have been decimated.

She noted that biodiversity is key to fertilising soil, recycling nutrients, regulating pests and diseases, controlling erosion and pollinating many of crops and trees:

> And it is knowledge of biodiversity – notably by farmers responsible for their families' health and well-being – that can ensure food availability during periods of crisis, such as civil conflicts, natural calamities, or disabling diseases.[2]

Whilst it may be longer term in effect, not only can business activities harm biodiversity, but clearly, a lack of biodiversity can ultimately affect the overall levels of business in the world. As a consequence, it is not an area that business managers should treat in a light manner.

The UN Montreal Protocol on Substances that Deplete the Ozone Layer[3]

This protocol affects the production of substances that affect the world's ozone layer and provides for a timed phasing out of the production of these substances.

There are two treaties that constitute this area of activity under the auspices of the UN Environmental Programme. The first is the Vienna Convention for the Protection of the Ozone Layer, signed in March 1985, which encourages intergovernmental cooperation on research, systematic observation of the ozone layer, the monitoring of CFC production and the exchange of information.

The second is The Montreal Protocol on Substances that Deplete the Ozone Layer which was adopted in September 1987. It includes legally binding commitments for industrial countries to reduce their consumption of chemicals that harm the ozone layer. Also it provides for the phase out schedules to be revised subsequently on the basis of periodic scientific assessments. The protocol was adjusted to accelerate the phase out schedules. There have also been four subsequent amendments to introduce other kinds of control measures and to add new controlled substances to the list.

Governments are not legally bound until they ratify the protocol as well as the amendment. Unfortunately, while by 2009 all governments in the UN had ratified the protocol, ratification of the amendment and their stronger control measures lag behind. Over 196 countries have signed the protocol and only 171 have ratified its latest amendment (Beijing in 1999). Interestingly, the USA ratified reasonably quickly, but countries such as Russia and China only ratified the amendment in 2005 and 2010 respectively.

Why is the ozone layer regarded as important? The discovery of the ozone 'hole' in 1985 shocked the world. It is regarded as one of this century's major environmental disasters. Ozone depletion can also affect humans if they live in affected areas, because it leads to increased surface UV radiation, with likely increases in some forms of cancer. This radiation could also affect the growth of some forms of crop agriculture. Scientific concern had started in 1970 when scientists suggested that there was a possibility that nitrogen oxides from fertilizers and supersonic aircraft might deplete the ozone layer.

This concern was reinforced in 1974, when it was recognised that when CFCs finally break apart in the atmosphere they cause ozone depletion as do bromine atoms.

Since that time, measurement of the ozone layer over the Antarctic has shown it to steadily weaken. The ozone hole appeared first over the colder Antarctic because the ozone-destroying chemical process works best in cold conditions. The Antarctic has colder conditions than the Arctic, which has no landmass. As the years have gone by the ozone hole has increased rapidly and is as large as Antarctica. The hole lasts for only two months and is at its largest around September each year.

Since measurements started in the early 1980s the area of the ozone hole has increased, reaching 29 million square kilometres in 2000 and peaking at around 30 million square kilometres in 2006. Elsewhere, no holes have been observed, but there has been evidence of the ozone layer thinning over the North Pole and over Europe and other high latitudes.

The substances covered by the Montreal Protocol include 96 chemicals, of which the major ones are considered to be:

- halo-carbons, known as CFCs;
- halons, used in refrigerators, air conditioners, spray cans, solvents, foams and other applications;
- carbon tetrachloride, used as a solvent; and
- methyl bromide, used as a fumigant for high-value crops, pest control and quarantine treatment of agricultural commodities awaiting export.

The risk to the ozone layer is that these substances are gases which have long life spans. When present in the atmosphere, they can last from one year up to 100 years in some cases.

The Montreal Protocol differentiates between developed countries and developing countries. For the latter, consumption freeze dates are between seven to 19 years later than for developed countries, whilst the phase out of production dates range from ten to 19 years later than those of the developed countries.

How does this affect business? Clearly there is a direct impact upon the chemical industry, which used to be the producers of these chemicals, as well as those industries that used to be the users of these substances. The knock on effect of their being phased out could have some degrees of cost increases for the ultimate end users, although the benefit to the environment far outstrips these additional costs.

However, most indices and supply chain CSR questionnaires will make reference to these substances and although the protocols are binding on governments rather than companies, the questionnaires will ask companies whether or not their actions are in compliance with the Montreal Protocol.

Consequently, they are implying that companies should take active steps to ensure that facilities such as refrigeration units in catering establishments, and air conditioning units and fire extinguishing systems in offices that may use these chemicals are in compliance with the Montreal Protocol phasing out timescale.

Whilst the Montreal Protocol has been deemed to be highly successful in phasing out 98% of chemicals covered by the protocol, the knock on effect has been that the chemicals that have replaced them – such as Hydrofluorcarbons (HFCs) deemed to be ozone friendly – are seen as a risk in the form of greenhouse gases. HFCs are 20 times more potent than CO_2 and there is now a focus to limit their use because of their impact on climate change.

The UN Climate Change Convention of 1988

This resulted in the Kyoto Protocol of 1997,[4] referred to earlier. The protocol set binding targets for 37 industrialised countries and the European community for reducing greenhouse gas (GHG) emissions .These targets amount to an average reduction of 5% against 1990 levels over the five-year period 2008–2012.

The major distinction between the Protocol and the convention is that while the convention *encouraged* industrialised countries to stabilise GHG emissions, the protocol *commits* them to do so.

This protocol has been the subject of much argument between the world states, over the extent to which GHG (other than the ozone depletors) actually results in climate change. Whilst the protocol was established 14 years ago, the US has never ratified it. The protocol came into force for all its ratifiers when at least 55 of the parties to the original convention (with emissions amounting to 55% of the 1990 benchmark) had ratified it. Up to early 2004, 127 countries had ratified it, but this still represented only 44% of the 1990 emissions. Key to the protocol coming into force was the ratification by the Russian Federation in October 2004, which took the percentage to 61%.

Following ratification by Russia, the Kyoto Protocol entered into force on 16 February 2005. In what was very much a landmark step, after a landslide victory of December 2007, the newly elected Australian Prime Minister, Kevin Rudd, signed documents for Australia to ratify the Kyoto Protocol on climate change, reversing the previous administration's years of refusal.

The convention was designed to consider how to address the rise in the average temperature of the earth's surface caused by the past 150 years of industrialisation involving the burning of ever-greater quantities of oil, gasoline and coal, the cutting of forests and certain farming methods.

The impact of these activities has led to increases in 'greenhouse gases' in the atmosphere, such as carbon dioxide, methane and nitrous oxide, whose increased presence in the atmosphere has led to the global temperature rising to artificially high levels.

Perhaps at this stage it would be helpful to explain what the 'greenhouse gas effect' is. Life on earth is made possible by energy from the sun, normally in the form of sunlight. Only about 70% of sunlight reaches the earth's surface through its outer atmosphere. When it reaches the surface, this energy is converted into a milder form of infra-red radiation. Eventually, this radiation escapes back into space, but it is delayed by greenhouse gases, including water vapour, carbon dioxide, ozone and methane. All of these occur naturally and have made up around 1% of the earth's atmosphere. They act like a blanket or a greenhouse roof, trapping in the heat and enabling the earth to be around 30°C warmer than it would be otherwise. What is now happening is that human activities (causing CO_2 emissions and other gases) are making the blanket thicker. This is the 'greenhouse gas effect' that is warming the Earth's atmosphere at dramatic rates. For those readers that seek more detailed information on the greenhouse gas effect and its economic effects, the Stern Review[5] is the seminal (and highly influential) report on the subject. The following is a summary of its findings:

- *Temperature change* – Carbon emissions have already pushed up global temperatures by half a degree celsius and if no action is taken on emissions, there is more than a 75% chance of global temperatures rising between two and three degrees celsius over the next 50 years.
- *Environmental impacts* – There will be continuing examples of extreme weather patterns, melting glaciers will increase flood risk and crop yields will decline, particularly in Africa. As a result of rising sea levels, 200 million people could be permanently displaced, whilst up to 40% of species could face extinction.
- *Economic effects* – Extreme weather could reduce global gross domestic product (GDP) by up to 1% and a two to three degrees Celsius rise in temperatures could reduce global economic output by 3%. To stabilise our world economy at manageable levels, emissions would need to stabilise in the next 20 years and fall between 1% and 3% after that, which would cost 1% of GDP to achieve.

The report's recommendations for action included:

- *Demand and supply* – Reduce consumer demand for heavily polluting industrial outputs, promote cleaner energy and transport technology and improve the efficiency of global energy supply, as well as reducing further deforestation to alleviate this source of carbon emissions.
- *Government action* – Create a global market for carbon pricing, including extending the European Emissions Trading Scheme globally. In addition, to work with the World Bank and other financial institutions to create a $20bn fund to help poor countries adjust to climate change challenges and to work with Brazil, Papua New Guinea and Costa Rica to promote sustainable forestry.

The report was written after what had been the warmest decade of the last millennium (the 1990s) with 1998 being then the warmest ever year. Since then, the World Meteorological Office has stated that the warmest 13 years of average global temperatures have all occurred in the 15 years since 1997. Arctic ice levels in 2011 are the thinnest they have ever been.

The consequences of altering the climate are likely to result in plant and animal extinctions, rising sea levels, changes in agricultural yields and changes in world population levels.

As stated earlier, the Kyoto Protocol includes powerful and legally binding measures to address these issues, involving emissions targets for 2008–2012 against benchmark figures of 1990 emissions. These targets cover the six main 'greenhouse gases':

- carbon dioxide;
- methane;
- nitrous oxide;
- hydro fluorocarbons;
- perfluorcarbons; and
- sulphur hexafluoride.

The Kyoto Protocol also gives individual states specific targets for achievement, involving reductions on emissions for some states (such as the then 15 states of the EU, that had a target reduction of 8% and the USA, with a target reduction of 7%) and increase in emissions for some states (such as Iceland, Australia and Norway). To achieve these targets, the protocol expects the signatories to have domestic policies and measures in place.

The protocol then became more complicated for the layman to understand. It enabled countries to offset their emissions by establishing carbon 'sinks' (involving renewing forests, as well as establishing new ones) and enabling emissions trading between countries.

There are international standards for the measurement of these gases – known as the Greenhouse Gas (or GHG) Protocol.[6] The GHG Protocol is the most widely used international accounting tool for government and business to, quantify and manage greenhouse gas emissions. It was the result of a decade-long development between the World Resources Institute and the World Business Council for Sustainable Development. It provides the accounting framework for nearly every GHG standard and programme, including the EU Emissions Trading Scheme and the Climate Registry – and is used as the basis for carbon footprints prepared by individual companies.

Does it matter to business? Certainly, the world after Kyoto came into force has a different economic profile, not only for the users of resources that produce 'greenhouse gases', but also for the individual corporations, as well as individuals.

There is a renewed focus on environmentally friendly transportation methods, a renewed consideration of nuclear fuel as a power source and a new focus on energy conservation measures, including the use of technology such as people-sensitive lighting in offices, as well as a review of the use of air conditioning and building insulation systems. Balancing these actions are the costs of introducing greenhouse gas measures and there is concern that this may shift the balance of trading advantage to those producers based in the USA.

The 'commitment period' of the Kyoto Protocol (the only legally binding global agreement on emissions) closes at the end of 2012. The pressure has been on to establish a 'second commitment period' running from 2012. This pressure has come from the EU as well as developing countries. The latter are particularly concerned that climate change could affect their living standards and their economies.

The original protocol had a goal of limiting temperature increases to 2°C above pre-industrial levels (the 1850 average). However, small island states, such as the Maldives, which will be among the first to be submerged by rising sea levels caused by global warming, want the target reset for the second 'commitment period' to a rise of no more than 1.5°C. Instead, there was pressure from the developed world countries such as the US and Canada was that the protocol itself should be scrapped, leaving only voluntary pledges in its place. These could be quite wide ranging. Apart from the EU's carbon trading scheme, Australia is planning to introduce a cap-and-trade system for emissions trading, Canada and Mexico are discussing something similar for North America and China has announced carbon targets for the first time.

The gulf between rich and poor countries was a key reason that two climate change summits – in Copenhagen in 2009 and Cancun in 2010 – failed to create the successor to Kyoto. One of the issues was how to curb emissions from industrialised countries, whilst accepting that developing countries needed to move through an industrialisation period, which would inevitably create more emissions than previously. One proposed initiative was to create a fund to enable the developing world to adapt to the effects of climate change and invest in low carbon technology. However, developed world countries such as the USA were unwilling to pay for such a fund.

The Durban summit in 2011was designed as a last-minute attempt to create the successor to Kyoto and expectations of this being achieved were low, having experienced failure in the two previous summits. However, as a result of extending the summit for a further two days, the obstacles were removed. Talks on a legal binding commitment covering all countries will begin in 2012 and end by 2015, with a legally binding global commitment coming into effect by 2020. In addition, the Kyoto Protocol is extended until at least the end of 2017 and perhaps as far as 2020 (when the global agreement proposed above is due to enter force) but the precise period is to be agreed in 2012. For the time being, Kyoto Protocol participants must submit quantified emission limitation or reduction objectives for review by May 2012.

The EU will place its current emission-cutting pledges inside the legally binding Kyoto Protocol, which was a key demand of developing countries. Management of a fund for climate aid to poor countries was also agreed, though how to raise the money was not. The Green Climate Fund is planned to gather and disburse finance amounting to $100bn (£64bn) per year to help poor countries develop cleanly and adapt to climate impacts.

Even so, the negotiations were close to stalling. The conclusion was delayed by a dispute between the EU and India over the precise wording of the 'roadmap' for a new global deal. India did not want a specification that it must be legally binding. Eventually, a Brazilian diplomat came up with the formulation that the deal must have 'legal force', which proved acceptable. Such are the ways of climate change conferences, where 'the haves' and 'the have nots' stand on opposite sides of the fence and guard their positions jealously.

The next three years to 2015 will undoubtedly face more of the same obstacles. The first came two days after the summit concluded, when Canada announced it would formally withdraw from the Kyoto Protocol. Canada was one of the earliest countries to ratify the protocol, but had been the subject of much criticism because it had not implemented many of the actions required to meet its 2012 target. If it had remained as party to the protocol, failure to meet its obligations under Kyoto would have led to fines of $13.6 billion.

However, there is now greater confidence in a legally binding agreement being delivered. For the first time, nations such as Brazil, China, India and the USA, which contribute significantly to global GHG emissions, have agreed to accept legally binding targets on GHG from 2020. Canada's minister for the environment said when announcing withdrawal from the Kyoto Protocol: 'We believe that a new agreement that will allow us to generate jobs and economic growth represents the way forward.' The inclusion of China and the USA in the way forward under the Durban platform will negate Canada's criticism that two of the world's largest polluters – the USA and China – were not covered by the Kyoto agreement. The global commitment to setting up the Green Climate Fund is a significant step, which will enable a common approach covering both the developed and developing nations.

The World Conference on Sustainable Development – Johannesburg World Summit 2002

This summit[7] took the issues of the environment into the realms of sustainability and its results assumed that the earlier initiatives and their resulting protocols were taking, or would take effect. Taking place ten years after the first summit at Rio, this summit was termed Rio+10.

This summit was billed as 'The Implementation Summit'. As a consequence it focused on six areas through which improved sustainability could occur throughout the world:

- access to modern energy services and energy efficiency;
- access to safe drinking water and sanitation;
- reducing infant mortality and the impact of HIV;
- improving agricultural productivity;
- reducing the biodiversity loss; and
- developing global economic and financial rules systems and markets to support sustainable development.

The summit did not result in protocols, as in the manner of previous summits or conferences, but instead called for:

- national governments to formulate national strategies for sustainable development by 2005;
- international institutions, such as the World Bank, to contribute to the implementation process through their actions;
- the establishment of a strengthened UN Commission on sustainable development to promote implementation and share best practices;
- the summit also recognised that the commission, with its dialogue with governments and major corporate groups would be 'an appropriate venue to promote corporate responsibility and accountability'.

Regrettably, the USA did not attend, after President George W. Bush boycotted the summit.

So what was the impact of this summit on business? The hope was that sustainable development would also lead to enlarged and increased world markets, but, as with previous summits, it takes many years before world governments shuffle into a line with a consistent approach. The next summit, billed Rio+20,[8] will be held in Rio in 2012.

EU regulations

In this area, the EU is leading the way to implement UN regulatory measures (many of which are often driven by EU member states such as Sweden). The EU has developed its Environmental Action Programmes (EAPs), of which the sixth, published in 2002, focused on actions to be delivered by 2012. This EAP[9] focused on four environmental areas:

- climate change;
- nature and biodiversity;
- environment and health and quality of life; and
- natural resources and waste.

The relevance of the EU's approach is that it has developed programmes that are actionable, using thematic strategies to tackle environmental issues that require a holistic approach because of the complexity of the issues, the diversity of the groups involved and the need to find multiple and innovative solutions.

For the sixth EAP, seven thematic strategies were introduced, covering the following subjects:

- clean air for Europe;
- soil protection;
- sustainable use of pesticides;
- protecting and conserving the marine environment;
- waste prevention and recycling;
- sustainable use of natural resources; and
- the urban environment.

There are two examples of the EU taking these thematic strategies and developing strong action plans to implement the required international programmes.

REACH

In late 2003, a proposal for a new EU regulatory framework for chemicals was adopted which came into force on 1 June 2007. Under the new system called REACH (Registration, Evaluation and Authorisation of Chemicals)[10] companies that manufacture or import more than one tonne of a chemical substance per year would be required to register it in a central database. This regulation aims to improve the protection of human health and the environment while maintaining the competitiveness and enhancing the innovative capability of the EU chemicals industry.

REACH is intended to give greater responsibility to industry to manage the risks from chemicals and to provide safety information on the substances. This information is then passed down the chain of production.

The reaction from the chemical industry to this framework has been strong, involving claims that REACH would affect innovation and that European manufacturers would be placed at a competitive disadvantage. In addition, it was claimed that one of the major benefits – the reduction in occupational health diseases – would not happen. Similarly based comments have arisen from the down stream users of chemicals such as the electrical components industry.

The European Union Greenhouse Gas Emission Trading Scheme (EU ETS) and the EU Directive on the Energy Performance of Buildings

In January 2005 the European Union Greenhouse Gas Emission Trading Scheme (EU ETS), which was targeted at the high carbon intensive industries, commenced operation as the largest multi-country, multi-sector GHG emission trading scheme worldwide, in line with the requirements of the Kyoto Protocol. It is important to note that it is not the only such scheme – similar schemes exist in California and New South Wales in Australia. Both examples are the more remarkable given that their national governments had not signed up to Kyoto when they were launched – Australia did so only in 2007.

The EU ETS requires national authorities to have an infrastructure in place, covering areas such as legislative changes, monitoring and registry issues. The UK had to have this infrastructure in place for those companies and public bodies that are affected, in time for the start of this scheme, but it was not necessarily as well organised as it might and companies found some difficulties in the administration and reporting on their trading of carbon allowances (known as Certified Emissions Reductions, or CERs).

Nevertheless the EU ETS has become the largest emissions trading market, with companies being able to trade allowances if their emissions reductions schemes are efficient or buying them if they are not. Over 11,000 European installations across a wide range of sectors were part of this trading market. The allowances are set by their national governments in the first place and this allocation was not as easy or as efficient as at first thought. This became apparent when the price of carbon (at one time as high as €30) collapsed to €0.50 in mid-2007. This was when it became clear that the allocation methodology was not as effective as needed, so that large emitters were not forced to buy credits as had been expected.

However, this was the first phase of the ETS, running until December 2007. Phase 2 commenced with a recovery in the forward price and some sound evidence that the cost of carbon is being taken into account in terms of investment decisions and pollution behaviour. The total allocation of carbon allowances is about 10% below what member states had requested. Phase II continues until 2012 and there are already plans in hand to consider how the ETS should be developed and expanded.[11] This could include airlines as well as shipping (both significant contributors to emissions) being subject to ETS trading – regarded as one of the major ways of addressing those sectors not covered by the ETS which are regarded as significant carbon emitters. However, national governments are planning their own initiatives linked to carbon trading and the UK's Climate Change Act 2008[12] set a series of carbon budgets with the intention of achieving a 60% cut in emissions by 2050. Included in what is now known as the Carbon Reduction Commitment (CRC) are medium-sized installations, such as supermarkets.

But the earlier EU ETS scheme covers high fossil fuel users such as energy industries, steel producers, oil refineries, cement manufacturers, ceramics and brick manufacturers and paper manufacturers. Their first consideration has been to ensure they are able to measure their own GHG emissions and then to initiate investments to reduce their emissions. This impact knocks on to their customer base.

However, this impact can go beyond EU boundaries, as a result of the UN's Clean Development Mechanism. This enables emission-reducing investment to be made in developing world countries. If EU companies make such investments, these will create credits that can be traded, creating opportunities for investments in emissions-reducing countries that can be achieved at a lower cost than in the EU. Economies such as India, China and Brazil have been benefiting from such investments. However, there is concern that this diverts emissions reduction activity away from EU installations. Nevertheless as the Stern Review pointed out, carbon trading is a key element in combating climate change and it is necessary to explore every means to achieve this objective.

In January 2012, the ETS was extended to include planes flying into and out of airports within the EU. The new legislation requires all airlines, including those of non-EU countries, to pay for their CO_2 emissions in an effort to encourage airlines to use cleaner fuels and to economise on fuel use. Those who do not comply would face steep fines. This legislation has brought strong opposition, including from both the Chinese and the US governments. The Chinese airlines have claimed it will cost them an extra £79 million a year. US airlines have already increased fares to cover these extra costs. The opposition from the US government has been very strong and Congress is passing a Bill that will put the EU on notice over its mandate for airlines worldwide to pay for carbon emissions from their planes while flying in Europe.

There is likely to be considerable political wrangling over the EU's move. This is not surprising given that there is lobbying within Europe over a much larger emissions target. Shipping is regarded as one of the bigger contributors to emissions (the UK's Committee on Climate Change has estimated that it will account for up to 10%

of the emissions allowed under the 2050 target). Currently there are no means to encourage shipping operators to reduce the emissions generated from their fleets. If the ETS is successfully applied to aviation, then it will not be long before shipping emissions come under the regulatory spotlight.

However, whilst the ETS focuses on the high-energy consumption industries, a linked EU regulatory measure will have a far wider impact on all forms of industry. This is the EU Directive on the Energy Performance of Buildings.[13] This is designed to promote:

- the improvement of the energy performance of buildings within the EU through cost effective measures; and
- the convergence of building standards towards those of Member States which already have ambitious levels (which will mean a significant stretch for some countries).

To deliver these objectives, there are certification schemes affecting new and existing buildings, regular inspection and assessment of heating and cooling systems and measurement of energy performance of buildings.

For businesses, this directive has far-reaching implications for all those that own, operate and develop buildings in the EU. There are minimum energy performance requirements, designed to focus on what is probably the most important area: final energy consumption. Research has shown that improved energy efficiency in buildings could reduce carbon emissions from buildings by 22%.

The final assessment of the sixth EAP

The European Commission is required to publish a final assessment of its action plans. It considers that the plan's major accomplishments in the field of environment during the past ten years have included:

- the extension of the Natura 2000 network to cover almost 18% of the EU's land area;
- the introduction of a comprehensive chemicals policy; and
- policy action on climate change.

However, it realistically concluded that there is progress to be made in implementing agreed EU objectives and rules and in improving biodiversity protection, soil and water quality. Also it asserted that the decoupling of resource use from economic growth has not led to a decrease in overall resources use.

Going forward from the Sixth Plan, the EU's environment policy is now integrated into the Europe 2020 Strategy for smart, sustainable and inclusive growth with a vision towards a resource efficient Europe by 2050. As part of this strategic focus, early in 2011, the EU published two climate change documents – 'The Roadmap for Moving to a Competitive Low Carbon Economy in 2050' and 'Energy Efficiency Plan 2011' (EEP). They include important statements – and new legislative requirements.

The roadmap focuses on the required performance for the 2020 and 2050 emissions targets. The former include:

- 20% emission reductions;
- 20% renewables in the EU's energy mix; and
- 20% energy efficiency.

The EU should achieve the first two, but not the third. The EU 2050 objective is an 80–95% emissions reduction over 1990 levels.

The EU currently anticipates only half of the 2020 energy efficiency target will be reached and so achieving the 2050 objective is exercising minds. Attainment assumes energy technology developments (low carbon energy sources, carbon capture and storage, smart grids and hybrid and electric vehicle technologies) deliver *fully* on time. For example, the power generating sector is planned to reduce emissions by 93–99% by 2050!

Additionally the roadmap highlights improving land use productivity (reducing non-CO_2 emissions), improving vehicle fuel efficiency and reducing emissions in the built environment. The last includes buildings' energy performance. It also highlights the potential of significant investment levels and jobs created with this low carbon strategy.

The EEP's short-term focus is to correct 2020 shortfalls and it states that the greatest energy-saving potential lies in buildings, with transport second. The effectiveness of national states' efficiency targets is questioned and the commission will review progress in 2013. If it is likely that national states will not achieve the 2020 target, then legally binding national targets will be imposed.

EEP focuses on three key areas – public sector, low energy buildings and industrial energy efficiency.

The public sector, with 17% of EU GDP and 12% of EU building stock, is tasked to lead by example. This includes introducing energy efficiency into public sector procurement, renovating public buildings to higher energy performance, implementing 'energy efficiency on the ground' (linked to The Covenant of Mayors, signed by 2,000+ EU cities) and energy performance contracting as part of building refurbishment. Under a proposed directive on energy efficiency, issued in June 2011, an annual 3% of buildings over 250 square metres owned by the public sector and not meeting minimum energy performance standards are to be renovated to meet these standards. Public bodies are to be prohibited from renting or buying buildings if they do not meet these standards.

The focus on low-energy buildings is because around 40% of energy consumption is in houses, office and shops – two-thirds being space heating. Measures considered include district heating; tackling the landlord/tenant responsibility for upgrading energy performance; investment in training schemes to develop the skills necessary to introduce energy-efficient building solutions; and using energy service companies (ESCOs) as the catalyst for renovation.

Industrial energy efficiency will primarily be addressed through ensuring efficient generation of heat and electricity with increased focus on use of cogeneration, such as municipal waste treatment plants and district heating. Large companies will have mandatory regular energy audits and eco-design requirements for industrial machinery and equipment are likely to be introduced.

EU waste legislation

There are many different forms of regulations and directives emanating from the EU on the subject of waste. As has already been mentioned, it is one of the seven thematic strategies of the Sixth Environmental Action Plan.

Waste is a key factor for the EU. Each year, 1.3 billion tonnes of waste is created, of which 40 million tonnes are hazardous. These figures continue to increase. However, some countries, notably Germany and the Netherlands, have taken action and the amounts of waste generated in these two countries fell during the 1990s.

The plan for the Sixth EAP[14] was to see the amount of waste going to 'final disposal' falling by 20% by 2020 and 50% in 2050. The focus is on three areas:

- *Waste prevention:* involving improved manufacturing and reduced packaging.
- *Recycling and re-use:* including materials as diverse as batteries, end-of-life motor vehicles, electrical and electronic waste and packaging. This involves member states setting legislation on waste collection and re-use. Some EU countries are already recycling over 50% of their packaging waste. However, the UK is some way behind.[15] In 2003, it recycled 17.9% of plastics and 65.2% of paper, with total packaging recycled of 46.8%. However, total waste generated fell by 11.3% between 2004 and 2008. Also, the proportion of waste to landfill in the UK decreased by 11% between 2004 and 2008.
- *Improving final disposal methods:* recognising that some waste can only be disposed of, the focus involves improving the methods of disposal to minimise the environmental impacts.

What this means for business is a likely increase in the costs of waste handling, until such time as technology can be used to reduce effectively the amounts of waste generated. It also means that companies will need to develop a culture within their management and staff that upholds the message that waste of any form is an unrecoverable expenditure for the company.

One example of this is the Waste Electrical and Electronic Equipment Directive (WEEE Directive).[16] This is designed to reduce the impact of electrical and electronic goods on the environment, by increasing re-use and recycling and reducing the amount of WEEE products going to landfill. Producers are responsible for financing the collection, treatment and recovery of waste electrical equipment and distributors are obliged to allow consumers to return their waste equipment free of charge. WEEE came into force in the UK in January 2007 and retailers such as Comet have invested in sophisticated recycling systems, such as collecting old fridges when delivering new replacements and have a central collection system to take these old products to a recycling centre.

UK legislation

In the main, UK legislation on environmental maters follows that of the EU, but the UK Government is attempting to position itself as cutting edge in this field and this is reflected by the then Department of Trade and Industry's (DTI)) long-term strategic vision – 'Our Energy Future – Creating a Low Carbon Economy' – published in 2004.

This looked ahead to 2050 and included a significant goal of cutting the UK's CO_2 emissions by some 60% by about 2050 with 'real progress by 2020', as well as meeting the security related challenge of maintaining the reliability of energy supplies.

As with all things political, things change. The DTI's replacement, the Department for Business, Enterprise and Regulatory Reform (BERR) produced its own white paper in 2008 on how to meet the energy challenge. This focused less on targets and more on how to deliver them. There was recognition that renewable energy was not going to be the sole means of delivering the reductions and the government began its return towards using nuclear power[17] as a means of delivering energy that had no carbon emissions. The responsibility for nuclear power – and energy as a whole – was transferred to the Department for Energy and Climate Change (DECC) in 2008.

Carbon reduction commitment energy efficiency scheme (CRC)

One of the first actions of DECC was to introduce the CRC. This was legislated under the UK's Climate Change Act 2008. It was designed to introduce a mandatory carbon emissions 'cap and trade' scheme for organisations that were large but too small and insufficiently carbon intensive to be included within the EU's carbon emissions trading scheme. The scheme was long term – with seven phases lasting until 2043 – a timing in line with the UK Government's overall targets of reducing greenhouse gas emissions by 2050 by at least 80% compared to the 1990 baseline.

The cut-off criterion for these organisations was whether or not they had half-hourly electricity metres that had a total consumption of 6,000 MWh in 2008. If so, then they were liable to report their total property energy use as part of CRC. In April 2010 around 20,000 UK organisations were required to register their property-based energy consumption. However, not all of those registered would be full participants, dependent on their energy usage. Those who were full participants would then begin recording annual consumption of all fuels used in their properties[18].

The complexity of the draft guidelines had many energy and environmental managers scratching their heads and it was a somewhat 'gold-plated sledgehammer', which involved severe penalties on companies for non-disclosure or mis-reporting. At the end of each year, the Environment Agency (which administers the CRC) publishes a performance league table of all those participating in the scheme. In addition, at the outset of the scheme it was intended that organisations would purchase 'carbon allowances' at the beginning of every year which would be recycled at the end of every year, based on their position on the performance league table. Those above mid-table would get back some, all, or more than all of the money they had spent on carbon allowances; the reverse would be true for all those below mid-table. The scheme was intended to be revenue neutral, with the sole objective of encouraging organisations to reduce their emissions.

In October 2010, the UK Government delivered its Comprehensive Spending Review, announcing areas of planned cuts to deliver £83 billion of savings. One of the surprising aspects of this statement was that one major change was not announced to the House of Commons, but was to be found in the Spending Review Report document. This was the scrapping of recycling payments under the CRC and the retention of funds generated from participants' purchase of allowances to boost public finances. The CRC went from being a revenue-neutral scheme to being a tax generation vehicle, with the government receiving £12 for every tonne of carbon declared under CRC. Other aspects remained essentially unchanged, especially the Performance League Table. The only change was that that payments would not commence until the second year of reporting (i.e. in October 2012).

The first Performance League Table was published in October 2011. Its results were quite revealing. First, the government had anticipated that 20,000 organisations would register for CRC –11,000 organisation registered in the first phase. Secondly, the government had anticipated around 5,000 CRC participating organisations – there were 2,100. Lastly, in the Comprehensive Spending Review, the Chancellor announced that revenue from CRC allowance sales was expected to total £1 billion a year by 2014–2015. In fact, the 2010–2011 emissions reported under CRC amounted to about 61 million tonnes, which at the first phase price of £12 per tonne would result in revenue of £735 million. A reduction in energy consumption can reasonably be expected between 2010 and 2015, lowering the expected revenue take.

In terms of the organisations featured in the table, that with the largest absolute value of emissions was the Ministry of Defence (which demonstrates that the CRC covers all forms of organisations) whilst the next five include the 'big four' supermarkets (Tesco, Sainsbury's, Morrison and Asda) and BT.

Regardless of the changes in the scheme, the UK Government now does have a scheme that could help encourage energy efficiency and emissions reduction on a long-term basis. The questions for the future are whether the government would reduce the cut-off criteria to embrace more organisations in the scheme and whether it would modify the price of carbon allowances, either to reflect changes in the price of carbon traded in the open market (as a result of the EU's Emission Trading Scheme) or to increase tax revenues.

UK Packaging waste regulations

One of the UK's actions to support the EU's thematic strategy for waste was the introduction of supporting legislation. The Producer Responsibility Obligations (Packaging Waste) Regulations 2007 were introduced and have been revised subsequently. The UK Government produces regular packaging recycling targets. Every year, over 10 million tonnes of packaging are placed on the UK market. About half that amount goes to households and the other half is used in commerce and industry. The policy is to prevent packaging waste and minimise its impact on the environment at the end of its life, through more recycling.

The EU set a target of recovering a minimum of 60% of all packaging waste by December 2008 (of which 55% must be recycled) and maintained subsequently, with specific recycling targets for key materials such as glass, paper/board, metals, plastics and wood. The UK's targets for 2011 and 2012 are total recycling of 68.1% and total recovery of packaging waste of 74%.

A concluding thought about legislation

Often in my experience, legislation and regulation can be treated as 'a given' by business people, with an acceptance that costs may well rise, but that this will be the same for all businesses in the sector.

In the case of the environment, however, the direction of legislation is reasonably clear and companies should have long-term plans to respond to these issues in a manner that at least is cost neutral. They require also a time plan that takes account of the impact of legislation, rather than reacting to it once it takes effect.

A *McKinsey* article from 2004 focused on the need for companies to consider their position about the rising cost of carbon emissions:

> Concerns about greenhouse gases and global warming are no longer limited to environmentalists . . . managers can begin now to prepare their organisations for the changing economics to come. Executives should respond to investors by determining how carbon regulations will change costs and then communicate a clear response. [19]

Since the legislation is having a worldwide impact, those companies that are most effective and proactive in their environmental investment planning will be the ones that are most likely to generate competitive advantage.

Environmental policies

The area of environmental policy is one which is as long as the company's impacts in the environment are various! The environmental policies I have observed with our clients can run from one page to many, many pages. The best are summarised in one page – a good example is that of Alliance Boots plc, which sets out in one page a description of the areas of the company's impacts and the policies and intentions for each area, such as the following for global warming:

> We'll reduce both direct and indirect carbon emissions from the energy we use in buildings, transport and manufacturing operations.

As you can see it is a simple statement that a stakeholder can easily understand – and one that is capable of being challenged to establish whether the company concerned has delivered the required results.

This is one aspect of the environment that is particularly relevant to stakeholders. It is a highly quantified area of CSR and one where other companies in similar sectors can provide comparable benchmark data for the NGOs to review and critique.

One example of this benchmarking is that of the Carbon Disclosure Project (CDP).[20] This provides a coordinating secretariat for institutional investors with a combined $41 trillion of assets under management. On their behalf it seeks information on the business risks and opportunities presented by climate change and greenhouse gas emissions data from the world's largest companies: over 3,000 organisations (up 25% since 2007) in some 60 countries. It has completed its eighth cycle of such reporting. The carbon footprint of companies disclosing are reproduced on its website. These carbon footprints align to the greenhouse gas protocol and report in terms of:

- *Scope 1 emissions:* these occur from sources that are owned or controlled by a company, such as combustion facilities, combustion of fuels in transportation and physical or chemical processes.
- *Scope 2 emissions:* these are emissions from energy purchased and consumed by the company, but generated by another party – described as 'purchased electricity' for the purposes of the GHG Protocol.
- *Scope 3 emissions:* this covers all indirect emissions (other than from purchased electricity) that occur from sources that are not owned or controlled by the company. The most common examples include embedded carbon emissions from purchased materials and business travel in modes of transport not owned or controlled by the company.

But measurement only represents the outputs from the environmental policies. These will extend into each of the individual sub-sections and go into each in far more depth than the overall summary. But of all the policies, the key one is that relating to the environmental management system that is in place in the company, without which an environment policy is 'hot air'.

Environmental management systems

An environmental management system (EMS) is a means whereby a company can continually plan, implement, review and improve the process and actions necessary to meets its environmental goals. As such it is a highly process driven system, with the intention of supporting the incorporating of environmental considerations into day-to-day operations.

The US Environmental Protection Agency has a useful website on EMS[21] which describes a viable EMS as being:

- cost effective;
- economically viable;
- in harmony with government legislation;
- based on systems and performance; and
- focused on continual improvement.

The emphasis is that the EMS is based on the business's objectives, not vice versa and that it relates to people and actions, rather than words and aspirations.

Most environmental management systems operate on the following circular approach:

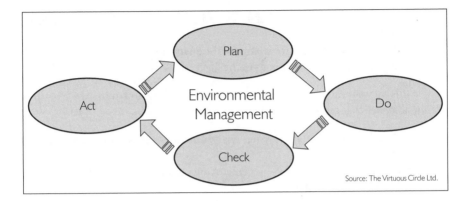

Source: The Virtuous Circle Ltd.

Each element shown above is intended to lead to continuous self improvement, based on the environmental policy:

- *Planning* – identifying environmental impacts and establishing goals, covering:
  - identifying the environmental impacts of activities, products and services;
  - determining legal and other requirements;
  - as a result, determining the priority environmental impacts; and
  - subsequently, determining environmental objectives and targets.
- *Implementation and control* – setting up the system and providing employee training and operational controls, covering:
  - organisational accountability, including structure and responsibility;
  - capabilities, including communication about the environmental targets and objectives and employee training to establish awareness about environmental issues and to deliver the skills and competencies necessary to deliver the environmental plan; and
  - establishing controls covering EMS documentation, document control, operational control and crisis management and response.
- *Checking and corrective action* – monitoring the performance (and ensuring corrective action is in place if performance is out of line with targets) involving:
  - ongoing measuring and reporting;
  - regular internal EMS audits;
  - non-conformance and preventive action; and
  - record keeping.
- *Management review* – undertaking progress reviews and modifying the EMS if required, include:
  - reviewing audit results, progress against objectives, changes in the nature of the business (facilities, activities, products or services and technology) and taking into account concerns of third parties about the business's environmental impacts;

- as a result, assessing the suitability and effectiveness of the business's EMS; and
- determining the need for change of the environmental policy, the objectives and targets or other elements of the EMS.

Whilst this may appear a heavily rigorous approach to those unfamiliar with it, there are sound beneficial reasons for following such a system:

- *Cost reduction* – by improving environmental performance and process efficiency.
- *Risk reduction or mitigation* – by enhancing compliance, preventing pollution and conserving resources.
- *Revenue protection and improvement* – by attracting new customers and retaining existing customers with concerns for environmental standards.
- *Maintaining and improving reputation* – by enhancing employee morale (including communicating with potential employees) and enhancing the image with the general public, government and investors.

Clearly offset against these benefits are the costs of running such an EMS and these costs will include the following:

- investment in the internal resources;
- training costs for dedicated EMS staff and employees in general;
- technical resource costs for the analysing of environmental impacts; and
- costs for corrective and preventative actions.

Environmental certification

Certification is *de rigeur* in the area of the environment, probably more so than any other aspect of CSR. The reason is clear when you look back in this chapter at the increasing amount of legislation affecting business's approach to environmental matters. Volume after volume of environmental legislation is concerned with setting targets for reductions – of ozone depletors, greenhouse gas emissions, energy and water resource usage and waste generated. As a consequence, a new business sector has developed focused on helping companies to measure these factors and helping business to introduce improvement strategies to reduce the likelihood of falling foul of penalties and fines.

But the area of certification focuses not on the measurement of environmental-related activities, but instead on the systems and processes in place to ensure they can be monitored and that, as a result, improvement programmes can be put in place to address any areas of failure. The two main certification systems are ISO 14000 and EMAS.

ISO 14000

ISO is the International Standards Organization, the central body representing 146 standards bodies worldwide. It was established first in 1906 as the International

Electrotechnical Commission. Since 1947, ISO has published more than 13,700 different standards, ranging from traditional activities such as agriculture and construction to the latest technology such as digital decoders and multimedia applications. In the world of management it is best known for its generic management standards – the quality management standard (ISO 9000) and the environmental management standard (ISO 14000).

ISO 14000[22] focuses on what an organisation does to

- minimise harmful effects on the environment caused by its activities; and
- achieve continual improvement of its environmental performance.

In fact, the ISO 14000 environmental standard, covers eight different areas of environmental management and are all based on the circular model of 'Plan, Do, Check and Act'. Whilst it is commonly called ISO 14000, in fact it is a family of standards, whose individual components include:

- ISO 14001 and ISO 14004 – covering environmental management systems.
- ISO 14040 – prioritising environmental aspects through life cycle assessment of the environmental performance of products.
- ISO 14062 – integrating environmental aspects in design and development, resulting in improvements of the environmental performance of products.
- ISO 14020 and ISO 14063, both concerned with communicating environmental performance, with former focusing on environmental labels and declarations and the latter focusing on environmental communication.
- ISO 14030 – monitoring and evaluating environmental performance of organisations.
- ISO 19011 – monitoring system performance through the auditing of environmental management systems.

The ISO standards are often criticised by managers because of their tendency to focus on the manuals that companies use to demonstrate their adherence towards ISO compliance, rather than their encouragement of improving performance.

However, as one of those that have been critical in the past, I recognise that ISO 14000 is the foundation on which environmental performance can be communicated. The standard ensures that there is consistency in how the company's system manages environmental matters and as a result gives confidence to the stakeholders that the information communicated to them is valid, accurate and capable of comparison.

Once this is in place, then the important task of discussing whether the environmental performance is satisfactory and how it can be improved has a concrete platform and can commence.

EMAS

The key aspect of ISO 14000 is that participation is voluntary on the part of the company concerned (although often made obligatory, rather than compulsory, by the actions of major customers, both business to business and retail chains). In contrast, the Eco-Management and Audit Scheme (EMAS)[23] although also voluntary, is driven by EU regulations and is wider in its brief than ISO 14000, including registration of performance.

Participation in EMAS extends to public or private organisations operating in the EU (as well as the European Economic Area (EEA) – Iceland, Liechtenstein and Norway), but organisations in other countries are considering implementing a similar programme. EMAS is considered to be a management tool for companies and other organisations to evaluate, report and improve their environmental performance. The scheme has been available for participation by companies since 1995 and was originally restricted to companies in industrial sectors. Since 2001, EMAS has been open to all economic sectors including public and private services. In addition, EMAS was strengthened by the integration of ISO 14000 as the environmental management system required by EMAS although it sees ISO 14000 as a stepping stone to EMAS certification.

To receive EMAS registration an organisation must comply with the following steps:

- conduct *an environmental review*;
- *establish an effective environmental management system* in light of the results of the review aimed at achieving the organisation's environmental policy;
- carry out *an environmental audit* assessing in particular the management system in place and conformity with the organisation's policy and programme as well as compliance with relevant environmental regulatory requirements;
- provide *a statement of its environmental performance* which lays down the results achieved against the environmental objectives and the future steps to be taken for continuous improvement.

The environmental review, EMS, audit procedure and the environmental statement must be approved by an accredited EMAS verifier and the validated statement needs to be sent to the EMAS Competent Body for registration.

Given the backing of the EU, it is perhaps surprising that, to date, there are only 7,800 EMAS evaluated sites (although this represents a 95% increase since 2004) in 4,600 EMAS registered organisations (up 40% since 2006). In contrast with ISO, EMAS can be seen to have a far narrower degree of influence and this may be reflected by the fact that the largest number of sites are in Germany (1,978), followed by Italy (1,710) and Spain (1,527) – the UK has 342 sites and France has only 21 sites. However, it is the fact that the EU is sponsoring EMAS that gives it its strength.

The EU provides promotional activities, with an EMAS help desk, EMAS workshops and conferences and awareness raising amongst local authorities, funding the EU's LIFE programme for innovative EMAS projects (as diverse as 60 church organisations in Germany becoming EMAS registered and the LEAP project in the UK, developing tools for local authorities to deal with green procurement). As importantly, the EU uses EMAS to improve the environmental performance of institutions that come within its authority, and it requires member states to promote EMAS on a national, regional and local level. This includes tax-related incentives, a good example of which was the introduction by the UK Government of the Climate Change Levy – a new tax on energy consumption – whose impact can be reduced by 80% if energy consumption reduction plans are in place, for which EMAS is used as the means of verifying the plan.

Surprisingly, EMAS has had less impact than might have been thought, given that the EU and the member states could use it as a means of encouraging companies to pay greater attention to their environment policies, as a part of their procurement screening process. However, to gain its correct level of influence, it needs to become stronger in member states such as the UK, France and the Netherlands, but it may well be too complex compared with ISO 14000 for this to occur.

Environmental performance measurement

When a company embarks on an environmental programme, a key output is the set of Performance Indicators (PIs) that a company produces in respect of its businesses' environmental impacts.

The environment can be seen to cover a very wide range of areas and producing KPIs could be seen as being a daunting task. However, the key task is to establish where its business impacts on the environment and a good example of how to approach this is to consider what measurements are required by the various CSR indices and surveys.

The key areas for measurement tend to be:

- energy usage;
- CO_2 emissions;
- waste generation;
- waste recycling;
- water consumption; and
- air pollution (if appropriate).

In addition, depending on the company's business sector, there will be additional areas such as the:

- use and extraction of timber (DIY retail, builder distributors, timber and construction industries);
- development and use of renewable energy (utility companies);
- use of sustainable agricultural and fishery products (food industries);
- extent of product stewardship (product manufacturers);
- environmental assessment of commercial loans (financial services companies);
- use of ozone depleting chemicals (users and manufacturers of temperature control systems); and
- use of hazardous chemicals – such as those on the UNEP 12 list or the OSPAR Priority list (for any company that uses such chemicals in their process or operations).

All of these quantified measures relate to the physical levels of the company's activity – for example on the basis of emissions per unit product sold. The challenge for an external observer is to assess what is a satisfactory benchmark for comparison of this data. In an article in *The Economist* on CSR Reporting, the example used was the Co-operative Financial Services (a company highly regarded in terms of its CSR approach), which 'aims to reduce its CO_2 emissions from energy use at less than 0.7kg per customer account' – which, *The Economist* commented, was a 'curiously meaningless statistical correlation'.[24] As an example, if the Co-op went online for all its transactions handling, this could reduce its CO_2 emissions significantly.

These indicators may seem relatively simple to measure for those readers who work for companies in industries with a long history of environmental regulation focus. However, companies that have seldom been under environmental pressure will probably be questioning where – and whether – to start!

Given the increasingly extending reach of environmental legislation, the key question for such companies is how to introduce a measurement system that is not burdensome.

One of our clients was a business-to-business support services company. We recommended that they develop a measurement system based on easily available information – such as utility bills from its accounting systems – and apply an Excel-based approach to identify measures such as energy usage and hence CO_2 emissions using the DEFRA emissions factors.[25] The latter was calculated using internal information such as business miles travelled by car and miles covered by air and train travel. Using this information, this client was able to report its emissions. Once this was in place, it enabled them to focus on those areas where they were shown to be weaker. It encouraged them to introduce greater use of technology to reduce such emissions, through extending its use of video and telephone conferencing.

The key message that this client took on board was that even for companies with the least environmental impact, the ability to measure key environmental indicators could help to identify strategies that could be beneficial both to the company's finances and in reducing its impact on the environment.

Environmental initiatives

Our experience of dealing with boards and senior management, relating to environmental matters, is that often they do not see the relevance of such matters to their business imperatives. We resolve this by describing environmental issues in business terms. Hence we discuss carbon emissions (often seen as 'hot air' by boards) in the context of energy efficiency and waste management in the context of materials utilisation. By referring to these issues in a context the board understands, we gain their attention and demonstrate the value added of pursuing environmental policies. It is only by doing this that management can start to innovate in terms of environmental initiatives.

Environmental initiatives are as important as environmental measurement. The latter describes how a company is performing, whilst the former describes how it plans to perform in future years. To ensure that such initiatives are effective, a key element is a training programme for employees in the company, to make them aware of environmental issues and ensuring that they reinforce any initiatives undertaken by the company that affect them, or which they can positively affect (an environmental initiative in itself for some companies).

Environmental initiatives – company examples

The type of initiatives will obviously depend on the nature of the business in which the company operates. For this purpose, I am focusing on a few companies that have been effective in developing environmentally based initiatives. These are set out below.

BAA

BAA is the owner and operator of some of the leading airports in the UK although it has been in the process of selling some of these because of monopolies legislative pressure. Its focus for CSR is amplified by the choice of the title for its programmes: 'Sustainable Development'. As part of this programme, it has focused on a variety of environmental areas:

- *Biodiversity* – It has developed a biodiversity strategy, following consultation with stakeholders including Defra, English Nature and Earthwatch. The strategy provides a clear direction and approach for how BAA manages its biodiversity resources and all BAA airports now have a local biodiversity strategy and biodiversity action plans in place. Its association with reputable external stakeholders makes this activity more credible.
- *Car sharing* – On a more direct basis, BAA has introduced car-share schemes for employees at its airports – not just employees of BAA, but also employees of the companies based at the airports. As an example, Heathrow's Commuter Carshare scheme[26] has entered its tenth year with more members than any other scheme of its kind in the UK. Since its launch in April 2001, the staff car-share scheme has grown to 2,500 members from all the companies located within the airport by 2011 – probably the largest single car-sharing database in the UK. Sharing the commute to and from work is seen to benefit the environment by lessening transport costs whilst helping to reduce congestion and vehicle emissions around Heathrow. The benefits are a reduction in distances travelled by car, and a CO_2 reduction, together with a fuel reduction. Interestingly, BAA has used permits for the availability of staff car parking spaces as a means of helping to encourage (or reinforce) the approach. As a result, local congestion and car parking requirements have also been reduced.
- *Environmental awareness* – In developing Terminal 5 at Heathrow, its 3,000-strong workforce were encouraged to consider the environment with a series of environmental awareness days using a customised double-decker bus to advise workers how they can do more in their workplace (and at home) to help the conserve the environment. A key priority for Terminal 5 is recycling

with a target of recycling 80% of all waste materials. To ensure the workforce sees that it is not only they that are expected to act responsibly, the company specified that one-third of the steel structure for the main terminal building was to be made of recycled steel.

B&Q

B&Q (part of Kingfisher) is probably one of the most highly regarded retailers in its approach towards the environment. It has produced a series of milestones demonstrating its environmental initiatives. Currently, its environmental initiatives cover seven areas – timber, paint, peat, detox, climate change, organics and end of life.

These milestones stretch back over 18 years, from the requirement that all timber suppliers identify their timber sources and the development of independent forest certification in 1990, through to extending its mileage reduction programme by shipping directly sourced products by boat from Rotterdam in 2002. Its programmes have been extensive, but here are a couple of exemplary examples:

- *Sustainable sources* – B&Q's focus on environmental matters started in 1990 (as the result of a series of media enquiries) and it subsequently introduced its first environmental policy. That same year, it asked all its timber suppliers to identify their source of supply and began work with the World Wildlife Fund for Nature to discuss the concept of independent forest certification. In 1991, it launched its timber policy and commenced auditing of timber sources from information provided by suppliers, including visits to forests in Malaysia, the Philippines and Papua New Guinea. In 1993, it set a target that all timber should come from known sources and in that same year, banned the purchase of mahogany from Brazil, because it was discovered to have been extracted illegally from forests belonging to indigenous people.
- *Supplier screening* – In 1995, it introduced QUEST – Quality, Ethics and Safety – a supplier screening programme, assessing the quality environmental and social performance of its supplier base and working with its suppliers to reach the standards it set.

Centrica

Centrica is perhaps better known as the owner of British Gas, which distributes (although, until recently, had not produced) gas and electricity. It has focused on environmental stewardship.

British Gas has developed a series of environmental stewardship programmes, designed to help its 44 million customers worldwide to be more environmentally responsible through the use of energy products and services. Its approach has been to provide information and advice to enable its customers to make informed decisions about, for example, the way they use energy or transport, including energy efficiency at work and home. As examples of their approach, there are two programmes:

- *Environmental community investment* – The 'Here to HELP' is a community investment programme, working closely with seven leading charities and social housing providers to offer a £150 million package of investment into free energy-efficiency measures and additional support and services at home, targeted at aged individuals living in households in some of the most deprived communities in Great Britain.

- *Environmental education* – The 'Think Energy' programme offering free energy efficiency advice to schools, with a national Think Energy education programme for schools and a website offering energy advice and information, covering children from seven to 18 years of age. The website offers online activities, home surveys, topics, quizzes and a gallery of 'top tips', including exam tips for the older visitors to the site.

HSBC

For a bank with relatively few direct environmental impacts (as distinct from the impact of the projects in which it invests), HSBC decided in 2002 to make a US$50 million commitment – its largest ever contribution – to support the environment:

- *Investing in the environment* – this programme involved a five-year partnership, called 'Investing in Nature', with three charities – Botanic Gardens Conservation International (BGCI), Earthwatch and WWF – to solve some pressing environmental problems. Its goals are to clean up three of the world's major rivers, designed to benefit the millions of people who depend upon them, as well as help save 20,000 rare plant species from extinction. As part of its investment, it committed to sending 2,000 HSBC staff to work on vital conservation research projects worldwide and training 200 scientists to help protect some of the world's biodiversity hotspots.

- *HSBC climate partnership* – Investing in the Environment evolved into the HSBC Climate Partnership, but it now has four charity partners: Climate Group, Earthwatch Institute, Smithsonian Tropical Research Institute and WWF – again for a five-year collaboration. As part of the HSBC Climate Partnership, Earthwatch has set up Regional Climate Centres around the world where scientists and HSBC staff collect data and observe the impacts of climate change on the world's forests. Earthwatch also supports HSBC employees with online learning on climate change issues. Benefiting HSBC, these employees include those appointed 'climate champions' within the business to both influence others and to develop business projects designed to help reduce HSBC's impact on the environment.

Facebook

Greenpeace estimates that server centres already consume up to 2% of the world's electricity — about the same as the whole of Britain — and it expects that figure to rise to 5% by 2020. Gartner suggested in 2010 that 50% of today's server centres and major science facilities in the US have insufficient power and cooling.

Facebook is a high user of server centres – every time someone updates their status or stream an online video, they are connecting via several thousand data centres, each with thousands of computers.

Facebook set up its Open Compute Project as a collaborative effort to make its data centres more environmentally efficient and reduce energy usage. The Prineville, Oregon data centre is its first output and is claimed to be 38% more energy efficient than other facilities. Key is temperature control, in a building environment where cooling is needed to prevent servers from overheating. Prineville has been built to act like a giant intake vent, cooling and humidifying the air. The only disadvantage is the artificial wind that can sometimes be a bit blustery!

Massachusetts Institute of Technology (MIT)

Like Facebook, MIT has significant computing power which is costly to run and cre-ating significant levels of emissions. It recognised that purchasing green power locally is expensive (especially because of significant transmission line losses) and that its computing facilities did not need to be located close to the place of study. However, the alternative of most renewable energy sites is that they are very remote and imprac-tical to connect to a national electrical grid. However, they can be easily reached via an optical network and such sites would provide independence from utility com-panies and the savings in transmission line losses (up to 15%) can pay for the cost of moving computing facilities to renewable energy sites.

To take advantage of this direction, MIT has invested in a new zero-carbon data centre in Holyoke, Massachusetts, to be managed and funded by the four main part-ners: MIT, Cisco Systems, the University of Massachusetts and EMC. It opened in late 2011 and is a high-performance computing environment designed to help expand the research and development capabilities of the companies. Why was Holyoke chosen? It has a very large hydroelectric dam, offering a ready source of cheap, rela-tively clean hydroelectric power – renewable energy for MIT right on its door step! The scheme offers an energy efficient data centre and it will also bring innovation and jobs to the city (including its schools).

Water – the food industry

Water affects us environmentally in different ways. Water courses can flood, causing social and economic devastation. Flooding can often be exacerbated by building domestic and commercial properties on flood plains. Such occurrences tend to affect urban populations – and typically are more damaging in developed countries than in the rest of the world.

But the reverse of too much water – water scarcity or drought – is a greater threat to mankind across the world. The latest edition of the UN's *Global Environmental Outlook Report*[27] (GEO-4) forecast that by 2025, 1.8 billion people would be living in areas of absolute water scarcity and that two-thirds of the world's population would be subject to 'water stress'. Indeed, water scarcity is regarded as the next most signifi-cant environmental issue after climate change – and it goes hand-in-hand with it. As a result, companies are being challenged to do what they can to conserve their own water usage. One of the biggest consumers is the food industry – in the UK, this represents 10% of the total industrial water usage. Consequently, companies, either individually or in industry-wide consortiums, are taking initiatives to reduce their usage.

- *Water management policies* – In 2007, companies like Coca Cola, Nestlé and PepsiCo established their own water management policies, recognising that they are at risk, not only in terms of their own production capability, but also from public protest from developing countries (including India) where water scarcity has provoked public outcry against companies.
- *Industry-wide voluntary agreements* – In 2008, 21 UK companies signed a voluntary agreement, brokered by the Food and Drink Federation, agreeing to cut their water consumption. Their target is a reduction of 20% by 2020, compared with their 2007 usage. This relates to water used during process manufacture and does not include liquid in the products themselves. Their expectation is that they will save 140 million litres of daily water consumption. Not surprisingly, it will also save these companies money – estimated at savings of £60 million per annum.

A concluding thought on environmental initiatives

Few companies can afford a donation of $50 million as HSBC has done, but the key question to ask yourself about your business is one posed by Michael Porter: 'Are we creating as much value as we can?' Environmental initiatives demonstrate that a company is determined to do more than just comply with regulations. Through such initiatives it can demonstrate commitment to environmental improvement and can develop its reputation amongst relevant stakeholders.

The question to ask is 'What can my company do?' It need not be a mega investment but should be appropriate to its size, culture and business sector. As an additional benefit, it will also help to improve the motivation and commitment of its employees – a subject to which we will turn in more detail in the next chapter.

Sources

1 Further information about the Convention on Biological Diversity can be found at: www.biodiv.org.

2 A speech given by Louise Fréchette, UN Deputy Secretary General in New York on World Food Day, 16 October 2004.

3 Information about the Vienna Convention and the Montreal Protocol can be found on the United Nations Development Programme website at: www.undp.org/.

4 Information about the Kyoto Protocol can be found on the UN's website for the Framework Convention on Climate Change at: www.unfccc.int.

5 The Stern Review (more correctly known as the *Stern Review Report on the Economics of Climate Change*) can be downloaded chapter by chapter from the UK's National Archives website at: webarchive. nationalarchives.gov.uk/+/www.hm-treasury.gov.uk/sternreview_index.htm.

6 Information about the Greenhouse Gas Protocol can be found on the GHG website at: www. ghgprotocol.org/.

7 Information about the Johannesburg Summit 2002 can be found on the UN's website at: www.un.org/ events/wssd.

8 Details of this summit are on its website at: www.earthsummit2012.org/.

9 Further information on the Sixth EAP can be found on the EU's website: ec.europa.eu/environment/newprg/final.htm.

10 Detailed information about REACH can be found on the EU's website: ec.europa.eu/environment/chemicals/reach/reach_intro.htm.

11 Details of the review, including the consultation papers can be found on the DEFRA website: www.defra.gov.uk/environment/climatechange/trading/eu/future/review.htm.

12 Details of the Climate Change Act 2008 are to be found on the DECC website at: www.decc.gov.uk/en/content/cms/legislation/cc_act_08/cc_act_08.aspx.

13 The Defra website has a section detailing this directive and the UK's involvement in it: see www.defra.gov.uk/environment/energy/internat/ecbuildings.htm.

14 Details of the waste thematic strategy as part of the Sixth EAP can be found on the EU's website at: ec.europa.eu/environment/waste/strategy.htm.

15 Details of the UK's recycling statistics can be found on the Defra website at: www.defra.gov.uk/statistics/environment/waste/.

16 Guidance on the UK's WEEE recycling approach can be found on the BIS website at: www.bis.gov.uk/files/file54145.pdf.

17 Details of the UK Government's views on the use of nuclear energy can be found on the DECC website at: www.decc.gov.uk/en/content/cms/meeting_energy/nuclear/nuclear.aspx.

18 A summary of the initial proposals for CRC can be found in TVC's *Inside Track* newsletter at: www.thevirtuouscircle.co.uk/INSIDE%20TRACK%20NEWSLETTERS/newsletter_No.15/newsletter_15.html.

19 'Preparing for a low carbon future' – *McKinsey Quarterly*, 17 Novembers 2004.

20 The carbon footprints of the companies who disclose under CDP are available at: www.cdproject.net/response_list.asp?id=5.

21 The US Environment Agency's section on Environmental Management Systems can be accessed at: www.epa.gov/ems.

22 Details about the ISO 14000 Environmental Management Systems series can be found at: www.iso14000-iso14001-environmental-management.com/.

23 A summary of the EMAS programme can be found at: ec.europa.eu/environment/emas/about/summary_en.htm.

24 'Wood for the Trees' *The Economist*, 4 November 2004.

25 DEFRA's emission factors for company reporting of CO_2 emissions change every year because of changes in the energy sources to generate electricity. The latest version and guidelines for their application can be found at: www.defra.gov.uk/environment/economy/business-efficiency/reporting/.

26 Details of the Heathrow Commuter Car-share scheme can be found at: www.heathrowairport.com/portal/page/Heathrow%5EHeathrow+Commuter%5ECommuting+to+Heathrow%5EBy+car/24152606c2bcf110VgnVCM10000036821c0a/448c6a4c7f1b0010VgnVCM200000357e120a/.

27 A copy of the latest *UN Global Environmental Outlook Report* can be found at: www.unep.org/geo/.

CSR – the workplace

In my experience with clients, one of the critical factors in ensuring that the CSR strategy successfully supports business performance relates to how responsibly employees are treated – and how they are made to feel that their employer cares about them. Indeed, in a 2007 US survey,[1] the majority of Americans believed the most important thing a company could do to be viewed as socially responsible was to 'treat their employees well'.

This chapter encompasses all aspects of CSR that are involved in managing a workforce and extends to the management of temporary or contract staff, as well as subcontractors (such as those operating overseas, as in call centres).

Like the other chapters, this starts with the legislation relating to the workplace, but given that this is probably an area with which the reader may be more familiar, it requires a less detailed review. It will then move on to the nature of policies and practices that a company should have to demonstrate a responsible approach towards its employees, particularly in the manner in which it can build its employer brand with both current and potential employees.

Legislation for the workplace

The right of freedom of association for workers began with the Trade Unions Act 1871. Similarly, the beginnings of health and safety at work can be traced back to 1802 with the Health & Morals of Apprentices Act, which was the first attempt to regulate pauper children in the textiles industry. This was followed by the Factory Act 1819, which determined that no children under nine years old could work in cotton mills and that children under nine years in other factories should work a maximum of 11 hours per day. The role of the Factory Inspectorate started in 1842.

Given all this previous legislation, it is quite surprising that health and safety legislation was not extended to all workplaces until 1974, under the Health and Safety at Work Act. In 1975 these provisions were extended to offshore gas and oil workers.

Much of the background on which recent workplace legislation is based comes from the ILO conventions (including clauses relating to forced labour, freedom of association and the right to organise, equal remuneration, discrimination and minimum wage). However, current workplace legislation is driven much more by current attitudes and politics and is derived mainly from two sources: EU legislation and UK legislation.

EU legislation

The European Social Chapter has had a significant influence on the development of UK workplace legislations. The Social Chapter was an annex to the Maastricht agreement of 1991. It required EU member states to adopt common social policies and to implement the Community Charter of Fundamental Social Rights.

These rights covered free movement throughout the EU; 'equitable' remuneration; a maximum number of hours per working week; free association in trade unions and collective bargaining; professional training; sex equality; minimum health and security provision; employer–employee consultation and participation; a minimum working age of 16; minimum pension rights; and protection for disabled workers.

The then Conservative government decided to opt out from this annex, which meant that much of the UK's workplace legislation lags behind that of its European neighbours.

In the build up to the May 1997 election, there was much political argument about the impact of the introduction of the Social Chapter.[2] In one famous quote, Prime Minister John Major described it as a 'Trojan Horse' that would bring Britain back to the industrial relations problems of the 1970s. However, with the election of the Labour Government, Tony Blair decided to sign up to the Social Chapter in 1997.

The main aspects of EU workplace-related legislation that have been implemented as a result of this decision are detailed below:

- *Working hours* – The Working Time Directive (implemented in the UK in 1998) was a major piece of legislation determining the maximum numbers of hours that could be worked by adults. Workers cannot be forced to work for more than 48 hours a week on average, although young workers may not ordinarily work more than eight hours a day or 40 hours per week. Workers can agree to work longer than the 48-hour limit, but must sign a written opt-out agreement. Among other things, it also established that every worker was entitled to four weeks' paid annual leave – whether part-time or full-time.

  This directive relates to most categories of workers, including those employed on a temporary basis, although for some occupations there are still exceptions – working hours for doctors are being phased in and certain occupations that were originally excluded (including areas such as road, rail, aviation and off shore) have now been included.[3] However, where legislation about working hours for specific occupations already exists, such as the Road Transport Directive (which determines a driver's weekly hours), then this legislation takes precedence.

  European discussions on proposed changes to the directive have been ongoing for some time, including the scope for workers to opt-out from the maximum average 48-hour working week and whether or not time spent 'on call' should be treated as working time. However, in April 2009, the negotiations came to an end without an agreement being reached, but the European Commission has started a new consultation on reforming the directive and will be preparing formal amendment proposals for review in 2012.

- *Employment rights* – The 2008 Temporary Agency Workers Directive[4] (introduced six years after the EU published its first proposals) came into force in the UK in October 2011 under the Agency Workers Regulations 2010. Its aim is to establish comparable employment rights and conditions between those employed under a permanent contract and those employed under a temporary contract. The regulations provide all agency workers with the right to equal treatment over basic employment and working conditions (working time, overtime, holidays, public holidays and pay) compared to their directly recruited counterparts, after they have been in a temporary job for 12 weeks.

- *Staff consultation* – the Information and Consultation Directive of 2001[5] came into force in the UK in 2005. It gives all employees, in undertakings employing more than 50 people, the right to be informed and consulted systematically, through their elected representatives, on matters affecting their jobs and future employment prospects, including a company's strategy.

  The General Secretary of the TUC described it as 'potentially the most significant piece of employment legislation ever to be introduced in the UK', but there are no indications that this legislation has had any momentous impact, although it does ensure good business practice in communicating with workforces.

- *Discrimination* – whilst the UK legislation has been a leading light in discrimination matters, the EU's Employment and Race Directives have taken these issues into a wider European context. The Employment Directive of 2000 outlawed discrimination in employment and vocational training on the grounds of sexual orientation, religion or belief, disability and age and came into force under UK regulations in 2003 and 2004 (the latter being amendments to the Disability Discrimination Act 2004).

  The Racial Equality Directive of 2000 outlawed discrimination on grounds of racial or ethnic origin in the areas of employment and vocational training as well as in goods and services, social protection, education and housing.

In addition to these directives, there have been other EU agreements that have impacted on the management of workplace activities, although some are European rather than UK based:

- *The European Works Council Directive of 1994* – this required companies with Europe-wide workforces of at least 1,000 employees and at least 150 employees in each of two or more member states to establish a European Works Council agreement. This legislation does affect companies based in only one member state (such as the UK) even though it is the norm in countries such as Germany.[6] This directive had minor technical amendments in 2009 and the implementing legislation became effective in the UK in June 2011.

- *The Social Partners Framework Agreement on Teleworking of 2002*[7] – this is a voluntary agreement established by representatives of the EU, unions and business. It aims to address the growing popularity of this type of work, ensuring that teleworkers have employment conditions, health and safety (especially using equipment provided by the employer), training and collective rights that are comparable to those workers based at their employer's premises.

UK legislation

In addition to those aspects of workers' rights that are prescribed by the EU, specific areas of workplace legalisation continue to be derived from the UK Parliament, such as amendments to what were previously the Race Relations Act, the Disability Discrimination Act and the Equal Opportunities Act.[8] The government created the Equality and Human Rights Commission in 2007, to deal with the all-encompassing EU legislation. The Equalities Act 2010 now consolidates all three discrimination acts (see chapter 9).

However, the UK Government has been active in developing employee rights in other areas. The Work and Families Act 2006[9] aimed to help families to find a work-life balance. It considered:

- *Flexible working* – This legislation, introduced in 2003, gave parents with children aged under six or disabled children aged under 18 the right to request a flexible working pattern. Their employers have a duty to consider their applications seriously.
- *Maternity and Parental Leave Regulations 2002* – This legislation represents both a consolidation of previous legislation and an update of legislation setting out the law on maternity, paternity and adoption leave and pay, parental leave and the right to time off for dependants. Additional parental leave was introduced in 2011 as a result of the Additional Parental Leave Regulations 2010. These extended the right to request flexible working to parents of children under 18.
- In addition, the last Labour Government published its consultation paper Balancing Work and Family Life: Enhancing Choice and Support for Parents. The results of this consultation took the form of a ten-year 'family friendly strategy' including the introduction of a childcare approval scheme, the goal of longer paid maternity leave (extended to nine months from April 2007) and an out of school childcare place for all children aged between three and 14 between the hours of 8am – 6pm each weekday by 2010.

In addition to the area of work-life balance, the UK Government has been at the forefront of health and safety legislation with the Health and Safety at Work Act 1974 resulting in the establishment of both the Health and Safety Commission and the Health and Safety Executive.[10] These bodies have been instrumental in monitoring safety issues, as well as being responsible for implementing EU directives, such as the 'six pack of regulations' of 1993 that covered both the corporate management of health and safety (through the Management of Health and Safety at Work Regulations 1999, also known as the 'Management Regs' which placed a legal duty on employers to carry out a risk assessment as a first step in ensuring a safe workplace) as well as other elements covering heating, lighting and ventilation at work; the safe use of computer screens and keyboards; handling heavy or awkward loads; rest breaks; and personal protective equipment.

In the UK, the levels of executive pay have come under increasing scrutiny (usually in relation to the median pay levels of all employees in a company). The study by the High Pay Commission[11] argued that the high salaries of UK executives are 'corrosive' to the UK economy. Although its name suggests a government body, the High Pay Commission was in fact set up by a pressure group with backing from the Joseph Rowntree Charitable Trust. Its focus aligns with the thinking behind the BIS consultation on remuneration and it is highly likely that, during 2012, legislation will be introduced requiring greater transparency on executive pay (including that of the senior management directly below the executive directors) including comparison against median pay levels.

In December 2011, the Treasury announced that it had launched a consultation on a proposal that the eight highest-paid employees in 'managerial' positions in Britain's 15 largest banks (outside boardroom level, whose bonuses are not made public) would have to reveal their remuneration packages. This is linked to its efforts to tackle 'unacceptable' bank bonuses. It is expected that this consultation will be implemented and that reporting will be retrospective, with disclosure for the first year beginning on or after 1 January 2012.

Workplace policies

With such a wealth of legislation surrounding the workplace in both the UK and the EU, it is hardly surprising that many management systems and policies are designed to comply with the various elements of legislation.

To start, let's look at the various policies that emerge from the individual indices and then at how the HR function has been able to contribute to the development of the CSR programme in a company, especially where this is outside its direct area of responsibility.

Workplace management systems and targets

There is no workplace management system laid down by an outside body; instead, the focus is on measuring and setting targets about key performance indicators relevant to the workplace. These represent an overview of the HR strategy within an organisation and the targets will very much depend on the nature and the needs of the organisation.

Typically, these targets at their most basic could be objectives such as improving the employee retention rate, but they could extend to objectives such as increasing the percentage of women (or staff from ethnic minorities) in management roles.

Even with this basic example, the relevance of having employee retention as an objective depends on the risks and opportunities associated with a business. So, for example, in a new company, this may be a highly relevant target to support business objectives, but in a call centres, staff 'burn out' is a regrettable fact of life; increasing staff retention amongst certain grades may actually be counter to the business need, and may result in reduced productivity. This highlights the need to ensure that work-place targets relate to the needs of the business.

The key issue is that the management system for the workplace has taken into account all the relevant risks and opportunities associated with the business and has identified specific CSR targets relevant to each of them. As importantly, these risks and opportunities (and the relevant CSR workplace targets) should be reviewed regu-larly – and ideally be in the public domain, as an element of the transparency of the business and its handling of its workforce.

Communications and consultation policies

In delivering these objective, and quantifiable targets, the issues of communication and consultation are highly relevant. They can take many forms, and the relevance of each form depends on the nature of the risk that is present in the business. Issues include:

- health and safety;
- remuneration and training matters;
- confidential grievance procedures (relating to employment conditions) in the form of whistle blowing systems;
- employee satisfaction surveys; and
- worker representation, including unions and works councils.

What is important is that these means of communication and consultation are not just a way to listen; if appropriate, they may result in a change of practice or policy. The key issue is the extent to which the views of employees – as the internal stake-holders – are taken into account.

Freedom of association and collective bargaining policies

This covers the extent to which the company allows its employees to have freedom of association, and, if appropriate, collective bargaining. This aspect of workplace CSR is not normally a challenge in the UK and Europe, but is far more significant if the company has a US subsidiary or operates in the developing world.

For companies operating in the USA as well as other developed countries, this can be difficult. Companies may have to adopt different views about freedom of associ-ation in the UK than in the US. In the former, employees have the right of freedom of association (even if the workforce does not exercise this right). However, in the latter, whilst the right exists constitutionally, freedom of association is a right that some workers feel they cannot claim.

The Executive Director of Human Rights Watch (Kenneth Roth) made a state-ment on this issue to a senate committee in a testimony entitled 'Unfair Advantage: Workers' Freedom of Association in the United States under International Human Rights Standards':

Human Rights Watch found that freedom of association is a right under severe, often buckling pressure when workers in the United States try to exercise it. Violations of this right occur across regions, industries and employment status because US labour law is feebly enforced and filled with loopholes. Some workers still succeed in organizing new unions, but only after surmounting major obstacles.[12]

The consequence of this approach is that many international companies have to check with their US operations before signing up to International Accords such as the Global Compact or the International Sullivan Principles, both of which include freedom of association within their text.

Of course, it should not usually be a problem to ensure that a policy that is accepted by the board in the UK or Europe should be applied in the USA. The difficulty arises where the company operates in a decentralised manner and the operational management are given individual freedom to operate within their own cultures.

In such instances, the country operations will argue cultural differences – and more relevantly, competitive disadvantage – for following the norms accepted by the industry in their local country rather than the company's global policy.

The position for companies with US subsidiaries can be reconciled, as most corporate HR functions require their developed world subsidiaries to adopt the same labour standards. In this case, the corporate organisation accepts that the 'potential' competitive disadvantage of accepting freedom of association is a price they are willing to pay for being in the US market.

The problem is slightly different when a company has a subsidiary in a developing country. A good example is the massive growth of foreign investment into China – responsible companies operating in China include Ford and Volkswagen (where the latter produces more cars in China than they do in Germany).

China has a state-run trade union that rejects the ILO Convention on Freedom of Association.[13] Workers trying to acquire a freedom of association run the risk of being imprisoned. Bearing in mind the increasing influx of developed world companies investing in China, how do such companies justify their dual standards?

The issues are a challenge that most companies do not find easy to address. The argument tends to be that they encourage consultation with their workforce, which enables them to provide some form of representation. Certainly their overall approach to workforce management is likely to be at the same standard as that of their operations in other parts of the world. But from the viewpoint of an external stakeholder such as an NGO this is often an area that attracts intense criticism.

The question that such companies face is whether or not they are willing to stand by their principles in seeking commercial opportunities in developing countries. This is not an easy question for a business manager to answer, but it is a necessity if the company wants to avoid being treated like a pariah by some of the NGOs. Later in this chapter, examples are given of how two companies have addressed the issues of offshoring (currently a hot topic for debate) in their transfer of call centres from the UK to India.

At the end of the day, the decision will be based on the reputational risk to their company from having taken this investment decision. They can mitigate that risk by demonstrating how their overall workplace policies and practices will improve their employees' quality of life. If this is true, then they should make considerable efforts to demonstrate this to offset adverse criticism from NGOs and unions (the latter often claim that jobs are being taken away from their country because of lower employment standards in the developing world).

Diversity

One of the key issues about the diversity element of workplace CSR is that it will often have different interpretations around the world.

In the USA, diversity[14] has been described as having up to 26 different elements, covering the normally accepted elements of gender, sexual orientation, race, age, disability and religion and extending through measures of diversity in terms of employees who are single parents, those caring for aged parents, and those with young children right through to the more extreme measures of diversity for those individuals of an introvert or an extrovert nature.

Not only do US companies consider the extent to which their workforce represents a diverse workforce and have policies in place to ensure no member of a diverse group is treated unfairly, it will also support the establishment of diversity groups within its workforce. As an example, when a client requested information for a CSR survey about its diversity policies, its US subsidiaries provided the minutes of its Hispanic workforce group, its Gay/Lesbian group and its New Fathers Group as evidence of its diversity approach.

In contrast, for those countries operating in the Middle East, the issue of legal frameworks may arise. Often such legal frameworks are based on religious law, usually concerning the presence of women.

If a company wishes to set up an operation in a Middle East state it has to take this framework into account in determining its workforce. Usually, women are not permitted to work alongside men. If a company is technology based, its challenge may be that there will not be a sufficiently skilled workforce available in the country. Consequently, they will need to transfer the relevant staff from their European or US locations.

The difficulty that this poses is that their recruitment transfer programme may include an explicit requirement that there are no jobs for women as part of the programme, which may be regarded as a form of discrimination by those of employees based in the US or Europe.

The message is clear, diversity is culturally defined, and for a company that is multinational, its diversity policy has to act as an umbrella under which its various subsidiaries can operate in a manner appropriate to culture and the legislative framework.

So how does a company establish a diversity policy? One of the first questions asked in CSR surveys is whether there is a board-level individual who champions diversity. In its own right, this may seem an innocuous question, but given the paucity of HR directors who are members of the main board, this is often a challenge for companies. Another question will be whether the board represents a diverse mix.

Beyond that, there is the question about the extent to which there are policies relating to diversity. In the UK, most companies that are of sufficient size are likely to have such policies. Indeed, if your company does not have policies in place for gender, ethnicity, disability, age, sexual orientation or religious belief, then you may be leaving yourself open to legal action from your employees.

Assuming there are policies in place, the issue is the attitude of the company towards diversity. If it regards it as purely a compliance issue, then it is unlikely to gain as much from it as if it has considered that there is a business case for developing diversity polices.

A good example of a company that identified a business case for having a diversity approach was Centrica. It wanted to ensure its workforce reflected a diversity profile in terms of disability – roughly 7% of individuals in the UK have some form of disability. It decided to pilot a programme of recruiting more people with disabilities in its British Gas call centre in Oldham.

Initially, there was resistance from the incumbent management – along the lines of 'I'm being set performance targets and you're trying to define how I should recruit my workforce'. Yet, with support for the management in terms of how to manage people with disabilities together with investment by the company in providing the additional adjustments to enable those individuals to perform their tasks without discomfort (as simple as providing different types of chairs or larger monitor screens), the programme was implemented.

The results surprised the incumbent managers; they included higher productivity, lower absenteeism (something these managers had felt was one of the risks) and longer retention levels. Centrica's HR Director had proved the business case; as a result, the company extended its programme – using the previously reluctant management to champion its more enlightened approach.

What this example shows is that not only can a business case be made for diversity, but also that the adjustments required were not of a significant nature – except in so far as developing a change of attitude may be considered to be a considerable investment.

A similar case holds for religious orientation. One of the big challenges in this area is providing employment for Muslims. The business case here is relatively easy to justify, based on the increasing levels of skill shortage that are emerging in the UK as our population becomes progressively older.

How should Muslims be integrated into a workforce? Arguments include the old ones about their looking different – in terms of both clothes and beards – and their religious practices being different, from fasting during the daytime hours of Ramadan through to different times of religious festivals.

Yet one study helped demonstrate that the adjustments necessary to accommodate an increasing Muslim workforce were not exceptionally costly for a company to implement. They included the simple measure of providing a room for prayers on a Friday (it is easy enough to nominate a meeting room for that purpose) through to allowing Muslim staff to take time off to observe religious festivals and to work in lieu during the accepted UK Christian festivals of Christmas and Easter. The example given in the study (referring to First Group[15]) highlighted that in an increasingly round-the-clock business culture, such flexibility could actually benefit the non-Muslim members of the workforce, as well as those Muslim members.

Of course, the real issues cover not only the need to provide adjustments, such as those already discussed, but also to ensure that the employees treat all their colleagues with respect. This is dealt with in the surveys by questions such as: 'Is there cultural awareness and diversity training provided for staff?' One utility company has provided a wide range of training and awareness programmes; these have developed an interest in the different backgrounds of the organisation. This has resulted in better treatment of all individuals, including a reduction in what may be regarded as harassment.

Much of the discussion so far deals with the treatment of employees already within the workforce. Other aspects of diversity policies relate to employees in transition – from the recruitment stage, through training and development, promotion and on to departure – redundancy, sacking or resignation.

In terms of recruitment, this is an area well covered by legislation in the UK – at least in terms of recruitment advertising – but the real issues of recruitment lie with face-to-face interviewing.

When I was a director of Manpower plc in the 1980s, a member of my London management team recounted the tale of a client ringing up for a temp with a particular skill and intonating over the phone that a black person would not be a suitable candidate. The manager in question handled the call perfectly, suggesting that with great charm that, with such specific needs, it would be helpful if she discussed the issues face to face. The client readily agreed to such a request, overwhelmed by her very charming voice, only to be totally pole-axed when she arrived at his office, dressed in her African tribal costume (not her normal mode of office dress) and asked 'Now what was it that you were saying about the colour of the candidate?'

Such racial issues still continue and the diversity policy is intended to ensure not only that an advertisement is fair, but also that the interviewing and selection process is fair. A BBC research study[16] involved sending identical CVs to a range of jobs advertised over a ten-month period. The only differences between the CVs were the names used for the applicants, covering typically white European, Asian Muslim and Black African origins. Those with white European names were between twice and three times as successful in securing invitations to be interviewed. The study followed US research which had shown similar results.

Training and development is similarly challenging in terms of diversity. One of the most underrated areas is that of developing staff that are single parents or carers of their own aged parents. How often do company training programmes involve either staying away from home for several days or being in work groups through to the evening? Most company development programmes involve courses that are likely to make it difficult for these staff to participate fully in developing themselves for their own and the company's benefit.

Instead, adjustments need to be made, such as online training that staff can do, either at their own desk or at home over evenings and weekends. The business case for a diversity policy that offers such adjustments should be unquestionable – it results in increased productivity and increased commitment and motivation on the part of the individuals concerned.

Diversity policies in terms of promotion are well publicised, largely through the 'Glass Ceiling' message that was promulgated by the Federal Glass Ceiling Commission of the US Department of Labor[17] which considered issues about making full use of the nation's human capital. This offered eight key recommendations for business:

- demonstrate CEO commitment;
- include diversity in all strategic business plans and hold line managers accountable for progress;
- use affirmative action as a tool;
- select, promote and retain qualified individuals;
- prepare minorities and women for senior positions;
- educate the corporate ranks;
- initiate work/life and friendly family policies; and
- adopt high performance workplace practices.

It made a further four key recommendations for government:

- lead by example;
- strengthen enforcement of anti-discrimination laws;
- improve data collection; and
- increase the disclosure of diversity data.

Are these 12 recommendations as valid today as they were 16 years ago? A 2011 US Government report, 'Women in the Federal Government: Ambitions and Achievements', published by the US Merit Systems Protection Board followed up a previous 1992 report that had examined this subject. The 2011 report found that women have made considerable gains since 1992, when they represented just 35% of the professional, middle-tier federal workforce. Females:

> now hold approximately 44% of the positions in both professional and administrative occupations. However despite these gains, women still only account for roughly 30% of the US's Senior Executive Service. Also women remain less likely to hold higher-paid positions – women are a majority of employees in professional and administrative occupations that have a median salary between $70,000 and $79,999, but remain a distinct minority in occupations with a median salary of $90,000 or above.

In terms of promotion, the issue of the glass ceiling is still there for women – particularly for those that decide to leave work to bring up their children and as a consequence are unwilling to relocate for higher paid jobs.

The business case is undeniable – companies are investing in developing women, only to lose them because of employment policies that are family unfriendly. The same can be said of other classes of diversity. Whilst increasing numbers of women are being seen on the boards of quoted companies (still too few, many would say) the same cannot be said of individuals from ethnic minorities. Promotion policies must take account of the individual's circumstances and ensure that promotion selection is based on the quality of the individual to enable the company to make full use of its human capital.

Redundancy and sacking, like recruitment advertising, are reasonably well covered by anti-discrimination legislation. The same cannot be said for resignation and the key issue here is for a company to monitor resignations from the perspective of diversity. Is a resignation really a hidden message that the employment practices are not sufficiently diversity proof? For example, is there a higher percentage of resignations amongst certain grades from individuals who are single parents?

In order to answer these questions satisfactorily a company needs a diversity measurement and monitoring programme. This will include profiling the workforce by the various relevant diversity characteristics (and these will vary by country), as well as including questions about attitudes towards diversity in the various employee surveys that occur. In terms of profiling the workforce, this measurement should include:

- the current workforce, including covering all grades of employee;
- new recruits (including those that applied, but failed to gain a job);
- those promoted;
- those on training and development programmes; and
- those made redundant, who have been sacked, or who resigned.

The question that most companies face is how should they benchmark this profile of their workforce? A typical question might be 'If we set up a new call centre in rural Pembrokeshire, how does this affect our diversity policy?' The implicit question relates to the company's overall measures of diversity such as ethnicity. The answer is relatively simple – you should benchmark each location's diversity measures against the available diversity profile in that location. If rural Pembrokeshire is a mainly white population, then that location's benchmark will be the profile of the rural Pembrokeshire population. However, where there are ethnic groups in the community, it is important that efforts are made to establish whether employment opportunities can be offered to the members of these groups in a reasonably easy manner.

The other issues of measurement relate to multinational companies. Measurement of diversity is an accepted – and legal – approach in western Europe, but in the USA, it is illegal to ask diversity questions about issues such as ethnicity or sexual orientation. This can be volunteered, but cannot be recorded on an employee's file. The same is true for French companies.

As a result, multinational companies always come out relatively poorly on surveys that seek to establish whether a company has a diversity programme in place by asking for a diversity profile. There is little that can be done except to disclose a diversity profile where it is legal to do so and identify those country operations where it is not.

Human rights

Human rights policies always use the UN Universal Declaration on Human Rights[18] as their background. As a consequence, many company managers assume such matters relate to business operations in the developing world. However, as can be seen from the earlier quotation, Human Rights Watch focused on the abuse of human rights in the USA in terms of the denial of freedom of association.

The UK Government introduced the Human Rights Act in 1998,[19] to reinforce the rights afforded individuals as a result of the introduction of the European Convention on Human Rights, first introduced in 1971. In many respects, this Act focuses on the responsibility of government and public authorities to be responsible to the rights granted under the convention. It also requires all UK Government legislation to be given a meaning that fits to the rights under the convention. However, the UK Government has given greater prominence to human rights by setting up the Equality and Human Rights Commission. This has been working primarily in the area of equality and ensuring that the Equality Act 2010 is embedded. Its work on human rights has been somewhat limited, in part because there is much political discussion about whether UK human rights law has been interpreted too liberally. The Coalition Government has given notice of its intention to redraft the Act.

Perhaps the best example of how such rights affect British business came with one of the first cases brought against a company, when residents around Heathrow Airport claimed a breach of their human right to 'a good night's sleep' as a result of night flights into the airport. Similar cases have been brought by fathers claiming a breach of their human rights because they have been denied access to their children.

So far, few, if any cases have been brought against companies in the area of employment. So, while a watching brief is needed, most human rights issues in the area of employment fall into the regions of the developing world. Surveys always ask if such policies exist, if training programmes are provided to help employees deal with aspects of these human rights policies, if the implementation of such policies are monitored and how non-compliance is remedied. A key issue is the extent to which policies, documentation and training programmes are translated into the indigenous languages –human rights practices are of little use if the recipient cannot understand them.

Most multinational companies will have few difficulties in addressing the issues that arise under the Universal Declaration of Human Rights. The main area of difficulty tends to be that of freedom of association with other areas being the right to equal pay for equal work and to form and join trade unions –specifically those rights that can be denied through a country's local legal framework. Another key area will be that of the local government's approach towards individual liberty, including freedom from torture.

This was the challenge that faced British American Tobacco with regard to its operations in Burma (Myanmar). In 2003 the UK Government made an exceptional request for BAT to reconsider its investment (gained through its merger with Rothmans in 1999) in Myanmar in a business that was 40% owned by the Myanmar Government. BAT's response to stakeholders who challenged it to withdraw from the country, arguing that foreign investment helped to keep the military in power, was that it:

> believe(s) that businesses can contribute to a positive future in developing countries by operating to internationally recognised standards, by setting an example and by influencing where a business can have influence, in areas such as employment standards, business practice, environmental management and community support.

In November 2003, BAT compromised, with what was described as 'a balanced solution', to meet the government's requirement while maintaining local employment prospects for its workforce of 500 employees. It sold its 60% share in its joint venture company to a Singapore-based investment company, but the agreement included a requirement to maintain high operating standards and the best possible job prospects for its employees.

Most companies faced with the same dilemma ultimately recognise that political pressure will determine the way in which they manage their multinational enterprises; greater effort needs to be made in how companies decide upon investment and divestment decisions in countries with poor human rights records.

Training and development

Here, the focus is on the extent to which a company has a medium-term workforce skills plan which includes the regular evaluation of employee performance. In terms of measuring such plans, indicators such as the amount of training invested upon each employee and the number of training days per employee are used to develop comparable benchmarks.

Also included will be questions relating to the extent to which the company has introduced knowledge management into the organisation. This is about how best practice is garnered and shared across the organisation, with the aim of increasing efficiency, supporting innovation and reducing risk through increasing the utilisation of the intellectual capital developed within the business.

This area of knowledge management is seldom addressed formally by all but the largest companies, but the range of tools that are considered applicable include directories (listing experts in various fields), intranet-based knowledge depositories, descriptions of best practice and learning networks.

In many respects, this area is seen as providing sufficient training to develop the necessary skills for the company's development, ensuring all categories of staff are given an equitable opportunity to develop themselves and ensuring that the knowledge gained within a company is retained and shared to the best effect.

Occupational health and safety

Occupational health and safety requirements are very much legislatively driven. This includes the extent to which the business has an Occupational Health and Safety

Management System in place across all the business and the extent to which the OHSMS is externally certified – usually according to OSHAS 18001. Although it may be easily assumed because of the nomenclature that this is an ISO standard, it is in fact generated through the US Occupations Safety And Health Act, which established OSHA (the Occupational Safety and Health Administration) although it was designed to be compatible with ISO 9001 and ISO 14001.

OSHAS 18001[20] combines a variety of different standards, including British Standards and Australia/New Zealand standards and includes the requirement for job safety analysis, assessing safety issues relating to workplace and work activities, determining a study of the hazards and the extent to which the precautions are adequate. The system should include the following:

- monitoring of OHS data;
- ongoing identification of hazards and risks;
- staff training on safety;
- identification of a clear responsibility for OHS, including the integration into line management responsibility; and
- involvement of employee representatives in OHS systems.

In addition to having a management system in place, the key question is the extent to which the company uses Key Performance Indicators (KPIs) to measure performance in terms of Occupation Health and Safety. These should relate to the nature of the business, but at their most basic should measure:

- fatalities;
- annual number of disabling injuries; and
- annual sickness rate.

One of the most important aspects from an internal management point of view is that there is consistency in terms of how these measurements are compiled.

Significant discrepancies in, say, health and safety performance between operations in different countries might be highlighted as a result of differences in government-required reporting. For example, in one country, any employee having a road accident on his way to work was treated as having had a work-based accident from the perspective of the government data collection service. The country operation took this method of calculating the data as the basis for submitting it to the group, with the result that the overall group reporting was badly distorted.

This serves to emphasise the importance of setting the definitions centrally, rather than allowing the local government definitions to set the basis for in-company reporting. Increasingly, multinational companies are setting a global standard for health and safety KPI measurement to enable consistent reporting at group level (whilst recognising that the local operation will compile government statistics in accordance with the local legislative requirements). This takes account of legislation in different countries.

Workplace benefits and attitudes

As well as reporting on the split between the permanent, temporary and contract components of the workforce, companies are also expected to report on how the remuneration and benefits vary by the different categories of employees and within the relevant grades. A question often asked by the likes of the Dow Jones Sustainability Index (DJSI) is the ratio between the pay of the chief executive and that of the median employee. In itself, this may be somewhat meaningless, especially if the company has a workforce made up largely of blue collar manual operatives. However, the benefit of such a measure comes through tracking it over time, when the extent of executive pay escalation can be seen in a very transparent manner.

As part of this approach, surveys will also question the extent to which there are regular attitude tracking studies relating to levels of employee satisfaction, covering the following issues:

- reward and recognition;
- leadership (at all levels);
- team collaboration;
- personal development opportunities;
- job satisfaction;
- working environment; and
- identification with corporate values and strategy.

Ideally, these studies should be benchmarked against an industrial sector average (for which some trade associations provide a confidential comparative database) or if this is not available, based on year-on-year performance.

Redundancy and redeployment

This last element focuses on the extent to which redundancy and redeployment policies are in place. The issue is whether there is unnecessary redundancy of skills, rather than developing approaches that ensure such redundant skills are recycled and redeployed in other areas of the business.

Redundancy is an area which few companies – or managers – take lightly. However, it is usually a commercial necessity and, as such, the CSR focus is on the extent to which such skills can be redeployed is a worthwhile effort and the manner in which such redundancies are handled.

Workplace initiatives

As you will have appreciated when reading this chapter, many workplace policies revolve around compliance and risk management (the latter include monitoring measures such as employee loss rates, etc.) However, if this were all that workplace CSR was considered to represent, then much of the CSR opportunity would have been missed.

This section on workplace initiatives will focus first on developing the employer brand as part of the CSR workplace activity and then move to other workplace initiatives that relate to broader CSR workplace issues.

The employer brand

This area of opportunity revolves around what is termed the 'psychological contract' that exists between employee and employer and, derived from this, the 'employer brand'.

The model of the 'psychological contract'[21] is well discussed and is grounded on evidence about how employees feel about their work and the impact that social employment practices have upon their attitudes and behaviour. The basic assumption is that in order to motivate and retain employees, employers have to treat them properly and the evidence from research in both the USA and the UK is that this will be reflected not only in increased employee satisfaction and commitment, but also in higher productivity and profitability.

The proposition of the 'psychological contract' is that working relations rely upon a 'deal' between employer and employees, which is honoured by both parties and which will generate the trust upon which good working relationships are founded. The idea of being treated fairly with strong procedures underpinning the methods of management is an essential ingredient of the 'psychological contract'.

Whilst this is the essence behind the principle, the current state of employee motivation may suggest the 'psychological contract' risks being broken in the UK with longer hours and increased insecurity, caused by employees' increasing concern about uncertainties such as the future of final salary pension schemes. However, the CIPD undertakes an annual survey of employee attitudes, which suggests that over the past seven years, the majority of employees continue to feel satisfied with their work and less than 20% feel insecure.

This continued 'good feeling' can only be developed as a result of good communication from the employer about the issues and the decisions facing the company. It is based on the employer establishing a climate of trust and fairness and ensuring the employees believe the employer will deliver on the psychological deal.

The employee must be seen to be responsible both to other employees and to other stakeholders. If the employee believes they are being treated well, but are concerned that other stakeholders are being treated less fairly, then this will develop a state of uncertainty that will undermine the quality of the employee–employer relationship.

As a consequence, the employer should be using all the elements of the CSR performance to communicate approaches to all stakeholders in an open and honest way to gain the employees' trust.

The employer brand builds upon this trust – and its external communication. The employer brand can be best described as the offer that an employer makes to attract and retain its employees. Chapter 10 referred to studies that showed certain categories of employees will make decisions about which employer to approach for employment, based on their perception of how that employer conducts itself.

In the 1980s the oil industry's employer brand suffered significantly as a result of the Brentspar incident, the Exxon Valdez sinking and the confrontation in the Nigerian oil fields with the indigenous people. The negative publicity surrounding these incidents subsequently affected its ability to recruit sufficient numbers of skilled graduates. Much of its CSR activity has addressed both criticism from the NGOs and the need to build the employer brand amongst the young graduate population.

The company found that even its current employees were finding it uncomfortable to deal with the criticism that came their way – Shell employees were quoted as saying that they 'found themselves being blamed … Even their children were targeted at school'[22], where previously they had been respected as pillars of the community.

Similar experiences occurred with Nike employees when their company was accused of using sweatshop labour in its Far Eastern suppliers. They found similar discomfort, being asked – even over a barbecue – 'How can you work for Nike?'

This attitude of employees (existing and potential) toward a company's ethical reputation continues today. The CIPD survey of graduate workplace attitudes in 2001 showed that two-thirds of graduates stated that a company's ethical reputation would influence their decision whether or not to apply for a specific job, with roughly 25% saying it would greatly influence them. In the 2006 CIPD survey, over 90% of graduates said that they considered happiness, career development, challenging work, training and development, a good relationship with their manager and company culture as very important to them. The first four aspects could be considered fairly obvious but the relationship with their manager and the company culture reinforce companies' need to consider their reputation for good conduct and behaviour as being important in the recruitment of graduates.

Given that the employer brand represents the values of a company and reflects the offers made by it to its current and potential employees, there any many ways in which CSR should be used to demonstrate that a company is trustworthy and responsible.

To maximise the opportunities represented by the employer brand and its CSR activities, the HR department must demonstrate levels of strategy in terms of a more marketing-focused approach towards targeting the HR communications.

External communications

Apart from recruitment advertisements in their own right, most potential employees learn about a company by looking at its website. Having looked at over 200 corporate websites, we are still amazed by the silo attitude that the HR department appears to have towards using the CSR messages as part of its external communication.

Most corporate websites will have a careers section. This is the portal for potential employees to obtain information about possible jobs and possibly obtaining an application form. Yet few of these career sections attempt to reinforce the employer brand by highlighting some of the CSR activities in which the company is involved – whether or not they are workplace related.

Much greater thought needs to be given as to how the careers section of a corporate website demonstrates all the attributes of the employer brand, using CSR activities to illustrate the company's qualities of trust and responsibility.

The assumption appears to be that because the CSR activities are described elsewhere on the website, a potential employee will make the effort to go through that section in sufficient detail to draw the right conclusions. Yet, research shows that the length of time spent visiting a corporate website rarely exceeds five minutes – hardly time to gain an understanding of the company's approach towards CSR.

Internal communications

In one survey of the international employees of a client, we discovered that only 3% of them learnt about its CSR activities through reading either its CSR report or its annual report. Instead, more tailored communication mechanisms are required – including both specific CSR newsletters for employees, as well as the more regular company newsletter.

More than anything, they wanted to hear about their company's CSR activities from their own managers. Clearly they wanted them to 'walk the talk' and their direct manager's comments had greater credibility than the more formal approach from company newsletters, which were not seen as being an objective evaluation of the company's position. Consequently, the role of the HR department is to devise mechanisms whereby the line management feels comfortable in describing CSR to their staff.

One international computer services and outsourcing company is addressing this by providing online CSR training to its managers. This is intended both to enable them to communicate CSR effectively and to change their corporate behaviour in line with what is expected of them.

However, training is only one element of the communications approach. Managers must be given CSR information to be able to communicate it. CSR should be seen as a dynamic activity, rather than something that is reported once a year to the external stakeholders. It must form part of the regular manager briefing notes and there needs to be the facility for upwards and downwards communicating of information relating to CSR activity.

CSR initiatives

Demonstrating leadership commitment

One of the key ways to demonstrate that there is a culture of trust between an employer and employees is for there to be a leadership commitment to all aspects of CSR.

Adecco is probably the world's largest employment services company, incorporating both temporary services and permanent placement. It has shown itself to be concerned about demonstrating its approach as a responsible employer, with CSR newsletters and an international Annual Operating Review that incorporates a review of its social commitment activities.

However, perhaps the most significant of its CSR activities in the context of HR is its Chairman's Awards. Like many companies, awards such as this are designed to provide recognition to individuals in the company who have provided exemplary performance over the prior year. Yet, the significant aspect of these awards is the set of criteria that are used to judge the candidates, which are stated publicly in its operating review.

These criteria cover three elements. The first is not surprising (and is usually the basis for such awards) being the assessment of outstanding business performance (including innovation and creativity). The second is a commitment to Adecco's seven group 'values at work', that include social responsibility and good citizenship, suggesting that the senior management expect its staff to demonstrate commitment to these values whilst at work. It is the third criterion that is unusual – community involvement outside of work. This reflects the senior management's expectation that the individual conforms to the Adecco Group's values in their personal life.

As such, these awards send the message that it is the *actions* of people that matter, regardless of whether they are in *or* out of work. The fact that this is recognised by the awards, demonstrates that Adecco's senior management places great importance on these characteristics in its employees.

Developing diversity culture

Centrica, the utility company, sees diversity as part of its business approach, not only because its management considers that valuing and embracing diversity is simply the right thing to do for any organisation, but also because it believes it makes good business sense.

It brought its employee and customer strategies together in a single approach and it aims to be a truly inclusive organisation, both in the way it operates internally with its staff and partners and in the way it operates externally with its customers and other stakeholders.

It is developing its diversity strategy in relation to all stakeholders, moving from the more traditional equal opportunities approach (as was referred to earlier) to one of inclusion and valuing difference, aiming to promote activity across the company that will enable its staff to understand, reflect and serve the breadth of diversity in the communities in which it operates.

To achieve its desired aims with customers and communities, Centrica needed to ensure that its employees believe they are part of a diversity-focused organisation. To do this the company had to take initiatives that demonstrated its commitment towards this objective. It had three initiatives in place:

- *Equality and diversity* – It has developed group policies on these areas with specific policies on employing disabled people, including providing training and guidance for managers and employees on a variety of considerations, including explaining how to make workplace adjustments to support disabled employees, understanding visual impairment and dyslexia as well as the provisions of legislation on sexual orientation, religion and belief.
- *Work/life balance* – This is seen as an important aspect for diversity and equality

and Centrica's HR policies reflect the importance that the company places on providing a work life balance for its employees.

- *Centrica carers' policy* – This recognises the needs of employees that have long-term or permanent caring responsibilities. The policy recognises the importance of supporting employees whilst they are caring, to ensure that they can successfully manage the balance between domestic and employment responsibilities. At the heart of this policy is the recognition that the UK working population is becoming an ageing population. All of us have to recognise we may become working carers at some time in our careers. Its carers' policy aims to ensure that the company is able to recruit and retain employees who have assumed caring responsibilities.

Based on this approach to employees, it is developing its diversity approach towards customers, communities and suppliers. The key platform is the commitment that it has towards the two business principles – *diversity is the right thing for an organisation to do and it makes business sense.*

Using CSR to develop the employer brand

ARM is the industry's leading provider of '16/32-bit embedded RISC microprocessor solutions', which means it designs computer chips for leading international electronics companies to manufacture as components for equipment such as tablets or smart phones.

Although a FTSE 100 company (dependent on the vagaries of the stock market), its total workforce worldwide amounts to roughly 1,500 staff. As a cutting edge intellectual property company it is more reliant than most on the creativity, drive and goodwill of its employees in a company that has changed from having a small company culture.

To recruit and retain the calibre of employee it requires to maintain its status and growth, it has set out to have an employer brand that represents it as being a good and ethical employer.

Its approach to developing its employer brand has come through four areas of activity:

- *Self-betterment and training* – Providing on-the-job and formal training to promote and support the development of everyone both individually and in teams to achieve their potential (as well as contributing to its success).
- *Generous benefits* – As well as paying well, it offers a wide range of employee benefits including offering the opportunity to travel to and work in its offices around the world.
- *Disabilities and diversity/ equal opportunities* – Its policies and practices in these areas start from the perspective that any form of disadvantage or difference should not be seen as an inhibitor to any of its employees to gain the type of work opportunity they wish.

- *Employee involvement* – Its culture is that of participation and involvement, in which employees are consulted with and contribute to decision making processes. A consultation forum has been established for its UK offices, covering more than 500 employees and it uses a comprehensive worldwide employee satisfaction survey every two years to ensure that it is fulfilling the expectations of our staff.

Does this focus on using workplace CSR elements meet the business objectives? In looking at ARM's results, the answer has to be 'yes'!

First, in terms of retention of high-calibre staff, its turnover is consistently low at approximately 5% per annum. Secondly, in terms of being able to attract high-calibre recruits, third-party recognition (as well as high quality communications) demonstrates the quality of the company's employer brand. In recent times ARM has been ranked in the *Sunday Times* 'Best Company to Work For' list and was also named as the Employer of the Year in the Midlands and East of England region in the UK National Business Awards.

This type of activity is not limited to FTSE 100 companies. Happy Computers is a computer training company with 46 employees. Its founders set out to make computer training fun, creating a great place to work, providing excellent service to customers and being of social benefit to the community.

It was the winner of Business in the Community's Award for Excellence in 2004 because of an approach that includes:

- having its core values agreed by its staff;
- donating 45% of its pre tax profit to community based activity, including volunteering, cash and gift in kind;
- making work/life balance a priority for its staff;
- having an inclusive approach to its staff, with no requirement of qualifications for recruitment – its motto is 'Hire for attitude, train for skill'; and
- having positive approaches to other CSR elements such as the environment and ethical trading.

As a result, it has built its reputation, to the extent that in 2005 it was rated No. 12 in the UK in the *Financial Times'* Best Workplaces and has continued to win awards for its approach to its employees and the workplace.

Developing a culture of trust

Rio Tinto is one of the world's leaders in extracting and processing mineral resources. At the heart of Rio Tinto's implementation of CSR lies the group's statement of business practice: 'The way we work'.

Established after the result of many months of internal consultation and discussion it represents shared values from around the group, capturing policies and best practices against which it can measure and report its performance.

The document commits the group to transparency (consistent with normal commercial confidentiality), corporate accountability and the application of appropriate standards and internal controls. It is available in 18 languages and has been distributed to each of its operations. It forms a central support for all of its managers worldwide. It sets the basis for how group companies' employees should act. Every employee is responsible for implementing the policies in the document.

In an industry that has many critics because of some of the excesses that exist within its less responsible operators, this document and its application has been at the heart of developing a culture of trust that enhances the health of the organisation by integrating sustainable business performance within the context of corporate values, ethics and culture. As a result, Rio Tinto believes it has the basis for developing intangible, real assets as external goodwill and employee commitment.

Addressing significant employment changes

One of the most significant changes in the workplace in the late 1990s and the early 2000s has been the growth in outsourcing.

This started first with the growth of call centres in the UK, offering customer service (usually managed by the company concerned), often including high levels of temporary and contract staff (who were employed not by the company, but by third-party providers and employment agencies).

However, of late, offshoring has become more common, with these UK call centres being themselves outsourced, often to English language-speaking countries such as India.

Two companies have been the focus of media attention suggesting that there is an incompatibility between these developments and their stance on CSR – BT and LloydsTSB. Your view on this incompatibility depends on which end of the telescope you are looking! As an example, the argument from developing countries accuses the developed world of using social and environmental performance as a reason for not employing labour in their factories or offices.

BT's approach to these challenges was to commission SustainAbility, an independent consultancy, to explore service sector offshoring in terms of CSR.

It concluded that, on balance, offshoring's benefits outweigh its negative impact. However, it also put forward some important reservations concerning the way that offshoring is handled, covering practical measures to assist those in the UK who lose jobs to manage their transition and critical improvements that offshoring companies can introduce in the new areas of operations.

For BT, its ethical trading manager visited the call centres with an independent assessor from an Indian NGO before the announcement was made, looking at all aspects of working conditions against its own ethical trading standards. Their conclusion was that the companies they assessed met and exceeded its standards in the vast majority of areas. Pay for those call centres was in the top quartile of the local labour market (although this was considerably lower than in the UK). The working environment, training and technology were of the same standard as those in the UK.

In October 2004, LloydsTSB (now part of Lloyds Banking Group) made a similar decision to 'move' 1,500 jobs to Indian call centres. Like BT, it also adopted rigorous CSR-based vetting procedures before making the decision, although in their case, they went one step further in terms of being seen to be independent by inviting representatives of UK unions to visit the candidate call centre businesses with its managers. Again, the view was that the working conditions and benefits were at levels that met or exceeded standards in the UK.

For LloydsTSB, this change was part of a planned restructuring that meant none of its UK employees lost their jobs.

For all types of companies, significant employment changes have been part of their decision-making history, from the time when the Industrial Revolution changed the balance between rural and urban populations.

Developments in technology have always affected working patterns – both in the type of work (compare how many typing clerks exist today in the era of information technology with an office in the 1970s) and in the geography of the workplace. The question is not whether the movement of employment opportunities is in itself a socially irresponsible activity, but rather whether the company undertaking such a change does so in a responsible manner.

Concluding thoughts on workplace CSR

In writing this chapter, I became very aware that much of the focus of CSR in the workplace was on meeting legislative requirements and measuring HR indicators. I hope that by the end of the chapter, with its focus on Workplace initiatives, this balance has been redressed.

Being proactive in the workplace means much more than meeting compliance standards. In an era where the balance of the workforce is changing and technology means that much more value is being placed on the calibre of employees, the HR function has a vital strategic role to recruit, train, develop and retain the right quality of staff to enable companies to grow to their required objectives. This is particularly true for those companies that consider themselves to be part of a 'talent war' for skilled employees. It is also relevant that a recent study[23] has shown that organisations with 'high employee engagement have a higher degree of readiness to focus on CSR as a strategy to improve overall organisational performance and better meet the needs of employees and external stakeholders'. Perhaps this finding is relatively unsurprising since CSR is often delivered (or destroyed) by frontline employees!

In earlier chapters, you will have seen the importance of CSR in making a company attractive for the younger generation employees. CSR initiatives – and particularly those that surpass the expectations of the target employee audience – will help companies by improving both its skill base and the commitment of its employees – leading to improved bottom-line performances. As Del Boy says: 'You know it makes sense'!

Sources

1 The executive summary of this survey Rethinking Corporate Social Responsibility (commissioned in 2006 by Fleishmann-Hillard and the National Consumers League) can be found at: fleishmanhillard.com/2007/05/09/rethinking-corporate-social-responsibility-2007/.

2 Information about the impact of the Social Chapter on the 1997 election, can be found at: www.eurofound.europa.eu/eiro/1997/02/inbrief/uk9702109n.htm.

³ Information about the changes in the Working Time Directive's excluded sectors can be found at: webarchive.nationalarchives.gov.uk/+/http://www.dti.gov.uk/er/work_time_regs/exsectors.htm.

4 Information about the Agency Workers Directive is available at: www.bis.gov.uk/policies/employment-matters/strategies/awd.

5 Information about the Information and Consultation Directive is available at: www.eurofound.europa.eu/areas/industrialrelations/dictionary/definitions/INFORMATIONANDCONSULTATION.htm.

6 For information on Works Councils see: www.bis.gov.uk/policies/employment-matters/rights/info-con/ewc.

7 Information about the Social Partners' Framework Agreement is available at: www.worker-participation.eu/EU-Social-Dialogue/Interprofessional-ESD/Outcomes/Framework-agreements/Framework-agreement-on-telework-2002.

8 Further information about the recent developments in discrimination legislation in the UK can be found at: www.equalityhumanrights.com/about-us/.

9 A review of legislation affecting work-life balance can be accessed at: www.workingfamilies.org.uk.

10 A useful review of the future of health and safety can be found in 'Thirty Years On and Looking Forward: The Development and Future of the Health and Safety System in Great Britain', published by the Health and Safety Executive, October 2004.

11 More information about the High Pay Commission report can be found at: http://highpaycommission.co.uk/.

12 Testimony to the Senate Committee on Health, Education, Labor and Pensions by Kenneth Roth, Executive Director of Human Rights Watch, June 2002.

13 For a view of the issues facing unions in China (from the perspective of a union body), see 'Confusion at the ILO? China's Government elected to Governing Body ... as worker delegate' at: www.globallabour.info/en/2007/07/confusion_at_the_ilo.html.

14 'Diversity Today – Developing and retaining the best corporate talent' (1999) *Fortune* magazine, in association with the Society for Human Resource Management.

15 Chapter 3 of *Muslims in the UK: Policies for Engaged Citizens*. (2005) EU Monitoring and Advocacy Program of the Open Society Institute.

16 BBC 5 Live research broadcast on 12 July 2004.

17 'A Solid Investment: Making Full Use of the Nation's Human Capital – Recommendations of the Federal Glass Ceiling Commission', US Federal Glass Ceiling Commission, November 1995.

18 The text of the UDHR can be found at: www.un.org/Overview/rights.html.

19 General information about the Human Rights Act can be found at: www.justice.gov.uk/whatwedo/humanrights.htm.

20 A simple guide to OHSAS 18001 is found on the OSHA website, under the heading 'Health and Safety Made Easy'. Available at: www.osha-bs8800-ohsas-18001-health-and-safety.com/.

21 *Public and Private Perspectives on the Psychological Contract* Guest and Conway (2001) CIPD.

22 *Corporate Social Responsibility and HR's Role – A guide* (2002) Chartered Institute of Personnel and Development.

23 Review the press release from the Hewitt Associates 2010 Best Companies in Canada study at: www.newswire.ca/en/story/690971/research-from-best-employers-in-canada-study-builds-business-case-for-investment-in-corporate-social-responsibility.

The marketplace:
clients and customers

The term 'Marketplace' encompasses two elements for CSR: clients and customers and suppliers. For the purposes of most businesses, these two areas are treated as separate functions. To reflect this, each of these activities has been allocated its own chapter. This chapter deals with clients and customers and Chapter 16 looks at suppliers.

Perhaps it is important to define clients and customers at the outset. For this purpose, clients are those individuals (often organisations) that are either purchasing services from a professional organisation, such as a solicitor, or have a form of contract between them and the supplier. Where the supplier is a professional organisation, a form of legal contract also exists – either implicitly through a professional code of conduct or explicitly for the purposes of the service required. A customer is defined by the *Oxford Concise English Dictionary* as 'someone that buys' – most usually an individual consumer, without any written contractual relationship relating to a specific transaction.

The legislative background

Because of the existence of a client relationship of a contractual nature, most of the CSR marketplace focuses on the customer – on the basis that they are less well protected legally. Like most of CSR, legislation exists relating to customers. This is derived from two sources: the EU and UK law.

EU legislation

Consumer policy is regarded as a core component of the EU Commission's strategy objective to improve the quality of life of all EU citizens. This involves the development of legislative and other actions to promote the interests, health and safety of consumers, to ensure the proper integration of consumer concerns in all EU policies and to complement the consumer policy conducted by member states.

At international level, the Commission aims to ensure the proper application by countries of the same high levels of consumer protection and consumer safety as exist in the European Community. The Commission also aims to promote the attainment of higher standards of consumer policy and consumer safety in international forums and with third world countries.

Consumer protection started in 1975 when a European consumer programme was adopted by the Community for the first time. The main principles behind this consumer programme were:

- protecting consumers' health and safety;
- protecting consumers' economic interests;
- safeguarding consumers' rights to objective information on products;
- procedures for dealing with grievances of consumers; and
- involvement of consumer interests in the decision-making process.

Consumer protection was given the status of a full Community policy in the Maastricht Treaty. This was designed to address many of the consumer issues that have resulted from the development of a Single Market.

Of particular relevance is the issue of consumer finance and loans, since when taking out a loan, consumers are now able to choose between financial institutions from other member states for the most competitive rates. As customers are often vulnerable, with the 1987 Council Directive on Consumer Credit, the EU has created rules for the sale of credit to protect the consumer from unfair trading procedures. The 1987 Directive was amended in 1990 and 1998, based on minimum harmonisation. However, it was accepted that since the original directive was passed in 1987, the consumer credit market had changed significantly and that more needed to be done to encourage the provision of consumer credit across national borders. The EU decided that there was a need to harmonise the laws, regulations and administrative provisions of the member states for credit for consumers and, as a result, introduced the Consumer Credit Directive 2008, which came into force in the UK in February 2011.

Similarly, the combination of the Single Market with improved communication systems has resulted in great changes in consumer habits. The EU has responded to these in a number of ways. For example, the Distance Selling Directive aims to protect the consumer who buys through the internet or teleshopping. This directive provides for a 'cooling-off period', as well as insisting that the sellers provide adequate information for the purchaser. This means that customers who want to make contracts at a distance are protected, as are those consumers who do not wish to conclude such contracts.

Equally, the protection of the consumer from inadequate or unsafe goods has a high priority. Many items sold in the EU, including all toys, must bear the CE mark. This indicates that the goods comply with the safety requirements defined by Community legislation. Manufacturers must also indicate on the package or on the instructions any information or warnings which may be relevant to the use of the item which could help reduce the risk of injury. In the case of toy manufacturers, indication of a suitable or minimum age group or the necessity of adult supervision must also be indicated. Such information is intended to give the consumer the confidence that the toy will be of a certain quality and standard and not dangerous if used under normal circumstances when instructions are followed.

Examples of other areas where the EU has taken action to improve consumers' protection include:

- *Cosmetic products (1976)*: Prohibiting the use of certain chemical substances in cosmetics.
- *Price indication (1979)*: Protecting consumers by indicating the prices of food-stuffs and non-food products and also the unit price of products.
- *Advertising standards (1984)*: Protecting consumers from misleading advertising.
- *Labelling of foodstuffs (1979)*: Introduced to ensure that the presentation, label-ling and advertising of foodstuffs was regulated to prevent misinformation.
- *Protection when buying holidays (1990)*: The directive on package travel, package holidays and package tours.

The Amsterdam Treaty signed in 1997 famously opened the door to the negotiations for the enlargement of the EU, but the treaty contained important measures to improve the position of consumers by giving greater priority to the rights of con-sumers and ensuring that all EU policies (regardless of their main focus) are now examined for possible effects on the position of the consumer.

The second point required the European Commission to evaluate and consider any decisions from the consumer's point of view when putting forward proposals in any other policy area, such as agriculture, which may have an impact on consumer affairs. As a result of this treaty, the Consumer Directorate of the Commission became the Directorate on Consumer Policy and Health Protection. It has established ten basic principles[1] to ensure the rights of the consumer are protected:

- *Buy what you want, where you want it:* This enables consumers to shop without having to pay customs or additional VAT when they return home. This applies both to personal shopping and to purchases made by telephone or e-mail.
- *If it doesn't work, send it back:* This applies up to 24 months after delivery, if the product purchased does not conform to the agreement made with the seller. It applies not only to products that don't work, such as a TV set that breaks down, but it also applies to products that are not what they appeared when purchased, such as antique furniture that turned out to be reproduction.
- *High safety standards for food and other consumer goods:* This regulates every part of the 'food chain', from the farmer to the retailer.
- *Know what you are eating:* EU laws on food labelling let consumers know what they are eating, including ingredients that may cause allergies, as well as regu-lating which products can be called 'organic' and those products that can be labelled as coming from specific regions (e.g. Parma ham).
- *Contracts should be fair to consumers:* This prohibits all forms of unfair con-tracts specifically targeted at small print contract abuses.
- *Sometimes consumers can change their mind:* This enables consumers to cancel doorstep selling and mail order contracts within seven days of signing, It also bans inertia selling.
- *Making it easier to compare prices:* This requires supermarkets to provide 'unit prices' (per kilo or per litre) of products that are sold in differing sizes of packaging.

- *Consumers should not be misled:* This prohibits advertising that misleads or deceives consumers, including mail order or internet retailing.
- *Protection while you are on holiday:* This offers protection for holiday makers whose tour operators go bankrupt. In addition, it ensures that those holiday makers who decide to buy a time-share property while they are at the holiday resort have the opportunity to read the contract in their own language.
- *Effective redress for cross-border disputes:* This makes it possible for consumers not only to make cross-border purchases, but also to have means of redress in case of disputes. The Commission is currently setting up a swift means of resolving cross-border disputes, which will encourage customers to seek redress if their rights have been infringed. There is a proposed directive on access to justice. This will mean that the customer can seek redress from a competent body in the country of origin or in their own country, which will give assurances to customers in cross-border trade situations.

One example of the increasing influence (perhaps rather than the power) of the EU's Consumer Directorate is their calling together major toy manufacturers to voice their concerns about toy safety. This was highlighted after the world's largest toy manufacturer, Mattel, issued four product recalls in 2007 because of design faults which meant that pieces of the toys broke off; one child required hospital care.

The recalls prompted the EU's Consumer Directorate to embark on a review of its toy safety regulations. Whilst focused on toys, its real target was the safety standards in outsourced manufacturing operations in countries such as China. It has no jurisdiction over these matters, but it does have jurisdiction over the companies whose brands are attached to these products – Mattel has agreements with factories in China and Mexico for the manufacture of Fisher Price branded toys. It is by putting pressure on such companies that the Consumer Directorate achieves adherence to its principles. As a consequence of this review, the EU introduced the new Toy Safety Directive in 2009, which substantially amended the old directive across virtually all safety aspects, meeting the highest level of health and safety standards and improving the existing rules for the marketing of toys that are produced in and imported into the EU to reduce toy-related accidents.

UK legislation

Whilst the UK legislation on consumer protection goes back some 70 years, to the Agricultural Products (Grading and Marking) Acts of 1928 and 1933, the intent of the EU Consumer Protection approach is that the member states should follow the EU's lead and implement the intent of the EU directives in the most appropriate manner for their own national marketplace.

There is, however, little opportunity for member states to vary from the EU directives, given the intent is to deliver the infrastructure for a single and unified market. As a consequence, there are few broad based pieces of UK consumer protection legislation currently in development that are not derived from EU directives.

The UK Government is implementing new regulations to take account of EU policies such as those embodied in the Ten Principles. One example is where loan companies conceal the true cost of a loan in their small print. The action to introduce regulations banning this practice was a considerable factor in the relatively recent court case,[2] in which a judge wiped out the debts of a couple whose £5,750 loan had spiralled to £384,000 as a result of failing to keep up the repayments on the loan.

In addition, the DTI (now BIS) launched a consultation in 2004 on a consumer strategy covering the next five to ten years – 'Extending Competitive Markets: Empowered Consumers, Successful Business'. This consultation was aimed at a wide group of stakeholders including consumer and business representatives and enforcers. It covered views on proposals for empowering consumers, improving consumer representation and complaints handling in the regulated industries, clarifying the law, helping consumers and business to resolve problems and improving the enforcement of a fair and safe trading environment. A commitment to bring forward proposals to strengthen and streamline consumer advocacy was reflected in the DTI Consumer Strategy, published in June 2005; a formal consultation on consumer representation and redress was launched in 2006. As a result, proposals were initiated that included the consolidation of existing consumer bodies into a single, coherent, consumer advocacy body and the introduction of new ombudsman schemes to resolve complaints where service providers had not been able to do so. This was finally implemented in 2008 with the creation of Consumer Focus, merging the National Consumer Council, energywatch and Postwatch. Consumer Focus is considered to be a more powerful consumer champion than its predecessors, with extended powers including that of demanding information from companies. Where companies and consumers are unable to reach agreement on complaints, an independent Ombudsman can step in with the legal power to enforce a resolution and provide compensation for consumers where appropriate.

Quasi-regulatory background

One development that is particularly relevant has been the way in which consumer representative bodies, such as the Consumer Association in the UK, have started to consider CSR issues in their evaluation of products – and the way in which they are communicating these findings on a public basis.

Which? magazine included CSR criteria in its 2003 tests on mobile phones and running shoes, whilst Consumentenbond, the Netherlands's main consumer association, has published 20 reports containing CSR information.

But the most striking step has been taken by *Test*, Germany's leading guide to consumer products, published by Stiftung Warentest (SWT). This assesses products on additional criteria, including whether the practices used in their manufacture comply with international social and labour standards and whether they are good or bad for the environment. SWT has developed a 20-page questionnaire, covering 39 different CSR-related categories that it sends to producers of the goods it is testing.

SWT's latest report (published in March 2011) was on the CSR practices of jean manufacturers. The full list of its CSR assessments was published in September 2011.[3]

CSR policies, management systems and performance measurement

In terms of policies and practices, much of the CSR focus lies with the extent to which companies have policies that ensure they and their staff comply with the consumer protection policies that are in force in the country or countries in which they are operating.

In this respect, the policies required include the extent to which the company and its staff are applying responsible selling and marketing practices. These policies will broaden dependent upon the extent to which such selling is regulated. An example is in the financial services industry, where the Financial Services Authority sets standards in terms of both selling and marketing practices and in the nature of the training required to be completed by any staff involved in such selling and marketing.

In addition to providing training for staff in terms of responsible sales and marketing, a company would be expected to have monitoring systems in place. These are designed to capture any complaints of irresponsible selling and marketing as well as being able to observe sales and marketing practices in the field to ensure they align with the company's CSR values.

Policies

Apart from having policies in place that relate to responsible sales and marketing, there are other policies that need to be in place that ensure a company is taking CSR into consideration in its development of sales and marketing. These policies are set out below.

Monitoring client/customer satisfaction and integrating feedback

This monitoring activity can vary from simple customer satisfaction surveys, through to more complicated opinion research surveys and mystery shopping exercises of branch locations, call centres and internet shopping.

As important is the way in which customer and client feedback (including complaints) are fed back into the product and service delivery process. Too often, complaints can be treated as being a nuisance, rather than as a means of improving the quality of approach and this is the area where the policy of integrating feedback should be focused.

A method of capturing customer loyalty that has been adopted by many companies in recent years is that of the Net Promoter Score (NPS). This is obtained by asking customers a single question – 'How likely is it that you would recommend our company to a friend or colleague?' – on a 0 to 10 rating scale, where 10 is 'extremely likely' and 0 is 'not at all likely'. Based on their responses, customers are categorised into one of three groups: Promoters (9–10 rating), Passives (7–8 rating) and Detractors (0–6 rating). The percentage of detractors is then subtracted from the percentage of promoters to obtain the NPS. However, whilst highly favoured, NPS does have its detractors, who argue that there is no or little correlation between NPS and future business growth. Its continued use by business executives is largely because it is easier to implement than more traditional customer satisfaction methods and easier to understand by those at the frontline.

Involving customers and clients

This is particularly relevant when it comes to those businesses that are providing services to their clients and customers. An example would be where the client or customer involvement in the delivery of the product actually forms part of the product specification, such as when a business defines the job skills and the interpersonal skills it requires from temporaries supplied by an employment agency.

This is more than undertaking opinion surveys – it means listening to customers and responding proactively. So, if customers indicate concern about the nature of the product being offered, then it makes sense to listen and modify your approach. A good example is that of McDonald's, which has recognised the objections being made about the problems of the fat content of its food products and has redefined its products to allow them to be considered as part of a 'healthy eating' diet. Of course, offering healthier options does not mean that customers will flock to buy them!

In this respect, it is important to consider how customers will react to CSR initiatives. We liken it to a person's approach to a jam doughnut. Why would someone buy one? Usually because they like the jam inside the doughnut. In this respect, the jam could be described as the brand attribute for a jam doughnut – take the jam away and it is not the same product. We observed these attitudes when TVC undertook consumer research for a large metropolitan public transport system. This had a reasonably high-profile CSR initiative which was highly valued internally. However, externally, customers commented their public transport service was failing to meet their expected brand attributes of a transport system: a system that was punctual, safe, secure and clean! For these customers, the brand attributes were what they were buying (the jam) and the CSR initiative was the dough that surrounded it. Without the basics, the CSR initiative was less valued.

A recent study[4] was carried out, in which consumers were asked to rate their purchase intentions for computer accessories after learning about a company's product quality and CSR activities. Descriptions of the company as having high product quality had a modest positive effect, but for a company with low product quality, the consumer's willingness to make a purchase actually *decreased* when it engaged in otherwise positive CSR activities. In this second case, consumers were wary of these activities, thinking that the company ought to give precedence to product quality. The product quality represents the 'jam' brand attributes, whilst the dough is the softer attributers relating to the CSR activities.

Products that are healthy and safe

An obvious requirement, given the legislative framework that exists for most industries selling in Europe, but there is a great value not only in ensuring that all products are healthy and safe but also communicating this to customers and clients.

Boots (part of Alliance Boots), regarded as the best known and most-trusted brand on the High Street, is a striking example of how a company can go to significant lengths to ensure the products it sells to its customers are both healthy and safe.

In all, Boots launches about 1,300 products each year and each will have been tested by Boots Product Development department to make sure that they are suitable for everybody, including the elderly, those with disabilities and those with allergies. This testing process includes bench testing and also utilises a bank of 9,000 volunteers, whose profile enables Boots to cover all aspects of its customer base, at the same time ensuring that all aspects of consumer health and safety are covered.

Environmental stewardship of products and services

This is an area that is coming into close focus, as companies recognise their approach has to take into account the impact of their products and processes. Such attention is not only about the products that consumers purchase, but also the way in which the ancillary services available to consumers are used (or abused).

For example, one area of considerable concern to supermarkets has been the way in which their shopping trolleys can often be taken away from their retail locations to be left a scar on housing estates or worse still, dropped into local canals or rivers. This is an area that many supermarkets have focused upon, providing additional staff to collect trolleys to stop them being taken away after the stores are closed, as well as introducing pay-for-use trolleys to act as a deterrent.

Another example from the supermarket sector is the way in which companies such as Tesco provide facilities for its customers to recycle products that have been bought at the store (as well as from other retailers) by providing recycling services for products as diverse as Christmas Cards, mobile telephones and inkjet cartridges.

But in another area, the financial services industry addresses the issues of investments in and loans being made to projects in developing countries that may be at risk of being associated with human rights violations. In one report,[5] financial services companies were found to be relatively unaware of the impact that human rights risks can have in their reputation and highlighted the need for financial services firms to improve their risk management approach to projects and practices that may associate them with human rights violations. The report indicated that there was a lack of formal processes or regulations to help such companies manage these risks. This report was written after the establishment of the Equator Principles (EPs),[6] which had been evolved at the instigation of the International Finance Corporation and designed to set out the framework under which financial lending institutions would ensure that the projects to which they made loans met the necessary environmental and social international standards. Similar initiatives have been introduced by investors focusing on responsible investment by their fund managers. By 2011, 72 financial institutions in 27 countries had officially adopted the EPs, representing over 70% of international project finance debt in emerging markets.

In early 2005 the then UN Secretary-General invited a group of the world's largest institutional investors to join a process to develop the Principles for Responsible Investment (UN PRI).[7] Individuals representing 20 institutional investors from 12 countries agreed to participate in the Investor Group. The group accepted ownership of the principles and had the freedom to develop them as they saw fit. As of late 2011 over 900 investment institutions are signatories, managing assets of approximately US$30 trillion.

Quality standards for customers and clients

These standards can be internally driven, but the commonly accepted best practice approach is to have some form of external verification, usually based on ISO 9000: 2000 (previously known as ISO 9001, 9002 and 9003) which is primarily concerned with 'quality management'. This relates to what the organisation does to:

- fulfil the customer's quality requirements and
- applicable regulatory requirements, while
- aiming to enhance customer satisfaction and
- achieve continual improvement of its performance in pursuit of these objectives.

As with ISO 14001, this approach is process driven. The issue is the extent to which the employees in a company regard customer quality as their overwhelming objective. In other words, are the employees truly committed to customer quality, or is ISO 9000 is used purely as a process, with no internal culture of putting the customer first?

Performance measurement

In a sales and marketing environment, performance measurement is part of the normal working operation. However, the area that is not normally part of the working day is the public communication of such measurement results. Yet, if a company wishes to demonstrate its transparency, this will be required – at least to the extent that the company's stakeholders believe that it is being open and honest about its performance. However, it is generally accepted that information considered to be commercially confidential is not normally expected to be communicated to the public at large.

So what indicators would be expected? These will include an indication of the levels of complaints received (perhaps on a unit basis, such as per 100 customers), indications of customer and client retention levels, results from mystery shopper exercises and an indication of the trends in customer satisfaction surveys, as well as industry specific measures (such as the numbers of product recalls).

The key issue is that any information that is provided is capable of being compared, either with outside benchmarks or with internally defined data, so that stakeholders can evaluate the company's performance.

Customer and client initiatives

For a business function such as sales and marketing, which is often accused of having initiatives being developed by the bucket load, the development of CSR objectives for customers and clients is quite challenging to achieve, without their being described as part of marketing 'spin'. However, developing such initiatives is feasible, although sometimes the marketing function requires being restrained from its enthusiasm from seeking 'unique sales propositions' that transgress CSR principles of transparency. Four areas of initiative will be covered.

Customer diversity

Here the focus is the extent to which a company has built customer diversity into its marketplace approaches. Marketplace diversity refers to the extent to which a company approaches its market so that all parts and categories of that market can access and acquire the products and services on offer.

Such diversity measures need not only be about making the products and services accessible to the wide range of individual consumers, but also relate to the extent to which business-to-business products and services are realistically available to SME's as well as to the larger clients. Probably the leading players in addressing marketplace diversity are the financial services companies, although other industry sectors are beginning to address this requirement – or more realistically, this market opportunity.

Most major banks will address the issue of customer diversity in some manner (often described as financial inclusion) and the examples given here, whilst specifically about LloydsTSB, can be found in other retail banks. The issue for banks in this country is that technology has tended to help eliminate those aspects of personal service that were common in the early half of the twentieth century. So for example, the availability of banking services in rural communities has diminished. Similarly, the issue of having an increasing ethnic population has meant that not only have the numbers of languages grown exponentially, but so too have the numbers of different cultures, resulting in greater difficulty for bank employees to communicate effectively. In addition, the issue of poverty is strongly linked to having a bank account – the old adage is that 'being poor means no bank account and having no bank account means that you're poor!' As a result, there is much focus in British banking on financial inclusion, as well as demonstrating responsible behaviour through their responsible lending approaches.

Some of the measures to address financial diversity are driven by government initiatives, such as the launch of Universal Banking Services in 2003, linking basic bank accounts with the Post Office (driven by the government's desire to pay social security benefits directly into a bank account). However, banks like LloydsTSB have created their own initiatives – in their case supporting the Money Advice Trust and helping to implement the Money Advice Debtline.

Similarly, initiatives to assist bank employees to understand the needs of those customers with disabilities have involved employee training. The banks have been at the forefront of making adjustments in branches to help those customers with blind or deafness impairments, as well as using Typetalk facilities to contact branches from a customer's home.

In addition the bank has focused on supporting under-served markets, not always through its own resources. For example, it has been active in supporting community credit union groups and community finance initiatives, often involving social partnerships in regeneration schemes.

In the area of ethnic businesses, the bank has undertaken training for its managers to help them develop their cultural awareness, as well as recruiting local multi-lingual staff to ensure the workforce reflects the cultural composition of the local community – especially where there is a high concentration of ethnic minorities.

In the broader context of small businesses, the bank has developed a range of services targeted at the various forms of small businesses, avoiding the 'one size fits all mentality' and providing support for newly formed small businesses through activities such as providing a business directory, detailing providers of the common forms of products and services required by a small company, as well as hosting business clubs to bring their small customers together.

Sustainable design

Product development is at the beginning of the sales and marketing cycle. The CSR focus here is on social and environmental impacts. Sustainable design is about taking a product, understanding its environmental and social impacts and developing a design that takes these impacts into account and minimises or eliminates them.

One example is mobile phones, many of which are discarded every time their owner upgrades to a new model. Some supermarkets offer mobile phone recycling as part of their customer service.

An alternative developed by scientists in Warwick University used sustainable design techniques utilising biodegradable plastic for the external casing. The plastic casing can be buried in the ground. Within the casing is a seed and when the casing biodegrades, the seed, which is a rose, germinates!

To be fair, some of the ideas for sustainable design require a high degree of lateral thinking in the product development stage. One tulip bulb container designed in Holland is made of cattle dung (apparently there is a large surplus of such material in Holland) and the container acts both to protect the bulbs when out in the ground and is a ready-made fertilizer when placed in the ground!

In a more futuristic mode, Philips Electronics Vision for the Future project designed a fabric that incorporates solar cells – and the power from a shirt made of fabric containing these cells can be used to power your iPod.

It is not all about electronics – Proctor and Gamble has developed a special version of Tide for consumers in countries who primarily do their washing by hand – typically those in the developing world, where washing can be both arduous and expensive, but also where clean clothing can contribute to better health standards. Its Tide 1–Banlaw (which means Tide 1 Rinse in English) has been designed to meet these needs and reduces the amount of water required by 60–70%. Use of Tide 1–Banlaw is further improved with P&G's PUR water filters, which were designed to be low-cost and manufactured with technology and ingredients based on municipal systems in developing countries.

But the biggest impact of sustainable design has come with the EU's Motor Vehicle End-of-Life Recycling Directive. This required (from 2006) the minimum percentage of the vehicle recycled to be 80% for reuse and recycling and 85% for reuse and recovery. These minimum levels are to be raised to 85% and 95% respectively in 2015. They have already had an impact for Ford Germany. By 2004, more than 300,000 vehicles had been recycled into 290,000 tons of metal. Similarly, it has been recycling waste tyres, working with a supplier to create air deflectors and splashguards from recycled tyres as well as recycling tens of thousands of used tyres from Ford vehicles into ergonomic floor mats to cushion the feet of the Ford plant employees who assemble the vehicles.

Customer boycotts

The issue of customer boycotts can vary from a small local fracas, such as consumers protesting about a large supermarket affecting the livelihoods of local stores (which in the main tend to be short-lived), to an on-going international organised programme. The magazine *Ethical Consumer* has a non-exhaustive list[8] of such ongoing boycotts (which it stresses does not infer any endorsement on its part). The list is interesting, particularly because of the indirect nature of some of the boycotts – for example, Anheuser Busch, the American brewery group, has been boycotted by an animal rights group, because it has a subsidiary, Seaworld in Florida, whose operations involve using captive performing Orcas (killer whales). Many of those on the list are promoted by single issue NGOs, such as the Burma Campaign or People for the Ethical Treatment of Animals (PETA).

In terms of cultural differences, consumers in the North American market can be the most demanding of companies, as was demonstrated in a presentation given by Business for Social Responsibility at the European Conference on CSR which included the chart below.[9]

But the fact that consumers (or more realistically, NGOs) can be demanding, does not mean that they are unwilling to modify their stance if they see the other party moving in their direction.

PETA is a worldwide activist movement, supported by many celebrities, such as Paul McCartney, and most food companies probably view it with a fair amount of

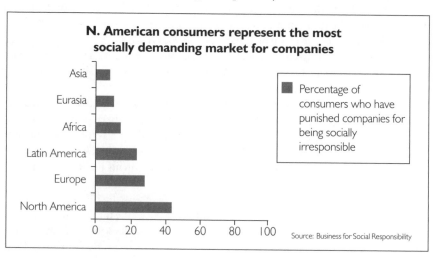

trepidation. But unlike some activist groups, it will enter into discussions with those companies it is boycotting, if it believes it has the ability to change their animal welfare practices. The burger industry is a case in point. PETA Europe declared that there is 'currently a campaign moratorium on this boycott due to improvements in welfare that McDonalds has agreed to while PETA is still in talks with them'.

Getting to this point has involved a lot of pain for McDonald's and Burger King. Whilst McDonald's has a global commitment to animal welfare governed by its Animal Welfare Guiding Principles, it was criticised in the late 1990s because these principles were seen to apply largely to its US and UK operations. One tactic used by PETA involved partnering with Trillium Asset Management – a billion dollar ethical fund manager – which resulted in the joint shareholder proposal to adopt and enforce consistent animal welfare standards internationally.

McDonald's website states that its principles now apply to all the countries in which it does business with a programme of technical standards and comprehensive audit procedures to implement these guiding principles in meat processing plants together with the establishment of an independent expert Animal Welfare Council.

In getting to that agreement, what may have seemed at the outset as a minor irritant became a massive sore that affected McDonald's reputation. Not only did organisations such as PETA use 'Mickey taking' terms such as 'McCruelty' to get their message across (not as bad as Burger King being entitled 'Murder King'), but they also had to face the outcome of what became known as the McLibel trials.

This case was brought by McDonald's against a group of protesters in London that distributed leaflets outside McDonald's outlets. The court case against five protesters began in 1994 and ended 30 months later. It became one of the longest running trials in English legal history, remarkable in its own right, because the ultimate two defenders were denied legal aid and had to fund their own defence

The verdict was unexpected for McDonald's. The judge ruled that the defendants had shown that they (McDonald's) 'exploit children' with their advertising, falsely advertise their food as nutritious, risk the health of their long-term regular customers, are 'culpably responsible' for cruelty to animals reared for their products, are 'strongly antipathetic' to unions and pay their workers low wages.

The defendants then took the UK Government to the European Court of Human Rights to defend the public's right to criticise multinationals, claiming UK libel laws were oppressive and unfair. In February 2005, six years after the defendants last appeared in court for their appeal, the European Court ruled they did not receive a fair trial as guaranteed under the Human Rights Convention, because of the lack of legal aid available to libel defendants and that their freedom of expression was violated by the 1997 judgment.

Whilst the European Court activity did not involve McDonald's directly, it has kept the case in the public eye and has sullied their reputation.

As noted earlier, McDonald's has since modified its Animal Guiding Principles and has produced new ranges of food, designed to mitigate the claims that it was selling food containing high levels of fat, particularly to younger generations. The latter has become a significant focus for consumer action and has seen other food retailers (such as Starbucks) providing healthy eating alternatives.

What is perhaps significant in recent years is the increased involvement of media organisations in consumer issues. Sometimes these are through consumer watch programmes –representing the editorial policy of the media concerned – and sometimes they are through programmes produced by third-party production houses and aired by the media.

The latter is the case with the food-related programmes aired in 2006–08, which featured celebrity chefs who aimed to affect consumer opinion and as a result influence caterers and supermarkets in terms of the quality of food they were selling to consumers.

One example is that of Jamie Oliver, the chef and restaurant owner, who has had two consumer-related campaigns. One focused on the quality of school meals available in the UK and the other criticised the quality of fresh chickens available in supermarkets. In the first case, Mr Oliver was successful in encouraging caterers to improve the healthy eating content of school meals. In the second, he was encouraging consumers to pay more for free range or organic alternatives. The outcome of this campaign has been that the likes of Sainsbury's in the UK has started to provide information about the range of chickens available in their supermarkets to ensure that their customers can make the choice most suitable for them.

What these developments highlight is that the media are now taking up the responsibility for airing and helping to address issues that affect consumers' well being.

Lessons to be learned

What are the lessons to be taken from customer boycotts? Can companies take positive action – and how do they cope where the action taken against them directly affects their business?

The first action for a company is not to underestimate the strength or vociferousness of the activist groups concerned – regardless of their size – and most importantly, not to ignore any boycott threats.

The second is to listen to what is being said by the public – many subsequent boycotters will be ex-customers and are likely to have made their views known in less assertive mediums, such as customer satisfaction surveys.

The third is for a company to assess the risks of such a boycott – which means fully understanding the nature of the boycotting organisation and the extent to which its views are, or can become, mainstream. The message here is to make sure that the company avoids having to swallow unnecessary economic consequences by fully understanding the risks beforehand.

The fourth action is not to neglect the social or environmental aspects of the activist complaints – most boycotts today tend to be about these areas. A company should aim to develop an early warning system to identify what issues are likely to develop over the next three to five years.

The fifth is to be ready to acknowledge the need for changes – and in this area be prepared to be faster to respond – and when the response is made, consider going further than the activists expect. It helps in this respect if your company is not the first target in its market. Burger King suffered provocative ads in the early 2000s once

McDonald's had agreed its animal welfare standards. Its reaction to these ads (the'Murder King' campaign) was to announce that it would exceed the animal welfare standards set by McDonald's. The response from PETA's President is interesting:[10]

> The only way to avoid cruelty in meat production is to go vegetarian, but today Burger King has taken giant steps to improve the lives of millions of animals. We are ending our Burger King protest and examining other chains, such as Wendy's, as potential targets for improvements in animal welfare.

PETA even asked its supporters to write to Burger King's CEO to thank him for the initial improvements and urge him to do more.

Actions such as this are not unusual for NGOs that have seen that their corporate targets are prepared to have a two-way dialogue. For example, Heinz was criticised by dolphin lovers who boycotted tuna processors because dolphins were being caught and killed along with tuna. It responded by saying that it would only purchase tuna from fishing boats that adopted safe (for dolphins) fishing practices. Together with this public statement, it put a 'dolphin safe' logo on its cans, with the apparent activists' acquiescence.

Just because your company is not a food manufacturer, do not assume you are safe.

The fashion retailer Abercrombie and Fitch declared it would boycott the use of Australian wool, after being targeted by PETA, which is focusing on unacceptable sheep rearing practices in Australia and live sheep exports.

Similarly timber merchants (including builders' merchants such as Wolseley and DIY retailers such as those belonging to Kingfisher) have been targeted by NGOs about the presence of timber in their stores that did not come from FSC (Forestry Stewardship Council) sources. On one occasion, the NGOs decided to bring along large inflatable chainsaws which they set up in the customer car parks as a means of drawing the attention of the customers and the media to the need to sell only forestry conservation products.

Plan A

It was difficult to decide whether Marks and Spencer's Plan A[11] should feature under the environment or elsewhere. In the end, it is featured under customer initiatives because this is where I see it is focused.

Plan A is Marks and Spencer's five-year, 100-point 'eco' plan, established in 2007 (it has since been extended to 180 commitments to achieve by 2015, with the ultimate goal of becoming the world's most sustainable major retailer). It sets out to address what it sees as some of the biggest challenges that its business faces (and also impacts on the world at large).

It has been praised because of its scope and criticised because of its marketing (largely, this criticism has come from other retailers). Whether you like it or hate it, it is having an impact and the cleverest part of its presentation is the assertion that there is no Plan B. As such, the company has gained the moral high ground over its competitors and gained the acclaim from its customers for taking what may be perceived to be a forthright action.

The plan comprises what the company calls its five pillars. These are the five key areas where it believes it can make its business both more sustainable and kinder to the environment. These (and their overall objectives) are described below:

- *Climate change* – to become carbon neutral by 2012.
- *Waste* – to send no waste to landfill.
- *Sustainable raw materials* – to extend sustainable sourcing.
- *Health* – to help customers and employees live a healthier lifestyle.
- *Being a fair partner* – to help improve the lives of people in its supply chain.

The intention of the company is that it will work with its customers and suppliers to address these issues. As an example of the underlying commitments behind each area, the following relates to waste. The company promises that it will:

- set targets to reduce food waste from its stores; and
- stop sending the remaining food waste to landfill. Instead, it plans to use environmentally friendly, harder working alternatives like composting and 'anaerobic digestion' – using waste from its stores and farms to generate green energy.

Managers from other companies in its sector comment that the company has to do this anyway. They suggest that often the commitments represent activities that were already at least partially in place before being brought together as a 100-point plan. However, by taking this step, Marks and Spencer has been able to position itself as one of the leaders in the sustainable development arena.

Does it matter if it is partially a marketing exercise? In my opinion, 'No'! Marks and Spencer has used its commercial muscle to drive these issues into the public spotlight and if it profits from doing so, then so be it. Certainly, when the then Chief Executive, Sir Stuart Rose, talked in March 2008 of the issues concerning the provision of plastic bags in its stores and their decision to charge customers 5p for each bag they requested, he did so under the aegis of Plan A. Without that banner, he would have been unable to grab the attention of the media and the general public. The company deserves credit for that – only if they were to use Plan A in a more blatantly commercial manner should they be rightly accused of 'spin'.

Sources

1 'Consumer Protection in the European Union: Ten Basic Principles'. European Commission, Health and Consumer Protection Directorate-General: 20 July 2004.

2 'Judge writes off couple's "unfair" £400,00 debt' *The Times*, 29 October 2004.

3 The list of products and the CSR criteria associated with each is available in German at: www.test.de/themen/bildung-soziales/special/
Unternehmensverantwortung-Sozial-und-oekologisch-produzieren-1313426-2313426/.

4 Bhattacharya, Korschun and Sen *Leveraging corporate responsibility: The stakeholder route to maximising business and social value* (2011) Cambridge University Press.

5 'Banking on Human Rights – Confronting human rights in the financial sector' A study undertaken jointly by F&C Asset Management plc and KPMG LLP UK, September 2004.

6 Details of the Equator Principles can be found on the Equator Principles website at: www.equator-principles.com

7 Information about UNPRI can be found at: www.unpri.org.

8 The list (including companies such as Boots, Johnson & Johnson and Kentucky Fried Chicken) can be found on the Ethical Consumer's website at: www.ethicalconsumer.org/Boycotts/CurrentBoycottsList.aspx.

9 'Are Americans From Mars? CSR in North America.' Presentation given at the European Conference on CSR, Maastricht, 8 November 2004 by Kate Fish, Managing Director, Europe, Business for Social Responsibility.

10 The copy of the press release can be found on PETA's specific site for the Burger King campaign: www.murderking.com/release.html.

11 Details of Marks and Spencer's Plan A (including its progress) can be found at: plana.marksandspencer.com/about/the-plan.

The marketplace:
the supply chain

The way in which a company manages its supply chain and the standards it expects of its suppliers is one that is becoming an increasing focus for the CSR spotlight. The reason for this is that when those companies who have been leaders on CSR began to feel that they had come a long way towards getting their own (internal) house in order, they realised there were pressures on them regarding their (external) partners. These pressures included their methodology for selecting suppliers and also whether they might be at risk of presenting themselves as corporate citizens, whilst importing imperfect practices from their supply chain.

The best-known example is the series of attacks on Nike for the use of sweat shop labour in its suppliers' sports wear factories in the Far East, where the standard of their supply chain practices had serious issues. These attacks had a direct impact on their brand reputation and on revenues (although the company has done much to improve its supply chain standards). However, it is not only the retail and manufacturing companies that have seen this pressure. Those companies outsourcing their work, whether it is to call centres in Bangor or in Bangalore, have been the subject of similar questioning.

The pressures for companies to ensure their supply chains conform to their own CSR standards are coming from investors (concerned about potential hidden risks), NGOs (concerned that companies were condoning unacceptable practices by purchasing from 'irresponsible' suppliers) and clients and customers, who saw the immediate supplier as having a responsibility to them that the supply chain was 'clean'.

The legislative background

There is no direct legislation that requires companies to review the standards in their supply chain – even food companies purchasing from abattoirs or food processors rely on their suppliers to meet their own legal duty to sell them food fit for the purpose.

However, the nature of supply chain CSR is to ensure your suppliers apply the same standards as your company upholds. Hence the underlying legislation to which the suppliers are expected to conform is both the international legislation and the national legislation of your country of operation. However, it is reasonable to accept that suppliers will face country-specific legislative differences that will need to be taken into consideration.

In terms of labour legislation, you would be expecting your suppliers to conform to ILO Conventions about the use of child and forced labour. Yet, if your home base is within the EU, it would not be reasonable to expect your Far Eastern suppliers to conform to EU labour legislations such as the Working Time Directive.

Similarly, in terms of environmental measures, you would expect your suppliers to conform to the UN's Montreal Protocol – and it would be reasonable to expect these suppliers to conform to greenhouse gas emission controls, such as the Kyoto Protocol. This would be more difficult to manage if your suppliers are primarily based in the USA, which did not ratify this protocol.

CSR practices, management and performance measurement

In reviewing a company's supply chain policies and practices, given the lack of legislative procedural direction, the scene is being set by supplier appraisal programmes from large companies, usually multinational enterprises, as well as government procurement departments.

The following are the subject areas covered in one such appraisal questionnaire – it is worth noting that the example given did not come from a European site, but from the headquarters of its Far Eastern region, indicating that the extent to which CSR in a multinational company crosses national boundaries. It also indicates the extent to which multinational legislation impacts upon all aspects of a multinational company's behaviour.

This supply chain questionnaire covered:

- the provision of an equal opportunities policy;
- compliance with ILO Conventions, and the Universal Declaration of Human Rights;
- quality assurance programmes and accreditation (e.g. ISO 9000);
- the provision of an Environmental Management System, and its accreditation;
- measurement of energy, waste and water usage and air emissions; and
- the provision of a health and safety policy.

Other questions that were specific to the nature of the client company and the product area of the supplier were also included.

It can be seen that, with the exception of the Community, clients who are major multinationals are looking at their suppliers' CSR approach in exactly the same way as they would look at their own CSR in their internal operations.

The practices that underlie this supplier appraisal are likely to be more rigorous than if the supplier were to do it of their own accord. This is because the clients' procurement programmes are generally well resourced for evaluating suppliers' performance. The practices included in such an evaluation are set out below.

Practices for sourcing and evaluating suppliers

Undertaking environmentally and socially focused supplier programmes

This would include undertaking a risk/opportunity review to prioritise suppliers based on environmental and social (such as health and safety, employee practices, and human rights programmes) criteria, including requiring suppliers to provide regular updates on their environmental and social performance; engaging with them; offering them support to improve their environmental and social standards; and encouraging suppliers to carry these same environmental and social principles to their own supply chain.

Monitoring of suppliers' operations and facilities

Suppliers' operations and facilities should be monitored to ensure they comply with the client's supplier policy. This includes developing and implementing systems to monitor new and existing supplies to ensure they comply with the supplier policy (including the extent to which a supplier's activities are covered by ISO 9000) and in particular with the core labour standards (generally those of the ILO Conventions, but they would also relate to relevant health and safety standards).

Communication programmes

This includes communicating with suppliers and sub-contractors (as well as suppliers' employees). It also requires both internal and external audits of compliance (including confidential interviews with the suppliers' employees and the suppliers' own stakeholders). In addition, CSR-related training needs to be provided for both the procurement teams and their suppliers, providing compliance incentives and support and providing whistle blowing systems in the event of any employee being concerned about non-compliance.

Remediation plans

This involves having a remediation system in place to deal with any concerns identified in the supply chain (e.g. remedying areas of non-compliance with the broad supplier policy) in particular and having remediation plans developed in cooperation with suppliers in countries where labour rights may be a concern.

A programme sourcing local suppliers

This involves developing a sourcing programme for suppliers that are local to the point of use of the supplied materials. This has both an environmental impact (including reducing CO_2 emissions by reducing journey miles) and an economic impact to the local communities. This is not only focused on a company's operation in a developing country using local supplies wherever possible, but is increasingly being used as a part of government policy in the developed world.

For example, DEFRA in the UK has been 'encouraging' food retailers and food service providers to move to a local sourcing programme with the intention of supporting local British agriculture. This programme can be fraught with difficulties, including whether supplies of, say, tomatoes can be provided on a year-round basis, to the quality provided by the likes of Spanish growers.

Similarly, government initiatives need to be linked up. Using the same example, the UK's NHS has severe cost constraints on the provision of hospital meals. These would be unlikely to support the cost increase if a supplier follows DEFRA's recommendations and only sources local food produce throughout the NHS.

As can be seen from the list of policies and practices, a CSR supply chain programme by major companies is likely to have more impact on changing procedures within the wide range of British and European business than any form of legislation written in Brussels, because of the effect of the market power behind such a programme. It is for this reason that the NGOs are seeking improvements in the CSR supply chain performance of major national and multinational companies.

With this in mind, the types of performance required to evaluate CSR in the supply chain of a company are very much process driven. They will include key performance indicators (KPIs) such as:

- the percentage of supplier operations and facilities that are audited annually for compliance with the CSR supplier policy;
- the percentage of supplier operations and facilities that are accredited to ISO 9000 or other Total Quality Management systems;
- the percentage of suppliers with health and safety management systems in place;
- the average days' debtors (to ensure that the company is complying with best practice in paying suppliers); and
- (if appropriate) the percentage of purchases from local suppliers.

But whilst these KPIs will demonstrate the effective level of supply chain management, it is the initiatives that a company takes in this area that will reinforce and build on its reputation for a totally professional approach in this area.

Supply chain initiatives

In an area of business as highly commercial as procurement, it may be difficult to envisage whether there are CSR initiatives that would feasibly deliver improvements in the supply chain. However there are several ways to achieve such an objective. These are discussed below.

Working with NGO partners

The best known example of large corporates working with NGO partners is that of the Ethical Trading Initiative (ETI). The ETI is an alliance of companies, non-governmental organisations and trade unions that was set up to promote and improve the implementation of corporate codes of practice which cover supply chain working conditions. Amongst its corporate members are the leading names in British retail.

It was set up in 1998 to develop an agreed code that would set out the minimum labour standards that these corporates expected their suppliers to comply with. Its ultimate goal is to ensure that the working conditions of workers producing for the UK market meet or exceed international labour standards.

It was established as a tri-partite organisation when those companies leading the way in establishing their own codes found that they had neither the public credibility, nor the necessary experience and skills, to be seen to be sufficiently proactive in this area. They realised they needed the backing of other organisations operating in this field, particularly from trade unions and NGOs, with expertise in labour issues and overseas development, who were skilled in identifying and promoting good practice in code implementation.

Engaging with NGOs in such projects is not difficult to initiate, but it is difficult to maintain. The key to success is recognising that NGOs have their own agenda – and they most certainly will not kow-tow to corporates that want to do things their own way. As a result, a successful partnership requires agreement about the objectives of the project. It also requires an understanding that once the project is completed, each party has the option to go their own way, unless a new partnership agreement is established. Considering such a partnership as a joint venture would be a mistake – thinking of it more as 'ships that pass in the night' is a more realistic approach to the likely longevity of the partnership.

Working with other third parties

Some companies may not find it as easy to work with NGOs. In these circumstances, there are commercial services available. These are usually developed on an industry basis.

One example is WethicA[1] (Worldwide Ethical Alliance) which provides world-wide supply chain assessment services – particularly to the textiles industry. It was set up by five entrepreneurs of different nationalities (Sri Lankan, Danish, French, and Mexican) who decided to share their experience to support an international project in social responsibility. It provides its clients with social audits of the production sites they are considering using and provides these sites with detailed audits, including areas for improvement. The sites are then revisited three months later to review the improvements (assuming these have been put in place).

Sedex is slightly different. It is a not-for-profit organisation, almost in the form of a cooperative, owned by its members. These can be retailers and brands, individual production sites and companies who supply retailers from a large number of production sites.

Sedex[2] offers a Suppliers Ethical Data Exchange. This is a secure, web-based system enabling companies to input data on labour standards at their production sites. The Sedex system has been designed to allow companies who are in an existing trading relationship to share this information, saving time and money lost on duplicated information. As a result, companies are better able to drive and demonstrate improvements.

The development of Sedex has been supported by a group of UK retailers and suppliers, including Geest, Marks & Spencer, Northern Foods, RHM, Sainsbury's, Tesco, Uniq and Waitrose. As can be seen from this list, much of Sedex's focus was upon food production sites, although in recent years, it has broadened the range of supply sectors. Its members span over 150 countries and range from small independent farms to some of the world's largest retailers and consumer brands.

The Kimberley Process

The Kimberley Process is a multi-party agreement set up to tackle a tricky issue that individual companies or countries could not resolve on their own. The issue is that of 'blood diamonds' – those diamonds that were sourced from rebel movements, who used the funds to finance wars against the legitimate governments of the countries in which the diamonds were mined. The process developed a certification methodology for diamonds that were sold on world markets.

The process was run by certain NGOs and the World Diamond Council. But the process has lost value because of the failure to tackle alleged human rights violations taking place in Marenge, Zimbabwe. Global Witness, the civil society group, and one of the founder members of the process, decided in late 2011 that it could no longer support the certification scheme as it 'has become an accomplice to diamond laundering'.

This decision highlights the fact that multi-party agreements need something more than goodwill to survive and succeed with their objectives. Unlike Sedex, there was no formal global organisation behind the Kimberley Process. For supply chain measures to operate effectively, they require management and governance systems so that all parties can adhere to them.

Carbon disclosure project – supply chain

CDP has already been discussed in chapter 13. It has expanded beyond its initial brief to capture carbon emissions data from major global companies and has extended into an offer to companies to capture emissions data from within their own supply chain.

It does this by requesting the participating customer companies to identify key suppliers and then requests those suppliers to complete the CDP questionnaire and estimate their emissions relating to the customers in question.

This is likely to become more prevalent as companies proceed down outsourcing routes. A good example is that of Cloud computing offered by companies such a Google. For those companies that utilise the Cloud technology, they are effectively outsourcing their computer servers (and the emissions associated with them) to Google. If the supply chain aspects of their emissions are not captured, then outsourcing is a relatively easy way for a company to claim to have reduced its carbon emissions, which would be misleading.

Developing in-house initiatives

In-house initiatives tend to be commercially driven, as distinct from seeking to implement codes of conduct. In this respect, they will often be driven by one party, with the other(s) acquiescing.

A good example is the way food suppliers have responded to requests from supermarkets to reduce transport journey miles by changing their delivery process from a single drop approach to one of delivering the food products and collecting packaging or pallets to return to their depot. This ensures that the vehicles are not travelling empty on the return leg. Whilst supermarkets may declare that they worked jointly with their suppliers, the likelihood is that the customer was king in this decision-making process.

A similar example is where companies have changed the nature of the packaging of their materials to make them biodegradable – the long-term beneficiary is the client, for whom a reduction in waste recycling costs can be a significant benefit.

However, such in-house initiatives can be more balanced in terms of meeting the needs of all parties. Marks & Spencer aims to help suppliers help themselves. It has set local benchmarking groups to help its suppliers make improvements. An example where all have benefited is in Morocco, where a benchmarking group has been responsible for 1,000 workers completing literacy training. Benefiting employers and employees alike, this initiative has increased productivity by as much as 15% in some factories, as operators can now read instructions rather than rely on close supervision. Similar benchmarking groups have been set up by Marks & Spencer in Indonesia, India and Turkey. In the latter, Marks & Spencer suppliers have worked together to find creative ways of providing child care facilities. The benefits for employers have included a marked reduction in the turnover of skilled workers.

Closer to home, Marks & Spencer has been active in supporting UK farmers by introducing them to their end customers. In 2003–04, it ran a 'meet the farmer' initiative so that customers could talk to some of the people who supplied fresh local British produce. After a pilot programme in Kent, suppliers were invited to meet customers in 25 of Marks & Spencer's large stores around the country. Some of its more recent commitments include working with suppliers and partners to deliver training and education to 500,000 workers (if the supplier's workforce lacks education, then it is highly likely that there will be irresponsible practices in place), as well as working with food suppliers to strengthen their human resources practices.

Some final thoughts on the marketplace

The marketplace, comprising sales, marketing and procurement, is where CSR meets the commercial realities of business.

As can be seen from the pages of this chapter and chapter 15, much of the work is focused on complying with the various sets of legislation, either impacting directly on a company's work, or indirectly, as is the case with supply chain.

However, the examples of the initiatives, both for clients and customers and the supply chain does show that worthwhile programmes can be developed that are both commercially viable and also capable of building the reputation of the company concerned. Perhaps it is in the marketplace that the truly responsible company is most visible, as it transcends a 'tick-box' compliance mentality and moves forward with initiatives that both meets its needs and contributes to meeting the needs of its stakeholders.

Sources

1 More information about WethicA can be obtained at: www.wethica.com/.
2 More information about Sedex can be obtained at: www.sedexglobal.com/.

PART
4

What to do to make CSR
work for your business

Stakeholder engagement and communication

No matter what a company does in CSR, if it doesn't communicate it, then it is of no use. This chapter looks at methods of stakeholder engagement and stakeholder communication. Like all the previous chapters, there is no one correct answer – the solution has to be what meets the needs of your company best and in this area, those needs will undoubtedly take on board any considerations about budget restrictions.

The starting point is stakeholder engagement, from which you will be able to better understand the needs and attitudes of your stakeholders, before considering how to communicate with them.

Stakeholder engagement

A stakeholder is an individual or a group that can either affect the company, or is affected by the company's activities at any time, either now or in the future. This definition can include employees, suppliers, local communities, single issue groups, government and the wider society – as well as shareholders. A similar, but more explicit definition of a stakeholder came from a conference in the City and was quoted in the media column of the *Financial Times* on 14 September 2004:

'Anyone that can b***er up your business.'

Stakeholder engagement is the means by which a company determines firstly the views of its stakeholders regarding its method of operations and then moves on to engage those stakeholders in discussing the issues and considering the possible range of solutions.

The process follows a reasonably well-defined path, identifying the stakeholders, understanding the issues, prioritising the issues from a company perspective and initiating a stakeholder engagement process to involve those key stakeholders in consideration of the issues. Reasonably well defined, but perhaps not so easily executed in practice! The process is graphically described in the flow chart overleaf.

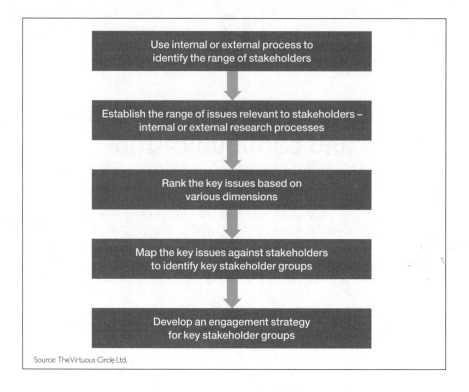

Source: The Virtuous Circle Ltd.

Identify the stakeholders

There are several alternative approaches to achieving this task. For one client, we held a workshop with senior managers from various functions, with a view to:

- identify which stakeholders (by individual name or by category) they had had contact with; and
- discuss what other groups of stakeholders are relevant to the company – even if they have not yet been in contact.

What we discovered was that the stakeholders had very diverse views – not an area that is commonly discussed within a company. As a result, there is little cross-fertilisation of views about who the stakeholders are, or even what kind of questions they ask. More importantly, when the views of the internal and external stakeholders were compared, it became apparent that there was a lot of inconsistency, largely because, in the past, the company did not have any shared views on stakeholders – except in times of crises.

There is often a very narrow view of stakeholders from an internal perspective. In our report for the RSA on 'Public Engagement by Science Based Companies in the UK',[1] what was striking was the extent to which the companies we interviewed did not see the end users of their science-based products as their customers. Instead, they viewed the end user as being a stakeholder of their immediate customers, such as the

NHS. This was in addition to those customers who bought their products as components to be converted into another product for use by a more distant end user. In other words, they did not attempt to understand the views or attitudes of a major stakeholder group – the end-user customer.

An alternative way to identify stakeholders is to use the social science approach – 'public engagement'. This starts from the premise that anyone can have a worthwhile view about a company's operations and products. Public engagement is described as a way for companies to explore and develop their relationships with investors, customers and the wider public.

This involves discussion and debate among the many interested parties who shape the business environment. Public engagement is considered to be a different approach because all parties can contribute to the agenda for discussion. An example of such an engagement was the genetically modified (GM) debate, the government's nationwide public debate on GM crops, which was conducted on an independent basis. It attracted more than 37,000 responses and 1,200 e-mails.

The problem with such an approach from a corporate perspective is that of organising the process without allowing the budget to run away to excess, as perhaps can be seen from the numbers who responded to the GM debate. There is also the risk that such a public engagement is orchestrated by activists – this was the criticism of the GM Debate by the Agricultural Biotechnology Council.

At the end of the day, perhaps the most important means of identifying and categorising the range of stakeholders that are important to a company is the old-fashioned method of monitoring any comments that come in from members of the public. These could include complaints or comments from customers, queries from interested parties such as members of the government, officials calling on their behalf, or calls made from members of the local community regarding practices relating to company premises that are local to them. These comments and queries are generally handled by different departments in a company and are not usually collated. This is different to the other types of stakeholder where there may be more regular and relatively formal contact, such as with staff representatives, union officials, or NGOs who may be in regular contact with the company or the trade bodies with which it works. For all of these potential stakeholders, the important task is to find a way to identify when comments or queries have arisen and to establish the degree of risk associated with each stakeholder group, in order to determine its degree of criticality to the business. Achieving this level of understanding requires a high degree of management coordination – and ideally will need some sort of software database, probably utilised over the corporate intranet.

Understand the needs and views of stakeholders

Again there are several ways to establish the needs and views of stakeholders. The first approach is to use the functional manager workshop, as described earlier, to develop an internal view of the stakeholders' needs and views. In our experience, this approach needs to be somewhat structured, since it can be a process that is almost alien to managers in a company. To help them in the process, it is best to provide the dimensions in which they can consider the individual stakeholders and their likely views – these dimensions include the:

- impact on individuals;
- impact on society at large;
- need for development that would benefit individuals; and
- need for development that would benefit society at large.

Again, our experience shows that while this is a very worthwhile exercise to get managers thinking about stakeholders and their needs, the output may leave a lot to be desired. The audience needs to be prompted about the nature of the issues that the stakeholders may consider as being relevant. The following represent the range of prompts that we used to describe the possible positive and negative impacts of the company. As you will appreciate, this is not an exhaustive list:

- *Community-linked examples* – traffic, smells, night noise, waste generation, employment, investment in the community, local sourcing, etc.
- *Environment-linked examples* – waste disposal, packaging, water usage, power used, recycling, etc.
- *Workplace-linked examples* – working hours, inflexibility, working conditions, training, remuneration, employment.
- *Client and customer-linked examples* – environmental damage, unsafe products, misleading advertising, inappropriate sales practices.
- *Supply chain-linked examples* – pay suppliers slowly, ignore local producers, involve local producers, work with suppliers to develop environmentally friendly approaches.
- *Health and safety linked examples* – standards of health and safety, visitor safety.
- *Investor-linked examples* – what are the key things that investors look for – succession plan, remuneration linked to performance, company knowledge, management.

Another alternative we used with one client was to look at the websites of its closest competitors. This enabled us to map out the issues seen to be relevant by its competitors against those that the company itself featured on its own website. For those issues not covered by the client company, the questions to be asked were: Why do its competitors consider these issues to be significant enough to be reported upon – does this mean that they represented issues that the company had missed, or were its own activities sufficiently strong to mean that these issues were genuinely not considered to be critical? Similarly, by looking at the websites of the NGOs and government bodies with which they had had some form of dialogue, we were able to identify areas that they considered to be important. We undertook a similar mapping exercise between the NGO issues and those of the company. It allowed the company to understand current NGO issues and to determine some of the areas that NGOs would be focusing on in the next 12 months. In each case, our role was to prick the bubble of complacency that companies can surround themselves with because of their introspective approach to issues that are of public interest.

Another approach is to engage directly with a range of stakeholders to ascertain their views. There are many different ways to achieve this objective and the choice will depend upon the budget available, the number of individual stakeholders who are constituents of an individual category and the nature of the likely issues. The alternatives methods of engagement include:

- a public meeting;
- focus groups;
- workshops; and
- interviews through opinion research (both quantitative and qualitative).

Most companies would favour a mix of focus groups and opinion research interviews, if only because the process is more manageable. Increasingly, the view from NGO's is that a more public engagement process (referred to earlier) can deliver better results – although the jury is probably still out on that debate!

However, what is extremely illuminating is that a mixed approach – where both internal and external stakeholders are invited to express their views – the results can be mismatched.

The internal stakeholders will have a more insular view of what they think stakeholders are thinking, often focusing on the current messages that are being promoted by the company. External stakeholders have a much more catholic approach, looking at how they expect the company to behave, as well as considering the relevance of its current areas of activity.

In this respect, the survey of external stakeholders will have a longer time horizon than that of the internal stakeholders and their vision will be unencumbered by issues such as budget availability, which often limits the views of internal stakeholders.

In addition, what becomes readily apparent, particularly when taking a survey of employees as internal stakeholders from within a multinational company, is the extent to which a range of diverse opinions can exist.

These opinions will show that differences in groups often depend on their experiences and cultural background. In a recent survey of an international client's employees, we found several differences in attitudes between:

- corporate staff and staff from operating companies;
- staff located in the UK, those in the USA, those in Europe and those in the rest of the world;
- younger staff with fewer years' service and those that are older with longer service periods; and
- senior management and board members and those staff of lower grades.

A similar reflection on differing cultural norms was given by Business for Social Responsibility in a presentation at the European Conference on CSR.[2] As can be seen, US respondents viewed the way in which companies treated their employees as being particularly relevant to them, but were less interested in social and human rights issues, or those of the environment (which was where the European interest

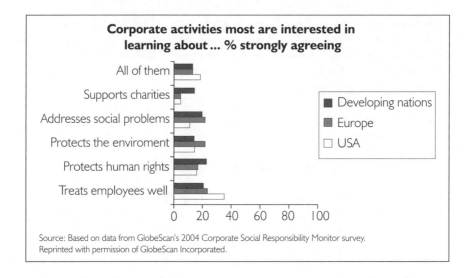

Source: Based on data from GlobeScan's 2004 Corporate Social Responsibility Monitor survey. Reprinted with permission of GlobeScan Incorporated.

was strongest). In contrast, human rights were regarded as being particularly important by respondents from the developing world who regarded addressing social problems and treating employees well as being significant. They were also the only group who thought that support for charities was of relevance.

These differences are further exacerbated when the views of clients are compared with those of NGOs. The critical question is how does a company both take on board all these views and also decide what is right for them to focus upon? It is important to prioritise.

Prioritising the stakeholders' issues

Prioritising the stakeholders' issues is a key task for any company. However, it should not be regarded as being a uniformly accepted task. NGOs and pressure groups will not readily accept that their views have less importance to a company than those of another part of society. This dilemma is something that has to be accepted and planned for by the company as part of the prioritisation process.

This has to take the form of a risk management activity, whereby the range of issues is assembled. Some measure of risk or opportunity needs to be placed against each of them. Some form of assessment is then required to establish the probability of the risk that is ascribed to each view.

In terms of assessing the value related to each issue, these are best undertaken on the basis of scoring various dimensions for each issue, of which the following are those we tend to use:

- ethical (relating to possible infringements of the code of ethics);
- financial (relating to issues that will impact on the financial performance);
- reputation (relating to issues that will impact upon the company's reputation); and

- potential for future regulation (relating to issues that may have the potential for subsequently becoming regulated).

The scoring should cover a range from 'no direct or indirect impact on each area' to 'there is a strong likelihood that this issue would have a direct or indirect impact of significance on the company'. When we undertake this approach, we use a five-point score to cover the range of these possibilities and with a total of 20 possible points (covering each of the four dimensions) which enables the evaluation of each issue against the following criteria:

- score of 0–6: low priority issues, probably no action required;
- score of 7–13: medium priority issue, monitoring required to ensure the view does not move into the high category;
- score of 14–20: high priority issues – commence engagement with stake-holders.

These scores will then enable you to identify those issues that need to be addressed, as well as those that can be put on review until the issues are considered again.

These then need to be mapped against the various stakeholders to establish which stakeholders (individuals or in groups) relate to the highest-ranking issues and, as a result, identify which stakeholders you need to establish a stakeholder engagement process. This identification can again be undertaken using some form of scoring approach, of which the following (based on a three-point scale) is a useful example:

- 0 – has no impact as a stakeholder;
- 1 – the organisation is likely to be low priority for stakeholder engagement with limited ability to have impact;
- 2 – the stakeholder can have a moderate impact on the company, which from time to time may be on their agenda;
- 3 – the stakeholder can have a high impact on the company, which is likely to be high on their agenda all of the time.

Once this prioritisation of stakeholders has occurred, then decisions can be made as to the nature and scope of the engagement with the key stakeholders.

It should be noted that this is a stakeholder-focused approach and provides a method to identify the potential impact of a risk occurring, compared with the CSR risk management model described in Chapter 13, where the focus is on the ability of the company's employees to manage both the impact of the risk and the probability of its occurrence.

Initiate a stakeholder engagement process

The nature of the engagement process can take many forms, all of which depend on the nature of the business and the stakeholder risks that are attached to it. Budget will be a factor, but this should be considered in the context of the perceived risks.

Engagement with employees

One aspect that should be common to all forms of stakeholder engagement is the engagement with employees. Yet here again, there will be different forms dependent on the business. These can cover the following methods of engagement:

Liaison with staff representatives

This should be conducted either directly or through a Works Council (which is an EU requirement for companies employing more than 1,000 employees across their operations in member states of the EU). In many respects, this can be one of the most effective means of engagement, because the liaison will be structured regarding respecting confidentiality (on both sides) and a structured means of communication to the workforce about any decisions made as a result of the liaison.

Employee focus groups

These can be extremely effective, because like the liaison with staff representatives, the discussion can delve deep into the real issues surrounding key factors relating to the business and its impact on employees or other stakeholders. However, unlike the liaison with staff representatives, these focus group discussions will be difficult to keep confidential and any results reached will only be communicated via the management. There will be little or no opportunity to use any staff input from these discussions as part of the message out to staff (unless this is agreed with at the start of the focus group).

Employee satisfaction surveys

These are probably the most common form of staff engagement, but are possibly the least productive in terms of establishing staff attitudes towards key CSR issues. This is because these surveys usually cover a wide range of employee/HR-related topics, from management style, through to remuneration packages, etc. CSR questions can be added to these surveys, but they would tend to be general in nature, rather than delving in depth about some of the CSR issues.

Employee CSR surveys

We have used this approach where a company has already used employee satisfaction surveys. We provided an intranet-based employee survey that went into depth about several CSR alternatives that the management wished to consider, as well as establishing the extent to which individuals were aware of the company's CSR activities.

It also includes a discussion about how individuals receive information about CSR and the ways in which they would prefer to learn about such news. In terms of preference, this approach stands above the employee satisfaction survey, but probably should be used in conjunction with employee focus groups, so that views that are identified through the survey can then be explored in more depth using focus groups.

Engagement with external stakeholders

In terms of external stakeholders, there are also alternative methods, which will also depend upon the nature of the stakeholders and the range of issues that need to be covered. These methods include:

One-to-one discussions

This approach is particularly useful where the key risks are related to one group of stakeholders who are represented by one or a few organisations. For example, where the key stakeholders are society at large, but where bodies such as Greenpeace or Friends of the Earth stand 'in loco parentis' for society. In such circumstances, a discussion with such NGOs is both practical and beneficial, provided you as the company representative are both willing to listen and to act on the results of the discussions.

One Chief Scientific Officer of an NGO said that he was very willing to enter into discussions with a company (on the basis that he saw the issues as being relevant to the NGOs agenda) provided the discussion was two way and he felt there was some chance of a positive result. His dissatisfaction came from discussions with companies where he felt that he was being told the facts of life from a corporate point of view.

This highlights both the opportunity and the risk of such an engagement approach. If this dialogue is conducted in an open and constructive manner, both parties will contribute and positive results are likely to be forthcoming. However, if this form of dialogue is not achieved, then relationships will sour and the likelihood is that the stakeholders will be alienated.

As a result, companies should only enter into such a dialogue if they are willing to take active criticism on board and to consider changes in approach, which are reasonable to meet the needs of both society and the environment.

Workshop or focus group discussions

This is probably the most common method of stakeholder engagement, partly because the approach is so cost effective. However, there is a risk that this activity can be seen as a market research exercise, where the individuals participating in the focus groups are listened to, but they are not engaged in a dialogue that involves both parties. To ensure the engagement occurs, the discussion should be facilitated, ideally by a third party, to ensure objectivity and independence.

Perhaps the best example of such discussions was practised by British American Tobacco, when developing its first CSR report. As a major worldwide producer of tobacco products, many people questioned whether such a company could ever be socially responsible.

However, BAT has turned the argument on its head. It acknowledged that its products constitute a risk to public health, but it also recognised that the public continue to purchase its products and that, failing a total world ban on tobacco products, it will continue to sell tobacco for many years to come. As such, its position is that:

If a business is managing such products, we believe it is all the more important it does so responsibly. Governments, societies and companies must together address the best ways of ensuring responsible management of such products, which millions of adults, balancing pleasure and risk, are likely to go on consuming and expect to buy at quality and fair prices.

When the first dialogue programme took place in 2001, significant groups such as the anti-smoking lobby declined to participate.

The dialogue only continued on the basis that the stakeholders contributed to ways in which BAT could become and be seen to become more responsible. The company did not try to convince people that tobacco is good for you, but rather that tobacco product producers and sellers should recognise their responsibility to society.

In this stakeholder engagement programme, the focus was on the development of the company's Statement of Business Principles, which BAT has now adopted as its over- arching business conduct procedure. In 2002, 145 stakeholders were invited to participate in the discussions, of which 82 chose to do so. The programme was facilitated by a Director of MORI and the Director of the Institute of Business Ethics, with BAT's independent verifier, Bureau Veritas, acting as the independent monitor and verifier. A great deal of internal work was undertaken on the Business Principles, before the discussions occurred.

The discussions themselves took place under Chatham House Rules to ensure that no comments could be attributed to individual organisations. However, to BAT's credit, it did publish non-attributed verbatim comments in its CSR report. These comments ranged from the complimentary – 'Excellent document' from a scientist – to critical – 'Like reading an insurance document' from a consumer to 'Lots of people are happy to take your money, but not take any responsibility' from an NGO.

BAT's dialogue process continued, developing the discussion into new areas of CSR as the company and its stakeholders became satisfied that appropriate action was taking place in the areas that had been discussed.

This reflects an important principle in such focus or workshop discussion. The attendees will only contribute – and continue to contribute – if they believe the company has both the intent and the willingness to act on their views.

The BAT model represents a significant CSR amount of investment, but given the product its sells and the company's worldwide exposure, particularly in developing countries in terms of both sales and growth of the raw material, it has been a successful exercise. Similar exercises with smaller companies, or with less controversial products, would not represent such a sizable investment, but would be likely to contribute similar incremental levels of understanding of stakeholder attitudes.

Public engagement

This method of engagement is extremely direct and is most appropriate for those companies where the issues facing them are regarded by the public as being controversial. As a consequence, as well as learning the views of the stakeholders, there is also an opportunity to be seen as an open communicator with the audience concerned and, as a result, to help that audience form a better opinion of the company concerned.

One of the best examples of such an engagement process was that undertaken by BNFL, which undertakes the reprocessing and production of plutonium in its main UK site at Sellafield. The view of the public at large was that its operations were unsafe and created dangerous pollution, although this perception was not shared by the BNFL workforce or (largely) by the communities around Sellafield, where a high proportion of people had direct or indirect knowledge of site operations and their impact.

As a consequence, BNFL conducted its National Stakeholder Dialogue process, involving about 1,000 members of the public that had an interest in the way BNFL conducted its operations. It used an independent convenor and facilitation that has proved particularly well-suited to considering the increasingly complex and controversial key issues associated with BNFL's activities.

BNFL has profited from this process by learning that the traditional approaches of engagement used by the organisation were not as sensitive or respectful of external stakeholder views as they could have been. In addition it began to appreciate that trust can only be developed through pro-actively seeking 'outside-in thinking'. These lessons could only be achieved through the commitment of many stakeholders and their respective organisations.

But what has changed as a result? BNFL believe their directors, managers and other employees have begun to appreciate the value of 'outside-in' thinking. There has also been a change in the way BNFL engages with stakeholders. It has moved away from the adversarial and into the constructive form of engagement. In addition, there was a change in perception about how the company provided information to the public, making business and technical information more accessible, being capable of being questioned and understood, as well as changing the way the company was perceived, more towards 'trust' and 'respect' for all parties' views and opinions.

As may be expected from the description of this process, it has not been a low-cost investment on the part of BNFL, but given its circumstances, it is clear that the use of this form of stakeholder engagement was both appropriate and effective. The level of appropriateness depends on the level of risk associated with the company's activities in the first instance.

Opinion surveys

This is a common approach, using opinion research methods to determine stakeholders' views on a set of CSR issues. Its attraction is that it represents a cost-effective way of gathering the views and opinions of as many groups of stakeholders as are required, including on both a national and an international basis. The model we use is our CSR Brand Quality Survey, shown overleaf.

The approach focuses first on understanding the respondents' views of the industry of the client company, because attitudes towards a company's CSR are determined by expectations of the industry. As an example, stakeholders will expect more of a supermarket retailer than they will of a support services company.

The next step is to establish the current perception of the company's CSR status

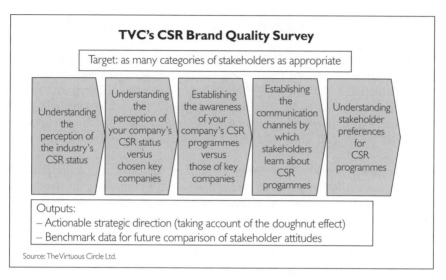

TVC's CSR Brand Quality Survey

Target: as many categories of stakeholders as appropriate

Understanding the perception of the industry's CSR status

Understanding the perception of your company's CSR status versus chosen key companies

Establishing the awareness of your company's CSR programmes versus those of key companies

Establishing the communication channels by which stakeholders learn about CSR progammes

Understanding stakeholder preferences for CSR programmes

Outputs:
– Actionable strategic direction (taking account of the doughnut effect)
– Benchmark data for future comparison of stakeholder attitudes

Source: The Virtuous Circle Ltd.

against chosen key companies and, as part of that, establishing the awareness of any existing CSR programmes. Many companies assume that because they are active with their CSR programmes, all its stakeholders will be aware of them. This leads to the next step, which is to identify how stakeholders learn about CSR programmes. Too often, a company will fail to use the stakeholders' preferred communication channels. As a result their messages will disappear into the ether – a CSR investment that is effectively being wasted.

Whilst much of the early parts of the Brand Quality Survey focus on activities that the company has up and running, the last and most important part of the survey addresses what the stakeholders' preferences are for CSR programmes. In our experience, these can often be different from these promoted by the company's senior executive, whose attitudes may be different because they do not have the same cultural ethos as those of their stakeholders.

An example of this difference occurred in one such survey we undertook for a client, where the stakeholders that were the subject of the survey were consumers of their service, of whom one-third came from ethnic minorities.

Their attitudes were found to be significantly different from those of the board, which could best be described as being made up of white Anglo-Saxon males. As a result, some of the existing CSR programmes, which were viewed with satisfaction by the board, were viewed as being less than satisfactory by their stakeholders.

This survey also highlighted what we term the 'jam in the doughnut effect', where the jam in the centre of the doughnut represents those activities that the stakeholders regard as being the core attributes that a company should provide – often equivalent to the hygiene factors for any product or service.

The ring of the doughnut represents those less-tangible CSR activities that can enhance the status of the company in the eyes of the stakeholders. However, unless the company is addressing the core activities (the jam in the centre of the doughnut) then the impact of those on the ring are ineffective, because they are seen as either gloss or peripheral.

We have used this form of survey technique with a wide range of stakeholders – government and NGO officials, clients, suppliers, investors and the media – increasingly on a worldwide basis. The findings show the differences between the different groups of stakeholders as well as between different cultures, different nationalities and different interests of individuals. More than anything this highlights the importance of developing individual CSR programmes that address the different stakeholders and their areas of focus.

A good example was the stakeholder survey we undertook for a company in a highly regulated market. The output was in the form of a very lengthy slide presentation, one slide of which is shown below. The stakeholder groups covered were employees (from the board to recent graduates), investors and external stakeholders (largely NGOs). The information on the slide shows three areas of conflicting stakeholder needs. Charitable donations were seen as a high priority by employees – but as a much lower priority by investors. The latter had not said this should be a low priority, but, from the detailed information we had from their interviews, the question they were asking was 'tell me how it contributes to company performance!'

A similar conflict came in terms of having a carbon footprint statement, with employees and external stakeholders seeing it as a high priority, whilst investors saw it lower down. Again, from the interviews, the investors made the very strong point that this company was in a low risk area regarding emissions and the company should not overplay its position.

The last area of conflict came in terms of having a code of business ethics. The company did have a very strong code, but its employees were relatively complacent about its importance. However, both the investors and the external stakeholders saw it as of vital importance, especially given the company was in a highly regulated industry.

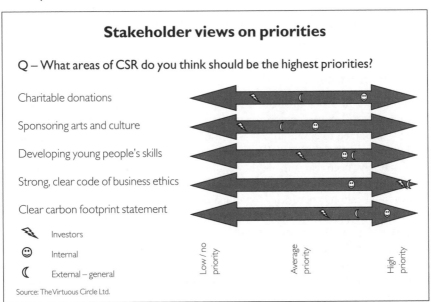

The benefit of these results to the company concerned was that they were able to prioritise their CSR activities and tailor their communications to the needs of their stakeholders. Of course, when there are conflicts of interest, only the company can decide which stakeholder group has priority, but this decision can then be made on the basis of the business model and the key business drivers.

Some last thoughts on stakeholder engagement

The process followed above covers the understanding of the key issues from the stakeholders' perspective, prioritising them and then engagement with the stakeholders to discuss how these issues can be best addressed. There are two important lessons to be learned out of this process.

The first lesson is to recognise that not all the issues can be addressed by a company. A good example of that is BAT's approach, which does not take into account the banning of smoking that some anti-smoking NGOs believe should be part of every responsible company's approach. The company's business objectives are paramount, although they should be set in a responsible context.

The second lesson is to recognise that all the stakeholder engagement processes tend to be a narrow-cast approach, limited to representatives of stakeholders, rather than to all the stakeholders included in the category. As such, the need to consider the broad-cast communications programme for all stakeholders is an essential consequence to the stakeholder engagement process.

Stakeholder communication

One of the key tenets about successful CSR is that companies should not only behave in a responsible manner towards society and the environment, but also that they should be seen to be doing so.

Why communicate?

We are aware of major financial services companies that have provided matched funding (running to six figure amounts) to its employees' volunteer community activity, but failed to communicate why they were doing so. As a result investment analysts were unconvinced and questioned the benefits of such funding. The questions may have been relevant, but they could have been dealt with more easily if there had been adequate communication in the first place.

Communication is necessary to reduce risks of any adverse action by key stakeholders, particularly government departments or NGOs who may suspect that a company is being less than responsible in some of its actions. Communication is also necessary to build a company's reputation amongst its stakeholders for any initiatives that it is taking that are over and above what is expected in its sector.

This is especially true of a company's investors. The book value percentage of the market value of FTSE 100 shares fell from 79% in 1975 to 39% in 2003. Put another way, the value of a company's share that is based on intangible assets and hence represented by its reputation (and its relative level of perceived risk) has risen three-fold from 21% to 61% in that period.

In this context, the value of non-financial information has become much more important in valuing a company's shares, as was evidenced in a piece of research by PricewaterhouseCoopers.[3]

This research looked at the 2001/2002 accounts of Coloplast, a Danish company with a strong reputation for the levels of financial and non-financial information it provides. PwC dissected this set of accounts and produced two sets of accounts: one which considered pure financial reporting requirements and another which included an extended range of non-financial data.

It took these two reports to the investment analyst team at Schroders (giving each member of the analyst team one of the two versions of the report) and asked them to produce both a forecast of revenue and earnings and a recommendation for the stock.

The results showed that the average revenue and earnings forecast for those with the financial and non-financial data was actually lower than those with just the financial data. However, despite the lower forecast, those with the complete information set were overwhelmingly in favour of buying the stock, whereas 80% of those with just the financial data recommended selling the stock.

This variation showed that although the process that underpins decision-making in Schroders is built on financial, any confidence attached to the estimates is underpinned by the non-financial data that is provided.

As the author of the report says:

> This case study reveals the magnitude of the economic benefits that can accrue to companies that offer a more comprehensive picture of corporate performance.

This message was amplified in an article in *Harvard Business Review*,[4] which discussed how model behaviour affects market power. The article concluded with the following paragraph:

> To be credible, global companies' social responsibility efforts must show that the companies have harnessed their ample resources to benefit society. Some may argue that corporations have no business expending resources on activities that lack a profit motive. That is short sighted. If consumers believe that global companies must shoulder greater social responsibility, executives do not have much of a choice, do they?

Ways to communicate?

The accepted form of stakeholder communication is some form of CSR report and/or a CSR section on the company website. In many respects this has come about out of custom and practice with the leading companies.

However, there is a need to review this approach to ensure that, first, we are not cutting down a rainforest purely to create CSR reports and secondly, that our CSR communications are targeted means of communicating with the stakeholders in the manner they find most effective. In addition, they need to cover the information they find most useful for their purposes. It also needs to take account of the often immense number of requests from stakeholders and investment analysts trying to evaluate a company's CSR performance.

A company must consider its CSR information and communication strategy up front – otherwise it will be overwhelmed by information requests that can be over-whelming once it has stepped onto the CSR escalator.

Clearly some form of CSR report must be sent to key stakeholders, particularly those government officials and key NGOs that, from our research experience, place a high value on its presence and its content.

However, the question is the size and scope of this report. Some CSR reports that we have read are extremely heavy and we question the extent to which they are read fully, except perhaps by CSR aficionados! That being the case, then there is a strong argument to have a limited-scope hard copy report, accompanied by a web-based version, with access to more detailed statistics and KPIs than are included in the hard copy version.

Similarly, a much simpler version of the CSR report should be targeted at indi-vidual groups of stakeholders. Ford in the UK produced a small four-page A5 sized summary which it made available to any potential and existing customers who visited its dealer showrooms. In its summary, it is made clear where further information could be accessed. Tesco also uses such a summary for its customers. Lloyds TSB has had both a report and a review – the former is very much CSR process-related, while the latter takes a stakeholder approach, using case studies and quotes from relevant stakeholders. Similar approaches should be developed that are tailored to those communities' local to a company's principal operating sites.

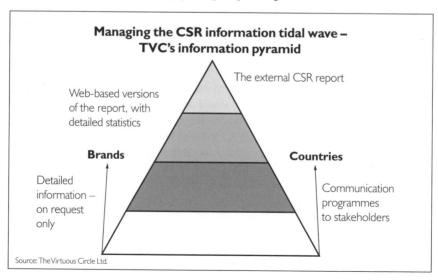

Managing the CSR information tidal wave – TVC's information pyramid

The external CSR report

Web-based versions of the report, with detailed statistics

Brands

Detailed information – on request only

Countries

Communication programmes to stakeholders

Source: The Virtuous Circle Ltd.

A company also needs to decide how much information should be made available to stakeholders, as some companies have received requests that could be considered to be unreasonable as to the amount of information they require.

In this respect, there is a lot to be said for telling stakeholders that all the information that a company is willing to provide is available by accessing its website. Not only would such a policy make it easier to manage requests from stakeholders, but it would also represent significant savings in terms of the man hours required to sort through such requests.

If the company is a multinational (or even if it has a significant presence in several regions in the UK) then specific communication programmes should be targeted at specific stakeholders both geographic and cultural.

If a CSR programme is to be embedded as part of a company's business process, then it should not be assumed that a CSR report centrally produced in Manchester will be of interest to stakeholders in Memphis or Melbourne. The same can be said for UK companies who have significant regional footprints.

Another issue that a company must consider is whether it is better known for its corporate brand or its product brand. For example, BT's corporate brand is now the same as its product brand, so it is quite acceptable to have its CSR communication programme based around its corporate branding.

For multi-brand companies, it is not sufficient to rely solely on centrally coordinated CSR communication – it must relate to the subsidiary brands. This example goes further than the parent company to brands who are manufacturing entities such as Volvo or Ford. Ford took its CSR communication further by developing communications that were targeted at specific stakeholder groups (e.g. customers visiting showrooms).

Man Group took this in the development of its 2007 Corporate Responsibility Report. It produced one overarching report, as well as three supplements – Man's People, Man in the Community and Man in the Environment. Each had additional detail to that included in the main report. As a result the company was able to send targeted information in response to specific requests from different interest bodies.

As was mentioned earlier, for many companies, the way forward has been to produce a summary hard copy report, whilst making much more detail available on all aspects of CSR on its website. Apart from saving costs and making the CSR report more readable, the advantage of this approach is that CSR communications can become much more dynamic and up to date.

Similarly, if a company manufactures multiple consumer products, how does the consumer understand the CSR approach of the parent company? For example 'Test' in Germany is starting to provide CSR information as part of its product evaluation process. Clearly 'Test' believes that consumers do not have enough information about the CSR practices of the manufacturers behind the products they purchase on a regular basis.

Equally in terms of providing information there is a risk that communications are seen to be an annual affair, linked to the corporate reporting cycle. Yet, providing regular updates is an important way to ensure that CSR is a topical issue for stakeholders.

As an example, BT hosted a series of discursive articles on its website that it described as 'Hot Topics'. These often included a vote on the topic by visitors to the website, which ensured that stakeholders knew that their views were being listened to. This has now been changed to its 'Better Future Blog'. Articles are posted and readers then have the opportunity to feedback their comments. However, this can be challenging if readers only post a few comments, which would tend to negate the benefit of having such a blog.

Perhaps the best example of such ongoing dialogue (and its challenges) was the approach that Shell adopted. Its CSR section of the website included a feature called 'Tell Shell' – which are now described in a less interesting way as 'Shell Dialogues'. This allowed anyone to post their views on Shell's activities and behaviour – the only veto that Shell takes on items that are posted are those that are abusive, or whose publication could have legal implications. By doing this, Shell shows its stakeholders that it listens – and shows that it goes one step further and responds with appropriate action.

The last area of stakeholder communication is that of employee communication. Two factors need to be considered here.

The first involves current employees. In one piece of employee CSR research we undertook, it was very clear that the main CSR communication was aimed at senior managers, with little penetrating to the wide numbers of staff beyond this tier of management. If a company considers that much of its stakeholder relations occur at its front line, then communicating with all levels of staff is essential. What this research also showed was that formal methods of communication such as the annual report or the CSR report did not get through to these groups of employees – to put it bluntly, they did not regard these documents as 'their type of read'. In addition, it was clear that they set more store in what they heard from their line managers than what they read.

Consequently, for these employees, CSR communication has to take a place in regular manager briefing sessions – which makes it all the more important that CSR is seen as a topical issue, rather than an annual report – as well as through employee-targeted hard copy or intranet newsletters. This will also require a CSR training programme for managers to help them communicate more effectively, as well as dealing with employees' questions on CSR in an adequate manner.

It is essential to consider ways of communicating with younger employees and those with fewer years of service, who will have differing levels of interest and different areas of focus This communication should link strongly with the messages they received when they were first recruited.

Communicating a company's CSR performance to potential recruits can be vital, especially if the company wants to secure new employees from the younger and better-educated marketplace. The company should consider how its recruitment communications take account of the CSR activity that is going on. Being able to display a caring face can be as important to potential recruits as demonstrating that employees have a good social life if they are part of the team.

Where this often falls down is on the careers section of the website which, in our experience, regularly fails to include CSR information that is relevant to potential recruits. This is often because the person responsible for this section makes the assumption that if a potential recruit wants information about CSR then he or she can click across to the relevant part of the website. In fact, most potential recruits are either not aware of the existence of the CSR section, or do not have time to spend surfing a company's website. Companies need to review the careers section on their websites to ensure the relevant CSR messages are readily accessible. It is the first port of call for many recruits and represents a significant opportunity to get across key messages about the company's CSR attributes to attract the type of staff that will be committed to it.

CSR and the Business Review

Now that there is a regulatory requirement to produce a Business Review is the CSR report still necessary? The reality, as can be seen from the previous discussions, is that they are two different documents, targeted at two different sets of audiences.

The Business Review is designed solely for the benefit of the shareholders, with other stakeholders being incidental beneficiaries of the information contained within it. The CSR report is designed for a wider range of stakeholders and will have to address a wider range of issues than the Business Review.

In this respect, there is also likely to be a significant difference in the time horizon for the two sets of reports. The Business Review reflects the typical investors' time horizon – anything from three months to five years. In contrast, the CSR report should have a longer time horizon addressing issues such as environmental impacts that may have a horizon of 10 to 20 years and those of employee development, given that employment represents between 40–70% of most organisations' costs. In that context, the Business Review reporting of non-financial indicators is likely to be a subset of the range of CSR indicators that would be reported by a company.

The Business Review will focus on the non-financial risks, whereas the CSR report also considers some of the non-financial opportunities that a company may exploit (e.g. having a more diverse customer base).

The decision of whether to include CSR information in a Business Review will depend on the company's business model. This determines to what extent the CSR elements are material to the company's key business drivers. This choice will obviously vary by the sector in which the company operates, but the following is a generalised perspective on whether information should be included in the annual report (ARA) or the CSR report.

For the environment, the likelihood is that greenhouse gas emissions should be in the annual report, whilst water use would probably be found in the CSR report unless business critical and waste management and environmental prosecutions would probably be found in the CSR report.

For the community, the only information that should be found in the annual report is the amount of financial donations – described by their purpose (although this is likely to change as part of the BIS consultation proposals). However, if the company has a significant community footprint – as do, for example, extraction industries and food retail supermarkets – then it is reasonable to provide case studies of the community activities in the annual report.

Business integrity measures relating to bribery/facilitation payments procedures should be commented on in the annual report, whilst reference to the code of conduct is more likely to be found in the CSR report.

Employee matters relating to diversity and health and safety should be commented on in the annual report, whilst some employee performance indicators should be in the annual report with more in the CSR report (including comments on policies and activities).

Human rights and supply chain matters are most likely to be found in the CSR report, unless the company operates in countries known as 'ones to watch', in which case some commentary is appropriate.

For customers, it is almost essential that some customer-related performance indicators should be seen in the annual report, whilst policies and processes should be covered in the CSR report.

As a consequence, our recommendation to companies is that where they have already produced a CSR report, they should continue to do so, alongside the Business Review. What is required is that they should undertake a mapping exercise, so that they can identify what elements of non-financial data can be included within the CSR report and what summary information should be included in the Business Review.

Yet our experience of supporting clients in the preparation of their Business Review strategy suggests that they have been often looking at it from purely the perspective of governance. However, once the Business Review is published by a company, it will have a very significant impact of the company's reputation, as can be seen from the following chart:

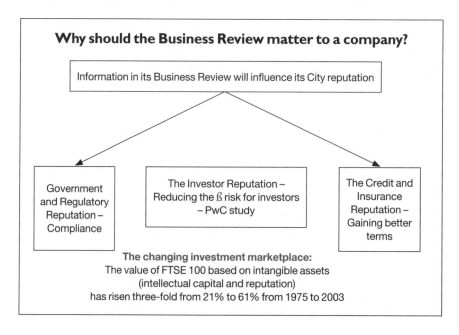

Why should the Business Review matter to a company?

Information in its Business Review will influence its City reputation

| Government and Regulatory Reputation – Compliance | The Investor Reputation – Reducing the ß risk for investors – PwC study | The Credit and Insurance Reputation – Gaining better terms |

The changing investment marketplace:
The value of FTSE 100 based on intangible assets
(intellectual capital and reputation)
has risen three-fold from 21% to 61% from 1975 to 2003

Many companies have seen the Business Review as being relevant primarily to shareholders – and indeed, as was evidenced by the PricewaterhouseCoopers study referred to earlier in this chapter, the availability of non financial indicators will have a significant impact on how a company's share price is evaluated.

Yet, once published, the Business Review will be used extensively by other financial intermediaries, including lenders and insurers, as a means of assessing the risk inherent in dealing with a company. Similarly, our research has shown that government and regulators rely extensively on CSR reports (where available) to develop their views on a company and their perception of its reputation as being a responsible operator. The Business Review will add to their evaluation and those companies that do not produce CSR reports will be surprised at the extent to which their Business Review will influence the attitudes of government and regulatory body officials towards them. In addition NGO officials will use Business Reviews to develop their own views on the validity of a company's reputation.

For those companies not yet producing a CSR report, there is the opportunity to review their whole corporate communication programme, including considering how the Business Review should mesh with a possible CSR report and any CSR reporting on their web. It offers them the possibility of setting their CSR and Business Review reporting into a more targeted approach that involves more effective use of the available information channels, without replication and in the most cost-effective manner, as can be seen from the following chart. A critical factor to consider is the level of information available in each resource. Hence a key discussion at the outset of developing the CSR strategy is to determine how the Business Review and CSR communication process should be mapped and combine them with other information sources, such as those accessible through the company's website.

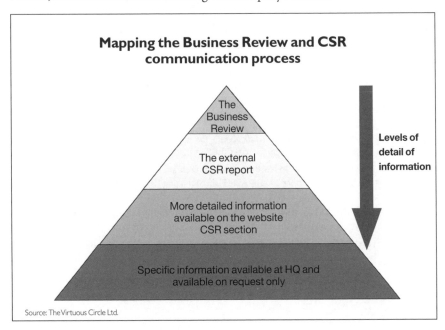

Mapping the Business Review and CSR communication process

The Business Review

The external CSR report

More detailed information available on the website CSR section

Specific information available at HQ and available on request only

Levels of detail of information

Source: The Virtuous Circle Ltd.

Some final thoughts on stakeholder communication

In drawing up our route map, we placed CSR communications at the end. Yet, in many respects, it needs to be considered at the beginning of the development of the CSR strategy.

To get to the end of the route map will have involved much effort, much thought and many discussions. To deliver a return on this investment will require having a communications plan that is effective in targeting the stakeholders and ensuring they understand the company's CSR messages. Too much CSR effort is expended without delivering the right levels of return, because there is insufficient thought about developing the right communication programme at the outset.

As well as ensuring that investment is made into the communication process, effort should also be made into ensuring the information content is relevant to the stakeholder audiences. An *Economist* article[5] about CSR reporting acknowledged that:

> ... the stories which companies are now telling in these reports are of interest to a widening audience and that they do have a real bearing on a firm's ability to raise capital and recruit the best employees.

However, it also went on to criticise those reports that commented on irrelevant issues, or failed to comment on those that are material to the company's business:

> Story-telling is all very well, but unless it is relevant to a company's performance, it is best left to fiction writers.

Once the programme is up and running, then it needs to be reviewed – CSR does not stand still and neither do the stakeholders! In the final chapter we will move to review where CSR might be going in the next five years.

Sources

1 S. Emery and T. Hoskins *What's there to talk about – Public engagement by science-based companies in the United Kingdom* (2004) Royal Society for Arts (The RSA).

2 'Are Americans From Mars? CSR in North America.' Presentation given at the European Conference on CSR in Maastricht on 8 November 2004 by Kate Fish, Managing Director, Europe, Business for Social Responsibility.

3 'A Tale of Two Reports.' Alison Thomas, Director of Research of PricewaterhouseCoopers' Value Reporting Team, European Business Forum Online, Autumn 2003.

4 Holt, Quelch and Taylor 'How Model Behaviour brings Market Power', *Harvard Business Review*, August 2004.

5 'Corporate Storytelling' *The Economist*, 4 November 2004.

18

The future of CSR

CSR – Where it's going?

Shortly after the millennium, there were questions about whether CSR was a flash in the pan. Was it an overreaction to company fraud in the 1980s and 1990s? Was the environmental thing being over-egged by NGOs? When, in 2004, we undertook research for one of our clients amongst external stakeholders we found that 80% of corporates agreed strongly that they had seen CSR grow as a subject for business discussion over the past five years. Furthermore, all of them (100%) expected to it grow even more in importance over the next three to five years. But there were certainly critics around – not the least of which was *The Economist*, whose 2004 comments have already been discussed. By 2008, *The Economist* had mellowed. Its special report on CSR[1] commented on examples such as M&S's Plan A which 'demonstrates that CSR is booming'. It returned to its critical sentiments towards CSR, but in a more accepting fashion, by stating that: 'None of this means that CSR has suddenly become a great idea. This publication has often argued that it is misguided, or worse. But in practice, few big companies can now afford to ignore it.' The report describes how CSR has developed, by identifying that 'CSR is now made up of three broad layers, one on top of the other'. It describes the first as corporate philanthropy – 'the most basic' – whilst the second is risk management. The third it describes as the 'trendiest layer of CSR' – helping to create value, and more importantly, creating a factor of competitive advantage.

But in the four years since the second edition of this book was published, the world has been through a maelstrom. Economically, we have gone through the collapse of Lehman Brothers and the ensuing banking crisis, the Eurozone crisis and we are now facing a severe double-dip recession. In 2011 we had societal changes such as the Arab Spring and the Occupy Movement against capitalism and bankers in particular (which breached the hallowed walls of Wall Street and St Pauls, London). We have had ethical issues in the form of the phone hacking scandal in the UK, and web hacking by Wikileaks (claiming to act on behalf of society) and by mysterious neo-governmental bodies (supposedly in China) hacking into major companies' secure computer systems. We have also had environmental disasters, such as the Deepwater Horizon explosion in the Gulf of Mexico and the thinning of the polar ice caps, alongside the delays to creating the successor to the Kyoto Protocol. Politically, the world has changed, with China becoming the world's second economy and the BRIC nations taking their role on the world stage alongside nations who think their own world role is sacrosanct. In the UK, we are planning the 2012 Olympics with the intention that it is the greenest ever Olympics and has a strong emphasis on diversity.

So, asking: 'Where is CSR going?' at the beginning of 2012 is a big challenge. Critics of CSR may suggest it has a small role to play in a world with these major challenges. Supporters may say that it is precisely at a time of such challenges that CSR will play a significant role because of its underlying focus on responsible practices.

However, the *McKinsey* Global Survey of 2011[2] – 'The Business of Sustainability' – states that: 'Many companies are actively integrating sustainability principles into their businesses, according to a recent McKinsey survey, and they are doing so by pursuing goals that go far beyond earlier concern for reputation management'. The implication is that more executives are seeing CSR or sustainability as integrated into their business processes and decision making, with a focus on those activities that offer the highest value potential. The top reason for addressing sustainability is seen as improving operational efficiency and lowering costs, which has succeeded corporate reputation, the leading reason in 2010. The areas where over 60% of respondents say their company is taking action are those of energy efficiency and waste reduction. The top-two process areas where respondents claim sustainability has been completely or mostly integrated are those of mission and values and strategic planning.

The survey concludes with the comment that: 'The choice for companies today is not *if,* but *how,* they should manage their sustainability activities. Companies can choose to see this agenda as a necessary evil – a matter of compliance or a risk to be managed while they get on with the business of business – or they can think of it as a novel way to open up new business opportunities while creating value for society.'

Evidence from reports by organisations such as *The Economist* and *McKinsey* surveys suggests that CSR has become an accepted (and acceptable) part of the management agenda. Even with the political, social, ethical, economic and environmental upheavals of the past few years, it is clear that CSR is an embedded part of the business fabric. However, the real question is: How will it move from here? What changes can we expect in terms of the position of CSR in management thinking over the next years – where will it be by 2020?

The legislative future

Legislative and CSR elements

The individual CSR elements have been the subject of a wealth of legislation designed to change corporate and individual behaviour in areas such as health and safety and employment law, as well as the protection of consumer interests. It is unlikely that additional legislation will be forthcoming in the next few years in these areas, with the exception of diversity (as the UK's Equality Act starts to impact) and human rights (with more emphasis from the EU).

However, there will be ongoing developments in terms of environmental legislation. Given the international pressure to address environmental issues, the driving force will that of EU legislators.

In particular, the EU's two climate change documents – 'The Roadmap for Moving to a Competitive Low Carbon Economy in 2050' and 'Energy Efficiency Plan 2011' – will begin to be interpreted into legislation. As a result, across all operations in the EU, businesses should anticipate:

- increased energy costs from the change in utilities' profit linkages;
- increased use of energy and carbon taxes – similar to the Carbon Reduction Commitment Energy Efficiency Scheme (CRC);
- energy audits (linked with incentives for companies to introduce energy management systems);
- advanced equipment replacement cycles, leading to increased investment.

In addition, the UK Government has set a floor on the price of carbon (essentially to encourage investment in renewables) but this is likely to affect the payments companies make to the government under the CRC.

Legislation and reporting

An area where legislation is likely to have significant impact is in the area of reporting. However, this is unlikely to be related to CSR reporting, since the EU retains its voluntary approach.

Instead, the major changes will come through annual reporting by companies listed in the UK. The BIS consultation and the FRC proposed changes will have a dramatic effect on the nature of annual reports. The focus will be on ensuring that only material CSR factors are reported upon in the new Strategic Report. This will ensure that more time is spent within companies considering how the CSR activity and its strategy align to its business model, key business drivers and business strategy. This will result in added importance for the key CSR activities and greater recognition of the part they play by the board. It is also likely to mean that companies will have to provide more information on the less material CSR activities on their websites.

In addition, there will be renewed focus on the remuneration packages of executive directors and those immediately below them. Within this focus will be the need for listed companies to include non-financial metrics as criteria for the annual and long-term bonuses. This is a potential minefield as choosing the wrong metrics could either deliver the wrong type of performance improvements, or be a distraction for the executives that are set to gain from them. Companies need to spend time considering which non-financial metrics are most relevant to achieve longer term improved performance for the company and base their remuneration packages on them.

The other area of reporting where legislation will have an impact is that of green house gas reporting. The UK Government is required under the Climate Change Act 2008 to consider requiring companies to report on their greenhouse gas emissions.

DEFRA launched a consultation on mandatory reporting in 2011. Its proposals have not yet been published, largely, we suspect, because their implementation will tie in with the publication of the narrative reporting proposals following the BIS consultation.

At this point, we consider it highly likely that all listed companies and all large unlisted companies will be required to report on their emissions. The extent to which this will require covering a wide range of fuels (including those from the supply chain) is uncertain, but hopefully the focus will be only in scope 1 and 2 emissions, which for many companies will be challenging. Anything beyond that would cause a major headache for most companies!

Of course, the real unknown is whether integrated reporting will come into being. If the IIRC pilots over the next few years prove to be successful, then the 'big four' accountancy practices will encourage the IASB to implement integrated reporting as an Accounting Standard. If this were to happen, then the EU would follow past practice and establish a directive to implement integrated reporting across all EU member states. However, if this were to happen, the implementation timescale is likely to be towards 2020. Interestingly, Puma, the sportswear company, published its first Environmental Profit and Loss Account in 2011. This represented an economic valuation of the environmental impacts caused by GHG emissions and water consumption along its value chain. By identifying the most significant environmental impacts, Puma hopes to develop solutions to address these issues, consequently minimising both business risks and environmental effects. Such profit and loss accounts could well form part of an integrated report (although whether they will sit well as an inclusion, rather than as a separate report is still to be seen).

However, the key issues relating to stakeholders' views of corporate reporting will not be determined by the amount of regulation or guidance that is in place. The ways in which companies have addressed the requirements of non-financial reporting is divided into several camps – those that see the value of non-financial reporting and are embracing it in a whole-hearted manner, those that see it as compliance and are being minimalist and those that are still trying to fathom it all out and who will probably follow the approach adopted by leaders in reporting.

The likelihood is that, overall, the quality of such reporting will improve as companies recognise the competitive pressures from investors, seeking greater information quality and stakeholders, seeking better understanding and improved transparency. Even now, our clients are commenting that they need to improve their performance in areas where they report, in common with their competitors, as well as extending the range of their reporting to cover those areas addressed by their competitors, but not yet by themselves. This 'keeping up with the Joneses' will serve to improve the quality of reporting and provide greater opportunity for corporate comparison.

My view is that by 2020, there will be a global acceptance amongst companies of the need to provide good quality relevant CSR-related information as part of their corporate reporting. In addition, it is likely that as companies' reporting begins to settle down (and they become familiar with the requirements) they will move from interested observers to introduce some form of comparison tables across companies within sectors. This initiative would encourage companies to benchmark their performance in the non-financial areas and bring greater transparency both for shareholders and for other interested stakeholders.

The trends in indices and frameworks

For what is becoming a global part of business, there are an incredible number of indices and surveys relating to CSR, all of which replicate each other to some degree or other.

The nearest means to a common set of measures that meets the needs of governmental and NGO bodies is the UN GRI. Having been upgraded to its G3 format[3] with many more sector-specific guidelines than was the case originally, GRI is now in the process of establishing its G4 format.

What is of special interest is the way the EU (which other states use as a benchmark for their own actions) is focusing on frameworks such as GRI as their 'approved' standard for reporting. In its recent 'Communication on CSR strategy', it also highlighted ISO 26000 as one of the standards which it expected European enterprises to comply with.

There remains the need for convergence amongst reporting frameworks and this may come to fruition over the next few years (especially if Integrated Reporting comes into force). This would be beneficial for those responsible for reporting, provided it does not lead to boiler plate approaches.

Future CSR issues

For companies considering moving onto the CSR escalator (as well as those already on it), it will be important to identify what will be the issues that will be at the foreground of CSR over the next five years or so. It will be equally important for those companies to decide how they will address these issues so that they can gain a competitive benefit from having done so. The following are some areas that companies should include in their planning.

Climate change – and forms of green energy

Perhaps the story about climate change is that the world is moving to tackle it, but slowly. As such, the likelihood is that our environment will change faster than we would like.

Already, climatologists have identified that 13 out of the 15 warmest years in recorded history have occurred since 1997, with drought resulting as a consequence. At the same time, heavy flooding (usually caused by torrential rain storms) and sizeable snow storms have affected the people and economies of developed communities. These events are likely to continue over the next five to seven years.

Businesses must anticipate and plan for such events. They need to ensure their production facilities are secure from flooding – the floods in Bangkok in 2011 were devastating for its population, but also they wrecked the supply chains of many companies who had electronic manufacturing bases in the city. Similarly, companies with water-intensive processes need to have conservation plans in place in the event that their operational centres suffer from drought conditions. This issue will be particularly significant for companies involved in agriculture or food production and their actions will include finding alternative locations from which they can source raw materials if climate change affects growing conditions.

The issue of renewable energy remains a challenge for the developing world. Not only is it more costly than traditional forms of energy generation, but the time taken to develop such sources is likely to be lengthy. In the meantime, nuclear power seemed to be growing in favour as a carbon free energy source – at least, until the disaster at Fukushima reminded us that it does have potential dangers. It is probably the best source of alternative energy in terms of power generation, but it is fraught with issues and is the subject of much discussion by the general public as well as NGOs.

No one green energy source will meet our needs. The likelihood is that what will be required is a combination of energy sources, together with concerted efforts to reduce energy consumption with new products such as electric vehicles as well as making existing energy consumption more efficient. To achieve improved energy efficiency will require inducements to encourage change. This could be in the form of subsidies (as is the case in the UK with electric cars) or taxes (as is the case with the CRC). Either way, the tax payer pays. All in all, a big challenge!

Corporate trust

The Occupy movement of 2011 may have had little clear view of what it sought to achieve, but its underlying message is one that has become far clearer over recent years – the extent to which the public distrusts big businesses and especially the financial world.

To address this lack of trust, companies will need to be more transparent (particularly in areas such as executive bonuses) and demonstrate higher standards of corporate governance. Issues such as phone hacking affect more than the Murdoch family and News International. They can be interpreted as a demonstration of a malaise in business standards overall.

Sir Martin Sorrell, CEO of WPP, the world's largest advertising company, was interviewed in 2011 for BBC's Desert Island Discs. His view on CSR is relevant. Whilst he doesn't like the phrase 'corporate social responsibility', he commented that if you are in the business of building brands for the long term, you will not do things that offend society and the environment. However, if the focus is on the short term, you will have a different approach.

His interpretation is correct. The challenge is for companies to encourage more long-term thinking on the part of their executives. The first place to start is to consider their incentives. The changes that will happen over the next few years will be gradual, but will involve the move from short- to long-term incentive structures with criteria that reflect longer-term value generation.

Addressing world poverty

A continuing issue which remains is that of world poverty. The impact of the tsunami waves in December 2004, the floods in Bangkok, in the Danube and in the Bangladesh delta have raised the world's awareness about the issues faced by the developing world (and the less economically fortunate in the developed world) and the extent to which such countries could deal effectively with major natural disasters, as with these tragic events. Yet, the numbers dying as a result of the 2004 tsunami are fewer than those dying in the developing world as a result of poverty and its resulting knock on impacts, such as malnutrition and poor health. The current increase in prices for agricultural products (claimed by some to be caused by the move to bio fuels) will have a greater impact on world poverty than any single natural disaster.

The approach developed by, amongst others, the then Chancellor Gordon Brown towards addressing poverty in the developing world by providing interest repayment holidays, was one of the first major international initiatives to tackle the cause of poverty. It is still too early to gauge how successful this approach has been. But it seems to be going the way of other international initiatives, which get bogged down by national governments who are less forthcoming with their money than they are with their words.

Regardless of political will and its resulting action, there will continue to be pressure on companies to consider how they can support economic development in the developing world. The solutions will include how companies can change their procurement policies to include suppliers in the developing world; how they can invest in these regions to foster other forms of economic development; and how they can provide support in developing the knowledge and expertise of the population in such countries. Whilst there is the recognition by companies that they can have a role in supporting local population in the redevelopment of their affected regions, they need to put the interests of their shareholders first and if they see political inaction in this area, they will follow this lead.

Water – a source of potential poverty

Water has been touched upon in relation to the impact of global warming. However, there is also the increasing growth of economic development in countries such as China and India which will mean that water will become a scarce commodity for many of the world's population. An issue that needs to be actively considered by companies is the likelihood of a water shortage – not just for their own operations, but also for the communities in which they exist.

Water supply and sanitation were part of the Millennium Development Goals identified within the Johannesburg Summit. This is not surprising, bearing in mind that 2.4 billion people around the world have no form of sanitation, and 1 billion had no supply of drinking water – out of a total population of over 7 billion.

People treat water as a free commodity, but if its availability changes then individuals and companies will have to consider what they may need to do differently. Already, the UNEP Finance Initiative has convened a study about the risks of water scarcity and its impact on the risks for financial institutions in terms of their projects and investments in the developing world.

Water will increase in price, as alternative sources are sought. A key measure for many companies in the future is the way in which they act to reduce water consumption.

Health

Nutrition and health is a similar issue that companies will need to take into account. Obesity features on almost every news bulletin nowadays. Unless checked and reversed, this aspect of health will have a significant impact on our healthcare costs, as well as issues such as staff absenteeism. Increasingly, the well being of staff is a subject of questioning in CSR indices and SRI surveys. How far companies can go to encourage employees to change their personal lifestyle is difficult to gauge, but they need to think about how they can assist their staff to become healthier, both for their own benefit and for that of the company.

Ethnic minorities

Immigration, especially where religion is involved, has been an issue that can divide society and this has been the case throughout history. In the UK, discrimination has occurred against immigrants from ethnic minorities such as the Huguenots, Jews from central Europe, West Indians and even Irish settlers.

The challenge is how business can integrate immigrants and ethnic minorities – both as workers and as customers.

A current issue is the growing ethnic profile of the European society and, in particular, the growth in the percentage of the population represented by the Muslim religion and the antagonism towards them (fuelled by the Muslim fundamentalists amongst them who have carried out terrorist attacks on society). The results of a *Sunday Times* survey[4] showed that Muslims are viewed with high levels of disapproval across Europe, especially in Sweden, where 75% of Swedes questioned said there was 'definitely a lot' or 'rather a lot' of disapproval of Muslims. Remarkably, this is a country where only 0.3% of the population was Muslim. In the UK, the survey found that there was a more positive approach (although 39% of those interviewed had similar levels of disapproval). Here, Muslims represented only 3% of the population. One third of the population is under 16, compared with one-fifth for the nation as a whole.

These children tend to have a lower level of academic achievement than the rest of the population and a population growth rate that is significantly higher. Yet, in a time when the working population is ageing at a rapid rate, companies need to consider how they can attract and train such members of our society. If members of the growing Muslim population retain their current economic deprivation into the second decade of the twenty-first century, then our society will lose valuable skill opportunities. In addition, there will be possible social consequence as a result of the different economic standing of ethnic groups. It is in the interests of companies to develop positive action and promote changes in attitudes towards Muslims.

In this context it is interesting that major UK banks have been active in providing Shari'a bank accounts to ensure Muslims can operate satisfactorily within the financial system – not only does it represent business opportunities, but also their actions help to promote economic development (and avoid potential social disruption) within the Muslim community. In addition to this business opportunity, companies will need to consider ethnic minorities as a source of potential recruitment and find ways to attract such talent into their organisation in a manner that is inclusive.

Ethical shopping

Perhaps one thing that climate change has achieved is that consumers have become more aware of the source of their purchases – and the journey miles involved in their distribution. As a consequence, a BBC report[5] suggested that shoppers are more concerned about green and ethical issues, including buying local products and paying extra for ethically produced goods, or those considered to be kind to the environment.

This movement is likely to continue, but as ever, the answer is not as simple as it seems. One study about the carbon footprint of flowers grown in East Africa, compared with those grown in the Netherlands showed that although the journey miles were considerably greater, any carbon emissions were offset by the additional heat required for propagation in the Netherlands. Similar studies have been undertaken that look at vegetables from the developed world. Young's Seafood ships prawns from the UK to Thailand to be peeled by hand. The company claims that not only is this approach more economically efficient, but it is also more carbon efficient to peel by hand in the Far East and then ship the peeled prawns back to the UK. Such arguments have added weight when taking into account the job creation that is achieved through the globalisation of our consumer goods manufacturing markets.

One question that companies will have to consider is the extent to which this ethical shopping approach will continue to build favour in a time of an economic downturn. Will the ethical consumers be part of the mainstream of the developed world's consumers or will they focus more on the price of their purchases than on their sourcing?

A world economy

In the early years of the millennium, one of the words bandied around disparagingly was 'globalisation'. This was used to indicate that companies were at risk of taking advantage of the working population in the developing world. The thought was that it was the developed world's duty to safeguard those in the developing world.

Over the next few years, people in the developed world will have to recognise that their own position has changed. The BRIC states (Brazil, Russia, India and China) have grown significantly in the last decade. It is estimated that BRIC economies will overtake G7 economies by 2027. The CIVETS group of countries – Colombia, Indonesia, Vietnam, Egypt, Turkey and South Africa – are being touted as the next generation of countries to succeed BRIC and who knows what the economic output of the Arab Spring of 2011 will be, in countries whose economies were designed to benefit the few rather than the many.

What will such a geo-economic change mean to CSR? First, it will be necessary to understand that different business cultures may emerge that may conflict with the responsible business approach of companies in the developed world. Secondly, the working population in such countries may have different attitudes to aspects such as workers' rights and fair employment practices. Thirdly, standards of corporate governance may be significantly different to those of the developed world.

To overcome such differences, it is essential that multinational companies use their economic weight to set examples of the standards that should be expected of newly emerging companies in the rest of the world. We have spent the past 250 years learning from our mistakes in industrial and commercial development, and we cannot expect the developing world to learn such lessons without our benevolent guidance.

Gaining competitive advantage for business

But as was noted earlier in this chapter, the real focus for the future is how companies start considering using their CSR activities to develop competitive advantage for themselves. This competitive advantage will come from addressing three groups of stakeholders:

- employees;
- customers and clients; and
- government (and NGOs).

The pressure will be to establish the real value of what a company is doing in the CSR area. Moves such as Marks and Spencer's Plan A demonstrates how being seen to behave responsibly means that companies can create competitive advantage for themselves – but it takes a fair degree of confidence for business leaders to step into these areas without fearing the reaction of their shareholders. To achieve a realistic evaluation requires both putting CSR business-related measurement processes in place and training employees fully in CSR – and using it to commercial advantage. With CSR business-related measurement, many KPIs are developed to meet external standards. More needs to be done to demonstrate the correlation between CSR KPI indicators and business performance, along the lines of the 'From People to Profits – The Attitude Chain' described in Chapter 10.

In the case of employees, we still see sales departments (especially national and global accounts) that are not adequately prepared to answer client and customer queries. They find it difficult to turn their companies' CSR activities to their advantage to ensure that customers chose their products or services, in a market where prices between competing companies are level with each other. Sales staff have to understand how they can use CSR information to their benefit.

Developing business knowledge of CSR

Once this training and evaluation is in place, there will be greater spread of the best practice that is beginning to develop in companies. To ensure this begins to flow, the CSR professional is likely to be required to take on board a more influential and authoritative role. The government introduced the CSR Academy[6] (now run under the auspices of Business in the Community and renamed the CR Academy) to provide a training structure for individuals taking on these roles. The academy started first by identifying the scope of the CSR job. The following charts show both the range of skills and competencies required to manage the CSR activity within a business and the nature of the CSR characteristics required to involve the various functions within a business in an integrated CSR business process.

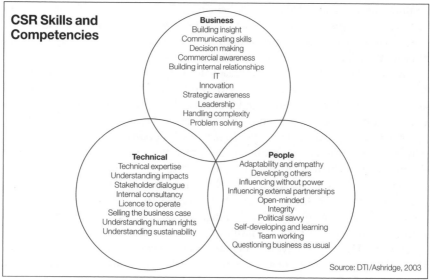

CSR Skills and Competencies

Business
Building insight
Communicating skills
Decision making
Commercial awareness
Building internal relationships
IT
Innovation
Strategic awareness
Leadership
Handling complexity
Problem solving

Technical
Technical expertise
Understanding impacts
Stakeholder dialogue
Internal consultancy
Licence to operate
Selling the business case
Understanding human rights
Understanding sustainability

People
Adaptability and empathy
Developing others
Influencing without power
Influencing external partnerships
Open-minded
Integrity
Political savvy
Self-developing and learning
Team working
Questioning business as usual

Source: DTI/Ashridge, 2003

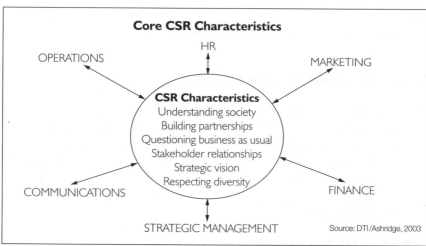

Core CSR Characteristics

HR

OPERATIONS

MARKETING

CSR Characteristics
Understanding society
Building partnerships
Questioning business as usual
Stakeholder relationships
Strategic vision
Respecting diversity

COMMUNICATIONS

FINANCE

STRATEGIC MANAGEMENT

Source: DTI/Ashridge, 2003

Clearly, developing CSR within a business so it can undertake the necessary evaluations and, as a result, share best practice is going to take time. It will require the development of the role of a CSR professional within a company. As we say to our clients when they ask us how long it will take them to introduce CSR into their organisation 'CSR is a journey...'

The academy has promoted the concept that CSR requires a professional approach. This has been taken up by many business schools which now include CSR management in their curriculum. This professional business-based approach is especially important if the CSR team is able to help the board to sell the value of these activities to investment analysts who are looking at their company's shares. When meeting with groups of investment analysts and CSR professionals, the same complaints seem to be forthcoming. The CSR professionals complain that when they have been to investor relations meetings, no one has asked them about their company's CSR activities. In response, the investment analysts say that no one has told them enough about the business relevance of these activities to enable them to decide whether it is important to factor them into their investment analysis.

The fault lies with the CSR professionals. They need to learn how to sell the benefits of their CSR activities in terms that investment analysts can understand and appreciate. The PwC research undertaken with the Coloplast set of accounts (described in Chapter 17) demonstrates the value of interpreting the relevance of non-financial CSR data to an analyst. In making this evaluation, there will undoubtedly be the realisation that some of the CSR programme is in fact adding nothing to the company's reputation or having little or no effect in reducing its risk.

Some sacred cows (usually the ones that senior members of the board feel very passionate about) will have to be sacrificed to make the CSR programme one that gives the company a competitive advantage across all spheres of its activity – and delivers improved share value as a result.

This has to be the objective of CSR practitioners over the next five years – to make all their programmes relevant to the company's stakeholders and, as a result, improve the financial performance and investment valuation of the company to the benefit of the shareholders. If this does not happen, then what is the commercial and financial point of developing and maintaining a CSR programme?

Making CSR work for your business

Much work has gone on in recent years to address the competencies required in a business to make CSR 'a way of thinking', including the development of the CSR Academy. This has established its Competency Framework to describe how managers need to act in order to integrate responsible business decision making. This framework consists of six key competencies:

- understanding society;
- building capacity;
- questioning business as usual;

- stakeholder relations;
- strategic view; and
- harnessing diversity.

This framework offers a very helpful guide to use with training managers in the development of their CSR knowledge and activity.

In addition, in our experience, we find it helpful to describe those key elements for a CSR programme to be successful in the form of a short sharp description of key activities that need to be addressed. Hence, the following represent the 'Seven Steps to Heaven' in terms of making CSR work for your business:

- *Step one: Involve your employees* – probably the most important part of your business, ensure that they involved in and are part of your development of your CSR strategy.
- *Step two: Know your positioning* – knowing where you're at and where you want to be is critical for success in CSR.
- *Step three: Develop an issues based strategy* – understand what your stakeholders think about your company and its activities, build a strategy that is in line with your capability and culture and learn to anticipate CSR-related legalisation – but remember Rome wasn't built in a day!
- *Step four: Surprise and elate* – reputation doesn't come from doing the same as everyone else in your sector. Reputation is built by surprising your stakeholders with activities they had not expected of you. Develop initiatives in the relevant areas to surprise your stakeholders. Against each ensure you have considered the return on investment, so that every initiative is seen to deliver against business objectives, and can be justified as such to your staff and your shareholders.
- *Step five: Global/local* – remember the results from the research quoted in this book. CSR is culturally bound. Don't try to determine all the activities from the centre, but develop a corporate umbrella of policies and practices under which your local operations can develop CSR actions that are right for their market and their culture.
- *Step six: Leadership* – Ensure that your employees and your stakeholders see that there is total commitment towards your CSR strategy from the very top of your organisation, as well as from every level of management within your organisation.
- *Step seven: Communicate* – Influence all your stakeholders, especially those that are key to your business, by communicating your activities to the relevant audiences to enhance your corporate reputation.

Remember that when you get on those seven steps, like an escalator, there's no way off, and no way back. In that respect, you have to anticipating building continuous improvement into your CSR programme for your business!

By following these steps, you should have:

- committed staff;
- satisfied stakeholders; and
- informed shareholders.

Some final thoughts

Throughout this book, I have attempted to put CSR into the context of meeting business objectives. I don't believe there is any other way in which a company should view it. But I recognise that others view it differently. At a conference on ethics in food and agriculture (with an audience of mainly academics, a few NGOs and two business people, including myself) the academics took a pure view of the issues, the NGOs took what may be considered to be an evangelical view and the business people took a pragmatic view.

Differences exist and these will continue to fuel CSR debate and growth. The subject has come to prominence over recent years largely because of a lack of trust – the general public does not trust business people to take decisions that are in the long-term interests of society as a whole –just look at the differing attitudes about corporate approaches towards climate change.

It has probably ever been thus. The difference is that today's world accepts that the establishment and its institutions should be questioned and challenged. The factors that have caused NGOs to flourish and have forced governments to consider the ways in which businesses behave (even though they are one of their biggest tax payers) will remain influential. This will continue until business can demonstrate through activities such as their CSR programmes that they are taking account of how their behaviour influences their long-term impact on the society and environment.

Having taken my MBA in the early 1970s, I recognise the changes that are moving through business education. In those days, there were no ethics courses on my MBA curriculum – now, most major business schools include them, often at the instigation of the students who are facing up to reality and making their older lecturers face the culture of modern society. Today, leading business schools like Harvard and London have significant research programmes into CSR and the benefits it can bring to all stakeholders – again something that would not even have been on the curriculum in my student days.

If what I see around me today continues then I am confident that business will grow and prosper – responsibly and without impacting adversely on society and its environment. Certainly there will be mistakes – business grows through its mistakes – but they will not be left to drift to the detriment of stakeholders. There will be a greater recognition of the need for a company to have a 'licence to operate' and to recognise its responsibility to its stakeholders.

As a result, it is increasingly likely that profit and responsibility will begin to live as equal partners through the actions of the wider business community, rather than just through the actions of those activists seen to be committed to the role of business in society.

Sources

1 '"Just Good Business" – *Economist* Special Report on Corporate Social Responsibility' – 19 January 2008.

2 The full survey can be found at:
www. Mckinseyquarterly.com/ The_business_of_ sustainability_McKinsey_Global_Survey_results_2867.

3 The latest GRI guidelines can be found on at: www.globalreporting.org.

4 *Sunday Times* 19 December, 2004 – quoting a report researched by GfK Worldwide on behalf of the *Wall Street Journal*.

5 'Shopping lists get more ethical' – BBC News website – 17 December 2007.

6 For more details on the Academy, visit the BitC website: www.bitc.org.uk/cr_academy/

Glossary

AccountAbility's AA1000 Assurance Standard   The AA1000 Framework was developed by UK-based AccountAbility to address the need for organisations to integrate their stakeholder engagement processes into daily activities. The framework provides guidance to users on how to establish a systematic stakeholder engagement process that generates the indicators, targets, and reporting systems needed to ensure its effectiveness in impacting on decisions, activities, and overall organisational performance. Provides a systematic, inclusive and credible approach to improving social and ethical accountability and overall performance.

Asset-based development   A development strategy that recognises that the possession of tangible assets – land, buildings or a dedicated income – is the key to achieving the goals of self-sufficiency, independence and sustainability which underpin community based regeneration organisations.

Assurance management system   A formalised system(s) that a company uses to provide confidence that all information for a particular purpose is of an acceptable quality and that it addresses all risks. In the case of corporate responsibility, such a system would assure information relating to community, environment, marketplace and workplace.

Balanced scorecard   A management system (not just a measurement system) that enables organisations to clarify their vision and strategy and translate them into action. It provides feedback around both the internal business processes and external outcomes in order to continuously improve strategic performance and results. When fully deployed, the balanced scorecard transforms strategic planning from an academic exercise into the nerve centre of an enterprise.

Benchmarking   A comparison of environmental and social management processes, performance and reporting. Benchmarking can be used to provide detailed comparisons of operating divisions within a company or companies within a particular sector. Benchmarking can also enable comparison of global trends between highly diverse organisations and sectors.

Bonus pool   Everyone shares a single bonus pool based on the company's performance as measured by the key business drivers they feel are critical to the success of the company, for example, customer satisfaction, supplier satisfaction, quality and operating profit. Employees are eligible for the bonus depending on their job grade or any other pre-agreed criteria.

Brand metrics   Brand metrics help companies strategically grow their brands by providing decision criteria based on an ongoing understanding of how a brand is performing, both internally and externally, helping to sustain organisational focus and communications and leading to the allocation of resources more effectively on an ongoing basis.

BREEAM   Building Research Establishment Environmental Assessment Method (BREEAM) – an industry measure of energy and environmental performance of commercial buildings.

Bribery and corruption   The use of gifts or rewards to gain a business advantage in countries where it is illegal. Can include facilitation payments, which relate to gaining access (e.g. obtaining goods from a port and usually relate to payments to government officials – US law permits such payments whereas other countries (e.g. the UK) treat them as illegal.

Business case   This is the outcome of cost–benefit analysis weighing up commercial gains against the losses incurred by a course of action undertaken by a company. It is commonly adopted to refer to the positive business rationale for working in the public interest and includes direct and indirect impacts over the long run.

Business in the Community CR Index (BitC)   An index developed by Business in the Community which seeks to assess corporate performance in the field of CSR.

Business in the Environment Index (BiE)   BitC's annual index of corporate environmental engagement benchmarks companies against their peers and whole industries against each other, on the basis of their environmental management and performance in key impact areas (usually produced in association with the CR Index).

Business evaluation process   A method of measuring business performance.

Business Review   Legally defined in the UK as the narrative report section of an annual report. The legal requirement for a Business Review stems from the EU's Account Modernisation Directive.

Caux round table   A member organisation that provides principles for ethical and responsible corporate behaviour.

Certified compliance   Independent verification of reaching a desired performance standard.

Child labour   A type and intensity of work that hampers the access of school age children to education, harms their health and development and deprives them of their childhood or self-respect.

CITES   The Convention on International Trade in Endangered Species (CITES) of Wild Fauna and Flora is an international agreement between governments. Its aim is to ensure that international trade in species of wild animals and plants does not threaten their survival.

Code of ethics   A management tool for establishing and articulating the corporate values, responsibilities, obligations, and ethical ambitions of an organisation and the way it functions. It provides guidance to employees on how to handle situations which pose a dilemma between alternative right courses of action, or when faced with pressure to consider right and wrong.

Collective agreements   Agreements on pay and working conditions reached with a recognised body representing a group of workers, typically a trade union.

Community   The interface between business and society, which can be both positively or negatively affected by its activities, contributing to social inclusion or exclusion on a local and global level.

Community development venture capital fund   A venture capital fund, run for profit, targeted at under-invested communities.

Community investment strategy   Community investment can include cash, staff time (including employee volunteering) gifts-in-kind and management support.

Community strategy A strategy to strengthen the company's reputation and standing in the local community by building relationships with key stakeholders.

Corporate citizenship The management of the totality of relationships between a company and its host communities, locally, nationally and globally. Often used as an alternative term for CSR or corporate responsibility.

Corporate governance The system by which business corporations are directed and controlled. The corporate governance structure specifies the distribution of rights and responsibilities among different participants in the corporation, such as the board, managers, shareholders and other stakeholders and spells out the rules and procedures for making decisions on corporate affairs.

Corporate reputation Corporate reputation impacts on a company's performance and its value. A good corporate reputation has to be earned by the tangible things the organisation does – higher quality products, better customer service. Reputation can be enhanced through better management of the emotional attachment that stakeholders have with the organisation.

Corporate social responsibility (CSR) and corporate responsibility (CR) Used interchangeably, CSR and CR refer to a company's positive impact on society and the environment through its operations, products or services and through its interaction with key stakeholders such as employees, customers, investors, communities and suppliers.

Corporate values The purpose of the organisation's existence and against which it wants its activities to be judged by employees, customers, suppliers, investors, communities and governments.

CSR issues Relate to the environmental, social and community aspects of a business operation.

CSR management system A system that translates the CSR policy statement into implementation of actions towards achieving the policy objectives and progress review. The results are either renewed or fresh actions agreed to achieve the objectives.

Crisis management A management process devised to handle recognised potential threats to an organisation.

Cultural awareness and diversity training Training programmes devised to sensitise and raise awareness among employees of potential cultural and other diversity differences in both their workplace and marketplace.

Decent work Productive work in which rights (specifically those contained in the International Labour Organisation's Declaration of Fundamental Rights at Work) are protected, which generates an adequate income, with adequate social protection. It also means sufficient work, in the sense that all should have full access to income-earning opportunities.

Direct or indirect political contributions Donations or gifts in kind to support the objectives of a recognised political party or lobby group.

Disability/disabled persons Disabled persons are people of any age who have a permanent and substantial physical, mental or emotional impairment in an area of social relationship important to their everyday life including: childrearing, education, employment, other occupations, communications, living and leisure activities.

Discrimination   Unequal treatment based on ethnicity, gender, sexual orientation, religion, physical disability or age in the workplace.

Diversity   Diversity recognises that people from different backgrounds can bring fresh ideas and perceptions which can make the way work is done more efficient and products and services more valued. A socially aware company seeks to encourage a mix of races, sexual orientation, religions, physical disabilities, ages and sexes within the workplace.

Diversity agenda   The issues surrounding sexism and racism in the workforce, including under-represented groups.

Diversity profile   A company record of the age, ethnic composition, gender and number of people with disabilities in its workforce.

Diversity proofed   An organisation which has policies and programmes in place for the selection and equal treatment of all staff, regardless of their gender, ethnic origin, age, disabilities or sexual orientation.

The Dow Jones Sustainability Indexes (DJSI's)   Launched in 1999, the DJSIs are the first global indexes tracking the financial performance of the leading sustainability-driven companies worldwide. Based on the cooperation of Dow Jones Indexes and SAM they provide asset managers with reliable and objective benchmarks to manage sustainability portfolios. Currently 51 DJSI licenses are held by asset managers in 14 countries to manage a variety of financial products including active and passive funds, certificates and segregated accounts. In total, these licensees presently manage €2.8 billion based on the DJSI.

Eco-efficiency   The delivery of competitively priced goods and services that satisfy human needs and bring quality of life, while progressively reducing ecological impacts and resource-use intensity throughout the life cycle to a level at least in line with the Earth's estimated carrying capacity. In short, creating more value with less impact.

Ecosystem   A community of plants, animals and their physical environment, functioning together as an independent unit.

Ecological footprint   The size and impact of the 'footprints' on the earth's ecosystems made by companies, communities, or individuals reflect a number of interlinked factors, including human population numbers, consumption patterns, and technologies used.

EMAS   The Eco-Management and Audit Scheme (EMAS) is a voluntary initiative designed to improve companies' environmental performance.

Employee community involvement   Employee involvement with the communities in which a company operates via donations, gifts in kind, supplying professional services, use of company premises or employee volunteering.

Employee share ownership plan (ESOP)   A plan that allows employees to participate in their businesses on a significant scale in a tax efficient way. An ESOP is a combination of an employee benefit trust (EBT) and a share distribution mechanism that is approved by the tax authorities.

Employee programme   The specific means of enabling employees (includes contractors) to achieve the objectives and targets where set. It includes a description of the measures taken or envisaged to achieve such objectives and, where appropriate, the deadlines set for implementation of such measures.

Employee satisfaction surveys Canvassing employee opinions on workplace issues using questionnaires or focus groups.

Environment The world's ecosystems and natural resources that can be directly and indirectly affected by a company's operation, products and services.

Environmental audit An audit of the company's environmental performance measured against its key performance indicators conducted by an accredited external body.

Environmental Management System (EMS) The EMS is that part of the overall management system which includes the organisational structure, responsibilities, practices, procedures, processes and resources for determining and implementing the environmental policy.

Environmental performance management Environmental performance can be managed and measured using key performance indicators (KPIs) obtaining organisational certification by external bodies (e.g. International Standards Organisation (ISO 14001) or using EMSs).

Environmental stewardship Considering and influencing the environmental impacts that arise directly or indirectly from a company's products, processes or services, such as the need for recycling of materials.

Equal opportunities Creating a climate where everyone is treated equally regardless of gender, race, ethnicity, age, sexual orientation or disability.

ESG Environmental, Social and Governance – a term that broadens CSR to include corporate governance. The term is often used in investment circles, and links to socially responsible investment.

Ethical Trading Initiative (ETI) The ETI is a UK initiative launched in 1998. Managing an organisation's supply chain in a socially and ethically responsible manner. Specifically it seeks to encourage a shared approach to the sourcing of good and services that leads to a raised standard of living for workers around the globe, particularly focusing on suppliers in developing countries.

Ethics Branch of philosophy concerned with the systematic study of human values. It involves the study of theories of conduct and goodness, and of the meanings of moral terms.

Ethical Investment Research and Information Service (EIRIS) EIRIS is a charity set up in 1983 with the help of a group of churches and charities which all had investments and strong convictions of what they thought was right and wrong. They needed a research organisation to help them put their principles into practice when making investment decisions. EIRIS provides the research into companies used to assess their suitability for inclusion into FTSE4Good.

Ethnicity The cultural characteristics that connect a particular group or groups of people to each other. Sometimes used a synonym for minority groups.

EU multi-stakeholder forum on CSR A series of round table meetings on CSR first reporting to the EU Commission in July 2004.

Experts directories A compilation of expert's credentials and contact information in many different fields, often available on the web.

Fair trade A trading partnership that aims at sustainable development for excluded and disadvantaged producers. It seeks to do this by providing better trading conditions, by awareness raising and by campaigning.

Focus group   An open-ended, discursive research approach used to gain a deeper understanding of respondents' attitudes and opinions. Typically involve between six to ten people and last for one to two hours. A key feature of group is that participants are able interact with, and react to, each other.

Forced labour   Certain forms of forced or compulsory labour constituting a violation of the rights of man referred to in the Charter of the United Nations and enunciated by the UN's Universal Declaration of Human Rights.

Formal knowledge   The unique knowledge embedded across an organisation is an essential success factor in our rapidly evolving knowledge economy. Formally capturing, cataloguing, and sharing knowledge improves business processes, realises efficiencies, increases productivity, and mitigates uncertainty and risk. The result is improved profitability, performance, and market share.

Freedom of association   The freedom of the individual to join a recognised trade union or other body undertaking collective bargaining or negotiation with employers on workplace issues on behalf of its members.

FTSE4Good   A set of tradable indices for the UK, Europe, the USA and the world that screen companies against a range of indicators that are focused on the areas of environment, human rights, and stakeholder relations.

Gender issues   To do with gender and equality in the workplace.

Gifts in kind   Company support to a charitable or community-based organisation that is non-financial, such as employee volunteering, goods and/or services.

Global Compact   An initiative of the UN Secretary-General, Kofi Annan, the Global Compact calls on companies to embrace ten universal principles in the areas of environment, human rights and labour standards.

Global Sullivan Principles   A voluntary initiative set up by the Reverend Sullivan in 1999, it encourages companies to support economic social and political justice wherever they operate.

GMO   A genetically modified organism.

The Global Reporting Initiative (GRI)   The Global Reporting Initiative (GRI) was convened in 1997 by the Coalition for Environmentally Responsible Economies (CERES) in partnership with the UN Environment Programme (UNEP). It was established to elevate sustainability reporting practices to a level equivalent to those of financial reporting, while achieving comparability, credibility, rigour, timeliness, and verifiability of reported information. GRI has undertaken this work with the active participation of corporations, environmental and social NGOs, accountancy organisations, trade unions, investors, and other stakeholders worldwide.

Greenhouse gas emissions   Gaseous pollutants released into the atmosphere through the burning of fossil fuels and through other avenues that amplify the greenhouse effect. The greenhouse effect is widely accepted as the cause of global climate change. Gases include CO_2, CH_4, N_2O, HFCs, PFCs, SF_6, and other CO_2 equivalents.

Grievance procedure   An agreed procedure to ensure that grievances which members of staff may wish to express about their conditions of service, or any other matter relating to their employment, are dealt with as fairly, efficiently and as speedily as possible.

Hazard Analysis Critical Control Point (HACCP)   A food safety management system based on a systematic hazard analysis of each step in a food production process, with the objective of identifying those points which are critical to food safety – the Critical Control Points (CCPs).

Harmonised CRM database   Assembling customer relationship management (CRM) information in an agreed and accessible format.

Human rights   Those individual freedoms, defined in international standards such as the UN Universal Declaration of Human Rights (UNUDHR) that allow people to lead a dignified and independent life free from abuse and violations and which can be directly and indirectly affected by a company's operations, products and services.

Indigenous land rights   The recognition of rights of indigenous peoples to specific lands which they occupy.

International Labour Organisation (ILO)   The UN specialised agency that seeks the promotion of social justice and internationally recognised human and labour rights. The ILO was founded in 1919. It formulates international labour standards in the form of Conventions and Recommendations setting minimum standards of basic labour rights: freedom of association, the right to organise, collective bargaining, abolition of forced labour, equality of opportunity and treatment, and other standards regulating conditions across the entire spectrum of work related issues.

ILO Convention on Core Labour Standards   The ILO has define core labour standards that include freedom of association, rights to collective bargaining, prohibition of forced labour, minimum wage, freedom from discrimination and equal pay for equal work.

ILO Tripartite Declaration of Principles concerning multinational enterprises and social policy   The aim of this Tripartite Declaration of Principles is to encourage the positive contribution which multinational enterprises can make to economic and social progress and to minimise and resolve the difficulties to which their various operations may give rise.

Informal knowledge/learning networks   Much of the knowledge generation and social learning in development takes place in networks. These networks, now increasingly going online, thus have an important role to play in facilitating social learning and the improvement of development practices.

Insider trading   Using privileged company information to reap an unfair gain on the stock market.

Internal environmental audit   A management tool comprising a systematic, documented, periodic and objective evaluation of the performance of the management system and processes designed to protect the environment. It can be carried out either internally or by an independent consultant.

ICC Business Charter for Sustainable Development   The International Chamber of Commerce (ICC) has developed 16 principles on environmental responsibility, appropriate for enterprises of all sizes.

Intranet-based knowledge repositories   Information storage about prior business situations that employees and teams can access to help tackle recurrent or new problems.

Investor perception studies   Perception studies are a valuable strategic planning tool for investor relations officers. They are a highly efficient means of gathering information to support IR decision making from establishing message strategy to delineating target audiences and the most appropriate communications vehicles.

ISEA   The Institute of Social and Ethical Accounting (ISEA) or AccountAbility is an international, not-for-profit, professional institute dedicated to the promotion of social, ethical and overall organisational accountability, a precondition for achieving sustainable development.

ISO 9001   The International Standards Organisation's (ISO's) main standard for quality systems covering design, development, production, installation and servicing organisations.

ISO 14001   These are specifications regarding the Environmental Management System (EMS) that has been laid down by the International Standards Organisation (ISO). They are used to certify organisations that have taken the environment into consideration by establishing systems that continually reduce environmental impacts.

Knowledge management   Knowledge management relates directly to the effectiveness with which the managed knowledge enables the members of the organisation to deal with today's situations and effectively envision and create their future. Without on-demand access to managed knowledge, every situation is addressed based on what the individual or group brings to the situation with them. With on-demand access to managed knowledge, each situation is addressed with the sum total of everything anyone in the organisation has ever learned about a situation of a similar nature.

Key Performance Indicator (KPI)   A Key Performance Indicator (KPI) reflects the performance and progress of a business. It is measurable and can be compared to a standard, such as a budget, or last year's figures, and acted upon.

Kyoto Protocol   In December 1997, more than 160 nations met in Kyoto, Japan, to negotiate binding limitations on greenhouse gases for the developed nations, pursuant to the objectives of the Framework Convention on Climate Change of 1992. The outcome of the meeting was the Kyoto Protocol, in which most of the developed nations agreed to limit their greenhouse gas emissions relative to the levels emitted in 1990. Subsequently, there were summits ending with Durban in 2011, convened with the objective of replacing the Kyoto Protocol with a global legally binding treaty to come into force after Kyoto ended on 2012.

Leverage   Leverage: enhancing the company's brand reputation through socially responsible attitudes and behaviours.

Local Exchange Trading Schemes (LETS)   Community-based mutual aid networks in which people exchange all kinds of goods and services with one another, without the need for money. They are an organised form of barter.

Lifecycle analysis   This is a method to quantitatively assess the environmental impact of a product from the procurement of the raw materials through the production, distribution, use, disposal and recycling of that product, these being the stages which constitute the product's lifecycle.

Lifecycle planning (LCP)   A detailed examination of the full lifecycle of a product, process, system or function. Taking as an example the case of a manufactured product, a lifecycle analysis involves taking or calculating detailed measurements during the manufacture of the product, from the extraction of the raw materials used in its production and distribution, through to its use, possible reuse or recycling, and eventual disposal.

Licence to operate In CSR terms, a company's 'licence to operate' is conferred by the society in which it operates and within which it should minimise any adverse environmental or social impacts.

Lifelong learning All learning activity undertaken throughout life, with the aim of improving knowledge, skills and competence, within a personal, civic, social and/ or employment-related perspective.

Marketplace Corporate responsibility in the marketplace is the application of responsible behaviour in managing business and consumer relationships from product development to the buying, marketing, selling and advertising of products and services. It includes consideration of the supply chain and clients and customers.

Materiality Information, often, but not exclusively, accounting based, which is viewed as significant to tine management of a business.

Mis-selling A failure to provide best advice about a product or service to consumers that results in an actual loss to the recipient.

Modal shift This refers to the proactive employment of shipping methods which are efficient in ensuring that the amount of goods transported per worker is large while the impact on the environment resulting from each amount transported is small.

Money laundering Illegally generated funds passed through the accounts of a legitimate business.

Monitoring The process of regularly collecting information to check performance against certain criteria.

The Natural Step The Natural Step is an international organisation that uses a science-based systems framework to help organisations and communities understand and move towards sustainability.

NGO Non-government organisation.

NOx Nitrous oxides.

Ombudsman An independent body set up in any sector, often by government, to arbitrate on customer complaints about goods or services.

OECD Guidelines for Multinational Enterprises The OECD Guidelines cover competition, financing, taxation, employment, industrial relations and environment, science and technology. So far, 34 countries are co-signatories.

The Organisation for Economic Cooperation and Development The OECD is a club of some 30 countries in which governments discuss, develop and perfect economic and social policy.

OHS Occupational health and safety.

OHS Management System An OHS management system provides a framework for managing OHS responsibilities so they become more efficient and more integrated into overall business operations.

Occupational Health and Safety Assessment Series (OHSAS 18001) A certification scheme for occupational health and safety that unified the existing schemes and created an auditable specification based on ISO 14001.

Ozone-depleting chemicals In 1990, the major governments of the world agreed to adopt the so-called Montreal Protocol which called for a phasing out of those chemicals with the greatest ozone-depleting potential (primarily chlorofluorocarbons) by 1995 and a gradual phasing-out of chemicals with a lesser ozone-depleting potential (primarily hydrochlorofluorcarbons) during the first decades of the twenty-first century.

Payroll giving Payroll giving allows company employees to contribute a percentage of their salary direct to a charitable organisation which may also be matched by the company.

Peer group KPI comparisons Benchmarking a company's key performance indicators against those of its peers.

Perception metrics Perception metrics diagnose how the brand is perceived by customers and key stakeholders and include brand relevance, awareness and preference, among others.

Performance metrics Performance metrics diagnose the brand's impact on business performance and range from price premium to loyalty to lifetime value of a customer. Performance metrics should lead to a quantitative assessment of gains in customer satisfaction, organisational performance and workforce excellence.

Plan A The term used by Marks and Spencer to describe its five-year, 100-point 'eco' plan. It has five pillars (climate change, waste, sustainable raw materials, health and being a fair partner). The company uses this banner with both its customers and suppliers to achieve changes in each of these pillars. It is famous also because of the converse as described by the company – 'There is no Plan B'.

Portfolio theory Portfolio theory explores how risk averse investors construct investment portfolios to optimise expected returns for a given level of market risk. The theory quantifies the benefits of diversification. Each portfolio on the efficient frontier offers the maximum possible expected return for a given level of risk.

Precautionary Principle Enshrined in the 1992 Rio Declaration on Environment and Development. This principle is an ethical principle that states that if the consequences of an action, especially the development of science and technology, are unknown, but is judged by some scientists to have a high detrimental risk, then it is better not to undertake that action rather than risk the possible negative consequences.

Process best practice Best practice guides, training and diagnostic tools, relating to product development, production, inventory and supply chain management, purchasing, and customer relationship management.

Public domain Information that is currently available in an external publication or on an external website, and has been promoted by the company in some form and is publicly available.

PVC Polyvinyl chloride (PVC) is commonly referred to as 'vinyl' and the two names can be used interchangeably. Vinyl resin can be combined with a wide range of other materials such as plasticisers, stabilisers, lubricants and colorants depending on the requirements of the end product. Not all vinyl products use the same combination of materials.

Real options method   Real options capture the value of managerial flexibility to adapt decisions in response to unexpected market developments. Companies create shareholder value by identifying, managing and exercising real options associated with their investment portfolio. The real options method applies financial options theory to quantify the value of management flexibility and leverage uncertainty in a changing world.

Renewable resources   Non-finite resources such as biomass, wind, forestry, solar and geothermal.

Reputation assurance   Managing risk via reputation management techniques, strategic social responsibility programmes, performance measurement and communication of commitments and performance internally and externally.

Responsible care   The American Chemistry Council has implemented responsible care, a voluntary programme to achieve improvements in environmental, health and safety performance beyond levels required by the US government.

Responsible purchasing preferences   Purchasing products with a lesser or reduced negative effect on human health and the environment when compared with competing products that serve the same purpose. This comparison may consider raw materials acquisition, production, manufacturing, packaging, distribution, reuse, operation, maintenance, and disposal of the product.

Risk analysis   A detailed analysis and identification of the major factors likely to impact the future of a business, both internally and externally.

Risk management   Identifying the key risks, explore how they might arise through various circumstances or scenarios, track those risks overtime, gauge whether the company has been successful in managing risks and therefore make it a less critical issue.

Risk management system (RMS)   A robust and dynamic risk management system which identifies current and potential risks to reputation, establishes appropriate controls and contingency plans, continuously monitors performance and provides early warning of developing issues.

SBU   Strategic business unit.

Scenario planning   Forecasting based on different assumptions about the company's future internal and external environments.

Scorecard target bonus   A scorecard bonus is arrived at by establishing an overall weighting formula with a maximum point total and then you divide the achievement of that maximum total into the number of success criteria to arrive at a bonus formula.

SEE   Social, environmental and ethical – an alternative term for CSR – see also ESG.

SEE   The Society of Environmental Engineers.

Sexual orientation   Heterosexual, bisexual, transsexual, gay or lesbian.

SME   Small and medium-sized enterprises (SMEs) are defined by the European Commission as independent enterprises that have fewer than 250 employees, and an annual turnover not exceeding €40/£25 million or a balance-sheet total not exceeding €27/£17 million (extract from the 96/280/EC, European Commission Recommendation of 3 April 1996).

Social Accountability 8000 (SA8000) The objective of SA8000 is to ensure ethical sourcing of goods and services. SA8000 is a voluntary standard and can be applied to any size of organisation or business across all industries. The standard can replace or augment company or industry specific social accountability codes. SA8000 sets basic standards for: child labour, forced labour, health and safety, freedom of association and the right to collective bargaining, discrimination, disciplinary practices, working hours, compensation. It is often used as a screening method of suppliers certified to this standard by a company's procurement department.

Social capital The features of social organisation, such as networks, norms, and trust that facilitate coordination and cooperation for mutual benefit.

Social exclusion People or areas that suffer from a combination of linked problems such as unemployment, poor skills, low incomes, poor housing, high crime environments, bad health and family breakdown.

Social inclusion The proactive enabling of access of people who are disadvantaged in some respect to employment, education and training.

Social impact assessments (SIA) Analysing, monitoring and managing the social consequences of a company's activities or developments.

Social Performance Indicator (SPI) Social performance indicators include human rights, labour practices and decent work, managing the impacts on communities in areas affected by activities and product responsibility.

Social reporting A report on a company's impacts on society.

Socially Responsible Investment (SRI) Socially Responsible Investment (SRI) is integrating personal values and societal concerns with investment decisions. SRI considers both the investor's financial needs and an investment's impact on society. With SRI, investors can put their money to work to build a better tomorrow while earning competitive returns today. Four key SRI strategies have evolved over the years: screening, shareholder advocacy, community investment and social venture capital.

SOX The Sarbanes Oxley Act – the US law designed to ensure companies follow good corporate governance, including having codes of conduct. Developed in the wake of Enron and other well known corporate scandals.

SOx Sulphur oxides.

Stakeholder Stakeholders are those who either affect, or are affected by, the activities of a company. They include customers and consumers, employees, trade unions, business partners, lenders and insurers, investors and analysts, sector/industry experts government, regulators, host communities, local and international NGOs, the media, and suppliers etc.

Stakeholder dialogue Meetings organised by the company and focused on marketplace issues or areas of concern identified by stakeholder groups, demonstrating how the dialogue influenced corporate strategy, direction or thinking.

Stakeholder engagement Communicating and obtaining feedback from customers and consumers, employees, trade unions, business partners, lenders and insurers, investors and analysts, sector/industry experts government, regulators, host communities, local and international NGOs, the media, and suppliers.

Strands of diversity   Separating diversity into its various elements (e.g. race, gender, sexual orientation, age, disability, etc.).

Supplier programme   The integration of social and environmental factors into the procurement process of an organisation. It can take the form of information exchange, help and encouragement to suppliers, and co-stewardship agreements.

Supply chain   The supply-chain encompasses every effort involved in producing and delivering a final product or service, from the supplier's supplier to the customer's customer.

Supply chain management   Supply-chain management includes managing supply and demand, sourcing raw materials and parts, manufacturing and assembly, warehousing and inventory tracking, order entry and order management, distribution across all channels and delivery to the customer.

Sustainability   Sustainability is a business approach that creates long-term shareholder value by embracing opportunities and managing risks deriving from economic, environmental and social developments. Corporate sustainability leaders harness the market's potential for sustainability products and services while at the same time successfully reducing and avoiding sustainability costs and risks. Often spoken in the same breath as CSR.

Sustainable development   Development which meets the needs of the present without compromising the ability of future generations to meet their own needs.

Systems dynamic methods   The methods of systems thinking provide us with tools for better understanding difficult management problems. The methods have been used for over 30 years (Forrester 1961) and are now well established. However, these approaches require a shift in the way we think about the performance of an organisation. In particular, they require that we move away from looking at isolated events and their causes (usually assumed to be some other events) and start to look at the organization as a system made up of interacting parts.

Talent attraction   Using a company's reputation for social responsibility to attract and retain a skilled workforce.

Total Quality Management (TQM)   Total Quality Management (TQM) is a structured system for satisfying internal and external customers and suppliers by integrating the business environment, continuous improvement and breakthroughs with development, improvement and maintenance cycles while changing organisational culture.

Transparency   Being honest and open in all communications about an organisation's activities. Also Transparency International – an NGO whose brief is to help companies ensure they operate in an open manner – especially in developing countries where bribery and corruption may be rife.

Triple bottom line   Measuring company performance based on its combined contribution to economic prosperity, environmental quality and social capital.

United Nations Environmental Programme (UNEP)   UNEP has developed information and training for environmental impact assessment that includes guidelines for developing countries.

UN Global Compact   A call to businesses of all sizes in all countries around the world to help build the social and environmental frameworks that will support the continuation of open and free markets, whilst giving people the right to share in the benefits that can come from a global economy. Companies that sign up to the Compact are required to provide annual statements of their progress in these areas. Established first in 1999.

United Nations Universal Declaration of Human Rights (UNUDHR) Its aim is to set basic standards for the protection of the rights and freedoms of the individual. It prohibits any distinction in the enjoyment of human rights on grounds of race, colour, sex, language, religion, political or other opinion, national or social origin, property birth or status (1948).

Universal accessibility The requirement to develop websites so that they are accessible to all (e.g. with large print and facilities for those who are colour blind).

Visible minorities A visible minority is a number of people from an identifiable minority ethnic background.

Voluntary Principles on Security and Human Rights Governments of the US and the UK, companies in the extractive and energy sectors ('Companies'), and non-governmental organisations, all with an interest in human rights and corporate social responsibility, have engaged in a dialogue on security and human rights.

Vulnerable groups Human rights law has long recognised that certain groups need special protection. Such groups include landless peasants, marginalised peasants, rural workers, rural unemployed, urban unemployed, urban poor, migrant workers, indigenous peoples, children, elderly people, women and the disabled.

Web-based, harmonised feedback channels Internet based methods for obtaining stakeholder interaction.

Whistleblowing Whistleblowing is speaking out in the public interest, typically to expose corruption or dangers to the public or environment. Can also be intended to relate to internal whistle blowing within a company to alert the board to malpractice at lower levels in the company.

WBSCD The World Business Council for Sustainable Development (WBCSD) is a coalition of major international companies united by a shared commitment to sustainable development via the three pillars of economic growth, ecological balance and social progress.

Workforce diversity profile Monitoring the age, ethnic background, gender and number of people with disabilities in the company workforce.

Work/life balance To recognise the benefits of adopting policies and procedures to enable employees to adopt flexible working patterns, helping staff to become better motivated and more productive because they were then better able to balance their work and other aspects of their lives.

Workplace The total working environment into which people are recruited. It is in the workplace that people are developed both as professionals and as individuals, and where staff can function as free and diverse individuals with entitlement to all employment rights.

Zero emission of waste Reducing the amount of landfill disposal to less than 1% after all by-products of business activities and any other products generated (total quantity of waste discharged) have been dealt with by a variety of other methods.

About The Virtuous Circle

Established in 2000, The Virtuous Circle (TVC) is a management consultancy specialising in reputation and risk. It has extensive experience in corporate responsibility, corporate reporting of non-financial information and risk management working with national and international businesses.

Activities undertaken include development of:

- Codes of ethics
- Strategy development
- Risk management
- Stakeholder research and engagement
- Competitive positioning
- Report writing and design
- Evaluation, research and design of CSR websites
- KPI development and collation
- Audits and verification
- Embedding
- Indices' submissions – DJSI, BitC and EIRIS
- Policy development
- Cause-related marketing
- Annual Report and Accounts – Business Review

Typically, its client base consists of blue chip national and multinational companies and the sectors it has worked in include:

- Retail
- Distribution
- Support services
- Utilities
- Property
- Heavy manufacturing
- Distribution
- Automotive
- Food services
- IT
- Financial services
- Professional services

Taking as its starting point a client's business objectives, TVC's approach has the aim of developing solutions for business which positively impact on business performance.

Complementing its corporate work, TVC also works with non profit organisations and major UK institutions on CSR research.

It has published research reports in association with The Work Foundation, the Royal Society of Arts (RSA), the Chartered Institute of Personnel and Development (CIPD) and contributed research reports that have been published in research-based compendia published by the Accountancy Standards Board.

Further information on The Virtuous Circle can be obtained on its website, www.thevirtuouscircle.co.uk or by e-mail to its Chief Executive, Tony Hoskins – thoskins@thevirtuouscircle.co.uk

Index